MODERN MARRIAGE AND FAMILY LIVING

MODERN

Edited by MORRIS FISHBEIN, M.D.

Contributing Editor, *Postgraduate Medicine;* Editor, *Excerpta Medica;* Medical
Editor, *Britannica Book of the Year*

and RUBY JO REEVES KENNEDY, Ph.D.

Professor of Sociology and Chairman of the Department, Connecticut College

With the advice of ERNEST W. BURGESS, Ph.D.

Professor Emeritus of Sociology, University of Chicago

and CHARLES H. PAGE, Ph.D.

Professor of Sociology, Smith College

Introduction by JOSEPH KIRK FOLSOM, Ph.D.

Professor of Sociology, Vassar College

NEW YORK

MARRIAGE

AND FAMILY LIVING

OXFORD UNIVERSITY PRESS · 1957

PRINTED IN THE UNITED STATES OF AMERICA

PREFACE

THIS book is a pioneer effort among college textbooks; it integrates to a degree not previously achieved the approaches of sociology, anthropology, psychology, economics, medicine, and biology in a unitary science of family living. The constant aim has been the preparation of a functional marriage textbook in which all personal and social aspects are covered.

Marriage is a personal arrangement between a man and a woman. These two, however, may legally enter into this arrangement only after complying with stipulated rules and regulations and after obtaining the permission of the state. Marriage, thus, is both personal and societal.

The family is bound together by blood and legal ties as well as by emotional, psychological, and social ones. The usual family is composed of a married pair and their offspring who live together on an intimate face-to-face basis. In the family situation the individual has his deepest and most intense personal emotional experiences, such as birth, puberty, marriage, and death. The family provides the setting for the development, expression, and expansion of the personality of the human being. In the family the pattern of personal interaction is unique and especially meaningful to the individual because of the kinds of bonds uniting the members of this group.

Society, too, has much interest in the family since it normally constitutes the only approved means by which human propagation occurs. The family serves as one of the main channels for transmitting the culture from generation to generation and is, therefore, important in perpetuating the society's way of life. The family, thus, is both personal and societal.

This book presents an analysis of both the personal and societal aspects of marriage and of the family. The family is viewed as a fundamental institution of society as well as the main primary group in which human beings expect to attain personal satisfactions. The comprehensiveness of the treatment is attested to by the wide range of fields in which the authors are specialists.

Modern Marriage and Family Living is not intended to encourage any objective other than successful marriage. The increase in divorce during the last score of years has been alarming. Divorce might well be considered a disease affecting marriage. As with physical diseases, prevention is the supreme objective. The importance of marriage and the maintenance of the family as the center of life and living for the continuation of our democracy are so great that the inclusion of factors making for successful marriage in the college curriculum would now seem to be a necessity.

This publication stems from the wide circulation and use of *Successful Marriage* published by Doubleday in 1947 and on which this volume is based. Various professors, and notably Charles H. Page of Smith College, had suggested that much of the material in the earlier volume might be invaluable as a core of a standard college curriculum on marriage, provided certain modifications were made and the sociological aspects of marriage appropriately introduced.

The editors wish to acknowledge their special indebtedness to Professor Gerald Leslie of Purdue University for his work in preparing the selected references and in assisting Professor Kennedy in the formulation of the topics for further thought following each chapter.

MORRIS FISHBEIN
RUBY JO REEVES KENNEDY

February, 1957

CONTENTS

ILLUSTRATIONS

CONTRIBUTORS

ADA HART ARLITT, Ph.D. from the University of Chicago, is currently Professor Emeritus of Child Care and Psychology in the Graduate School of Arts and Sciences of the University of Cincinnati. She has been associated with Tulane University, the University of Chicago, Bryn Mawr College, and the Mental Hygiene Clinic in Cincinnati. Dr. Arlitt was an advisory member of the Committee on Parent Education and staff consultant of the White House Conference on Child Health and Protection; a member of the governing board of the National Council for Parent Education; and National Chairman on Parent Education of the National Congress of Parents and Teachers. She is the author of numerous books and articles in her field.

MILTON L. BARRON, Ph.D. from Yale University, is Associate Professor of Sociology at The City College of New York. His fields of specialization include intergroup relations, retirement problems of old age, and intermarriage studies. Dr. Barron is the author of *The Juvenile in Delinquent Society*.

HOWARD F. BIGELOW is Professor of Economics at Western Michigan College, Kalamazoo, and has specialized in family economics and in consumer economics. He is the author of *Family Finance* and has contributed to many periodicals.

JAMES H. S. BOSSARD is Professor of Sociology and Director of the William T. Carter Foundation at the University of Pennsylvania, from which institution he received his Ph.D. He is the author or co-author of more than thirty books in the field of marriage and child development. His recent books include *The Sociology of Child Development, Parent and Child, Ritual in Family Living* (with E. S. Boll), *Toward Family Stability, Family Situations* (with E. S. Boll), and *Marriage and the Child*.

HENRY A. BOWMAN, Ph.D. from Yale University, is Associate Professor of Sociology at the University of Texas. He was formerly the head of the Department of Marriage Education and the Division of Home and Family at Stephens College. In his work he has discussed preparation for marriage with thousands of college students, and has written extensively in the field. Among his publications are: *Marriage for Moderns* and *The Family and You.*

LEE M. BROOKS, Ph.D. from the University of North Carolina, from which he retired in 1955 as Professor Emeritus (Sociology), has specialized in sociology of the family and community and in the field of criminology-penology. His wife, Evelyn C. Brooks, has researched and co-authored some of the more important publications such as *Adventuring in Adoption.* Publications have included study manuals, textbooks such as *Readings in the Family* (with E. R. Groves), and research volumes: *The North Carolina Chain Gang* (with J. F. Steiner and R. M. Brown). He has contributed numerous articles to sociological, educational, and religious journals. He has held visiting professorships in all parts of the country and is presently (1955-57) teaching at Whittier College. Retirement ended a decade or more of associate editorship of *Social Forces.*

MURIEL W. BROWN, Ph.D. Psychology, Johns Hopkins University, is Parent Education Specialist in the Children's Bureau, Department of Health, Education and Welfare, Washington, D.C. She was formerly with the U.S. Office of Education first as Family Life Education Specialist with the Home Economics Branch of the Vocational Education Division and more recently as Program Specialist in the Division of International Education. As a staff member or special consultant, she has worked with the Pennsylvania Department of Public Instruction, the California State Department of Education, the Tulsa Public Schools, the Department of State, The World Federation for Mental Health, the Josiah Macy Foundation, and the Ford Foundation on assignments in the United States and abroad.

ERNEST WATSON BURGESS is Professor Emeritus of Sociology at the University of Chicago, where he received his Ph.D. in 1913. He has been secretary of the American Sociological Society, president of the National Council on Family Relations, and a member of many educational commissions and research bodies in Chicago. Professor Burgess has contributed many articles to periodicals in the field of sociology. He edited *The Urban Community* and *The Human Side of Social Planning.* He has written the *Belleville Survey, Lawrence Social Survey, Function of Socialization and Social Evolution, Introduction to the Science of Sociology,* and *The City.* His recent books include *Predicting Success or Failure in Marriage, The Family,* and *Engagement and Marriage.* He is at present conducting research into problems of old age and has written several books in this field.

KINGSLEY DAVIS, Ph.D. from Harvard University, is Professor of Sociology and Sociological Institutions at the University of California at Berkeley. He has taught at Smith College, Pennsylvania State University, Princeton University, and Columbia University. He is currently a member of the Executive Committee of the American Sociological Society and of the American Eugenics Association, a director of the American Population Association, vice president of the Population Reference Bureau, a fellow of the American Association for the Advancement of Science and of the American Statistical Association. Most of his professional work has been done in the field of population analysis and comparative international statistics. He has published a number of scientific articles in the sociology of the family and marriage. His books include: *Human Society, Population of India and Pakistan, Modern American Society,* and *The Pattern of World Urbanization.*

M. EDWARD DAVIS, M.D., is Joseph Bolivar DeLee Professor and Chairman of the Department of Obstetrics and Gynecology in the University of Chicago School of Medicine. He is Chief of the Chicago Lying-In Hospital. He has written a book for nurses in the field of obstetrics and is also the author of a popular book called *Natural Child Spacing.*

LESTER W. DEARBORN is Director of the Boston Marriage Counseling Service, and President of the American Association of Counselors. His counseling work also extends into the fields of marriage and the family and the psychology of the personality. He is the author of many periodical articles and a member of the American Psychological Association, the American Vocational Guidance Association, and the American Association of Marriage Counselors.

The late ROBERT L. DICKINSON, M.D., author of *Human Sex Anatomy,* was honorary chairman of the National Committee on Maternal Health. He was distinguished as an investigator of problems related to marriage and wrote many books and articles on obstetrics, diseases of women, and sex problems. He illustrated his own writings.

EVELYN M. DUVALL, Ph.D. from the University of Chicago, is a Consultant on Courtship, Marriage, and Family Life. She was formerly Director of the Association for Family Living and Executive Secretary of the National Council on Family Relations. Her writings include *Family Living, Facts of Life and Love: A Guide for Teen-Agers, In-Laws: Pro and Con, Saving Your Marriage* (co-author), *Leading Parents Groups,* and *When You Marry.*

O. SPURGEON ENGLISH, M.D., is Professor and Head of the Department of Psychiatry, Temple University School of Medicine. His books include *Emotional Problems of Living* (with Dr. G. H. J. Pearson), *Psychosomatic Medicine* (with Dr. Edward Weiss), *Fathers Are Parents Too* (with Constance J. Foster), and *Introduction to Psychiatry* (with Dr. Stuart M. Finch).

MORRIS FISHBEIN, M.D., was editor of *The Journal of the American Medical Association* and of the other publications of the Association, including *Hygeia,* from 1924 to 1950. He is now editor of *Postgraduate Medicine* and *Excerpta Medica,* and he acts as consultant editor for several other medical publications. He has written many books and articles in the field of medicine, including *The Modern Home Medical Adviser,* to which he contributed largely and which he edited, and the various editions of *Successful Marriage.* Dr. Fishbein is also Medical Editor of the *Britannica Book of the Year.* He holds the position of Clinical Professor of Medicine in the University of Illinois School of Medicine.

JOSEPH K. FOLSOM is Professor of Sociology at Vassar College. He is author of *The Family and Democratic Society,* and other writings on family life, personality and culture, and education. He was Chairman of the National Committee on Parent Education, a director of the National Council on Family Relations and of the American Eugenics Society, and is an affiliate member of The American Association of Marriage Counselors, Inc. He is a student of the family life and personality of Russian, British, and other cultures.

J. P. GREENHILL, M.D., is widely known as the author, with Joseph B. DeLee, of a textbook on obstetrics and other books on obstetrics and gynecology. He has been for many years associated with the staffs of the Chicago Lying-In Hospital, the Cook County Hospital, the Michael Reese Hospital, and other hospitals in Chicago. He is Professor of Gynecology at the Cook County Graduate School of Medicine. His books on obstetrical and gynecological problems have wide use by the medical profession in the United States and abroad.

ALAN F. GUTTMACHER, M.D., is Director of the Department of Obstetrics and Gynecology of Mount Sinai Hospital, New York, and Clinical Professor of Obstetrics and Gynecology at Columbia University. He was formerly Associate Professor of Obstetrics in the Johns Hopkins University Medical School and chief of obstetrics at Sinai Hospital, Baltimore. He has written many articles and several books for the medical profession on problems related to childbirth.

ELIZABETH B. HURLOCK is Associate in Psychology in the Graduate School of the University of Pennsylvania. She was formerly with Columbia University, where she obtained her Ph.D. She specializes in child and adolescent psychology and is Secretary-Treasurer of the Division on Developmental Psychology and representative to the American Psychological Association Council. Her writings include the textbooks *Child Development, Child Growth and Development, Adolescent Development,* and *Developmental Psychology.* Her books for parents include *Modern Ways with Babies, Modern Ways with Children, Guideposts to Growing Up,* and *Baby's Early Years.*

G. LOMBARD KELLY, M.D., is President Emeritus of the Medical College of Georgia, where he was also Professor and Dean. His published books include *Sexual Feeling in Woman, Sex Manual, for Those Married or About To Be, Sexual Feeling in Married Men and Women.*

RUBY JO REEVES KENNEDY, Ph.D. from Yale University, has been professor and chairman of the Department of Sociology, Connecticut College, since 1945. In her work she has specialized in human relations, problems of marriage, and mental deficiency. In addition to many articles contributed to sociological publications, she is the author of *The Social Adjustment of Morons in a Connecticut City* and 'Single or Triple Melting Pot?—Intermarriage in New Haven, 1870-1950,' *American Journal of Sociology* (July 1952). Doctor Kennedy has been closely associated with the publication of this book, having aided in the development of the outline, selection of authors, reading of the material to which she gave critical consideration, preparation of the study topics, and reading of the proof.

MIRRA KOMAROVSKY, Ph.D. from Columbia University, is Professor and Chairman of the Department of Sociology at Barnard College. She was formerly associated with the faculties of Skidmore College and Yale University. She has been a frequent contributor to sociological journals and her major publications include the following books: *The Unemployed Man and His Family; Leisure: A Suburban Study* (co-author); *Women in the Modern World: Their Education and Their Dilemmas.*

EARL LOMON KOOS, Ph.D. from Columbia University, is Professor of Social Welfare at Florida State University. He was formerly with the University of Rochester. He has served as Research Fellow of the Josiah Macy Jr. Foundation and as Consultant in family life with the Hogg Foundation for Mental

Hygiene. He has specialized in family life problems. In addition to various articles, he is the author of *Families in Trouble, Sociology of the Patient, Marriage,* and *The Health of Regionville.*

WILTON M. KROGMAN, Ph.D. from the University of Chicago, is Professor of Physical Anthropology in the Graduate School of Medicine at the University of Pennsylvania. He is also Director of the Philadelphia Center for Research in Child Growth. As an anthropologist he has specialized in physical anthropology and child growth and development. His books include *Growth of Man* and *A Handbook of the Measurement and Interpretation of Height and Weight in the Growing Child.*

CHARLES E. MANWILLER, Ph.D. from the University of Pittsburgh, is a member of the International Council on Religious Education, the Foreign Policy Association, and Pittsburgh Chapter of the Religious Education Association. He is Chairman of the Research Committee of the Pennsylvania Branch of the National Association of Secondary School Principals, and Chairman of the State Committee on Education for Citizenship. As a curriculum specialist he was sent by the United States Department for educational work in Germany in 1953. He is editor of the research bulletin, *Pittsburgh Schools,* formerly a member of the Board of Directors of the Child Guidance Center of Pittsburgh, and has published many articles.

GEORGE J. MOHR, M.D., is Clinical Professor of Psychiatry at the University of Illinois. He is a member of the staff of the Institute for Psychoanalysis. Formerly he was Clinical Director of the Institute for Juvenile Research in Chicago. In September 1954 he went to Jerusalem for one year, during which he acted as Assistant Director of the Lasker Mental Hygiene Clinic and Child Guidance Center and also aided in the teaching and training of personnel.

EMILY HARTSHORNE MUDD, Ph.D. from the University of Pennsylvania, is Director of the Marriage Council of Philadelphia and Assistant Professor of Psychiatry, School of Medicine, University of Pennsylvania. She also is the principal marriage counseling investigator for the U.S. Public Health Service; principal investigator in alcoholism and marital conflict for the Pennsylvania Department of Health; member of the faculty for marriage counseling, Veterans Administration Resident Training Program for Psychiatrists in Philadelphia; lecturer, Bryn Mawr and Swarthmore colleges; chairman of the executive committee, Interprofessional Commission on Marriage and Divorce Laws and Family Courts (sponsored by the American Bar Association). Her major contributions in the field of sociology include *The Practice of Marriage Counseling* and *Readings on Marriage and Family Relations* (co-author).

JANET FOWLER NELSON, Ph.D. from Columbia University, has taught at both Columbia and New York Universities. She is currently Marriage Counselor and Program Consultant for the YWCA of Cleveland, Ohio. Dr. Nelson developed the Education for Marriage Program for the National Board of the YMCA, and has been associated with the National Staff of the Planned Parenthood Federation of America and the Caroline Zachry Institute. She is a member of the American Psychological Association, the National Council of Family Relations, and the American Association of Marriage Counselors, of which she is currently vice-president. Among her numerous books and articles are *Marriages Are Not Made in Heaven* and *Current Trends in Marriage Counseling.*

CHARLES H. PAGE, Ph.D. from Columbia University, has been Professor of Sociology at Smith College since 1946. He has been of great help in outlining the scope of this book, suggesting authors for various chapters and giving it his critical opinion. His special interests are social stratification, bureaucracy, and social and political theory. His writings include *Class and American Sociology, Society: An Introductory Analysis* (with R. M. MacIver), and *Freedom and Control in Modern Society* (co-editor).

EDITH L. POTTER, M.D., is Associate Professor of Pathology in the Department of Obstetrics and Gynecology at the University of Chicago and Pathologist to the Chicago Lying-In Hospital. She is distinguished particularly for research dealing with causes of stillbirths and deaths in the early days of life and has made many contributions toward reducing deaths in the prenatal period and in infancy. She is the author of many articles in medical publications and several books including *Rh: Its Relation to Congenital Hemolytic Disease and to Intragroup Transfusion Reaction, Fundamentals of Human Reproduction, Fetal and Neonatal Death,* and *Pathology of the Fetus and the Newborn.*

THURMAN B. RICE, M.D., was, at the time of his death, Professor of Public Health in the Indiana University School of Medicine. He was also State Health Director of Indiana. He has written a book of advice in the field of marriage counseling and many essays on public health.

GEORGENE H. SEWARD, Ph.D. from Columbia University, is Associate Professor of Psychology at the University of Southern California where she is consultant for their training program and to the Veterans Administration. She has contributed articles to many publications in the field of psychology and sociology on such subjects as psychosomatics, psychopathology, the reproductive functions, and social sex roles and social psychology. She is the author of *Sex and the Social Order* and *Psychotherapy and Culture Conflict.*

JOHN SIRJAMAKI is Associate Professor of Sociology at the University of Minnesota. He was formerly on the faculties of Yale University, where he obtained his Ph.D., New York University, and Vassar College. He specializes in contemporary American culture, the family, and the city. In addition to many articles in periodicals, he has written *The American Family in the Twentieth Century.*

WILLIAM CARLSON SMITH, Ph.D. from the University of Chicago, is Professor of Sociology, Dana College, Blair, Nebraska. He was associated with the University of Southern California, the University of Hawaii, Texas Christian University, William Jewell College, Linfield College, Lewis and Clark College, and South Dakota State College. During more recent years he has specialized in the problems of the stepchild, in studies of immigrants and their American-born children, and in the sociology of religion. His books include *The Ao Naga Tribe of Assam, Americans in Process: A Study of Our Citizens of Oriental Ancestry, Americans in the Making: A Study of the Assimilation of Immigrants, The Stepchild.* He has also contributed numerous articles to many sociological journals.

WARREN P. SPENCER, Ph.D. from Ohio State University, is Professor of Biology at the College of Wooster (Ohio). During the years 1936-7 and 1949-50, he was Research Associate at the California Institute of Technology and at the

University of Rochester during 1943-5. He has contributed many papers on genetics and animal behavior to the journals of biology and to the *Britannica Book of the Year*.

The late ANNA O. STEPHENS, M.D., was director of the College Health Service at Pennsylvania State College.

KATHARINE WHITESIDE TAYLOR, Ed.D., is Supervisor of Parent Education with the Baltimore Public Schools and has had wide experience as teacher, lecturer, and writer in the fields of parent education and marriage and family living. Her writings include *Do Adolescents Need Parents?* and *Parent Co-operative Nursery Schools* and the Science Research Associates booklet, *Getting Along With Parents*. She is on the Editorial Board of *Understanding the Child*, the publication of the National Committee on Mental Hygiene, and is a member of the American Association of Marriage Counselors and the National Council on Family Relations.

The late LEWIS M. TERMAN, Ph.D. from Clark University, was Professor Emeritus of Psychology at Stanford University. He was especially distinguished for a study of gifted children extending over many years. His published writings include *Measurement of Intelligence, The Intelligence of School Children, Stanford Revision of the Binet Test* (revised in 1937 as *Measuring Intelligence*), and five volumes of *Genetic Studies of Genius*. He was the originator of various tests. Those he wrote or helped to write include the Army Mental Tests used in World War I, the Stanford-Binet Test, the Terman Group Test, the Stanford Achievement Tests, and the Terman-McNemar Test of Mental Ability.

CHARLES F. WESTOFF, Ph.D. from the University of Pennsylvania, is a Research Associate in the Office of Population Research at Princeton University. He was formerly on the faculty of the University of Pennsylvania, and was subsequently a Research Associate in the Research Division of the Milbank Memorial Fund. His special interests and training include demography, particularly the study of fertility, on which he has published many articles.

INTRODUCTION

FAMILY LIFE—AN INTERDISCIPLINARY STUDY

Joseph K. Folsom

H E scoffs at the moon as Cupid's helper." Thus did a newspaper headline the report of a speech I made some eighteen years
ago on scientific preparation for marriage. Perhaps this was suggested
by the remark of a fellow sociologist who thought that courting couples
could learn from the moonlight more that was pertinent to their
situation than they could from the typical college course on marriage.

The fact is that I did *not* scoff at the moon, but I did advocate the
scientific analysis of certain feelings nurtured by the moon, believing,
as I do now, that if such feelings are worth anything they cannot be
injured by such an analysis. The fact is, also, that my fellow sociologist did not object to the scientific study of marriage and the family;
he merely doubted the value of one kind of college course that was
then being developed—one which selects miscellaneous materials
from several of the sciences in the effort to be extremely practical
and directly helpful to students in their personal approach to courtship and marriage.

However, the book now open before you is precisely this kind of
a course. It is a mixture of sociology, economics, anatomy and physiology, law, psychology, genetics, and philosophy of education, and
other scholarly disciplines. But it is also a unity, for it is centered
about marriage and the family. Its unity is concrete rather than abstract. On the other hand, any one scholarly discipline such as "sociology" is a mixture of many concrete problems, and its unity is on
the abstract level. We need both kinds of courses and books.

During the past thirty years this type of concretely centered course of study of marriage and the family, represented by this book, has proved its value. It has found its way into the programs of hundreds of colleges and high schools. It is inspired by the belief that *we should make all the relevant knowledge available, as quickly and simply as possible, and to the greatest possible number of people.* But this may mean a certain sacrifice of other educational ideas: the ideal of teaching things in the most logical order, the ideal of teaching people something only when they are ready for it, or when they have taken the proper "prerequisites," or when they are "sufficiently mature." Many times in life we have to choose one ideal over another. In effect the authors of this book have chosen the ideal of making knowledge available. They are saying in effect that they prefer to take the risks of discursiveness and of premature enlightenment rather than those of perpetuating ignorance. They are also saying in effect that it is better for you to look up a few words that you may not understand than for them to hold back their whole chapter for some more advanced or specialized book that you will probably never read, simply because you might not understand these few words.

In one respect, I feel, we may not have given as complete information as might be useful. This is in the matter of contraception. If so, the reason lies in the federal and state laws which prevent a full discussion of the subject. You as readers and citizens have the right to work for the change of such laws. You can change the laws so as to release knowledge, without changing your moral or religious beliefs about how that knowledge should be used. After all, the law permits chemists to teach their students how to make explosives and poisons; yet the students are still guided by their ethics and religion as to how such explosives and poisons may be used.

VALUES AND SCIENCE BOTH IMPORTANT

In this and many other matters, knowledge does not *dictate* choice, but tells us somewhat "cold-bloodedly," perhaps, what the choices actually are. You will learn from this book that marriage outside your faith, premarital intercourse, young mothers working outside the home, and some other "deviations from the normal," are risky, but much less risky than the speakers against these practices would have us think. You will probably gather that science can say very little, if anything, against masturbation, intercourse during pregnancy, and many of the so-called sexual perversions. But most of this "knowledge" is of a statistical character: it pertains to the mass or average of persons. It does not tell *you,* an individual with some definite personal or religious ideal, that you can violate this ideal with impunity. An ideal, or value, is something you will try to maintain in maximum safety rather than something with which you will take a calculated risk. The consequence of knowing more about the general or average experience is often to place greater responsibility upon your personal conscience and your understanding of your unique individual self.

THE IMPORTANCE OF SELF-KNOWLEDGE—COUNSELING

Socrates' dictum, "Know thyself," is more important today than when he said it. In this book there is no chapter on "self-understanding," yet the idea that people are different, and hence that it is important to understand oneself and others as individuals, is a kind of underground idea that runs through all the chapters. We often ask a lecturer what he would do about this problem of courtship or of child discipline, and he replies, "It all depends on the individual case." Then some of us, turning to our neighbors, mutter: "Humpf, he really doesn't know any more than we do." The lecturer may have given us some "on the average" statistics, but what we *do* about our problem will probably depend much more upon "the individual case," which we know but the lecturer does not.

Ideally, the lecturer should then become a counselor, or be followed up by a counselor, to whom we could describe our individual case. There is never time or proper atmosphere for this in the public question period following a lecture. It usually requires an hour or several in confidential sessions. Yet even in counseling, the main problem is the client's ability to communicate fully to the counselor; the counselor seldom can or should give definite "advice." What he does is to help the client better to understand himself and his problem so that the client is able to make the final decision himself. Hence the task of the counselor is not so much to teach the client general, on-the-average facts but to teach him how to analyze himself and his peculiar situation. He must teach him what to look for and how to get information.

In his chapter in this book Professor Koos suggests that middle-class people, isolated from the richer contacts with kinsfolk found in both upper and lower classes (and traditionally too proud to accept some services from social agencies), must learn to accept counseling. They need common sense and have it, but in these days of increasing conflict of values, common sense is not enough. Help is often needed to work through the dilemma between the need for security and the greater diffusion of interests in the middle-class family.

THE NEED FOR KNOWLEDGE OF, AND INTEREST IN, OTHERS

If problems are so much problems of individual self-knowledge, what is the use of a book like this, or, in fact, any book, since books give mostly general information? Partly because the first step in knowing yourself is to know others! You do not know whether you are tall or short until you have seen many other people and gained some idea of the average stature. As we said above, knowledge is not the only guide to action but it is one guide, and we have an unconditional right to it if it exists. A husband and wife may disagree on how often they wish sexual intercourse. The Kinsey report will tell them more authoritatively than ever before what is average for their age and characteristics. It will not tell them how often they *ought* to have intercourse, nor will it necessarily cause them to agree. But it will remove *one* possible source of disagreement, that is, ignorance of the general average. By silencing argument about known facts, scientific information reduces many a quarrel to the basis of tastes and values alone. I believe we are more likely to be honest about our tastes and values, and more generous toward those of another, when we can no longer use falsehoods and ignorance as weapons of debate.

Sometimes we know the "principle of the thing" but cannot apply it because we do not correctly perceive ourself or the person to whom the principle is to be applied. For example, we all believe we should marry for love rather than infatuation, but can we recognize love and infatuation when we see them, in ourselves or others? Professor Bowman's chapter gives some suggestions for developing this diagnostic skill. Apparently love and infatuation may *feel* the same; to distinguish them one must watch them over a period of time.

To you, an individual reader, several of the chapters in this book may seem highly specialized and hence irrelevant. After all, the men who want to adopt a child or who fall in love with a widow with children are small minorities. Of course, some women have Rh-negative blood, some crave extramarital relations, and some are determined to keep up a career at all costs. But you are not going to be one of these unusual cases, so why read about them? As to those deviations known as immoral, why write so much about them, why try so hard to understand and explain them? Do we not actually praise them with our faint "damns"?

Actually, every one of us is unusual. In some way or other each of us represents a very small minority. In some ways every one of us needs tolerance, understanding, or special attention. Thus it becomes a matter of giving unto others what we crave from them—although in different guise. To have empathy for other people's problems which seem strange and foreign to us is to become more fully human.

There is the converse side of this story. There is no one of us who will have perfect family life. We may be very happy, but there will be something lacking which will occasionally bring us sadness. There is the couple who have everything that love and devotion can give— except a child of their own.[1] There is the couple who invested years in common toil for a purpose such as a home in a certain place, or a special job or position, only to have it destroyed by fire or by the callous decisions of other people. Even a marriage which both partners would choose in preference to any they have ever conceived of in the past may be clouded by the failure and guilt of a former marriage. Sometimes it helps us to look outward upon others and to enjoy vicariously in others what we lack in ourselves. It is a common tendency to seek this vicarious satisfaction through our children, or through movies and fiction; much safer and more realistic is the cultivation of warm intimate friendships with many people of our own, older, and younger generations.

Genuinely to care about many other persons is to run the risk of more disappointments and heartaches, but also to court pleasant surprises and rich satisfactions. By *identifying* with others we enlarge our own selves.

Sometimes vocational ambition, snobbery, fear of being taken advantage of, or fear of extramarital relations by the spouse thins out and impoverishes these warm currents of friendship. One of the problems of marriage today is this area of close interpersonal relations surrounding marriage. Once these were mostly with kinsfolk or in-laws and more or less standardized. Now they are not. Obviously, hurtful relations are not likely to develop if friendships are maintained on a couple or family basis. But sometimes one spouse would rather not be bothered by a relationship which is much wanted by the other spouse. What then?

I think the only general answer is that in both the internal and external relations of marriage, we need more than ever before to develop

[1] Adoption often brings adequate compensation in such cases. See Chapter 33.

skill in human relations, or as Foote and Cottrell have called it, *interpersonal competence*.[2]

THE MODERN INDIVIDUATION OF MAN

What has the great world process of social change done to the character of human beings? As society becomes more industrialized, more urbanized, more the master of nature, more populous, do we become more neurotic, less aggressive, more monogamous; do we change from tradition-directed people to inner-directed and then other-directed, as Riesman[3] says?

The thing that is most significant is that we become more differentiated, more individuated.[4] For the extreme "patterns of cultures"[5] which could be seen by surveying the world from Bering Strait to the Cape of Good Hope, we must substitute the extreme "patterns of personality" which can now be found in a single city in an advanced society. Specialization of labor, differentiation of consumption, of recreation, and of intellectual fare, lead to differentiation of experiences, tastes, and values.

For example, the average American probably reads little, if any, more than the average citizen of other advanced countries, but the number of different books, magazines, et cetera, available to him is tremendous. This makes for less uniformity of mental content, so far as it is derived from reading.

Time was when a rural frontier mother could say, "I am sick of all this talk of choosing and choosing. . . If a man is healthy and does not drink, and has a good handful of stock, and a good temper, and is a good Christian, what great difference can it make to a woman which man she takes? There is not so much difference between one man and another." *

2 Nelson N. Foote and Leonard S. Cottrell, Jr., *Identity and Interpersonal Competence: a New Direction in Family Research,* University of Chicago Press, 1955.

3 David Riesman, et al., *The Lonely Crowd: A Study of the Changing American Character,* Yale University Press, 1950.

4 Cf. F. Müller-Lyer, *The Evolution of Modern Marriage,* Knopf, 1930; *The Family,* Knopf, 1931.

5 Ruth Benedict, *Patterns of Culture,* Houghton Mifflin, 1935.

* James G. Leyburn, *Frontier Folkways,* Yale University Press, 1935, p. 129. By permission.

THE NECESSITY TO CHOOSE

Family life today requires many difficult choices seldom required of our forefathers. Will you marry before John goes into the service or wait till he comes back? Will you marry while John is still in college, letting Mary support them, expecting John to reciprocate later?

Traditionally in our society a woman might choose (1) marriage, which was rather uniform in rights and duties and practically indissoluble, (2) celibate spinsterhood, (3) religious orders, or (4) disgrace. Today she can choose marriage, which though legally uniform is of several varieties in terms of work, recreation, sex, and parenthood; she can choose divorce and remarriage, and more than one mode of spinsterhood. She no longer has to decide between marriage and a specialized occupation, but may choose many different ways of combining marriage with other activities and occupations. As illustrated by Professor Komarovsky's chapter, the multiplicity of choices creates new problems of how to manage them, and these call for individual creative solutions and sometimes for counseling.

When you choose a husband you also choose his occupation, but today it is not unthinkable that he might change his job for the sake of better family life. Today many wives have the problem of whether to be good "corporation wives" or to insist upon independence in ways of living even at the risk of the husband's rapid promotion. Choices of schools for children are becoming more complicated. Will you get a television set when you know that the average youngster, according to certain surveys, spends four hours a day at it? There are twenty-four hours in a day for everyone alike; and these four hours must subtract from something else. To be sure, television is educative. Have you enough confidence in your own firmness as a parent to control the programs and to prevent the absolute waste of time with which modern business threatens our youth? You deplore the brain-washing procedures of the communists; are you also aware of the occasional brain-scattering and brain-softening procedure of advertising in a free-enterprise country?

PREDICTIONS THAT UPSET PREDICTION

We have seen how statistical, on-the-average knowledge does not solve an individual problem but does provide standards which are indirectly helpful. This kind of scientific knowledge reached a high-water mark of precision in the predictions of marriage success by Terman (see his chapter in this book), Burgess, Cottrell, and Wallin.[6] Tests, that is, combinations of facts knowable at a given time, were discovered which correlated from +.50 to +.60 with a condition knowable only at a later time—the degree of success or happiness of the marriage. This is about as well as we can predict students' success in college from their entrance examinations. Nothing much to brag about, but still some basis for mass selection if not individual selection. Statistical scientists continually work to improve such tests. Do they hope eventually to be able to predict marital success or failure as accurately as one can predict the time of the sunrise? If so, what for?

Indeed this scientific development of tests leads to a logical and philosophical criticism of the kind of science they represent. Suppose everyone did know the test scores of all his or her potential marriage partners? What would be the result? Of course 50 per cent of persons would fall below the median test score; yet 92 per cent of persons eventually marry. Would any fewer people marry as a result, or would the high-scorers merely mate with the high-scorers, leaving the low-scorers to a predictably miserable future with other low-scorers? Would marriage, on the whole, be improved any by all this scientific prediction?

Obviously, the only hope of the tests is that they might help persons to correct faults and thereby improve their chances of happy marriage. If any *perfect* prediction were possible, which it isn't, we wouldn't want to hear it, just as we would not want to know the date of our death, if it were predictable, which it isn't. In matters of human hope and possibility the only function of a prediction is to *upset itself*. The prediction is a result of past facts, but once it is announced, it enters into the chain of events and becomes a cause. Thus a marriage might succeed because its failure was predicted!

A NEW TYPE OF SCIENTIFIC RESEARCH

These considerations are leading to a "new direction in family research." This is set forth by Nelson Foote and Leonard S. Cottrell, Jr., in their *Identity and Interpersonal Competence.*[2] The older research assumed that certain conditions were more or less fixed, and the problem was to *adjust* to them. Research was supposed to show the most

---

[6] Ernest W. Burgess and Leonard S. Cottrell, Jr., *Predicting Success or Failure in Marriage,* Prentice-Hall, 1939. E. W. Burgess and Paul Wallin, *Engagement and Marriage,* Lippincott, 1953. Lewis M. Terman, *Psychological Factors in Marital Happiness,* McGraw-Hill, 1938.

probable means of successful adjustment. The fixed conditions were sometimes in the environment, sometimes in the personality itself. But always something had to be adjusted to something else.

On the other hand, the new research assumes that everything is changing all the time. Each day a person is a little different from what he was before, and so are the other persons and the environment to which he is related. Hence the central problem is to teach skills in meeting new situations. The aim is not the adjusted person but the competent person. Interpersonal competence, as Foote and Cottrell call it, can be analyzed into six components: health, intelligence, empathy, autonomy, judgment, and creativity. Empathy is the ability to perceive situations as another perceives them, and thus to feel oneself into the other's role. Autonomy is the ability to maintain one's own standards and self-confidence in the face of pressures from others. Judgment is the ability to estimate the consequences of alternative lines of conduct; it develops slowly and is not the same thing as intelligence. Creativity is the "capacity for innovations in behavior or real reconstruction of any aspect of the social environment."

Ways to measure or estimate these traits are being devised. One promising method is role-playing. A person, acting in a group even in a constructed situation, reveals meaningful characteristics that do not appear in pencil-and-paper tests and private interviews.

The role of this new research is not to measure and classify persons as fixed entities but to show them how to change. The new research is closely related to the procedures used by both the Moreno and Lewin schools of "sociodrama," "group dynamics," and the like.[7]

I venture to predict that marriage and family counseling will become more dynamic and make greater use of group methods. Heretofore it has relied largely upon the confidential interviewing of each client separately. It was thought that only in such privacy could an upset person reveal his true self and what he really felt about his spouse. In a joint interview one or both spouses would hold back something or else they might quarrel in the presence of the counselor and thus be driven even farther apart by the shame of it all. Such was the theory. However, spouses who saw the counselor separately often came home and talked over what the counselor had said. Each stressed those

[7] J. L. Moreno, *Who Shall Survive?* Beacon Press, Revised, 1953. "Psycho-dramatic Treatment of Marriage Problems," *Sociometry*, 3:1-23, Jan. 1940. Kurt Lewin, *Resolving Social Conflicts*, Harper, 1948. Stuart Chase, *The Proper Study of Mankind*, Harper, Revised, 1956, Ch. 13.

things the counselor said which bolstered his own ego or seemed to cast reflections on the other. So the counselor was providing fuel for another quarrel anyway, even though it was not conducted in his presence. Now, perhaps, it would be worth trying as an experiment to have *only* joint sessions, so that everything said by the counselor to either party was heard by the other and could be objected to if one wished. A new vista is opened up. Moreno even has brought a quarreling couple together on a role-playing stage with the "other woman" with whom the husband was in love. We are not prepared to say that this all-cards-on-the-table method will work better than the conventional methods. *But to try out methods* is the very kernel of the new family research. It is action research.

THE PERMANENCE OF THE FAMILY

In the early part of the twentieth century it was said that the family was an institution of declining importance. Both in Russia and in America some thinkers predicted, on different grounds, that the family would wither away. But now as the century begins its second half, in both Russia and America, the family is still with us and going strong. Also we begin to see more clearly the reason it must remain. The question of how many functions are lost by the family, and how many are gained, is silly, because it all depends on how you define and subdivide "functions." More sensible is an estimate in terms of person-hours-per-year of time. It seems clear that on the whole people are not spending any less percentage of their time in the performance of family and household duties and in home activities. What if we have given up the baking of bread and the weaving of cloth in the home, and the children get more education in the school and other community agencies? The home is still the main base of operations, even for teen-agers; and as the average real income goes up the trend is toward more suburban living, better home equipment, and a greater variety of home activities. In Russia, reports show a strong family solidarity, partly as a result of outside pressures, and the government is encouraging home and family life. Like the green suburban grass advertised by a prominent manufacturer of lawn fertilizer, the family "never had it so good."

The luxuriant blossoming of family life in America still comprises a considerable amount of partner-changing (divorce and remarriage). Twenty per cent of our marriages are remarriages (including both death and divorce causes). A small but increasing minority of American children are affected by divorce. The divorce rate, however, is leveling off and is not accelerating toward the point where, as one of our Russian critics facetiously suggested, each woman in a certain city would have been at sometime the wife of every man therein.

As part of the new research, our task is not to make fatalistic predictions but to find out how to help people to make marriage successful, and that means happy and permanent. One researcher, after much observation of stable and broken marriages, found that the clearest difference between them was the sheer *will* to preserve the marriage.

In the broken marriages of years ago we saw much of drink, adultery, and cruelty. The breaking marriages of today still have to prove such faults as grounds for divorce. But the essential grounds of conflict are made up of incompatible personal wishes of many kinds.

If all persons agreed on what is right and what is wrong, this problem would be easier, as it was in earlier times. Few persons have the stubbornness to hold out against what spouse, kinsfolk, neighbors, and friends consider the "right thing." But today marital conflicts are much more like politics, that is, both parties are "right"; which means that each can find enough justification and supporters to continue the quarrel. It is an amazing spectacle to behold two bitterly quarreling mates, each believing himself or herself to be a saint. Thus there is a need for a new, modern type of sacrifice and resignation which gives up even what seems to be a great *good* for the sake of the greater good of marriage.

Henry Pratt Fairchild has pointed out that the real problem of life is not the choice between good and evil, but it is choosing the greater of goods or the lesser of evils.[8] The divorcés of today are not all weak and inadequate personalities and "bad actors"; many of them are simply persons who would rather be right than married.

Perhaps the new research will discover how to give quarreling mates the empathy to look each into the other's eyes and to feel the hurt that is there—in the other. Perhaps it will develop empathy with a possible future self looking back remorsefully upon the breaking of a loving, growing bond and doubting that it needed to be broken.

[8] Henry Pratt Fairchild, "But You Can't Have Both," *Harpers,* 168:438-47 (1934).

ONE

SOCIAL ASPECTS OF MARRIAGE AND

THE FAMILY

1 EDUCATION AND FAMILY LIFE

Muriel W. Brown

M. DE SALES, a French journalist, once wrote a clever essay on love in America. "America," he began, "appears to be the only country in the world where love is a national problem. . . Nowhere else can one find a people devoting so much time and so much study to the relationship between men and women." In a spirit of gay condescension he discourses on love, democracy, and cookbooks and finally concludes that someday love in this country will cease to be "a hunting ground for reformers" and become, "as everywhere else, a personal affair, very much worth the effort it takes to examine it."

As a matter of fact, there is no country in the world, including our own, where love is not both a personal affair and a national concern. We are not, as M. de Sales implies, willful children determined to make love "work" because we want more of the pleasure we know it can give us. We are seriously trying to learn what love is and how we can work *with* it. We are intent upon doing this because we believe that the hope of this troubled world lies, ultimately, in man's ability to experience and express love in appropriate ways in all of his relationships with other human beings and with God. We believe that the most central purpose of family life is to foster the growth of love and teach people how to use constructively the power it re- leases. Because of these beliefs, we feel obliged to try to find out how homes in which this kind of learning can go on are established and maintained. If this be "reform," let us make the most of it. Actually it seems to us more sensible to think of this "movement" as basic human education. Usually we call it family-life education or education for family living.

Education for family life is as old as the family itself. In the past, and in many parts of the world today, cultures have perpetuated their patterns of family living through systems of indoctrination which have left most of the people concerned in little doubt about their duties and responsibilities as sons, daughters, fathers, mothers, husbands, wives. With the total support of tightly organized societies, children have been taught by their parents the values and folkways of their forebears. Codes of conduct handed down from one generation to the next have been useful over long periods of time because the life situations in which they have been successfully applied have changed slowly during many centuries. Tradition, until recently, has been the force which has stabilized and given continuity to human experience.

As social changes take place with increasing rapidity, however, tradition inevitably becomes a less and less reliable guide for use in meeting new situations. This began to be true in the early days of our own history. England, France, and Spain were too far away from us to be able to impose their value systems on us for long. Survival in colonial America depended on ingenuity, adaptability, and co-operative action. Only by men and women who had learned to think fearlessly and creatively could this continent have been conquered and this nation built. The Yankee shrewdness which amuses and sometimes shocks the rest of the world is the inevitable result of our long apprenticeship in problem-solving. It has become our habit to challenge assumptions that seem unreasonable, to ask questions when we are in doubt, to try to find out what the matter is when something goes wrong, and to invent new solutions and create new possibilities when old approaches to problems no longer serve.

This dynamic approach to life has bred in us a great deal of self-confidence and a tremendous respect for the ability to co-operate effectively with change. As far as most of us are concerned, there is no forever Forbidden City in man's search for knowledge and for truth. If an aspect of life is puzzling, we explore it. If problems multiply in an area of special importance, we analyze them with special care. The heart may have reasons that reason does not know, but we expect that eventually reason will bring these to light.

PROGRAMS OF STUDY

In view of these considerations, it is not surprising that ours should be one of the first countries—if not *the* first—to develop a dynamic concept of education for family living and to implement this with planned programs of study. These programs seek the continuous improvement of family life through the intelligent application of insights, knowledge, and skills acquired to the everyday problems of the home and the family. They are sometimes described collectively as a folk movement because they have tended to develop in response to popular demand and because the people themselves who take part have so much to do with the organization and direction of so many of them.

Family-life education has been defined as that part of a total education which equips individuals for effective membership in the family so that each contributes to home and community life according to his capacity. Activities within this broad field are conducted under many different auspices, in many different ways. They include the programs for parents called, originally, mothercraft, then child study or parent education. They include homemaking education for children, youth, and adults—that part of home economics which is centered on home activities and relationships and enables the individual to assume the responsibilities of homemaking. They include the local, state, and national programs of marriage counseling, social hygiene, and mental hygiene which are developing soundly against sometimes heavy odds. They include the courses in marriage and family living now being given in many colleges, and a wide variety of offerings in the curricula of elementary and secondary schools (in addition to home economics)—the units on the family in most social-studies courses, the home-living units in the lower grades, the sex instruction sometimes given in science and health education, the classes in personality development and human relations. They also include a great many different kinds of community projects under the sponsorship of a wide variety of community groups.

Education for family living is carried on in the United States by an unknown number of governmental and nongovernmental agencies and organizations. It is also carried on by persons trained in many different professions, including particularly psychiatrists, lawyers, psychologists, social workers, teachers, pediatricians, sociologists, ministers, nurses, and family doctors. In 1948, 104 of our national organizations were emphasizing some phase of family-life education in their programs to an extent which justified their participation in the National Conference on the Family held during that year. This number did not include the 27 federal agencies and the 17 foundations also working in this area. Today there are undoubtedly many more groups active in both categories.

NATIONAL AGENCIES AND ORGANIZATIONS

Among the agencies and organizations most active in this field of education are the schools, colleges, and universities; the churches; the social agencies; the libraries; the co-operative extension services of federal and state departments of agriculture; and many large voluntary groups with nationwide memberships, both lay and professional. To give a reliable over-view of the principal channels and sources of leadership is probably impossible, so varied are the auspices under which activities in this field are promoted. At the federal level, there is a family-life specialist in the Extension Division of the U.S. Department of Agriculture. In the Department of Health, Education, and Welfare there are family experts in the Office of Education, the Public Health Service, and the Social Security Administration, which includes the Children's Bureau and the Bureau of Public Assistance. The total programs of both of these departments are geared to the study of problems affecting families in a number of ways. The interdepartmental Committee for Children and Youth, staffed by the Children's Bureau, is broadly concerned with family welfare and co-ordinates informally many of the activities of the constituent agencies in this general area.

Many national women's organizations, such as the General Federation of Women's Clubs and the American Association of University Women, stress home and family life in their programs of work and prepare materials for their members to use in studying family problems. The labor organizations are also emphasizing work in this field. The national church organizations are, of course, all actively interested, and the national social welfare associations are giving increasing attention to educational, as distinguished from therapeutic, aspects of both group work and case work with families.

Of the specialized agencies giving national, professional leadership in family-life education, the National Council on Family Relations is perhaps the largest and the most consistently interdisciplinary. Other important professional groups are the American Association of Marriage Counselors, the Planned Parenthood Federation of America, the Child Study Association of America, the American Institute of Family Relations, the Association for Family Living (Chicago). The National Congress of Parents and Teachers and the American Home Economics Association both have special departments which stimulate and guide their activities in parent education, child development, and homemaking. Several foundations have indicated their interest in education for home and family living.

The Groves Conference on Marriage and the Family is an annual meeting which provides opportunities for the presentation and informal co-ordination of teaching, research, and counseling in the family field. The chief professional magazine for family-life specialists is *Marriage and Family Living,* the journal of the National Council on Family Relations. *Parents' Magazine,* the outstanding popular publication in parent education, now reaches more than a million families each month. Commercial magazines for families are widely available through department and food stores and other business channels.

STATE ORGANIZATIONS

State governments participate in family-life education through state departments of health, education, and welfare, and through the Co-operative Extension Service in Agriculture in each state. A few state departments of public instruction have specialists in parent or family-life education on their staffs; all (including the Territories and the District of Columbia) have supervisors of home economics who give full time to the homemaking programs, including those for adults, sponsored by the public schools in their states. The Co-operative Extension Service in thirty states employs one or more full-time specialists in family-life education.

LOCAL GROUPS

On the local level, in city neighborhoods, in towns, and in country villages, one senses most vividly the great vitality of this movement. In these places, teachers, parents, home demonstration agents, health educators, social workers, youth leaders, and ministers of all denominations are engaged in a great, if informal, joint effort to help families improve their living. Here are courses in family living for children in school, classes and study groups for out-of-school youth and adults. Here are community projects, co-operatively organized, in which local family problems that can be generalized are studied in the light of new knowledge which bears upon them. There is probably no state today in which at least one community has not had at least one well-attended family-life conference, institute, or workshop for lay and professional people, sponsored by one or more local groups.

The following letter, addressed to a member of the staff of the Home Economics Education Branch of the U.S. Office of Education, shows the spirit and scope of many of these grass-roots activities. It comes from a minister in a small Midwestern city and says, in part:

We noted the increase in divorces in our county, rising to a high of 51 per cent. The Ministerial Association called in the lawyers of the county for a supper. We ate and talked and found a lot of common ground which perhaps most of us did not know existed to this extent. A committee on recommendations for a later meeting was appointed. I am chairman of that committee. The committee includes three pastors and three representing the lawyers: judge of the Common Pleas Court, judge of Probate Court, and president of the Bar Association. Our recommendations, after many committee meetings, are tentatively the following:

1. That a course be offered in all county high schools (city high schools too) which would study the related factors in harmonious marriage and happy family life. A course is now being offered in one of our high schools, with the approach from the health side; the course is given by the physical-education department.

2. That a course on "The Essentials for Success and Harmony in Marriage" (or some similar subject) be offered in —— periodically (probably 9 or 10 months out of the year); this course to be especially for premarried and newly married couples and others who may wish to attend.

3. That a counseling service be set up in —— to which all interested individuals and agencies may be referred; namely, all personnel directors in our factories, social-welfare agencies, school principals, county Bar Association, county health department, etc., would be solicited to refer people in need to this service.

In spite of our national tendency to explore and experiment, developments in this crucial area of education have taken place slowly. Each of the specialized programs mentioned has had to overcome opposition originating in ignorance, indifference, or fear. Several years ago two well-known women, one from abroad, the other an American, found themselves dinner partners at a banquet in New York.

"Your name is very familiar," the foreign visitor said to her neighbor. "May I ask what your work is?"

"Parent education," replied the American.

There was an awkward pause.

"Parent education!" the woman from overseas finally exclaimed. *"Really? How amusing!"*

The word amusing used in this connection is packed, of course, with hidden meanings. If she had fully spoken her mind that night, the guest from Europe would probably have said, as people in our own country still sometimes do:

Education for marriage and parenthood? Nonsense. A mother instinctively knows what to do for her baby because she loves it. The things people need to know to make a success of love, marriage, childbearing, and child rearing they must learn from experience. If one should feel the need of more information than he happens to have about any of these things, he can always turn to a book—or a friend. These are intimate, personal experiences with which each person has a right to deal as he sees fit. And, really, after all, how ridiculous to suppose that logic and reasoning have anything to do with love!

Even those phases of family-life education conservative enough to find their way into public-school curriculums have developed gradually. In 1841, for example, Catharine Beecher, the sister of Harriet Beecher Stowe, wrote an excellent textbook for use in women's colleges called *A Treatise on Domestic Economy*. It would be hard to paint a more inspiring, more comprehensive, or more practical picture of the duties, responsibilities, and privileges of the American homemaker. A succession of able home economists have enriched and enlarged upon the concepts introduced by Miss Beecher. Yet it has taken approximately one hundred years for leaders in home economics to establish homemaking as a functional area in American education and to demonstrate that the teaching of homemaking can be as vital, rich, and varied as life in the homes served by our schools.

Nevertheless, the United States has, at last, become "family-conscious." As the letter quoted earlier indicates, increases in juvenile delinquency and divorce following World War II have forced us to recognize weaknesses in our social structure which we have not been too willing to face in the past. Parents, at present, are the scapegoats, charged with every crime against children known to psychiatry. Riding high on the band wagon, radios, newspapers, magazines, even the chain grocery stores, are bombarding the public with information and advice on every conceivable phase of family living—child care and guidance, family relations, marriage, sex, and the technical problems of homemaking. Sometimes these and other special-interest groups make contributions to family education that are extremely valuable. Sometimes, unfortunately, they use the most subtle psychological tricks to sell bills of goods, playing mercilessly upon the emotions of worried people, chiefly upon their fears.

Because systematic education in the essentials of good family living has not been an integral part of his basic education, the average American does not know what to do about all this furor over his alleged failure as a homemaker. When his family is in trouble he seeks advice, not as a rule from those trained professionally to deal with problems like his, but from those in whom he has confidence for other reasons—relatives, the corner druggist, the bartender. Less frequently he goes for help to a clergyman, a labor leader, a ward boss, or a policeman.

A recent analysis of 6,422 letters received from women during a one-year period by Christine H. Hillman, an advice columnist writing for a popular monthly magazine, shows how urgent and widespread is the need for help with family problems. Of these correspondents, 87 per cent indicated a need for sex information, 73 per cent for birth-control information, 52 per cent for information about agencies which might help with specific problems, 30 per cent for legal advice, 23 per cent for information about venereal diseases, 22 per cent for help in deciding whether or not to get a divorce, 14 per cent for advice about how to get a second party to agree to marriage, 13 per cent for advice about how to prevent a divorce. Altogether, the lives of roughly 38,897 immediate relatives were affected by the decisions made by these "people in quandaries." [1]

Miss Hillman asks,

Why did these women write to an advice columnist? There appears to be one basic reason. It is because somewhere along the way someone has failed. That failure may lie in the home, the school, the church, the community, or in society itself. . . It appears, therefore, that the challenge for family-life education is there. Ways must be found to extend and enlarge upon the work now being done in classrooms, marital clinics, through counseling services, and in parent-education groups.

It would, of course, be naïve to imply that professional education has any easy short cuts to success in family development. The whole problem of learning in relation to life adjustment is extremely complicated, and to oversimplify it is dangerous. There are four principal

[1] Christine H. Hillman, "An Advice Column's Challenge for Family Life Education," *Marriage and Family Living,* 16:1:51-4.

sources of knowledge in the world—the findings of scientific research, the revelations of religion, the insights of artists, and the observations made currently and in the past by people in all walks of life. From these sources come the raw materials of understanding—facts, hunches, doctrines, opinions, descriptions of experience, problems. These raw materials are gradually brought together, evaluated, and organized into bodies or fields of knowledge, which have to be related to each other. It is then the business of education to deal with these syntheses, making generalizations, pulling out principles, showing how these may be used as guides and tools in solving life problems.

It has not been easy to organize knowledge pertaining to family life, partly because we have had little experience in dealing with the kinds of raw materials involved; partly because this whole area is so heavily mined, emotionally, that we have been afraid of it; partly because nature continues to operate, however blindly, without our intervention. As small increases in understanding have pointed the way to greater happiness and satisfaction in family living, interest in the study of this field has grown. We have begun to assemble our data from religion, from the arts, from the sciences, from life. This comprehensive book is in itself good evidence of the progress we have made. Already we know a great deal about human growth and development, and about the history of the family as a social institution. We have had some fruitful research on specific aspects of sex behavior. We know some things which seem significant about present-day family living in our own and other cultures. There have been spectacular developments in the technologies of homemaking. Unfortunately, the biggest lag is at the place where insight is most needed—the study of human relationships.

GUIDES FOR FAMILY ACTION

The important fact in this connection, however, is not that knowledge is still limited, but that we are not making full use of the knowledge we do possess. As in the case of the possibly fictitious farmer, "Our doin's need to catch up with our knowin's!" Three publications have suggested partial answers to at least three of the most basic questions it is possible to ask about family life: (1) What makes families strong? (2) What are families for? (3) What is *good* family living?

One of these publications is a report of a study made between 1940 and 1943 which seems to throw a good deal of light on the first of these questions.[2] It is an analysis of the experiences during this period of 62 low-income families living in New York City. In the 24 months of the study, these families had a total of 109 serious troubles. But here is the interesting thing: fourteen of them had no troubles at all during this time. When the investigator rated all of these 62 families on the quality of their family living, he found that, judging by his criteria, family troubles tended to increase as family organization weakened. The 14 families without troubles from 1940 to 1943 were average or better in the following respects:

1. Each person in the family knew his place or role and knew what to expect of each other member of the family. As one father put it, "If everybody has a job in the family and does it, we get along all right."

2. Each member of the family was willing to put the good of the family ahead of his own good.

3. Each family provided some means for family members to meet their needs and satisfy their interests within the family.

4. Each family had a goal or plan and was moving in the direction of it. Everybody in the family wanted this goal and was helping to reach it.

This study puts new substance into family-life education. It does not highlight any given system of family practices; it does show what some of the specifics probably are in successful family organization. Each one of these seemingly "fortunate" families had found out how to work together for something that seemed important to both parents and children. This joint striving toward common goals gave form, direction, and meaning to family life. So long as these goals or values were clear in the minds of those seeking them, the material circumstances of life could change again and again without disturbing family morale. Each such change was just a new challenge to "take what they had and make what they wanted."

It is in knowing *what to want* in family life that most young people contemplating marriage, and many married couples, are at a loss today. In helping them to find out, family-life education has, perhaps, its greatest opportunity for social usefulness. The most important goals for American families are goals which must be stated in terms of action. What should we expect families to do for their own members, for their communities, for their country, and for the great family of nations which is the world? In short, the second of our three key questions: What are families for?

[2] Earl Lomon Koos, *Families in Trouble,* New York, King's Crown Press, 1946, pp. 33ff.

Too often in the past the answers to this question have been unsatisfactory because they have not been based on knowledge and experience that were sufficiently broad. To be universally meaningful, they must be acceptable to the religious leader, the artist, the scientist, and the man in the street. The second of the publications mentioned earlier in connection with this question is a report of an attempt to get such a consensus.[3] This document was prepared in 1945 for the Woman's Foundation of New York by a committee of specialists in anthropology, education, psychiatry, psychology, religion, and sociology. It proposes a statement of the distinctive functions of family living in our society which is so far-reaching, yet so comprehensive and fundamental, that it may well serve as a platform or charter for programs of family-life education under any auspices, anywhere. According to this statement, these functions or tasks are to

1. Provide a way of living for members of the family group in which basic physical needs can be met and emotional security and personal fulfillment can be attained.

2. Provide in marriage for the achievement of a sustained relationship between a man and a woman in and through which they may seek fulfillment of their intimate, affectionate needs and desires.

3. Bear and rear healthy children in the setting of a home and of family life.

4. Provide the kind of family living which fosters the development and maturation of personalities able to maintain a democratic way of life in the family and in society generally.

5. Transmit, transform, and develop cultural traditions from one generation to the next, especially in the area of interpersonal relations.

6. Integrate, mediate, and interpret the demands (which the environment makes upon the individual) and the possibilities (which it has for him).

7. Provide a socially sanctioned situation in which cooperative living and division of labor can be developed according to the interests, needs, and abilities of the family group.

This brings us to the third question: What is *good* family living? If in our society we depend upon the family for certain essential contributions to personal and social development, then as far as we are concerned good families are families which make these contributions in a reasonably adequate manner. The purposes or tasks for family

[3] *The Place of the Family in American Life,* New York, Woman's Foundation, 1945, p. 15.

life just quoted are stated in terms of action. This action must be co-operative, since no single member of a family group can perform any one of these functions by himself. The *sine qua non* of good family living in our culture is, therefore, the ability to maintain co-operative relations among family members. We call relationships of this type democratic, meaning by that word not some vague form of friendly association, but a kind of behavior which frees the energies of the human spirit for creative, co-operative living.

A definition of democracy which seems capable of releasing untold amounts of energy for more effective living in families is the one found in the report of a study of democratic practice in American schools published by the Educational Policies Commission of the National Education Association.[4] On the basis of this definition, the democratic society is one in which:

1. There is cooperative action for the common good.
2. The welfare of each member is sought by all the rest.
3. All members take part, according to their ability, in planning, carrying out, and evaluating the results of group activities.
4. The experimental method of free inquiry based on faith in informed intelligence is freely used in solving problems.
5. Controversial issues are freely studied and discussed in order that truth may be discovered through the dispassionate examination of all available facts and many different points of view.
6. Each member has freedom with *responsibility* in action.

These three sets of conclusions dovetail neatly because they spring from the same basic philosophy. They are positive guides for family action. Their chief value is that they can never be used as formulas. They offer no ready-made solutions for family problems. Their purpose is to show us what the job is and how it can be done. Their full meaning becomes apparent only as we begin to work with them, delving for the facts behind the generalizations. How, for instance, are family roles determined? What are basic human needs? What can families do to meet these? What is emotional security? How is it attained? What does it mean to "achieve" in relationships? What can a family do to give children a true appreciation of the riches coming into our culture through the art, music, literature, crafts, and customs of all the people joining us from other lands? Can success and failure

[4] Educational Policies Commission, *Learning the Ways of Democracy*, Washington, D.C., National Educational Association, 1941, pp. 127-8.

in marriage be predicted? Can young people be taught *how* to love before they fall in love? How are habits of co-operative living formed? How does a family learn to discuss controversial problems? To what extent and how is it possible to educate children for responsible freedom?

These and countless other questions are the subject matter of education for home and family living today. Much of this education must be on-the-job training. The best time to teach the fine art of diapering, for example, is when a young girl or boy has a baby to care for. This does not mean, however, that everything waits for the wedding. Into adequate preparation for marriage and family living go a multitude of attitudes, skills, and abilities which are content for learning from infancy on up.

This seems to indicate that major responsibility for giving basic, systematic instruction in homemaking and family development must rest with the school. Among our many educational agencies, this is the only one in a position to offer fundamental education for family living to all of our people. This does not mean that full recognition is not given to the value of educational opportunities in this field provided by other agencies and many professions. The school alone cannot possibly meet all of the needs of family members of all ages for help with all kinds of family problems. As a matter of fact, the school can do little or nothing, even in its own technical sphere, without the wholehearted support of all other agencies and organizations able in any way to extend, interpret, enrich, reinforce, encourage, help direct and apply its teachings.

Clearly there is not yet agreement among the professions concerned about what the specific objectives of family-life education should be. The following statement from an unpublished 1947 memorandum of the U.S. Office of Education on the needs and purposes of family-life education at the secondary level is meeting with increasing favor as teachers and school officials experiment with ways of helping students to develop the insights and abilities listed:

1. An appreciation of the importance of the family in American life and some specific understanding of its functions as a social institution.
2. A specific understanding of what good family living means in terms of the student's own family experience.
3. A desire to establish and maintain families which are good by the highest standards the student can realistically set for himself.

4. A specific yet broad understanding of what the resources for family living are in the communities where students live.

5. The skills and abilities needed for finding these resources and using them effectively. These abilities include among others:

    a. The ability to buy wisely within the limits of family income.

    b. The ability to resist the propaganda, high-pressure salesmanship, and the trickery which now keeps so large a proportion of American families in perpetual debt.

    c. The ability to work effectively with other families to develop new resources, make better use of resources already available, and/or solve family problems of common concern.

    d. The skills of good housekeeping and home management.

6. The ability to maintain democratic relationships in family life—to be a good family citizen.

7. The ability to participate effectively in the establishing and maintaining of wholesome family-community relations.

8. The ability to recognize and conserve values in family living as family patterns change.

These are exciting goals but, at this point, it becomes necessary to face a fundamental question. The abilities listed are, for the most part, facets of a single, basic one: the ability to express in one's relations with other people the attitudes and values which characterize American democracy. What kinds of learning experiences help people develop and organize what kinds of value systems, and how is progress in this sort of learning evaluated?

It is generally understood that *knowing about* and *really knowing* are two quite different things. If family happiness and stability depend, in the last analysis, on the ability of family members to express certain qualities of personality in their relations with each other, then the study of personality development must have a central place in family-life education. And in studying personality development we can no longer content ourselves with the egocentric approach so commonly made in the past. Education for living in the democratic family in the United States in the middle of the twentieth century requires that we concern ourselves simultaneously with the effects of family membership on the individual at all stages of growth and the effect upon the family of the behavior of the individual family member.

It is indeed difficult, as Montaigne once remarked, to lay hold of "the many little nimble motions" made by two such active systems of variables. Recently, however, there have been a number of promising new leads. The 1950 White House Conference on Children and Youth has put Erikson's "ground plan" for normal personality development directly into the awareness of the social sciences. This concept makes sense both as a springboard for research and as a practical guide for people working with parents and children. For example, in this scheme the first developmental task for the newborn baby is the achievement of a sense of basic trust in the people around him and in the world in which he finds himself. Lacking this feeling of security, the infant becomes fearful and must draw heavily on energy needed for growth to protect himself in what probably seems to him a terribly dangerous environment.

Assuming that this hypothesis is correct, the most important thing that parents can do for a young baby is to learn how to feed, clothe, bathe, and love him in ways that help him to trust life. If his family can help him to "make the grade" in this special sense as he meets each of the major growth crises of life, the trusting baby will, in all probability, become the kind of person who can do the same thing, in due time, for his own children and for his marriage partner.

This White House Conference material has helped to make much more specific the parallel concept of family stages, the outstanding contribution of the 1948 National Conference on the Family, formulated by Evelyn Duvall and Reuben Hill. Much further work needs to be done in knitting the two together. A recent trend in family-life research is toward the study of the total family as a small group over periods of time sufficiently long to permit the tracing of developmental processes from their various beginnings as they weave themselves into the patterns of family and family-society interrelationships which they create. As this kind of research matures, ways will be found of exploring more effectively than is now possible the intricate problems of role determination in family life. We certainly need more insight into the causes of family tensions and better techniques for resolving those which arise from feelings of hostility, guilt, doubt, or shame due to deep-seated dissatisfaction with one's own family role and the roles of other family members.

What this new content will mean as it comes to enrich family-life education, we cannot yet really know. To be able to handle it, teachers will certainly need more intensive training than most teachers' colleges now offer in functional approaches to the study of child, group, and family development. More attention will have to be given to ways of helping people in positions of administrative leadership gain deeper insight into the meaning of human communication, and more skill in establishing human relations in which people can actually communicate with each other.

It will surely be necessary to develop better methods of helping teachers to understand themselves, particularly their own motivations, before we can expect them to be able to help students, on any educational level, understand better their own family behavior. Perhaps the task most immediately before us is to learn how to use more effectively some of the procedures and techniques already known. The sociodrama, for instance, is a method which has much more to contribute to emotional education than most of us know how to get from it.

Far as we still have to go, we have just cause for optimism as we review accomplishments in the broad field of education for family living in recent years. All of the familiar educational problems beset us in this as in other kinds of teaching—problems of motivation, ego-involvement, attitude change, carry-over into behavior. On the other hand, we see encouraging evidences of progress. We see an increasing number of co-ordinated family-life programs in schools reaching an increasing number of pupils. We see increasing richness of psychological and social content in these programs, with increasing emphasis on school-community co-operation in discovering the needs of students and their families. We see increasingly more dynamic and realistic methods of teaching coming into use. We see an increasing emphasis on educational aspects of the work of many other agencies and organizations serving families, and an increasing readiness for interdisciplinary co-ordination and co-operation in planning, executing, and evaluating joint family-life education projects.

One of the most interesting and significant of recent developments has been the growth in the number and effectiveness of community programs of education for home and family living under the direction of local family-life councils. As community concern is focused on local conditions of family living, communities are showing increasing initiative and ingenuity in meeting problems. One thinks, in this connection, of the successful family health program carried on under the auspices of the Family Life Program in Obion County, Tennessee; [5] of the fathers and mothers in countless places organizing study groups,

[5] Muriel W. Brown, *With Focus on Family Living* (Vocational Division Bulletin No. 249, Home Economics Education Series No. 28), Washington, D.C., Office of Education, 1953, pp. 66-93.

nursery schools or play groups, child-care centers, co-operative laun-
dries, and other services needed to supplement the efforts of individual
families to meet family needs. This, indeed, is democracy in action
since, by definition, a democracy is a society in which each citizen
helps to create the conditions under which he wishes to live. It is
also functional family-life education.

In the 1930s a little band of refugees from the dust bowls of
Arkansas and Oklahoma trekked north. They stopped on the out-
skirts of Wichita, Kansas, because they had no means of going further.
They lived as well as they could in the shelter they could find—
houses no one else wanted, tin shacks and old chicken coops. There
was no work to be had even for the most capable and the most willing.
At last the time came when children stayed home from school because they had no shoes to wear; when families huddled at night in
their ragged coats because they had not enough quilts or blankets to
keep them warm when the cold winds of winter blew across the
prairies.

A community family-life program was organized in Wichita in
1938, and among its other activities arrangements were made for a
teacher provided through the public schools to work with these families. The Lend-a-Hand Club previously organized by the families
themselves became a sewing class in which donated garments were
renovated and made to fit. Quilts were made for beds and rag rugs
for floors. Soon a full-fledged Self-help Center began to operate, with
hours of credit on clothing and other household necessities given for
hours of work on the project.

Finally the day arrived when it seemed not too farfetched to think
of better housing. All possible improvements were made in the homes
then occupied, with the help of the Vocational Education Department
of the Wichita Public Schools and many other co-operating groups.
Much conversation about buying, renting, and similar decisions revealed that no one in the Center knew much about housing. With an
initial loan of $300 from friends the group undertook to learn about
houses by building a little house in the manner of old-fashioned barn-
raisings. An attractive three-room dwelling was finished completely
and sold to a young family for $500, the details of financing being
also a part of the study.

In the short space of nine years this family-life-education project
developed to the point where Center families owned their own club-

house, belonged to the National Association of Credit Unions and the Blue Cross. The Lend-a-Hand Club long ago became the Source Class which studied and made recommendations to the membership concerning any new activities or policies the Center might be considering.

This experiment has been both a fulfillment and a promise. It justified the belief that people with meager resources can generate plenty of power to raise their own standards of living through thoughtfully planned co-operative action. It gave us a preview of what education may be like when we have learned to think, feel, and act more creatively about it and the concept of learning by doing has gained real respectability.

In many parts of the world, the same principles of community organization for better family living which operated in the Wichita program are now being applied in programs of village development. Families in places as far apart as the Lebanese province of Saneen, the South Pacific island of Palau, the village of Mit Halfa in the ancient valley of the Nile, the crossroads settlement of Tin Top, Texas, made famous by the Ford Foundation radio project, *The People Act*—families in all of these places are finding ways and means of dealing with problems of housing, health, sanitation, agriculture, industry, and education which have defied governmental efforts for generations.

Not long ago an African chief was discussing the United Nations. "The U.N.," he said, "that is the council which is sewing the world together in one piece." One of the most effective ways in which we can help with this "sewing"—which certainly needs to be done, and done quickly—is to give high priority here at home to the programs of education for democracy which we call education for home and family living. From homes which foster the growth of love and understanding between people flow, as David Mace once said, "tides of peace and sanity which renew from age to age the deepest purposes of life." To strengthen the movement which is bringing such homes into ever closer and more dynamic relationships with each other, in our own country and in other lands, must surely be the most effective answer to the destructive forces which, from time to time, marshal against us out of the dark night of time.

Topics for further thought:

1. In our society it is now considered desirable that every person of normal intelligence receive at least a high-school education. It is also expected that every normal adult will marry and have children. Discuss the potentialities for both the family and the school of the development of education for family life.

2. Is it to society's interest to educate women and men separately, or together? Should there be different kinds of education for the two sexes? Explain.

Selected reading references

Becker, Howard, and Hill, Reuben, *Family, Marriage, and Parenthood,* Boston, D. C. Heath and Company, 1954.
Contributions by specialists in the following areas: Contexts of Family Life; Preparation for Marriage; Marriage Interaction; Problems of Parenthood and Family Administration; Family Crises; and Prospects for the Future.

Kane, John J., *Marriage and the Family: A Catholic Approach,* New York, The Dryden Press, 1952.
A college textbook on marriage and the family written from the Catholic point of view. Integrates theory and research findings.

Landis, Judson T., and Landis, Mary G., *Building a Successful Marriage,* New York, Prentice-Hall, 1953.
A widely used book in preparation for marriage. Contains original research and chapters on mixed marriages and life insurance.

Landis, Paul H., *Making the Most of Marriage,* New York, Appleton-Century-Crofts, 1955.
Optimistic, constructive approach to dating, selection of the marriage partner, marital adjustment, and parenthood.

Levy, John, and Munroe, Ruth, *The Happy Family,* New York, A. A. Knopf, 1938.
A basic book for students of family life education. A psychiatrist writes about the dynamics of normal family living in a clear, practical, and hopeful way.

Peterson, James A., *Education for Marriage,* New York, Charles Scribner's Sons, 1956.

Interestingly written and supplemented by excerpts from case histories. Includes suggestions for use in analyzing one's own personality.

Witmer, Helen L., and Kotinsky, Ruth, editors, *Personality in the Making,* The Fact-Finding Report of the Mid-century White House Conference on Children and Youth, New York, Harper and Brothers, 1952.

The final summary of papers and reports on various phases of family, child, and community development prepared for the White House Conference by experts in many professional fields. Readable, authentic, and forward-looking.

2 AMERICAN CULTURE AND FAMILY LIFE

John Sirjamaki

THE family, although present in all societies, differs considerably as an institution among them. While always an association of adults of both sexes and their children, the number of spouses and their relations to each other, as well as the nature of their households and domestic life, vary with the types of their marriages. In all societies, the lawful procreation of children is restricted to wedded couples, but parents rear their young differently to prepare them for the life and culture of their particular societies. Parents and children also rely differently upon families for subsistence and companionship in various societies. Family and kindred predominate as social groups in some, especially nonliterate, societies whose members continuously live and work together. Such extensive association in families, however, seldom occurs in modern societies. In modern societies, the people participate in many institutions in addition to the family and they secure the necessaries of life from all of them, not solely or even largely from families. Societies make different uses of the family, uses which foster diverse sentiments concerning family, marriage, and sex. Thus the family, although it is a universal institution, varies in structure, functions, and values in societies throughout the world.

In every society, the family as an institution has a form and character fitted to the culture of the people. An institution means a group of people who are organized in accordance with cultural principles to carry on activities which fulfill certain of their basic individual and social needs as human beings. Spouses, children, and other relatives by blood or marriage, in various combinations, comprise such family institutions. They engage in practices which provide for their individual maintenance and group survival and insure the biological and cultural continuity of their society as well. Since these are indispensable functions, the society, by law and custom, prescribes nearly all their relations and activities, including courtship, form of marriage, rights and duties of spouses, upbringing of children, and recognition of kinship. A particular family institution thereby becomes standardized and obligatory for them. The family is, in addition, the basis of social structure in all societies. It is also closely aligned to other social institutions, inasmuch as the people participate in all of them and develop a consistent way of life among them.

THE AMERICAN FAMILY

This close relation between family and society also occurs in the United States. The family is specifically an American as well as a universal institution in that it organizes the sexes in marriage and regulates their domestic life in ways which concur with the social organization and culture of American society. Thus it espouses a democratic and companionate association of couples and an individualization of family members, parents, and children alike which is in keeping with American democracy. It is adapted to the economy as well, by its ties with the husband's occupation and income, by the occupational and social mobility of its members, by their small number, and by their possession of property as individuals. In the home, family activities are of a kind which reflect the cultural life of the society and the participation of members in all its institutions.

Since the American people are a large and heterogeneous population, not one but many family institutions exist among them. One must speak of the American family with considerable generalization. Ordinarily the term means the family of the native-born majority population, who support the concept of a specific family in their practices and laws. The cultural minorities of the United States have family institutions that differ from the majority family in degree but not in kind. As their members assimilate to American society, they adopt many or most of the practices of the majority family. Thus possession by all the people of a common core of family practices and values increases. Achievement of complete uniformity in families is unlikely, however, since their conditions of life differ and therefore their domesticity does also.

THE MAJORITY FAMILY

The American family possesses a social structure and marriage practices which produce distinctive family and kin groups in the society. The family is nuclear in form, being comprised of a pair of adults of both sexes and their own or adopted children, with occasional other relatives or other persons living with them in their household. Couples marry by their own free choice and upon the basis of mutual affection, without the initiative or subsidy of parents and without regard to preferred kinship ties between them; thus by random mate selection. They normally settle in a home of their own, or, in technical terms, in neolocal residence, wherever the husband's job requires or his income permits it, and separate from their respective parents' families or other relatives. The rule of neolocal residence has the effect of scattering adult siblings upon marriage, and it prevents the accumulation of relatives, except voluntarily, in one place, with the result that kindred do not comprise real groups and seldom act collectively in crises. Spouses owe their primary family loyalties to themselves and their children, not to parents and not to other kin groups. They typically regard their family as complete and autonomous in itself, which having begun with their marriage will end with their deaths or divorce. Except for filial and personal ties which they retain with parents and relatives, they otherwise dissociate their families from those of the latter, with the result that families of parents and children are discontinuous through successive generations.

These structural features, whether as cause or effect, provide the American family with certain salient traits. Since its independent nuclear character is so strongly maintained, the marital ties of husband and wife are magnified in it and are, indeed, its basis. Their status of matrimony imposes rights and duties by law upon them, but, much more than this, they make a home by their own enterprise which reflects their aptitudes and goals in marriage. They marry for love, and covet happiness in wedlock, and cultivate a companionate marriage accordingly in which they seek to fulfill these expectations. This involves not their love alone, however, but the entire organization of their domestic life. The spouses have consciously to develop their own private family culture, in which each performs the marital roles appropriate to his sex or to which experience or necessity inclines him, and to engage in such social and other activities as are congenial or possible to them. In this division of labor each is ordinarily motivated to do his part well because failure by him in his roles reduces the benefits of their marriage.

This concern with individual marriages causes spouses to keep their families small in size as most compatible with their marital goals. They want children, and believe them to be necessary to full family living, but desire them also to be relatively few in number. With limited progeny they can more fully incorporate them into the family group, maintain their home at a higher standard of living, and cultivate companionship among themselves. They also have currently a considerable appreciation of children as individuals in their own right, who they believe should be permitted to mature according to their natures, and not be treated as miniature adults. With this view, parents can better apply the standard when they limit the number of their children. The ability to control their fertility is of course due to their practice of contraception, but the planning and spacing of the arrival of children is due to their attitudes toward the family.

Spouses inevitably restrict or neglect the obligations of kinship by concentration upon their own families. In most societies of the world kin groups support and defend the nuclear families of which they are formed; they serve the latter as a second line of defense, as it were. So much have kin groups withered in the United States, however, that generally only lineal descendants at three generation levels and their families—grandparents, parents, and children, and their spouses and children—observe traditional ties of consanguinity, and even among them these are sometimes eroded. They often drift apart because they reside at great distances from each other or differ in occupation, income, level of education, or social class, which hinders their association; or they dislike each other as persons. Often spouses and parents-in-law feud and therefore lessen or eliminate their contacts. Many exceptions to these generalizations occur among native- and foreign-born cultural minorities whose family and kin groups continue relatively intact. Such extended family groups, however, persist because their members live in the same or adjacent communities, or engage in similar occupations, which facilitates communication among them, or they strive consciously to retain their family ties. In most cases sentiments of kinship are not enough to insure cohesion among relatives.

With the attrition of the kinship system, neither spouses nor children obviously acquire a strong sense of familism, that is, of identification with family and kindred and subordination to them as a dominant social group. Far from developing feelings of clannishness or surrendering their individualism, they hold an opposite attitude—that the family exists for them and not they for it. The family, in their view, has a function to develop the personality of its members by promoting their maturation and by enabling each member to cultivate his interests or aptitudes. Their desire for personal achievement is nourished by the sentiments of individualism which prevail in the society. The individualization of family members has been supported by legislation that has equalized the social and legal status of husbands and wives, and given children social rights which parents may not abridge. The family does not disrupt into anarchy because its members realize that their private goals are best achieved in harmonious, compact families, for which reason they hold the family in high respect.

ASPECTS OF MARRIAGE

Family living is so favorably regarded, indeed, that it induces a highly optimistic attitude toward marriage among Americans, which is demonstrated by their high rates of marriage. More than nine of every ten of them eventually marry, and the majority do so by their early twenties, at an age for first marriage which has declined perceptibly since the turn of the century. Seven of every eight divorced persons, whose numbers are currently large, remarry in time also. So high has the marriage rate been during the past fourteen years that the proportion of married population, nearly 70 per cent, and the number of families, about forty million, are at their all-time high in the United States.

This predilection for marriage indicates that Americans regard wedlock as a desired status of adult persons. Marriage permits spouses, in their view, to form a close community marked by companionship, mutual loyalty, sexual gratification, and parenthood, and quite unlike, therefore, any friendship or other association which they have. Accordingly they believe it to be a more mature and responsible way of life than is single status, which, in contrast, they regard as inferior and even as unfortunate when it continues too long in adults. Men and women alike, therefore, are reared to expect to fall in love and to marry in proper time, and commonly they hope this time will occur relatively soon in their adult lives.

These attitudes toward marriage are strongly reinforced by present methods of mate selection in the society. No other basis for marriage than the free choice and mutual affection of spouses exists, and they are expected to conduct their courtship with a romantic love which exalts their attachment for each other. Romantic love, indeed, supplies a cherished fillip to their association, and they prize its advent between them and cultivate it as a great emotional experience. They obviously expect it to continue in their marriage, and to insure it they insist, as noted before, upon the independence of their family and home.

Young people are trained to anticipate romantic love while they grow up, but particularly during the years following upon their puberty. At this time they begin to attend the places and events of school and community in cross-sex association, generally in pairs but also in groups, and thus to develop a desire and aptitude for such companionship. The term dating designates their temporary pairing as couples in this manner, which is the sanctioned and patterned way in which companionship between unmarried persons of opposite sexes occurs in the society. Individuals date with several or many persons as they grow up, and rehearse with them the sentiments of companionship and affection. In time, when they are of marriageable age or mood, they encounter some person with whom they fall in love and who reciprocates their feelings, and their dating transforms into courtship, and usually leads to their marriage.

Dating, as such, is not a unique American practice, but it is conducted in the United States with an industry and in a volume duplicated nowhere else in the world. Its role in courtship partly explains this, but it flourishes, in addition, because it provides young people with a means to have friends and acquaintances of both sexes, and to engage in social activities with them. Thus they have an opportunity to acquire social experience, develop social personality, and, in general, prepare for adult heterosexual life. Dating, therefore, fulfills social as well as libidinous functions for them. In its present bulk it is largely a twentieth-century development, and is a luxury afforded young people by the urban industrialism of the society, which permits them to stay in school and out of the labor force until at least their late adolescence.

In marriage spouses strive to perpetuate the love and companionship and such other expectations as they acquire during dating and courting. The personality functions of marriage are therefore paramount to them, and they consequently establish their family as an autonomous group in which to cultivate them. Their initial preoccupation with each other has inevitably to expand, however, to include their parenthood, upbringing of children, husband's employment, doing of household chores, and other family activities. They do not thus neglect the subsistence functions of the family, but they no longer accord them priority over the personal or qualitative aspects of their relation. Their attitudes are in keeping with the family's loss or sharing of functions with other institutions, and are made possible, in addition, by the high productivity of the economy which has substituted considerations of a standard of living for those of survival in most American homes.

FAMILY PROBLEMS

Families in various societies have types of problems which arise, at least in part, from their structures and values. As institutions families adjust to their societies, but they never fully accomplish this before changed conditions require still other accommodations by them; and certain stresses, or problems, occur in them through their lag in readaptation. Moreover, functionally fitted to specific purposes, they may be dysfunctional in other respects. Thus they have faults as well as virtues in being closely molded to the life and culture of their societies. It is instructive to know what these are in the American family, first, to test the generalizations concerning it made in this chapter, and, second, to illumine its traits further.

An initial and poignant problem of the American family at present is its high rate of divorce. About one divorce for every four new marriages occurs in the United States, or, in numbers, about 400,000 annually. This high rate of divorce suggests that something is seriously wrong with the family, and therefore contradicts the more optimistic appraisal which has been made of it. A denial of the gravity of the present avalanche of divorces should not be made: they represent the failure of spouses in marriage; they inflict hardship and suffering upon the persons involved in them; and they disrupt the orderly processes of family living and reproduction, and therefore threaten the security of the entire society.

Nevertheless the high incidence of divorces is partly accountable to the nature of the family as an institution. Inevitably many couples who marry for love and companionship fail to achieve these objectives with each other, whether for faults in themselves or in the conditions of the society which produce family instability. They place their marriages, moreover, on unsure foundations when they aspire to psychological satisfactions which are frequently defeated in this frustrating world. When they fall out of love and into discord, they must resolve their conflicts largely by themselves, as they have built their marriages upon husband-wife bases and lack the support of parents and relatives in salvaging their unions. In this extremity they suffer from limitations of the nuclear family, whose members are engrossed with each other, isolated from kin groups, separated from parents and their generation, and afflicted with endemic in-law problems. These traits, as already noted, in happier circumstances invest the American family with vitality and uniqueness.

Once seriously thwarted in their love and companionship, spouses are disinclined to continue in wedlock merely to keep their marriage intact, or to maintain a home for their children. Instead they believe increasingly that marriages which have failed in fact should be dissolved by law, and the mates set free to resume their lives apart or perhaps to marry other persons. These attitudes, of course, reflect the importance which couples ascribe to the personality functions in marriage, and their conceptions of its success in terms of their private happiness. While they do not disdain other benefits of marriage, such as domestic life, marital status, economic security, or merely that it last throughout their lives, they nevertheless regard these as material advantages which, however important, are secondary returns from matrimony. They want greater emotional satisfactions and security from marriage than it is ordinarily able to give them, and they often succumb to their frustrations as a result. When they divorce, they no longer are universally condemned by the society or treated as persons of defective morals, even if they are not entirely condoned for their actions. As a result of these developments the family has less staying power today than before, and has become a chronically unstable institution. Standards of living in the family are currently high, and superior to what they were in earlier American homes.

The stresses which adolescents experience, as an age group in the society and in their relations with parents, create a second problem which is, again, in measure referable to the family. No longer children but not yet grown up, adolescents exist between protected infancy and adult independence, and are without the sure rights and duties of one or the other. They tend consequently to alternate between these statuses in their activities and, indeed, are compelled to do so by the society. At this age, moreover, they strive for individualization and maturation, and physiological processes within and cultural pressures outside them urge them to these ends. But, being juvenile and immature, they are often uncertain of themselves and need the support of parents and the security of the home. Thus they waver between impulses of independence and dependence which lead many of them into conflict with parents and a few of them into delinquencies in their communities.

These tensions are a part of growing up which adolescents probably experience in all societies, but they differ in intensity and therefore in effect upon children according to their family and other circumstances of life. In the United States they are often serious because adolescents inhabit, as it were, two social worlds, one comprised of family and other primary groups, and the other of school and nonfamily associates, which make different and sometimes conflicting demands upon them. They love and depend on parents, who, in turn, care for them now as they have since infancy. But children are active in school and in events outside the home, in which they participate as individuals, and outside the company and authority of parents. With other young people they develop practices and values that differ in respects from those of adults. They become emotionally bound to each other, and collectively form a social group which rivals their families in influence upon some of their actions.

A scrutiny of parent-children relations at several stages of the family cycle will indicate the crises which adolescence sometimes brings families. While children are in arms or of preschool age, parents have nearly exclusive control of them, which includes supervision over their playmates. Parents are commonly eager in these years to rear their children as individuals, and to enjoy affection and companionship with them. In these purposes they are currently aided by numerous persons and agencies that provide help or advice concerning their children: pediatricians, psychologists, nurses, teachers, and other specialists in child care. At least some parents, moreover, read the books which these experts write, and rear the children by their precepts. In addition, parents have available an entire industry from which to purchase special foods and play equipment to provide their children with physical if not always mental health.

While children attend school, they leave the protected environment of the home and identification with the family. At school they associate with other children of their own ages, similarly separated as individuals from their families, with whom they form groups and engage in activities which, by adolescence, assume the semblance of a youth society and subculture, in distinction to the society at large and its culture. Parents know only a small number of the many persons with whom their children have contact, perhaps their teachers, some friends, and a few others, and appreciate but do not always fully comprehend their intellectual and social growth as individuals. Inevitably children grow apart from parents and supplement family groups with cliques and coteries of their age-peers.

Parents, of course, modify their relations and roles as children grow up, and understand, at least sympathetically, the attraction which friends and schoolmates have for them. Yet they find it hard to endure the emotional weaning of children from them, and their consequent weakened contacts with them. When this causes dissension between them, they have few experts to turn to for counsel, or even reliable books on adolescence to read, since scientific specialization in adolescence has begun only recently. Perhaps the reason for this is that adolescence is regarded as a less specific and significant age period than infancy and childhood, and its problems are largely social, and of the kind indicated here. It has therefore been less inviting and amenable to investigation.

To a large extent these dilemmas of adolescence have arisen, at least become aggravated, in modern United States. Before this century parents and children maintained a relatively continuous relation in the home, which often kept on intimately after the latter had married and founded their own families. This was particularly so with rural families, whose adults and children lived and worked together, and were more closely knit as a group than is common now. Parents therefore influenced, if they did not always control, the associations of children through adolescence. Children, moreover, were generally identified as members of families as well as individuals because parents and kindred were generally known and had a family reputation in their communities. Nor were children detached from families by schools as much as now, since these were local institutions with limited grades, whose pupils were the usual associates outside the classroom. Sons and daughters, in addition, tended to go into farming upon marriage, and occupational shifts did not cause rifts between them and parents.

An inability of family members to provide adequately for aged parents and other relatives is a third, and increasing, problem of American families. Or, stated conversely, elderly persons suffer in old age because, among other reasons, they lack reliable family ties, and are without the continuous companionship of children or relatives in their last years of life. By this time many families, particularly in the working class, have been broken by the separation or divorce of spouses, or the death of one of them, or internal dissension. Children are married adults and often unable or unwilling to care for aged parents in their own homes. While all aged parents are isolated from children to some extent, this is not, of course, always complete separation, particularly when they have maintained close ties with each other throughout their lives. In a minority of cases elderly couples, if in good health and financially independent, may actually enjoy their old age as a period when they are no longer responsible for children and are free to follow their own inclinations.

In its connection with the family old age has two major and, in a sense, opposing aspects. On one hand, the proportion of persons 65 years of age and older in the society has steadily increased owing to advances in standards of living and in medical care which enable more people to live to old age. On the other hand, family and kin groups have declined in size and diminished in functions, thereby also reducing their ability to care for these aged persons. To repair their failure in this respect, the society has instituted various social-insurance programs since 1935 to provide the aged with at least some means of income in their last years.

The cultural practices of the American family of course contribute to the domestic problems of elderly people. There are still other causes, however. Because of the early age of first marriages, American parents are about fifty or fifty-five years old when their children have grown up, married, and left home; and, in terms of their present life expectancy, they will live, on the average, for another fifteen or twenty years. Thus they have years in which to exist as a childless couple and to manage together in elderly companionship. They do not wholly lack ties with their children and their families, but association with them is often difficult because of personal or social reasons. Many elderly couples are loath to live with married children, moreover, because they went to retain their independence and control of their own homes. They know that two families seldom live amicably for long under the same roof. Even if parents wished to live with children or other relatives, often a place is not available in the apartments or small houses in which they are likely to reside.

SUMMARY

Families vary in structure, functions, and values in societies throughout the world. In America the family espouses a democratic and companionate association of couples with an individualization of family members. Cultural minorities in America gradually adapt to the majority pattern. In the majority pattern, the great kin groups that prevail in most of the world have withered. The family exists for its members—not they for it. Americans regard wedlock as a most desirable state. Present methods of mate selection reinforce this view. Divorces represent failures in marriage. Changing relationships in families have raised three problems: divorce, adolescent tensions and adjustments, and provision for the aged. These three problems of the American family are being studied seriously but solutions have not yet been found.

Topics for further thought:

1. In our society the institution of the family serves important needs of both the individual and the group. Is there any conflict between these two? Discuss their relationship.

2. Do you think there are any special aspects of the American family system which are likely to foster divorce, difficulty in adjusting to the conditions of youth and old age? Suggest ways of reducing and, perhaps ultimately, of overcoming these problems.

Selected reading references

Burgess, Ernest W., and Locke, Harvey J., *The Family: from Institution to Companionship,* New York, American Book Company, 1953.
Portrays the American family in transition from the large, externally controlled family to the small, democratic type built around the needs and satisfactions of family members.

Kirkpatrick, Clifford, *The Family: As Process and Institution,* New York, The Ronald Press Company, 1955.
Penetrating social-psychological analysis of the American family. Adjustment and maladjustment considered in terms of family types and the dilemmas which confront family members.

Ogburn, William F., and Nimkoff, Meyer F., *Technology and the Changing Family,* Cambridge, Houghton Mifflin Company, 1955.
An extended analysis of family change through the impact of material invention and technological development.

Parsons, Talcott, "Age and Sex in the Social Structure of the United States," *American Sociological Review,* October, 1942, pp. 604-16.
Sophisticated analysis of the American family, from the viewpoint of structure-function sociology.

Sirjamaki, John, *The American Family in the Twentieth Century,* Cambridge, Harvard University Press, 1953.
A well-written synthesis of existing theory and research on the American family. Written for the intelligent lay reader.

3 MARRIAGE IN MIDDLE-CLASS FAMILIES

Earl Lomon Koos

A DISCUSSION of the family life of a social class will of necessity be an incomplete one. One reason lies in the lack of available data, since students of the family have paid slight attention to the relation of family behavior to class membership. A second results from the sharp differences that occur in family life in one part of the country as contrasted with another. Belonging to the middle class in a New England village is often quite different from belonging to the middle class in New York City or in an Iowa community. A third reason is the variation of middle-class families in their economic and educational status. They have varying degrees of freedom to behave as other families behave. The discussion that follows stems largely from the author's own studies, together with the special studies of certain aspects of family life by authorities in various fields of human behavior. (See Selected reading references at end of chapter.)

THE SIGNIFICANCE OF CLASS MEMBERSHIP

In an open-class society such as ours, where people are relatively free to move from one stratum to another through their own efforts, the significance of class membership for the family lies not so much in the position in which the family is placed in the class hierarchy as in what that position means to the family. Social classes are in effect subcultures, for each class shares part of the thinking and behavior of the whole culture, but each also has its own ideals, ideas, attitudes, and behavior patterns. These in turn have both prescriptive and proscriptive power in shaping the behavior of the family. It is not enough, however, to say that class differences do exist, for this can easily be shown. What is important is that identification with a given class be shown to be important in determining how the family behaves. It is not difficult to show that this is often the case. The author found, studying family behavior in a New York community, that a certain school was offering dancing lessons to the teen-aged children at a nominal fee. The following abstracts from representative interviews indicate the prescriptive power of class membership (in the case of the middle-class parent) and its proscriptive power (in the case of the working-class parent).

Things are bad right now in our business, and the bills outrun the income. We've had to cut a lot of expenses to keep things going right here in the family. . . But here's this dancing class. I can't spare the twenty-five dollars this year at all, but whether I like it or not, I've got to. So I hold off another bill this month, and pay for the lessons. . . Why? Because that's what people like us do. Our friends and other people like us send their youngsters, and we feel we have to behave as they do. . . Don't let anyone tell you that your social position doesn't make you do things in a certain way! Any father in my shoes can tell you that it does.

In contrast, the working-class father made the following observation:

I want my kid to have a lot of things I never had. Take this dancing class at the school. I'd rake up enough dough, somewhere—maybe I'd have to give up a few beers, even—but that ain't all there is to it. Some things we just don't do, and one of them is make a sissy out of your kid by sendin' him to a *dancing* class. H——, if he went there on Thursday afternoons, and the boys at the plant found it out, they'd ride me to death. . . His mother don't feel about it like I do—she just says dancing classes ain't for the likes of us.

These are isolated and perhaps naïve examples; they do illustrate the important point outlined earlier: the real meaning of social-class membership lies in the effectiveness of that membership in determining family behavior. If this premise is acceptable, the remainder of this chapter can be devoted to outlining some of the characteristic patterns of middle-class family life. The importance of recognizing these for people planning to marry or already married lies primarily in the couples' not falling into the trap of "doing what the Jones's do" regardless of the cost to the family's own integrity and well-being.

MIDDLE-CLASS FAMILY LIFE

This discussion is limited to observations concerning middle-class family life. The serious student will develop contrasts with upper and working classes through a search of literature in the field of the family. Such phases as kinship, mobility, economics, family planning, and child rearing in the middle-class family are emphasized in this discussion.

Kinship. The middle-class family tends to center its thinking upon the family of procreation, that is, to include only the father, mother, and such children as ensue from the marriage. The extension of interest to the preceding generation and to collaterals such as uncles, aunts, and cousins is rarely great, and, as a result, the middle-class family is a sharply confined group of interacting persons. While this has certain advantages, it also has the disadvantage of lessening many of the psychological ties that give a richness to family life. The middle-class family finds itself, then, standing alone, with consequent disadvantages in time of stress. The lack of assistance, in terms both of morale and of actual physical and financial succor, often renders the family more vulnerable than it would otherwise be.

Status Needs. Because the middle-class family is isolated, it has a peculiar need to be like others of its own kind. Where there are extensive (and intensive) family ties, the family's values are shared with the large family and morale and status are strengthened. Where the family lacks these, this fundamental deprivation must somehow be overcome. It appears that in practice the middle-class family overcomes absence of external ties through an adherence to the ways of other families it considers to be like itself. Status is gained through the possession of material things, through belonging to the right organizations, through doing things the right way. That this is not always a conscious act in no way prevents its occurrence.

Mobility. The middle-class family often earns its living through professional, managerial, and other white-collar activities. As industrial developments have taken place at an accelerated pace, many of these families have found it necessary to move from one part of the United States to another. Others have moved as the result of choosing mates while away from home in college or in the armed services. In effect, this means that cultural roots are displaced, and that one or both parents (and often the children) must take on new ways of life that are inconsistent with their past experience. This often requires a readjustment of values and behavior, which is not always an easy matter. For example, a middle-class wife in a southern city stated her plight in these words:

In Massachusetts, John and I went to church if we felt like it, and mostly we didn't. When we moved to Georgia, John was told by his superintendent that we would be expected to join a church and to take an active part. This was really foreign to our nature and beliefs, and we've had to make some adjustments that aren't comfortable. . . I suppose this is what most Yankees have to go through with when they move to the Bible belt. . . Yes, you get used to it, but it puts you in a bad situation.

One other aspect of this cultural disparity resulting from mobility needs to be mentioned at this point. In contrast with other groups possessing less mobility, middle-class families are frequently composed of spouses with somewhat varied backgrounds. College friends, for example, become marriage partners without the strict regard for family characteristic of the upper class or for ethnic qualities characteristic of the lower class. As a result, middle-class marriages often require a significant amalgamation of backgrounds, which places some stress upon the marriage.

Economic Aspects. The middle-class family ordinarily finds itself possessed of sufficient income for the basic needs of life, but rarely has enough for luxuries. In this connection it should be noted that American advertising, by and large, is directed at the middle class and that much is directed toward making the luxury become the necessity. (One has only to scan the current women's magazines to realize how many items are emphasized as being necessary for the successful homemaker.) Technological advances contribute to the family's "need" for these luxuries. The introduction of new items, with an accompanying emphasis upon their real importance for the home, makes demands upon the family budget which are increasingly difficult to meet.

The end result is twofold. First, there is the constant need by the husband to increase his earnings, which means that the middle-class husband must see himself climbing the ladder of success—or be regarded as something of a failure. Second, there is the increasing tendency for the wife to work, either in the early stages of marriage or after the childbearing stage is completed. In the first of these situations, working outside the home is often required if the household is to be "suitably" equipped, and childbearing is delayed. In the latter, supplementing the husband's income is often a primary need, and the children are reared with the aid of institutional supplements (kindergartens and schools). This is not a state of affairs confined to the middle class, of course, but it is characteristic of that class because of the family's need to maintain standards which are often inconsistent with its ordinary income.

The need for "every tub to stand on its own bottom," as Robert S. Lynd has characterized the middle-class family, is further reinforced by two goals—owning their own home (except in large urban areas) and providing for the future through insurance. Both are objectives shared to some extent with other social classes, but again both are characteristic of the middle class in that status is unduly attached to their attainment.

Family Planning. In the past two decades, childbearing has become for most middle-class families a matter of choice. The improvement of contraceptive techniques has made it possible to limit reproduction. This fact, coupled with the increasing pressures to attain and to maintain status through a heightened plane of living, has resulted in smaller families and in families with the children spaced in accordance with the parents' wishes. (The great increase in births and the birth rate should not be considered as a denial of this statement. The increase is in good measure the result of depression-delayed childbearing and of the excess of marriages due to war.)

Whether or not the middle-class family today rears fewer children better is a question that cannot be answered, but it does raise the issue of the family's consideration of the child in this social class.

Child Rearing. The middle-class family exhibits distinctive characteristics in its child-rearing practices. In this social class, the child has a pre-eminent position in the family. From the moment pregnancy is recognized, much attention is paid to motherhood (and increasingly to fatherhood) as a career, at least temporarily. It has been said that in the middle class evidences of pregnancy are not hidden, but boasted about. (One evidence of this is the current middle-class practice of wearing maternity clothes long before there is visible evidence of the condition.)

The practices of childbearing and child rearing are pretty much standardized in this social class. Children must be born in hospitals, bottle-fed instead of breast-fed, attended by pediatricians, and dressed *à la mode.* Some of these practices are sound, but their significance lies in the fact that the rationalization for their use is "because that is what people like us do."

In general the middle class rears its children by the rule book. Lacking the support and guidance of an older generation, the mother resorts to baby books (for whatever age child) in an effort to be a good mother. This has its disadvantages, for there are significant changes from time to time in what is considered to be good practice. (From 1920 to 1950, for example, three distinct patterns of child rearing have been advanced by child psychologists and accepted in good measure by middle-class mothers.)

The child in the middle-class family has little utilitarian value. He is not expected to contribute to the family income or to provide for his parents in their old age. He is therefore to some degree an economic liability, and we may well ask why the middle class is so child-centered in its thinking. The answer lies in the high emotional value found in parent-child relations. Where the family members lack the larger numbers of relatives with whom to interact emotionally, those emotions are more specially focused between parent and child and are also intensified. In the small middle-class family, the concern of the parent for the child is a very real one. Parental aspirations are developed early (for the best companionships, the most advantageous education, the activities which will contribute most to personality development) and family activities are planned accordingly. This, in turn, creates financial and social demands of a high order.

As a result the middle-class child is pushed toward success to an exceptional degree. The *right* behavior is expected of the child, and his failure to fulfill these expectations leads to parental frustration. That these expectations are sometimes contrary to the dictates of nature is not surprising. The parents are likely to demand of the child behavior that is not consistent with his place in the developmental cycle and to feel a personal threat if he does not achieve that behavior. Behavior problems (for example, thumbsucking and masturbation) are likely to result from the pressures exerted by the parents, with an additional threat to the parents. All of this leads to a greater concern on the part of the parent, which is bolstered, most frequently, by the need to behave and to have one's children behave in the popularly conceived middle-class manner.

Diffusion of Family Interests. The middle-class family tends, because of its intense feeling of responsibility for the child's development, to make extensive use of institutional aids in the rearing of its children. The child is expected to participate in activities which are popularly assumed to contribute to his socialization; middle-class children therefore are likely to become members of youth organizations (Boy Scouts, Girl Scouts, the Y's) and are encouraged to extend their activities far beyond the limits of family activity.

Middle-class parents, too, participate freely in extrafamily activities, if for no other reason than their status-giving value. Parent-teacher organizations, for example, are composed largely of members of the middle class, as are garden clubs and museum associations. Some of these activities stem from the parents' feeling of responsibility for their children's welfare, others from the need to be accepted and recognized as substantial folks.

The result of this multiplicity of memberships, for both parent and child, is the diffusing of interests and the development of varied and nonfamily-centered loyalties. Family members, then, often fail to have the close contacts and identification which can be found outside the middle class.

Role Definition. In the middle-class family, roles tend to be clearly recognized. The father is the breadwinner, although this role is increasingly shared in certain stages of the family cycle (as has been indicated earlier). The mother is the rearer of the children, the social pace-setter, the manager of the home. It is the mother who makes decisions as to what friendships shall be formed and how they shall be pursued, and it is she whose decisions are paramount regarding child training. She is, in effect, the family purchasing agent, except in matters that are primarily of masculine concern, as, for example, the family car (and then the choice of color is left to her). The middle-class family tends, in considerable measure, to be mother-centered in its functioning and child-centered in its emotional interaction.

THE DILEMMA OF THE MIDDLE-CLASS FAMILY

The observations given in the preceding sections are necessarily broad generalizations. The reader is correct if he gathers from these an impression that the middle-class family faces something of a dilemma. Lacking extensive family ties it finds itself dependent upon its own few members for the rich emotional contacts inherent in family living. It also finds the diffusion of its members' interests necessary if they are to achieve status and to have the advantages believed due them. At the same time it is sensitive to the need for emotional security by its members, for this is emphasized in the literature of child rearing. A major result is the preoccupation with—and fear of failure in— the interactions of family life.

Equally important is the family's need to be independent and self-sufficient while it attempts to live in a society with increasingly complex demands and multiplying frustrations. Little provision is made by the society for aiding the middle-class family with its problems. For the working class, there are numbers of agencies designed to alleviate human problems. For the upper class, professional services are available, and the paying of ample fees makes them acceptable. The present development of community-supported agencies charging minimum fees will lessen this problem, but only as the middle class learns to use them without fear or sensitivity.

THE CHALLENGE TO THE MIDDLE-CLASS STUDENT

If middle-class family life is to be satisfactory, certain factors must be kept in mind: (1) the pressures that are inherent in American society (which dictate in unwarranted fashion what the family should do and be) need to be resisted where circumstances make them impracticable; (2) successful family living is essentially a matter of developing satisfying interpersonal relationships, which does not necessarily involve the use of outside groups—however attractive or necessary these are made to seem by their proponents; (3) child rearing involves a considerable measure of common sense, which makes the current ideologies less important than they are often held to be; (4) the increasing complexity of social life is such that recourse to professional services for help in maintaining the family's interaction need no longer be viewed as either weakness or failure on the part of the middle class.

SUMMARY

Middle-class families differ in various parts of the country. Identification with a given class is important in determining family behavior. The middle-class family stands alone without dependence on a large kinship. Status is gained through possession of material things. Changes in industrial development in various portions of the country require movement of families and adaptation to different local cultures. Family needs often require employment for the mother. Families tend to become smaller through limitation of childbearing. The child in the middle-class family has little utilitarian value. There is a strong push toward success. The middle-class family tends to be mother-centered. A satisfactory life for the middle-class family will require resistance to unwarranted demands and common sense in evaluating current ideologies.

Topics for further thought:

1. Middle-class families in our society have aspirations and patterns of behavior which are not experienced by other classes. Discuss some of the significant goals and methods of attaining them which are characteristic of the middle class.

2. Estimate the chances for happiness in marriage of the average member of the middle class. What are the main hazards and what are the prospects of meeting them successfully?

Selected reading references

Cavan, Ruth S., *The American Family,* New York, Thomas Y. Crowell Company, 1953.
> A standard sociological textbook on the family. Includes extensive analysis of family patterns among the various social classes.

Hollingshead, August B., *Elmtown's Youth: The Impact of Social Classes on Adolescents,* New York, John Wiley and Sons, 1949.
> The results of the author's detailed study of the impact of the social position of families upon the behavior of adolescents. Discusses all aspects of adolescent life.

Koos, Earl L., *Families in Trouble,* New York, King's Crown Press, 1946.
> Classic study of the problems of a group of lower-income families in New York City.

Koos, Earl L., "Class Differences in Family Reactions to Crisis," *Marriage and Family Living,* Summer, 1950, pp. 77-9, 99.

Shows how position in the class structure determines what conditions constitute family crises and how crises are met.

Warner, W. Lloyd, and Lunt, Paul S., *The Social Life of a Modern Community*, New Haven, Yale University Press, 1941.

A comprehensive analysis of the class structure of a New England city. Demonstrates the family patterns of different social classes.

4 RACE, RELIGION, AND NATIONALITY IN MATE SELECTION

Milton L. Barron

THERE are indications of a decline in the significance of ethnic factors in some aspects of American life. It is unwise, however, to underestimate the persistent influence of race, religion, and nationality background in marriage and the family. They still operate as important influences in courtship patterns and they serve to restrict the selection of a mate. Religious affiliation usually determines the kind of ceremony with which the marriage is solemnized. Ethnic factors orient many of the newlyweds' attitudes toward the home, and they supply many of the cultural practices within the home. They are central in the decisions regarding what will happen to the newborn child. Frequently they define the type and place of education for the child and delineate the circles within which both child and parents find their friends.

Ethnic factors in mate selection and the consequences in family relationships of choosing a mate either from within or outside one's ethnic groups obviously call for careful consideration.

ETHNIC GROUPS AND ENDOGAMY

All records show that in every society, historical or contemporary, primitive or modern, cultural restrictions limit the possible marriage partners available to each person. Among the many restrictions, endogamy or inmarriage is basic and universal. It defines the social groups outside of which marriage is either prohibited or generally avoided. In most societies, endogamy is customary with respect to race, religion, and, to a lesser extent, nationality background. To prohibit intermarriage along these lines, there are various types of taboo and social control: public opinion, religious doctrine and ritual, and legal proscription.

Racial Endogamy. In the United States, the most stringent form of social control, legislation, has been enacted against racial inter-marriage in thirty southern and western states. Six of these states considered the prohibition of racial intermarriage so fundamental that the laws were made part of the state constitutions. The lack of legis-lation against racial intermarriage in the remaining eighteen states need not be interpreted as evidence that such unions are socially approved or even that there is an indifference to them. It is more likely that racial minorities are such a negligible portion of the population or that intermarriages between racial groups are so few that the ques-tion can be ignored.

When there is such legislation and racial intermarriages do occur, most of the states' laws pronounce them null and void. In addition, almost all the laws provide penalties of imprisonment or fines, or both, for each party. Many laws also penalize those who issue mar-riage licenses for, or officiate at, racial intermarriages. After the adoption of the Fourteenth Amendment to the Constitution, the ques-tion developed whether or not state laws prohibiting racial inter-marriage denied to racial minorities the equality guaranteed them by the Amendment. Many cases testing the constitutionality of these laws have been tried in state courts. Invariably, until recent times, the laws have been held to be valid. The decisions in almost all cases were based on the position that there is no discrimination in the laws because they apply equally to whites and nonwhites. Furthermore the courts have held that although marriage is a civil contract it is one over which the state may exercise control with regard to those who may be permitted to enter the contract.

In 1947 in California a white and a Negro were refused a marriage license in accordance with the state law. The couple challenged this in the lower courts and then in the higher ones. The following year the state supreme court of California ruled that the state's law against racial intermarriage was unconstitutional and ordered the Los Angeles County Clerk to issue a license to the couple. This was the first time that any tribunal in the United States, state or federal, had declared such a law invalid. (In 1951, however, the California state senate defied the state supreme court and voted to keep on the statute books the law prohibiting marriages of whites with those of other races. The senate let the law stand by voting to postpone indefinitely consideration of an assembly bill that would have stricken the ban from the law.) Another sign of approaching liberalization of the legal restrictions against intermarriage appeared in 1948. That year the Human Rights Committee of the United Nations Economic and Social Council adopted a resolution deploring laws forbidding marriages between persons differing in color, nationality, race, or religion.

Religious Endogamy. While there are only informal pressures against nationality intermarriages, such as those exercised by relatives and friends, religious endogamy is subject to the powerful sanctions of ecclesiastical control. For example, Orthodox and Conservative rabbis in the United States have opposed marriages between Jews and gentiles as vigorously as their predecessors in Europe and elsewhere. True, American rabbis of the Reformed wing of Judaism were lenient in this matter for many years, and many of them officiated at mixed marriages. In recent decades, especially since 1909, there has been an unmistakable trend among these Reformed Jewish clergymen back to the traditional Jewish position. Virtually all of them now concur with other rabbis in the policy of officiating at a marriage between Jew and non-Jew only after the latter has become a convert to Judaism. In 1947 the Central Conference of American Rabbis, the official organization of Reformed Jewish clergymen, reiterated the position it had taken in 1909, declaring that mixed marriages (involving a Jew and a non-Jew) are contrary to the tradition of the Jewish religion and should therefore be discouraged by the American rabbinate. In case of a civil marriage ceremony the fact that the couple is already married by civil law does not obviate the necessity of conversion of the gentile party before a Jewish marriage ceremony can take place.

The policy of the Roman Catholic Church in the United States regarding religious endogamy is the most complex and conspicuous of all American religious groups. Therefore it calls for a more detailed analysis. Roman Catholic spokesmen continually deplore mixed marriage with non-Catholics, but their ecclesiastical policy reflects the outgroup preference of Catholic laymen for Protestants and other baptized Christians over non-Christians. Christians who are not Roman Catholics are considered to be heretics, but the Roman Catholic Church concedes that at least they are Christians if they have been properly baptized. Intermarriage with them (*mixta religio*) is not as undesirable as marriage with infidels (*disparitas cultus*) like Jews and Moslems. The Roman Catholic scale of preference goes even further. Among the least preferred groups, the infidels, a Reformed Jew is considered less undesirable in marriage than an Orthodox Jew. Permission to marry an Orthodox Jew who adheres strictly to traditional Jewish observances is more difficult to obtain from Catholic authorities than permission to marry a Reformed Jew.

Basically there are two reasons given by Roman Catholic authorities for their disapproval of religious intermarriage. One is that they wish to prevent cultural conflict and "the absence of intimate union and mutual harmony between husband and wife." The second reason is that they wish to avoid losses of two kinds to the Roman Catholic Church: of the Catholic party to intermarriage and of the forthcoming offspring of such marriage.

To ward off marital conflict and membership losses, the Roman Catholic Church has formulated explicit rules of procedure for both priests and laymen. First, priests are instructed to "use every endeavor to deter the faithful from contracting mixed marriages." Roman Catholic authorities tacitly recognize, however, that when a prospective mixed marriage is brought to the attention of the parish priest, little can be done to dissuade the couple. He must concentrate his efforts on the avoidance of loss to the Church and the minimization of marital conflict. Several requirements must be fulfilled before a Roman Catholic and a non-Catholic are allowed to be married by a Catholic priest. It is sinful to have a civil marriage ceremony, and no religious ceremony other than the Roman Catholic one is recognized. Furthermore, dispensation to forgo the difference in religion between the two parties must be obtained from the Roman Catholic hierarchy.

The dispensation is awarded only if there are "just and grave" causes or situations, such as follows: (1) the community in which the Roman Catholic party resides has a small Catholic population, thus restricting the choice of a marriage partner; (2) the Roman Catholic party is beyond the usual marriageable age and her chances of securing a Catholic husband are remote; (3) the Roman Catholic party is an impoverished widow who needs someone to support her; (4) there is reason to suspect that the two parties have been sexually intimate and if they do not marry, "worse things might happen"; (5) "worse things" have happened—the woman is pregnant; and (6) the couple will probably be married by a non-Catholic clergyman or by a civil magistrate if the Roman Catholic dispensation is not granted.

Another Roman Catholic requirement is that an antenuptial contract be signed by both parties. The non-Catholic must promise to allow the Catholic to practice his or her religion and to refrain from remarriage as long as the Catholic consort is still alive. Both persons must promise that no other marriage ceremony than the one to be performed by the Roman Catholic priest will take place, that they will maintain the position of the Church regarding birth control, and that all children resulting from the marriage will be brought up in the Roman Catholic religion. Violation of the promises concerning uninterrupted allegiance by the Roman Catholic party to Catholicism and Catholic training for the children may result in exclusion from participation in church activities, denial of a church burial, and even excommunication.

In many Roman Catholic dioceses, it is also expected that the non-Catholic party will take instruction in Roman Catholic doctrine and in the duties of married life. Frequently the Roman Catholic party is advised to attend these sessions. If the marriage ceremony is allowed to take place, the site is decided by the bishop. Until recently most bishops did not allow the usual church ceremony. It took place in the rectory, vestry, or outside the rail within the church. Unlike endogamous Roman Catholic marriages, the banns in mixed marriages are not published, there is no blessing of the ring, and the nuptial mass is omitted.

Protestant churches, with the exception of small sects like the Mennonites, who excommunicate any member marrying outside the faith, have not had formal systems for safeguarding religious endogamy. There have been three reasons for this lack: (1) the feeling that religion is essentially a personal matter and that the rights of individual consciences must be respected; (2) a sense on the part of Protestant ministers that in officiating at a marriage ceremony they are civil as well as religious authorities; and (3) the conviction that on an occasion which ought to be associated with all the sanction a religious rite can give to it, religious ceremony should not be withheld. Otherwise the couple will be compelled to consider their marriage purely as a civil contract.

This is not to say that most Protestant clergymen have been indifferent to religious mixed marriage. On the contrary, in 1932 the Committee on Marriage and the Home of the Federal Council of

Churches of Christ announced that "where intolerable conditions are imposed . . . persons contemplating a mixed marriage should be advised not to enter it." "Intolerable conditions" referred to the Roman Catholic requirement of a promise that the children born of intermarriages be reared as Roman Catholics. Increasingly thereafter Protestant laymen have been warned against marriage with Roman Catholics.

Despite these pressures and restrictions favoring endogamy in the Jewish, Roman Catholic, and Protestant religions, a survey of a national cross section of the readers of *The Woman's Home Companion* (March 1953) reported that four out of five women answered affirmatively to the question: Do you think mature, intelligent people of basically different religious backgrounds can have a happy marriage? Believing in the possibility of a successful intermarriage is not necessarily the same as facing a mixed marriage in one's own family. Therefore the next question in the survey was: If your own son or daughter wished to marry someone of basically different religious views, would you approve or disapprove of the marriage? Three out of five replied they would approve. In short, a smaller proportion of the respondents said they would approve of religious intermarriage for their own children than those who thought it could be successful.

Causal Factors in the Disruption of Endogamy. It is important to be familiar with the legislative, social, and ecclesiastical controls in support of ethnic endogamy. But it is equally important to understand the causal factors making for mate selection outside of one's ethnic group. What are the social and psychological forces that induce intermarriage?

Sociological studies in several American communities have revealed that an unbalanced sex ratio and numerically small representation lead some groups into considerable intermarriage. But even more important are the cultural similarities and the social proximity developed by the children and descendants of our earlier immigrant population. For example, residential propinquity, a well-known factor in courtship, not only because of the premarital associations it facilitates but also because of the economic and cultural similarities it implies, is a correlate of intermarriages as well as of ethnic inmarriages. Residential areas in the community are not always homogeneous with regard to race, religion, and nationality background.

Studies also indicate that young people of diverse ethnic groups are led into marital ties through occupational contacts, close association and common experiences in the amount, type, and locale of education, and recreational interaction. In other words, easy social contact and a cultural common denominator crossing ethnic lines may negate much of the prohibitive force of institutional control.

That is not all. Postadolescence and the premarital years in American society frequently constitute an age of rebellion against the more conservative values of parents. This, coupled with the conflict between generations and the emancipation from family control brought on by extramural and secular experiences in education and the economy, are conducive to intermarriage. For many young Americans, the cultural relativity to which they are exposed in the public-school system and the psychological association they construct between the intermarriage taboos and backwardness are also significant. A likely explanation is also to be found in the individualistic choice of a marriage partner embedded in the romantic complex of American culture. Lastly, one must give due consideration to the roles of self-hatred among some members of ethnic minorities and to the drive toward upward social mobility, both of which may find expression in marriage outside the group.

Patterns of Endogamy and Intermarriage—The Kennedy Study. What types of ethnic groups are more resistant to the breakdown of endogamy and what are the least resistant? What are the dynamics or trends of incidence and selection in intermarriage over the years? Sociologists who pose these questions in their community studies generally find that intermarriage occurs most often between nationality groups, less often between religious groups, and least often between racially defined groups. The most valuable study in this connection was conducted in New Haven and covered a long time span.[1] Marriage records in that community for 1870, 1900, 1930, 1940, and 1950 were analyzed, and over each time interval there was found to have been an increase in the percentages of those intermarrying in most—*but not all*—groups. The proportion of Protestants intermarrying with non-Protestants, and Roman Catholics with non-Catholics, for instance, declined slightly from 1930 to 1940. This is more significant than it may appear at first glance, largely because it upsets the arm-

---

[1] Ruby Jo Reeves Kennedy, "Single or Triple Melting Pot? Intermarriage Trends in New Haven," *American Journal of Sociology*, 49:331-9 (1944); see also "Single or Triple Melting Pot? Intermarriage in New Haven, 1870-1950," *American Journal of Sociology*, 58:56-9 (1952).

chair, speculative idea that intermarriage relentlessly increases in the course of time in a smooth, unbroken pattern.

The most interesting pattern discovered in the New Haven study is implicit in the concept of the triple melting pot. Negro-white intermarriages, on the one hand, have been virtually nonexistent. Nationality groups, on the other hand, have intermarried at a very high rate, but not indiscriminately. Rather they have tended to intermarry within the confines of the apparently hardening lines of religion. That is, Roman Catholic nationalities have intermarried with other Roman Catholic nationalities; Protestant nationalities have chosen other Protestants; and Jews, probably in large part because their religious and tribal traits generally coincide, have married other Jews. Thus New Haven has had the pattern of a triple melting pot.

The need for further knowledge is obvious. Community studies of the patterns of endogamy and intermarriage have been few in number and, like the New Haven study, concentrated for the most part on the Eastern seaboard. It is important to have a more adequate regional coverage before generalizing about what is happening in American society.

THE CONSEQUENCES OF MATE SELECTION

In comparison with ethnically endogamous couples and their children, how do those who intermarry and their offspring fare in size of family, personality development and interpersonal relations, religious affiliation and participation, and success and failure as measured by the criteria of divorce, desertion, and separation?

It is difficult to answer this question because research has been concerned mainly with religious intermarriage. Before the findings are considered, one should be aware that such research must challenge the already existing prejudgments of vested interest, social myopia, and wishful thinking. To be sure, few but racists and fundamental zealots now argue against intermarriage on the grounds of detrimental biological consequences. But there are many people who insist that in social and cultural affairs those who intermarry face insurmountable difficulties. As one leading clergyman put it recently:

Intermarriages undermine the stability of the home, increase the number of unhappy marriages, and bring children into the world with a rift in their souls which can never be healed.

Perhaps more sober and realistic is the view of another outstanding clergyman:

There are many who deprecate mixed marriages on simple practical grounds. Marriage, they argue, involves at best many problems and difficulties. Why complicate it still more? Why enter a union with a reduced chance of success? This would be an impressive argument if we could show that a majority, or even a dangerously high percentage, of intermarriages are failures. We do not, in fact, have reliable statistics; nor do we have a satisfactory way of measuring success in marriage. Everyone knows of successful intermarriages, and they are not so rare as to be labeled startling exceptions.

Also worthy of preliminary attention before considering the actual consequences of mate selection in family relationships is the relevant theory formulated by specialists in the field of marriage and the family: extreme differences in background should foster marital discord rather than rapport. They have suggested, for instance, that the element of mixture is a focal point for conflict in many cases of inter-marriage because it becomes the scapegoat for tensions that originate elsewhere in the marital relationship. It is an easy substitute ex-planation for a couple's poor adjustment in, for example, financial affairs. At the same time, however, the theorists have maintained that the consequences of any marriage depend upon the total situation and not merely upon the fact of mixture. That is, a marriage's inner solidarity is affected not only by its various parts but also by the influences of those with whom the couple has had and continues to have social ties. Theoretically no type of marriage contains within itself the germs of its own inevitable failure. Success or failure de-pends upon total adjustment rather than upon the mere elements of difference.

Accompanying this theory pertinent to the husband-wife relation-ship in intermarriage is the theory regarding the children of such marriages. Most prevalent is the notion that lack of adequate identifica-tion and the status of marginality and outcast are the burdens they must bear. M. C. Elmer has speculated that in order to avoid this situation, one adjustment probably at work in American society is the greater exercise of birth control; the number of children born of intermarriages must be less than the number born of inmarriages.[2] For those religiously intermarried couples who do have children there are known to be several alternative adjustments. An early European practice sanctioned by law in some countries and transplanted in-

[2] M. C. Elmer, *The Sociology of the Family,* Boston, Ginn & Company, 1945, p. 195.

formally to the United States is for the boys to follow the religion of the father and the girls that of the mother. Another practice is for all members of the family—parents as well as children—to assume the religious affiliation of one of the parents. Still another is for one parent and all the children to join one denomination while the other parent remains in his own. Next is the compromise alternative: The parents become members of a religious body like the Universalists or Unitarians and rear their children accordingly. Idealists try one of two other alternatives: Either the children are exposed to both of the parents' divergent faiths or they are allowed to make up their own minds when they reach the age of discretion.

Occasionally the problem of religious identification of children of intermarriages comes before the courts, and, in some of these cases, important precedents are established. For example, a test case in Texas was concerned with the legal validity of that part of the Roman Catholic antenuptial contract and promises signed by the non-Catholic in an intermarriage which states that "all children, both boys and girls, that may be born of this union shall be baptized and educated solely in the faith of the Roman Catholic Church, even in the event of the death of my Catholic consort. In case of dispute . . . the custody of the children shall be given to such guardians as to assure the faithful execution of this covenant and promise. . ." The decision in court was that the promises signed are not valid in law; they are only binding in good faith.

Another case in New Jersey dealt with the question of the religious affiliation of children of intermarriages in the event of a divorce. The mother, who was Jewish, had married and divorced a Roman Catholic. There were two children of the marriage, a ten-year-old son and a five-and-a-half-year-old daughter. The mother insisted on rearing them as Jews whereas the father called for his own religion. The Court of Errors and Appeals decided in the mother's favor after the father had contended that the right to control religious training is vested exclusively in the male parent. The court, rejecting this, cited the state law that each parent has an equal right in the matter and noted that in the divorce case the custody of the children had been awarded to the mother. Therefore she had the right to rear the children in the religion she saw fit.

The Landis Study. What systematic, factual information has sociological research uncovered about the consequences of intermarriage?

Landis at Michigan State College conducted the most fruitful study.[3] For three years he collected from the students in marriage lecture sessions information on their parents' marriages, such as age when married, occupation, education, religion, present marital status, whether either parent changed his or her religious faith at or after marriage, which parent took the responsibility for providing religious training, how much conflict over religion had been evident to the children, and the eventual faith taken by the children, the students themselves.

Of the 4,108 families whose histories were thus analyzed, Landis discovered that almost two-thirds of the parents had inmarried as Protestants, both parents were Catholics in 573 families, and in 346 cases Catholics had intermarried with 305 Protestants and with 41 persons having no religious faith. In 192 of these 346 intermarriages, each spouse retained his or her own religious affiliation after the marriage; in 113 of the cases either the Catholic or the Protestant changed to the faith of the other.

What about the divorce rates of the inmarrying and intermarrying parents? The Landis study showed that the rates were lowest in unmixed marriages—with Catholics first, Protestants second—followed by Catholic-Protestant intermarriages, and reaching the highest level in marriages in which one partner had no religious faith. Landis acknowledged that the divorce rate was not an accurate index of marital success or failure. Catholic-Protestant intermarriages seemed to have a better chance of avoiding divorce when one mate—particularly the Protestant wife or the Catholic husband—changed to the faith of the other mate. The divorce was affected by whether or not the mother in the intermarriage was Catholic or Protestant. There were three times as many divorces in intermarriages between a Catholic man and a Protestant woman as there were in cases in which the husband was Protestant and the wife Catholic.

Landis's explanation for this significant differential is that fewer factors make for tension in intermarriages in which the mother is Catholic. This is because the mother-role and Roman Catholicism are more likely to be constants or inflexible; the father-role and Prot-

[3] Judson T. Landis, "Marriages of Mixed and Non-mixed Religious Faith," *American Sociological Review,* 14:401-7 (1949). This study's significance has two limitations. First, it does not reflect a cross section of the American population, but rather it represents the background of young people in college in the Midwest. Second, because of the method used in collecting the data, the results shed light only upon intermarriages in which there are children. A study of childless intermarriages would probably show different results.

estantism, on the other hand, are more likely to be variables or flexible. Consider, for example, the religious training of the children. Landis observed:

In the American home the mother is more likely to be a church member and is more apt to take the responsibility for the religious instruction of the children. When a man who has no faith or is a Protestant marries a Catholic woman, he signs the ante-nuptial agreement and does not find it difficult to abide by the agreement when his children are born. He expects his wife to be responsible for their religious training. There is then no great cause for conflict in this type of a mixed marriage. If the mother is Protestant the marriage seems to have many more serious problems. The Protestant mother has agreed that the children will be baptized Catholic, and yet she can hardly bring up her children in a faith which she herself does not accept. Since the major responsibility for religious training falls upon her, she will probably bring the children up in the only faith she knows and believes in. This means that the agreement made before marriage must be scrapped. The Catholic husband is more apt to be a church member than the Protestant husband who marries a Catholic. It may be quite a blow to him to find that his wife will not have the children baptized into his faith. Conflict results since many Catholic fathers cannot give up without a struggle. The Catholic father not only has his own conscience to live with but he is also constantly aware of the attitude of his church and of his family when they see his children being brought up in the Protestant faith.

How were the children in Landis's study actually brought up? First, the data substantiate the previously mentioned theory of intermarriage adjustment by limitation of offspring. The students whose parents had intermarried had fewer brothers and sisters than those whose parents were not mixed. Catholic women married to Protestants had had 2.2 children on the average; Protestant women married to Catholics, 1.9; while couples in which both were Catholics had 3.6; and those in which both were Protestants had 2.7. The most common tendency was for the children, especially daughters, to follow the faith of the mother, this being true for approximately 75 per cent of the girls as compared with 65 per cent of the boys. This was consistent with the students' descriptions of the parental responsibility for religious training in their homes. The most frequent policy was that the mother took all responsibility for the religious training; the second most frequent policy was that the parents told them about both faiths but let them decide for themselves when they were old enough.

CONCLUSION

Conspicuous by their absence in the Landis study as well as in other studies are data about the consequences of intermarriages between Jews and non-Jews. Before sociologists can rest assured about the thoroughness of the knowledge regarding the consequences of inter-marriage, however, they must do more research on a larger sampling of socioeconomic groups in American society than that implied on the college level. They need to pursue studies of intermarriage among childless couples. More needs to be known, too, about the degree or lack of acceptability of intermarried couples by their relatives. Other studies should be made of inmarriages and intermarriages that have not ended in divorce or separation so that success or failure may be seen in terms of other meaningful standards. There is also a need for knowledge about intermarriages between members of different Prot-estant denominations and sects, for in these cases the problems of adjustment probably can be as great as those between the major religious affiliations of Roman Catholic, Protestant, and Jew.

One final task confronts American sociologists. It is to call atten-tion to the inconsistency of conservative attitudes toward intermar-riage on the one hand with activities in creating social and cultural conditions favoring intermarriage on the other hand. Sending children to public schools and to centers of higher education away from home, struggling against restrictive covenants, job discrimination, and quota systems, participating in interfaith activity, are but a few rep-resentative practices that lead inevitably to intergroup contacts and subsequently to love and intermarriage. The recognition of this dilemma is fundamental to any intelligent approach to the problem.

Topics for further thought:

1. Preferential marriage groups exist in our society and it is expected that an individual will find a marriage partner within his group. Relate this "patterning of marriage" to basic societal controls.

2. Discuss the relationship of this "patterning of marriage" to what is often referred to in America as increasing individualism and de-creasing family control.

Selected reading references

Barron, Milton, *People Who Intermarry,* Syracuse, Syracuse University Press, 1946.
The most comprehensive account in print of the status and problems of intermarriage. Research carried out in an Eastern community.

Black, Algernon D., *If I Marry Outside My Religion,* New York, Public Affairs Pamphlet No. 204.
Discusses simply and practically the various issues involved in choosing a mate outside one's religion.

Frazier, E. Franklin, *The Negro Family in the United States,* New York, The Dryden Press, 1951.
Contains considerable historical material on race mixture in the United States.

Freehof, Solomon B., "Report on Mixed Marriages and Intermarriage," *Yearbook,* Vol. 57, Philadelphia, Central Conference of American Rabbis, 1947.
Considers both marriage between persons from different branches of Judaism and marriages of Jews and non-Jews.

Schmiedeler, Edgar, *Marriage and the Family,* New York, McGraw-Hill Book Company, 1946.
Contains a statement of the Catholic point of view on marriages between Catholics and non-Catholics.

5 SOCIAL PSYCHOLOGICAL FACTORS AFFECTING FERTILITY: THE INDIANAPOLIS STUDY

Charles F. Westoff

IN 1938 a committee of population experts (demographers) and psychologists was organized to investigate the social and psychological factors affecting fertility. Interest in this subject had developed against a background of a declining birth rate in the United States and in Western civilization generally, which had reached an all-time low during the depression of the 1930's. The committee members hoped to find a significant amount of information about the motivations and interests of married couples regarding the planning and having of children and the factors responsible for differences in fertility. Such information would be helpful in the event that the development of a national population policy should be undertaken in the United States as it already had been in countries with low birth rates, such as France and Sweden. Although the birth rate in the United States made a sharp recovery with World War II and postwar prosperity without the development of a population policy of encouraging larger families, the scientific value of the study's results has not been lessened in any way.

The project, known as the Study of Social and Psychological Factors Affecting Fertility, was designed to provide answers to such questions as these: What proportion of married couples actually try to plan size of family, that is, practice contraception except when trying to have a child? What social and psychological factors affect the proportion of couples who practice contraception effectively? Which methods of contraception are employed? Why do some couples want and have small families and others large families? What factors combine to produce group differences in fertility, for example, among socio-economic classes?

As guides for the collection and analysis of data, the committee formulated 23 hypotheses regarding the influence of various factors on the proportion of couples practicing contraception effectively and on the size of planned families. Some of the variables presumed to be important were socioeconomic status, feeling of economic security, interest in and liking for children, the interference of children with personal freedom, conformity to group patterns, adherence to traditions, interest in religion, feeling of personal adequacy, and marital adjustment. The hypothesis on marital adjustment, for example, was stated as follows: The more satisfactory the marital adjustment, the higher the proportion of couples practicing contraception effectively and the larger the planned families. This hypothesis and the others related to size of *planned* families, that is, to the fertility of couples who successfully planned and had the number of children they desired. The committee emphasized *planned* families because it was especially interested in studying the kinds of factors that induce some couples to have small families and others to have large families, excluding accidental pregnancies.

For various reasons, the committee decided to restrict the study to native-white, urban, Protestant couples who had been married from 12 to 15 years (that is, who were married in 1927, 1928, or 1929) and who had never been previously married, the wife under thirty and the husband under forty at the time of marriage, and both at least elementary-school graduates. Following the selection of Indianapolis as the site for the Study, the committee developed and pretested schedules and questionnaires. Then an adjusted, representative sample of 1,977 couples was obtained and three interviews were conducted with the wife and one with the husband. Of the total 1,977 cases analyzed, 533 revealed a history of either complete or partial sterility, leaving for the detailed motivational and attitudinal analysis 1,444 couples who were physiologically able to have children. This summary relates to the latter group only.

Within the limits of this chapter a full discussion of the results of the Indianapolis Study is impossible. No less than 32 articles reporting the statistical results and analyses of the hypotheses have been published and, although the Study is now virtually completed (World War II caused delay in finishing the work), several reports may still be published. Here only a description of some of the basic data and a summary of the outstanding analytical findings are presented.

CONTRACEPTION AND FERTILITY PLANNING

Among the basic questions that the Study was designed to answer were the extent to which contraception was practiced and the kinds and effectiveness of birth-control techniques used.

With few exceptions the couples in the Indianapolis sample had all used some method of birth control at one time or another during their 12 to 15 years of marriage. There was, however, considerable variation in the methods employed and in the regularity and effectiveness of practice. Actually, there were no less than 22 contraceptive methods and different combinations of methods that were used in this sample to an extent sufficient for statistical analysis. But the most common methods were douche, condom, and diaphragm and jelly. For the wives, friends and relatives were the chief sources of information about the use of douches, husbands about the condom, and physicians about diaphragm and jelly.

The wives stated that the main reason they employed the particular method they were using before the interview was that they felt it was the most reliable one; but many of the wives who were using a douche reported that it was the only method of birth control they knew. Most of the couples had changed methods at one time or another during their marriage. This change from one method to another frequently followed an unplanned conception, and the couple wanted a more reliable method. The main reason for change, unreliability, was cited most frequently by couples who had switched from a douche to some other method and was cited least by couples using condom, diaphragm and jelly, or some combination of condom and douche. The reason offered by most of the couples who changed from condom to another method was that the condom interfered with their enjoyment of the sex act.

The actual effectiveness of the methods, as measured by comparative pregnancy rates occurring while the methods were being used, agreed with these subjective reactions. The most effective methods were diaphragm and jelly, condom, and withdrawal (and various combinations of these with each other and with douches). The least effective methods were the safe period or the rhythm method (partly because it was misunderstood) and douches used alone. There is definite evidence that the couples tended to gravitate toward the use of the more effective methods, although a significant proportion of the group were still relying on the less effective methods at the time of the interview.

Despite the fact that there was a high level of contraceptive practice among the couples in the Indianapolis sample, over half (53 per cent) of all the pregnancies experienced by the group were accidental or unplanned in the sense that they occurred while contraception was being practiced. An even greater proportion of the total number of pregnancies can be considered unplanned if those are included which began before the first use of contraception; these amounted to about 19 per cent of the total. In only 27 per cent of all pregnancies did the couples deliberately interrupt the practice of contraception in order to have a child.

These figures do not tell the whole story of the planning of births. The attitudes of the couples must be considered, since some pregnancies were not deliberately planned, although the couple may have wanted a child nevertheless. In addition, the sequence of planned and unplanned pregnancies is important. Thus, the fertility-planning status of couples who had had earlier, unplanned pregnancies but who deliberately planned the last pregnancy is quite different from that of couples who had accidental pregnancies after the last wanted one. A classification which takes attitudes and control practices into account was devised by Whelpton and Kiser and revealed the following distribution:

Number and spacing planned. This group constituted 28 per cent of the sample. These couples exhibited the most successful control of fertility in that they had no pregnancies that were not deliberately planned by stopping contraception in order to conceive. Nearly one-third of the couples in this category were deliberately childless; they had practiced contraception regularly during all (or nearly all) of their married life because they did not want a child. The average number of births to couples in this entire group was only 1.1.

Number planned. This group constituted 14 per cent of the sample and consisted mainly of couples whose *last* pregnancy was deliberately planned by stopping contraception in order to conceive but who had one or more previous pregnancies under other circumstances. The average number of births to these couples was 2.3

Quasi-planned. Couples classified in this group, over 31 per cent of the total, had not deliberately planned their last pregnancy, as had those in the two categories above, but they said either that they wanted their last pregnancy or that they wanted another. These couples had an average of 2.0 births.

Excess fertility. This group was composed of 27 per cent of the couples; they were considered as least successful in planning size of family, because they wanted neither the last pregnancy nor another. These couples had the largest families, with an average of 3.0 births per couple.

As indicated by the foregoing description, there is considerable variation in the practice of contraception in the general population. Almost all of the couples in the sample had at one time or another during their marriage practiced some form of birth control, although with varying degrees of regularity. Despite this wide practice of birth control, however, over half of all pregnancies were accidental. The reasons for this are complex; involved are such factors as the inherent differences in the effectiveness of the methods themselves, variations in the regularity and proficiency of practice, and, perhaps most importantly, differences in the intensity of the motivations of couples to prevent a pregnancy.

The practice of contraception was only one of the dependent variables in which the committee was interested. In the final analysis, the main interest was, of course, fertility itself. What factors account for socioeconomic group differences in fertility? What social and psychological variables affect the size of *planned* families? The following sections summarize some of the general findings pertinent to these questions.

SOCIOECONOMIC STATUS

Throughout the analyses of the Indianapolis Study, the authors were interested in differential fertility among the socioeconomic classes of the population. Traditionally, in the United States and in parts of Western Europe there has been an inverse relationship between socioeconomic status and size of family, that is, the poorer, uneducated, or lower classes have had the largest families. Many early theorists had speculated that this relationship might be due to differences in the average fecundity (physiological capacity to conceive) of these groups. Later evidence has indicated that the more widespread knowledge and use of contraception among the educated, white-color classes was the main factor permitting lower fertility, and has failed to support the hypothesis that there are class differences in fecundity.

The data from the Indianapolis Study threw further light on this matter. Evidence indicated that contraception was used more regularly and more effectively among the higher-income groups. Not only was the proficiency of use of any method better, but the higher-income groups used more effective methods. Douching, for example, noted as one of the least effective methods, was used much more by the lower-income group. As a result of these factors, the lower-income groups exhibited higher accidental pregnancy rates. On the other hand, when pregnancy rates were examined, no systematic relationship with income class was found in the *absence* of contraception. Thus, the inverse relationship between socioeconomic status and fertility was shown to reflect in large measure the differences among the classes in the practice of contraception.

The practice of contraception is, of course, only the means to family limitation. Also involved are the couples' desires, values, and interests with respect to children—in general, the kind of life they want to lead. Some couples are visibly more family-oriented than others. Thus, it is of interest to examine the factors responsible for differences in the size of *planned* families.

Perhaps the outstanding finding of the Indianapolis Study was that fertility and socioeconomic status varied *directly* among planned families. In other words, among couples who had exercised complete and effective fertility control (that is, the number-and-spacing-planned category), those at the higher levels had more children than those in the lower socioeconomic groups. The variable of income showed this relationship more clearly than any of the other socioeconomic variables such as occupation and education. This is the *opposite* pattern from that observed for *all* couples and supports the theory that the traditional inverse relation of fertility to socioeconomic status is dependent largely on group differences in contraceptive knowledge and practice. Actually, other studies of fertility based on wider and larger samples have indicated that the traditional inverse relationship has been altered; the higher classes no longer evidence the lowest fertility. This suggests the increasing popularization of birth control— a fact that makes the study of planned fertility even more important.

FEELING OF ECONOMIC SECURITY

Although socioeconomic status is an objective fact, it does not always have the same influence on people's feeling of security. For example, some college-educated, white-collar employees having an annual income of around $5,000 will feel economically secure, but others will not. How they feel will depend on a variety of things, including such factors as the desired level of consumption, the neighborhood they live in, the friends they have, their job security, their health, and so forth. This conceptual distinction between socioeconomic status and feeling of economic security was deemed of sufficient importance to require an independent hypothesis relating to feeling of economic security. An index of feeling of economic security was constructed and was analyzed in relation to size of planned family. The analysis showed that those couples who felt more secure economically had larger planned families, a relationship that was partly independent of socioeconomic status.

MARITAL ADJUSTMENT AND HAPPINESS

Inasmuch as the planning of children and the decision regarding the number of children a couple wants is the net reflection of two persons' attitudes, interests, and values, questions naturally arise whether couples who are happier and better adjusted in their marriages have more success in planning fertility and whether they have smaller or larger families than couples who are less satisfied with their marriages. There has been a traditional image in the United States (probably deriving from rural culture) of the large, happy family which, to some extent, conveys the implication that healthy, well-adjusted, happy couples have many children. The results of the Indianapolis Study do not support this idea. There is definite evidence, however, that marital adjustment, as reflected and measured by the couples' opinions of their marital happiness, agreement on family matters, and lack of desire to improve spouse, is positively associated with ability in preventing unwanted pregnancies. In short, the happier, better-adjusted couples reported more successful fertility planning. This relationship, of course, can and probably does work in two directions. On the one hand, a wife and husband who are happy and well adjusted in their marriage probably communicate better with each other on matters of birth control and the number of children they desire, and thus, as compared to a couple who do not discuss or cannot agree on such questions, are less likely to have accidental pregnancies. There is evidence, for example, that wives and husbands who replied that responsibility for contraception was on a fifty-fifty basis had considerably greater success in preventing unwanted pregnancies than those who stated that one or the other had the main responsibility for birth control. On the other hand, by virtue of their success in having the number of children they wanted, the couple's marital happiness and adjustment probably benefited.

The analysis of these factors in relation to size of family did not produce such clear-cut results. With respect to the total fertility of the sample of 1,444 couples, marital adjustment and happiness decreased as size of family increased. Among couples who exercised completely successful control in the planning of their children (the number-and-spacing-planned group), however, there was some slight, though not consistent, suggestion that the happier, better-adjusted couples had slightly larger families. Among this group, the couples who were deliberately childless, for example, show somewhat lower marital-adjustment scores than those who had several children. It should be emphasized, however, that no really important fertility differences by marital adjustment among couples who had successfully planned their children were found in this Study.

RATIONALITY OF BEHAVIOR

The discussion thus far has covered the three variables: socioeconomic status, feeling of economic security, and marital adjustment. There were 20 other variables represented in the hypotheses formulated for the Indianapolis Study, but the remaining part of this chapter will summarize only some of the more important ones.

One cluster of hypotheses is related to rationality of behavior and includes hypotheses on interest in religion, adherence to traditions, tendency to plan in general, and conformity to group patterns. Analysis of the last of these variables did not produce any conclusive results. As for the first three variables in this group, the results show that couples who were least interested in religion, who adhered least to traditional forms of behavior and values, and who exhibited the most tendency to plan in general tended to have the greatest success in planning fertility. In broader terms, this is interpreted to mean that the couples who were most rational in their behavior, that is, whose behavior was more the result of calculated choices between alternatives rather than the unquestioning acceptance on faith of the traditional behavioral standards of the group to which they belonged, applied similar standards to their fertility behavior. Thus, as one might expect from the fact that fewer unplanned pregnancies occurred to these couples, total fertility tended to decrease with increasing rationality of behavior. The relationship between these variables and size of family among couples who completely planned fertility, however, is not very strong. In general, couples who had a strong religious interest and couples who were inclined to be tradition-oriented tended to have slightly larger planned families; couples manifesting little tendency to plan their general affairs tended to have slightly smaller planned families. All of these associations, however, appear to be dependent somewhat on the socioeconomic status of the couples.

PERSONAL HEALTH

There were two hypotheses in the Indianapolis Study relating to health, or, more precisely, personal evaluation of health (since no medical data were obtained). One related to the health of the couple, the other to the health of the children. It had been hypothesized that the poorer the health of the couple and children, the greater the effective practice of contraception and the smaller the size of planned families. Actually, the opposite type of pattern prevailed in so far as contraception was concerned. Couples reporting good health for themselves and children had the most successful birth-control records. They did not differ systematically from the others, however, with respect to size of planned families. Again, there are interrelationships between socioeconomic status and health, fertility planning status, and fertility that indicate that the relationships of health and fertility behavior are not independent of those between health and socioeconomic status.

Another hypothesis of similar nature related to fear and anxieties about pregnancy and childbirth. The analysis of the data on this hypothesis indicated that fears of this nature were not a serious factor after the birth of the first child. It did appear to be operating to some degree among childless couples but, all in all, it was not a particularly significant variable among those studied.

PERSONALITY CHARACTERISTICS

At least two of the Indianapolis Study hypotheses were aimed at the relationship of personality characteristics to fertility behavior. Feeling of personal adequacy, one of the two, was measured by questions on self-confidence, inclination to worry, tendency to get upset, chance for self-expression, and the like. Analysis revealed that the more adequate personality or, more specifically, the more emotionally stable, self-confident, well-satisfied personality exhibited greater success in planning fertility than the less adequate personality. This relationship, however, depended to a large extent on the socioeconomic status of the couple. No association of any significance was found with the fertility of planned families.

The other hypothesis relating exclusively to personality was that couples who had an ego-centered interest in children would successfully plan fertility and would have smaller families. The phrase "ego-centered interest in children" was conceived to mean the use of children as a means for satisfying the parents' needs for ego satisfaction and was partly measured by a battery of questions relating to the couple's psychological dependency on their children and the feelings of security that they derive from having children love them. Although the hypothesis seemed to be rather promising, the variable itself was not measured adequately and the analysis with fertility planning and fertility showed only a very slight support of the hypothesis.

ATTITUDES TOWARD CHILDREN

One would assume that couples who have a strong liking for children would plan and have larger families than couples who are not particularly interested in children. Results indicated that the relationship, although definitely present, was not simple. It appeared that couples who had a strong liking for and interest in children would have *some* children rather than *none,* but there seemed to be no straight progression of size of planned family with this variable. Nevertheless, the net statistical relationship was one of the highest to be found with planned fertility in the entire study.

A hypothesis similar in nature to the preceding one related to the feeling that children interfere with personal freedom—a feeling that was presumed to lead to effective planning and small families. This was measured by questions on how much children interfered with visiting, going to the movies, entertaining, and other social activities. The analysis, however, actually revealed some indication of an opposite pattern. It was thought that the main reason for this unexpected result was that the couples had answered in terms of their current assessment of how much their children interfered with these activities, rather than in the context of their original motivations for planning the number of children they had. In other words, the answers were in terms of actual child care rather than fertility planning.

ADDITIONAL HYPOTHESES

A number of other hypotheses in the Indianapolis Study that will not be summarized here covered such diverse subjects as the effect on fertility behavior of migration, types of family and childhood situations, doubling-up of families in homes, parental preferences regarding the sex of children, the desire of children for brothers and sisters, feeling of economic tension, and husband-wife dominance. Two other hypotheses related to reasons for having a second child: a belief that an only child is handicapped and a desire to insure against childlessness in the event of the death of the first child.

SOCIAL MOBILITY

One important social-psychological area not included in the design of the Study was that of social mobility, or the movement of individuals up or down the ladder of occupational and financial success. It is plausible to presume that couples who are ambitious will exercise greater control over their fertility than those who are not especially oriented toward advancement and success. For those who are, the occurrence of a pregnancy at the wrong time in the husband's career is frequently regarded as disadvantageous, to say the least. Of course, the longer conception is postponed the lower becomes the probability of having a large family. Although hypotheses on social mobility were not included in the Study, the data provided some possibility for analyzing the relation of father's and son's occupations (son meaning the husband who was interviewed) and the occupational changes that occurred in the husband's work history. The analysis of these data in general supports the notion that upwardly mobile couples tend to plan fertility more effectively and to have smaller families, but there are many exceptions in the data and the various interpretations are complicated. All the participants in the Study were convinced that any future studies of social and psychological factors affecting fertility should definitely emphasize the factor of social mobility, and that data should be collected not only on occupational and other socioeconomic changes but also on couples' mobility aspirations.

THE STUDY IN PERSPECTIVE

It is appropriate to raise the question of the value and significance of the Indianapolis Study. What contributions has the Indianapolis Study made both to social science and to a better understanding of human fertility?

It should be emphasized that the Indianapolis Study was a pioneer effort in a previously unexplored field. It attempted to go beyond the collection of primary population statistics in order to investigate the complex motivations, personality characteristics, attitudes, and values that lie behind the planning for children and the ultimate size of the family. In an important sense, these research objectives resulted in a truly interdisciplinary effort that produced a useful integration of the interests and skills of demography with those of psychology and sociology. This co-operation has developed and today a new inter-disciplinary committee has been formed for the express purpose of carrying on research into the social and psychological factors affecting fertility.

Of more significance, however, is the nature of the Study's contributions to the knowledge of human fertility. For example, it provided the first large-scale profile of the extent and nature of contraceptive practice for a general population. It indicated very clearly that contraception as practiced left much to be desired with regard to effectiveness. One of the key questions to which analysis was directed was that of the connections between socioeconomic status and fertility. The analysis revealed that the high negative relationships between these two variables was due mainly to their joint relationship to the *planning* of fertility. In other words, when differences in contraceptive practice were held constant statistically, the inverse relationship between socioeconomic status and fertility virtually disappeared. In fact, just the opposite relationship appeared among couples who exercised successful fertility control; couples in the higher socioeconomic categories tended to have slightly *larger* families.

The Study was less successful, however, in its attempt to unravel the social-psychological variables that underlie these relationships. It did indicate that feeling of economic security was involved to some extent. Marital adjustment, rationality of behavior, and some of the personality characteristics studied were shown to have significant influences on whether contraception was practiced successfully but they shed little or no light on the understanding of the differences in fertility among couples who effectively controlled size of family. Only the variable on liking for and interest in children evidenced a fairly strong relationship and this relationship was shown to be mainly a distinction between childlessness and having some children rather than a guide to the size of family itself.

As with other relationships, the fact that the Study was conducted among couples married 12 to 15 years increases the difficulty of interpretation. For example, it is not clear in this case whether interest in and liking for children precedes the decision to have children or is a result of having children. In this specific instance, it is no doubt safe to assume that the relationship operates in both directions.

In conclusion, the Indianapolis Study, as with many other studies in new fields, probably raises more questions than it answers. One consequence of this fact is that a new study is now being planned which will focus more sharply on some of these questions.

Topics for further thought:

1. The effective use of contraception in planning family size seems to be related to socioeconomic status. What are the implications of this for changes in the size of our population?

2. Our culture stresses the values of individual happiness, personal achievement, and success. In order to reach these goals many married couples choose to remain childless at the risk of incurring societal disapproval. Discuss their dilemma from both the individual and the societal points of view.

Selected reading references

Kiser, Clyde V., "L'Enquete d'Indianapolis sur la fecondité," *Population,* April-June, 1950, pp. 271-90.

Kiser, Clyde V., and Whelpton, P. K., "Résumé of the Indianapolis Study of Social and Psychological Factors Affecting Fertility," *Population Studies,* November, 1953, pp. 95-110.

Kiser, Clyde V., "The Indianapolis Fertility Study: An Example of Planned Observational Research," *The Public Opinion Quarterly,* Winter, 1953-54, pp. 496-510.
The three references above present earlier summaries of the Indianapolis Study.

Whelpton, P. K., and Kiser, Clyde V. (eds.), *Social and Psychological Factors Affecting Fertility,* 4 vols., New York, Milbank Memorial Fund, 1946-55.
Findings of the Indianapolis Study published up to the time of publication of this book.

6 SEX AND THE SOCIAL ORDER

Georgene H. Seward

S EX was once viewed as one of the constants of human nature, an instinctual force struggling against social forces attempting to control it. More recently cultural anthropology has taught that human nature cannot be abstracted from its cultural context and that the only constant is the interaction between the individual and his society. Individual behavior must be interpreted in the light of the social frame in which it inheres. Consequently, to determine the role of sex in a given culture, one first must determine the basic values of that culture. Sex may carry the meaning of sin or pleasure, nurture or dominance, according to the prevailing system of values.

NORMS FOR SEXUAL BEHAVIOR

Even within the confines of Western culture wide diversity appears in the interpretation of sexual behavior from one subculture to another. In working-class groups, for example, more direct heterosexual activity is acceptable, in accordance with the greater permissiveness of impulse expression in general. In fact, status is acquired through early sexual experience. Masturbation, however, is more apt to be disapproved as a perversion among the underprivileged, and sexual outlets to be narrowly channeled in sexual intercourse with little variation in technique and foreplay. One investigation of lower-class urban Negro girls showed that the standard of sex morality corresponded more closely to the more lenient conduct expected of middle-class white boys. A different sex code prevails in the Italian slums of an eastern city, where a premium is placed on virginity at marriage. Strong legal and institutional sanctions uphold this ideal and equally strong sentiments support it. A "corner boy" who misleads a virgin incurs the severe censure of his group.

NORMS FOR SOCIAL SEX ROLES

In the social roles ascribed to the two sexes, cultural relativity is no less apparent than in the evaluation of sexual behavior. In most societies a definite sex line is established as regards what constitutes appropriate personality and behavior. Masculine usually means a higher dominance level. Men are more often expected to perform tasks involving direct contact with the environment while women must tend the home fires and care for the young. In societies where the sex-personality line is tightly drawn, the situation is fraught with risk of failure to fit into the prescribed mold and of consequent social punishment for deviation. Some cultures wisely meet this difficulty by providing safety valves for those likely to deviate. Examples are the institutionalized sex-role reversals of the *berdache* among the Plains Indians, the "manly hearts" of the North Piegans, the two-way exchanges of the Mohaves, and others.

In Western culture, fluidity has marked the history of social sex roles since the days of antiquity. Today, behavior expectancies change from one generation to the next, and even during the course of individual development there are shifts and discontinuities from one stage to another. What is appropriate conduct at one age level may be highly inappropriate a little later. For example, a boy with characteristics that carried status in the first grade (such as keeping quiet) may find his prestige lowered by the time he reaches the fifth grade by merely maintaining the previously rewarded trait. Analogous shifts in status occur among feminine personality patterns—the prepubertal little-lady ideal, for example, giving way to the good-sport and glamour-girl ideal at a junior-high-school level. These evershifting standards make it difficult for the developing boy and girl to know what is expected of them.

No less confusing are the adult sex roles that they are to emulate. The transition from a father-dominant to a democratic form of family structure is causing many dislocations and inconsistencies in the roles of both men and women. The situation is further complicated because changes in feminine social role and personality pattern are proceeding more rapidly for single than for married women. A common dilemma among college girls is that of deciding when to "play dumb" on dates and when to play up to the "modern" role that an equalitarian education demands. For married women the choice seems to be among three wifely roles: the traditional, the companion, and the partner, with the last outstripping the other two in popularity among the younger generation.

The cultural transition that is responsible for shifts and readjustments in the feminine role necessarily brings with it concomitant changes in the masculine. The loss of patriarchal status with its clearcut directives concerning economic support and authority in the home has sometimes shown a boomerang effect, resulting in role reversals rather than the adoption of a partnership. There seems to have been some tendency for women to usurp the abdicated masculine domestic authority, leading to extreme cases of dependency, or "momism." Recent studies of the father role, however, indicate an increasing recognition of the importance of companionship with the children and of sharing the disciplinary function with the mother.

CULTURAL DEFINITION OF SEXUAL DEVIATION

"Normal" sex and sex role behavior is relative not only to a given society but also to local areas and to age and ethnic groupings. The conflict and confusion inherent in the complex patterns that constitute our culture make it easy enough to understand the prevalence of sexual deviation. It is not so easy, however, to understand the particular forms the deviation may take. Two cases with the same label may have altogether different meanings in the history of the patient. For example, a theft may have been committed in order to obtain articles for a sexual partner, for fetishistic enjoyment, or merely for the perverse erotic excitement aroused by the danger. Widely different surface manifestations may reflect the same inner dynamics. In the case of a fetishist, burglary, theft, and assault may all represent the means of obtaining the erotic object on which his sexual gratification depends. People who deviate sexually are neither vicious monsters nor supernatural vampires. Sex offenders are chiefly people whose orientation toward their reproductive functions and social sex roles has not been properly channeled. In other words, they are anomalies of personality development. Biological maturation accounts only for sexual drive; learning, for its direction. Behavior that may be appropriate at one developmental period or at one time or place becomes a "perversion" in other circumstances.

Perversion of Sex Object. Since the biological end of sexual behavior is procreation of the species, the direction of sex interest toward objects other than the biologically adequate adult of opposite sex is a perversion. The commonest one is masturbation, in which the individual gratifies his sexual needs by stimulating his own genitals. Long before the sex organs are capable of reproductive function they have become the focus of interest to the child. This interest might be utilized constructively or destructively by society. (We may contrast the Marquesans, who encourage it among their children, with the generally negative attitude that prevails in our own society.) Autoerotic practices usually decrease as other sources of gratification become available. In cases in which such practices are continued into adult life generalization is not possible since masturbation is differently motivated in different personalities. For the neurotic who has failed to free himself from family ties, masturbation may represent an escape from the more exacting demands of heterosexual relations; for the well-adjusted person masturbation may be merely one of the many forms of sex play he enjoys, while for the celibate youth or aging widow it becomes a means of eliminating distracting tensions. Whether the practice is good or bad depends upon its significance for the person concerned. Absolutely good or bad effects have not been scientifically established. Where masturbation is a symptom of underlying maladjustment and represents a failure to grow up sufficiently to undertake adult sexual relationships, the treatment should be aimed at the underlying problem.

Another potential misdirection of sexual interest is toward members of the immediate family. To guard against this possibility and to insure co-operation between groups through exogamy, most societies have erected strong taboos against incest. Although conspicuous exceptions exist, such as the Egyptian Ptolemies, the incest taboo is almost universal. In the intimate family structure of contemporary Western culture strong incestuous tendencies have to be counteracted by equally strong social sanctions; as a result incestuous attachments are usually deeply repressed and do not ordinarily reach the point of overt expression. Even so, incest occurs more often than is commonly supposed, the chief offenders being widowers and their daughters. When incestuous relationships are begun in childhood they might be expected to constitute a serious threat to later adjustment. Whether or not traumatic aftereffects will follow, however, seems to depend on the existing security level of the child at the time of the experience.

Similar considerations hold for cases in which sex relations occur between children and unrelated adults. The child's later development is not so seriously threatened as might be supposed. Aggressions occurring before puberty do not seem to predispose the person toward the development of mental disorders in adult life. Contrary to popular belief, the child, far from being the pitiable victim of sexual attack, frequently acts as the aggressor, apparently deriving positive satisfaction from the experience. The chief danger to the child from such precocious sexual relationships lies in the possibility of acquiring negative attitudes toward sex that may be unfavorable for normal heterosexual adjustments and ultimately lead to homosexuality.

As for the adult participating in sexual associations with children, one frequently finds a timid soul whose inadequacy to cope with the complexities of adult relationships leads him to escape into the simpler intimacies with children. Mr. L, for example, was arrested at the age of thirty-eight for the fourth time for improper approaches to little girls. His background revealed a combination of browbeating on the part of his domineering father and oversolicitude by his mother that prevented him from developing normal feelings of self-esteem. With the building up of his confidence in himself his erotic interest in children disappeared. Lowering of inhibitions in senility or following the use of alcohol may also result in regression from adult adjustment patterns to the more infantile love of children.

One of the most common sexual aberrations in many cultures is orientation toward the same sex. The significance of this disorder varies with local circumstance. Intimate friendships between comrades in arms were glorified in ancient Greece and Persia, in Japan during the period of chivalry, and notoriously in Nazi Germany. Among certain preliterate peoples a homosexual stage is considered essential to the attainment of sexual maturity. The Keraki Indians of southern New Guinea provide an example in their "making-of-man" cult. They believe it necessary for boys to pass through a passive and an active homosexual stage before they are prepared for full adult sexuality. In our own society, temporary homosexual interests are regarded as part of growing up and are supported if not induced by the many sex-segregating influences to which the developing individual is subjected. This represents a passing phase that is reversible, giving way easily when heterosexual opportunities arise. Later in life, if unusual situations occur in which homosexual behavior is rewarded, the individual may revert to this form of adjustment. Prison life, for example, not only involves long periods of segregation of members of the same sex but it is so far beyond the pale of what is normal outside the walls that new customs are likely to develop. Social stratification is often along homosexual lines, with status differentials following proficiency in obtaining "gals." Similar social organization was reported for an institution segregating subnormal Negro and white girls. In this extraordinary context the scarcer Negro girls enjoyed superior social status which they expressed as aggressive behavior toward the white girls. The latter, in turn, responded with sexual interest. The social origin of the homosexual dominance behavior on the part of the Negro girls came out clearly when they dropped the masculine role they had assumed toward white girls in order to play the feminine role toward another Negro girl. From armies to monasteries, sex-segregated groups that remain an integral part of the larger social structure accept the official taboo against homosexual practices, punishing overt offenders, although there may be clandestine indulgence.

Although the weight of scientific evidence indicates that social factors are the most important in inducing homosexuality, genetic and hormonal factors also contribute to the condition. Where the biological distortion is extreme, homoerotic attachments are conceivably acquired more readily, but even in such cases the environment would have to provide the opportunity for the deviant learning. In other words, training may enrich natural predispositions or it may run counter to them. In either event, the training is the differential in the individual's ultimate behavior.

Cases of deeply embedded homoeroticism often have their roots in the early family situation and may reflect a variety of unwholesome influences. Failure of the parent to provide an appropriate sex model often leads to cross-sex identification, as does his failure to provide the child with an opportunity to try out appropriate sex-role behavior. Irreparable harm has been done by disappointed parents in their futile attempts to thrust upon the child the role of the desired sex. Little boys whose baby curls are kept too long or who are dressed up in sister's clothes for the amusement and admiration of female relatives may become the transvestites of the next generation. For example, Nancy's father wanted a son and her mother rejected femininity. In this family where everything desirable was on the male side Nancy naturally wanted to be a boy. She wore shorts, insisted that other children call her Bill, and refused to play the role of mother or little girl in "house." Her futile efforts to change her sex led her into conflict.

Perhaps the most convincing evidence of the importance of social factors in psychosexuality comes from the pseudohermaphrodites who show discrepancies between biology and behavior. In a review of 84 cases from the medical literature, Ellis concluded that although physical sexuality may be biologically determined, experience determines the more inclusive psychosexuality that ultimately develops. As an illustrative case S. M., with the anatomy of a male, was reared as a girl and completely accepted the feminine role. At the age of seventeen, failure to menstruate led to the discovery that "she" had undescended testes and predominately male secondary sex characters, while the only suggestion of female anatomy was a large clitoris. In this case the feminine social orientation began with an early identification with the mother entrenched by fear of the father.

The rarer perversions that have as their objects animals, corpses, nongenital parts of the body, inanimate objects, and others are the products of unfortunate conditioning no less than are the more common forms. The goatherds of southern Italy and Sicily who spend so much of their time with animals frequently have sexual relations with animals. Under the conditions of modern urban life, however, such a sexual orientation is symptomatic of severe pathology. Sometimes a perversion is the result of a single vivid association between a particular object and sexual excitement, although retraining may be a long, uphill process.

Perversion of the Sex Act. Perversion of the sex object is not the only way in which sexual deviation may occur. The means by which gratification is attained may include activities as irrelevant to biological mating as stealing, arson, and murder. More common perversions involve deriving erotic satisfaction from infliction of injury upon others (sadism) or the self (masochism). These distortions may occur in a homosexual as well as in a heterosexual context. Olkon and Sherman describe a transvestite male who behaved sadistically and also sought chastisement from his wife and family. A number of perverse attitudes may be combined in the same person, as in the case of J. S., a meek and mild middle-aged New Englander who was arrested for homosexual practices with little boys. The children were coached to act out the punitive role of the irate father. The background suggested a female identification, expressed in a childhood preference for girls' games for which the patient was severely punished. In this case, prefrontal lobotomy apparently relieved the obsessive, masochistic fantasies and anxieties.

Sexual satisfaction in some cases seems to depend on what is normally a preliminary step in the sex act, namely, exhibiting and viewing the genitals. Again the behavior must be evaluated in the light of the cultural setting. It becomes pathological only where there are social sanctions against genital display. Among the South African Bantu, for example, prepubertal boys may freely reveal the penis, even decorating it with bells, although after circumcision the glans must be concealed. In our own culture, where display of the sex organs is regarded as obscene, the genitals acquire correspondingly high valence and their demonstration becomes a distorted attempt to win social approval. The exhibitionist is often the shy, overconscientious, well-bred son of a domineering mother; he feels compelled to display his genitals in order to prove his masculinity. For example, a brilliant young scientist whose success in research was unparalleled had exhibitionistic compulsions. His mother's sexual frigidity and resentment at having borne a son rather than a daughter had led to this man's compulsions. The continual threat to his career and to his marriage was ended by suicide.

Analogous considerations hold for cases of voyeurism, where there is the reverse tendency to spy on others in order to see their genitals or to watch them perform the sex act. Like pornography, voyeurism is a cultural product of the secrecy with which sex relations are surrounded. The concealment generates excessive interest in the subject, and as "peeping Toms" timid, ineffectual, and sexually impotent men may find sublimation for the sexual needs they dare not express directly.

Behavior that is normal in one culture may be abnormal in another. The interpretation of a specific form of aberration cannot be understood categorically but only within the personality context of the individual patient. Sex offense is a symptom of total personality maladjustment. It may represent the gamut of emotional disturbance, including psychoneurosis, psychopathic personality, and, more rarely, psychosis. The basic cause, not the superficial symptom, should be treated. A physician does not treat a fever or a hallucination; he treats a case of pneumonia or schizophrenia. It is just as futile to try to cope with exhibitionism or homosexuality without discovering the underlying personality disturbance they represent. When the "treatment" is some kind of punishment, incarceration, castration, or other serious frustration, it is not only futile but harmful. Each offense should be handled individually. The psychiatric approach is no less important in dangerous cases in which segregation is necessary for the protection of the community. The more the hospital replaces the prison, the more may be expected in the way of personal and social reclamation of the sex offender. The ultimate ideal of prevention rather than reclamation may be hoped for only when intelligent social planning results in relieving individuals of the major sources of anxiety and hostility.

Deviation from Heterosexual Mores. Even in cases in which the individual's sex development has reached adult heterosexuality his behavior may be socially deviant though not biologically perverted. In our culture acceptable sex behavior is restricted to monogamous marriage. Frequent breaches of this requirement are bound to occur. In fact, the mores themselves are undergoing progressive change in the direction of increasing permissiveness of premarital intercourse, especially between engaged couples. Some observers have gone so far as to suggest more drastic modification of the mores in the interests of better adaptation to current realities. For example, K. Frankenthal remarked, "When an important part of the people does not live in marriage and a great number of women cannot find a mate, marriage can scarcely continue to be the only institution in which sex life is legitimate." In present circumstances, however, the unmarried mother and the illegitimate child continue to be symptoms of our social pathology.

Illegitimacy is often associated with culture conflict. Confusion between two sets of mores may go a long way toward explaining the high incidence of illegitimate pregnancies among girls of foreign parentage. During World War II parental neglect, manifested by poor social identification and inadequate sex instruction, was held responsible for the increase in sex delinquency among underprivileged teenagers. Similar background conditions were also found among lower-class unmarried mothers in an attempt to analyze the dynamics of anxiety at different social levels.

The results of parental neglect do not stop with the unmarried mothers; they unfortunately are transmitted by them to their illegitimate offspring. These children suffer from feelings of being unwanted. Other factors that contribute to the difficulties of children of unmarried mothers are the absence of a father figure and the general social rejection that occurs when their status becomes known.

If the stigma of illegitimacy were removed and the children born out of wedlock were afforded the same legal status and the associated inheritance rights and social security that other children enjoy, a big step would be taken toward the amelioration of one major social sex problem. Prevention through better education for sex living would of course represent a more fundamental attack.

Another form of deviation from the official institution of matrimony is prostitution. Here is a case to emphasize the importance of the individual approach to this social disease. The patient, a girl of strict religious training and good education, had to undertake the support of her two children after an unsuccessful marriage. Financial difficulties made it necessary for her to live in a neighborhood where prostitution was the norm. In this atmosphere she first indulged in some casual promiscuous relationships, later in prostitution. That the prostitution actually filled a deep emotional need was revealed by psychoanalysis. She harbored an unconscious hostility toward her father that found vent in her behavior. When a stronger motive was mobilized by pointing out the undesirable effects on her children, the practice was suddenly stopped despite a worse financial status. Thus the economic need was only a secondary factor serving as a rationalization for the primary unconscious motive. This case indicates the need for scientific handling of the problem.

Escape from the monogamous standard is sometimes sought in an extramarital affair. Although such irregularity may occasionally happen among the happily married it is more often an index of maladjustment. Sexual relationships outside of wedlock are paradoxically motivated less by sexual need than by the need for reassurance. They may also serve the purpose of working off unconscious hostilities toward the spouse. In any case, extramarital tendencies should be recognized as symptoms rather than causes of conjugal disharmony. The underlying factors may or may not reveal incompatibility so serious as to make the continuation of the relationship undesirable. However that may be, separation on the basis of symptom alone, no matter how legally and socially defensible, may break a marriage that could be saved and contribute needlessly to personal unhappiness.

CULTURE AND SUCCESSFUL MARRIAGE

Intramarital Disturbance. Even when there is outward conformity to the prevailing mores internal sources of tension may threaten to disrupt the marriage relationship. The friction may be reflected in impotence, frigidity, painful intercourse, or as any of a large number of related psychosomatic symptoms. The important point is that such disturbances are merely *symptoms* and not in themselves *causes* of the maladjustment. The underlying difficulty frequently has its roots in the ambiguity and confusion of current sex-role expectations. Formerly, personal happiness of the mates was subordinated to their obligations and duties to the larger grandparental family groups they represented. Under these auspices the erotic was paradoxically likely to be divorced from the marriage and driven underground in the more casual relationships with mistress or prostitute. In contrast, the contemporary family focusing on the personal relationship between married partners theoretically provides them with the opportunity of developing an intimate companionship in which the erotic supplies the vital spark. Actually, however, the new sex equality has too often merely opened up a new avenue through which the competitive pattern of the culture may find expression. We may have outgrown some of the authoritarian forms, but we have not yet grown up enough to accept the implications of the democratic family design.

Suggested Solutions. A variety of solutions for handling the problems created by the re-evaluation of sex roles has been suggested in recent publications. For example, Erich Fromm points out the fallacy of equating difference with deficiency. For him, equality of opportunity affords the basis for the development of differences, resulting in the fullest realization of individuality. In his opinion, sex differences in biological role have certain personality overtones which blend with those directly produced by culture, and so do not warrant casting men and women in different social roles.

Margaret Mead also stresses certain core differences between the sexes which she discovered in societies widely diverse in the surface patterning of social sex behaviors. In all, achievement appeared as the chief male preoccupation, while for women, nurturing activities were paramount. Unlike Fromm, Mead believes that social sex roles should follow these biological cleavages, with women finding their self-expression in the service areas while men remain free to engage in competitive achievement.

Agreeing with Mead's basic assumptions, F. Lundberg and M. F. Farnham would go farther in an effort to restore the balance between the sexes which was lost when the Industrial Revolution removed the feminine functions from the home. According to these authors, to re-establish woman's sense of personal worth it is not enough that she be permitted to follow her nurturing interests into the world beyond the home. Within the home itself, her unique and essential contribution of mothering should be elevated to a social status commensurate with that accorded competitive achievement. To implement this notion, the authors suggest recognition of successful childbearing and rearing by government subsidies and academic honors.

In view of the importance of culture in playing up or playing down whatever sex differences may be traced to biological process, any dichotomizing of social roles is risky for the individual. Greater differences may be found among members within one sex than between the sexes. This overlapping has led Mirra Komarovsky to comment with respect to education that woman's "nature" would be just as much violated by being forced into a "feminized" curriculum as by the so-called imitation of men. She suggests a rich and flexible offering in which the talents of individuals irrespective of sex are fostered.

The educational groundwork should be begun long before college age. If men and women are to develop co-operative attitudes and more harmonious marriages, they must begin their basic training in childhood. As little boys and girls they need to learn the distinction between biological and social roles, accepting their complementary biological functions, and at the same time respecting one another's freedom in the choice of social roles. While such education would not eliminate the problem of adjusting to changing and often confusing sex-role demands, in so far as it contributed to the achievement of the necessary role flexibility it would provide the individual with an important technique for successful marriage.

Topics for further thought:

1. Our society expects men to be "masculine" and women to be correspondingly "feminine." Exactly what does this mean? Discuss the advantages and disadvantages to the individual and to society of insisting on this distinction.

2. Why is there societal disapproval of the following forms of sexual behavior: masturbation by adults, homosexuality, prostitution?

Selected reading references

Ford, Clellan S., and Beach, Frank A., *Patterns of Sexual Behavior,* New York, Harper and Brothers, 1951.
Survey of sexual patterns among 190 different societies and among lower animal species. Throws considerable light on the nature of human sexuality.

Himelhoch, Jerome, and Fava, Sylvia F. (eds.), *Sexual Behavior in American Society,* New York, W. W. Norton and Company, 1955.
Subtitled, "An Appraisal of the First Two Kinsey Reports," this volume includes many excellent articles relating to the larger problem of sex and the social order.

Mead, Margaret, *Male and Female, A Study of the Sexes in a Changing World,* New York, William Morrow and Company, 1949.
A penetrating analysis of male and female behavior with particular emphasis given to contemporary America.

Mead, Margaret, *Sex and Temperament in Three Primitive Societies,* New York, The New American Library, 1950.
Anthropological study of three fascinating, preliterate societies. Indicates how cultural conditioning may modify or even reverse biological tendencies.

Murdock, George P., *Social Structure,* New York, The Macmillan Company, 1949.
A high-level research volume analyzing the sexual, marital, and familial structures of 250 human societies.

Seward, Georgene H., *Sex and the Social Order,* New York, McGraw-Hill Book Co., 1946.
Sophisticated analysis of the influences of social definition upon the facts of sex and sex functioning.

7 DIVORCE AND ITS EFFECTS

Kingsley Davis

LIKE everything else in marriage, divorce concerns not one person but at least two or more. Ordinarily, in connection with marital relations, one can assume that the marriage itself is considered valuable by both parties and that the aim of both is to preserve or improve it. But when a desire for divorce has been expressed, this assumption can no longer be made. For either the husband or the wife, or possibly both, the marriage itself is no longer valued. It is conceived rather as an obstacle to be eliminated, even at some mental or material cost.

The conflict of interest in divorce is at a minimum when both parties want a dissolution. Even in this case, however, plenty of room is left for possible bitterness and for disagreement over such matters as property settlements, alimony, and custody of children. In such cases the state, according to law, must play the unpleasant role of opposing a divorce which both parties want, at the same time arbitrating the conflict of interests over subsidiary matters.

The more typical cases are those in which one partner wants the divorce and the other really does not. Such a case strongly tempts neighbors and friends to take sides in the emotional struggle. Presumably a marriage counselor would attempt to remain neutral, simply trying to give the couple insight into their own motives and some knowledge concerning the possible psychological and social effects of their actions. But since people who do marriage counseling are usually sponsored by religious, social-work, or government agencies, their moral evaluation with reference to divorce is likely to be somewhat conservative and hence not strictly neutral. Consequently the partner who wants a divorce is likely to stay away from such advice. He is likely to feel that by traditional standards he is in the wrong unless he can show a morally acceptable reason for his goal. If he is merely bored with his mate or he happens to like someone else better, he may well fear a concealed opposition. He is more likely to rely upon his lawyer, who by profession is pledged to look after the interest of his client. Indeed, the lawyers do more marriage counseling and more intelligent balancing of interests than anyone else in divorce cases, ill prepared as they may be for this difficult role.

The truth is that divorce poses the problem of conflicting interest in an acute form. For this reason, once the decision to obtain a divorce has been made by one or both parties, the chief role of the marriage counselor refers no longer to marital adjustment but rather to a divorce adjustment. Those who believe that the incidence of divorce can be greatly reduced through the counseling of couples after they have already sought divorce are probably mistaken. By that time marital discord or ennui has usually grown too deep to be banished by verbal dissuasion.

Since divorce is an old institution and is embedded in the social structure in many ways, there already exist agencies for handling its different aspects. First, divorce is a legal matter, with an elaborate legal machinery and a traditional legal philosophy for handling it. Second, it is a cultural and statistical fact, with fluctuations in time which respond to concurrent economic and social changes. Third, it is an emotional and personal process, with psychologic and psychiatric ramifications. Finally, it is a moral fact, with official and unofficial attitudes toward it that are mutually opposed. All of these aspects must be kept in mind if divorce is to be understood.

DIVORCE AND THE LAW

When the legal aspect of divorce is mentioned, one naturally thinks of divorce laws. But the stipulations and intent of legislative acts, constitutional clauses, and established precedents are not the whole legal story. Another part of the story lies in the way the law is actually used, and for what purposes. Perhaps in no other field of legal practice is the divergence between the intent of the law and its actual use so great as it is in divorce litigation. American divorce law today ideally sets out to accomplish one goal but in fact accomplishes the opposite, and it rests its logic on one set of assumptions but in practice operates on a contrary set. This hiatus between law in theory and law in action is partly a result of the rapid changes in our society which have affected divorce attitudes and behavior much more than they have affected formal divorce law. But the hiatus is also due to the fact that much of our family law, including that of divorce, had its origin in ecclesiastical jurisprudence but is now applied by secular courts in a secular state. The ecclesiastical system from which stems our present family law, however, happens to have been one which did not admit of absolute divorce, whereas under modern secular law this has become the main form of divorce.

Sometimes it seems that the formal law of divorce has not changed at all, but only the social role and practice of the law. But actually during the last three or four decades there have been some changes, among which the following may be singled out for brief attention.

1. *An increase in the number of legal grounds and a liberalization of their interpretation and character.* Under the traditional theory, a divorce can be obtained only by the innocent party coming into court and proving that the guilty party has committed one of the unbearable faults which the state legislature had laid down as legitimate grounds for divorce. This view of divorce—known as the adversary theory—has never been 100 per cent pure; there have always been in various states grounds of divorce—impotency, insanity, epilepsy— which can hardly be construed as a matter of willful fault. During recent decades, however, the adversary theory has been shaken in new ways. Not only has the number of grounds of divorce tended to multiply under state legislation, but the nature of some of these grounds, either by definition or by interpretation, is contrary to the old view.

The most striking of the nonadversary grounds is incompatibility. During the nineteenth century several states allowed divorce for incompatibility of temperament, but the statutes were subsequently repealed. But in recent times three jurisdictions (Alaska in 1933, New Mexico in 1935, and the Virgin Islands in 1944) have included incompatibility among the grounds. Obviously, incompatibility is not a fault; it cannot be blamed on one party and not the other. A man can commit adultery, but he can hardly commit incompatibility.

In addition, at least six jurisdictions have amended their laws in order to permit divorce because of voluntary separation: Arizona (1931), Arkansas (1937), District of Columbia (1929), Louisiana (1932), Maryland (1937), and Nevada (1934). Eleven others do so on the ground of protracted separation, which at least in some cases may be voluntary. Such separation is certainly different from the old-style desertion. Like incompatibility, it is a mutual matter. Folsom states, "No charge of desertion nor assumption of guilt is necessary; if the parties voluntarily live apart for the given period, either may get the divorce on this ground alone." [1]

Still another modification of the adversary theory is reached through the cruelty channel. No less than 42 states allow divorce for cruelty. Eight of these specifically mention mental cruelty in their statutes, and virtually all the others (except Alabama and South Carolina) seemingly admit mental cruelty as a cause in actual divorce cases. While such cruelty appears to fit with the adversary theory, it actually does not to the extent that mutual contempt (that is, expressed incompatibility) is construed as fitting the definition and to the extent that the cruelty need not be intentional. Similarly, ten jurisdictions allow divorce for indignities suffered by the plaintiff. Generally, the indignities need to have been intentionally inflicted, and so this cause does not overlap with incompatibility to the same extent that mental cruelty does, but its liberalizing effect is nevertheless plain.

These changes in the grounds of divorce therefore represent an adjustment of American legal theory in the direction of actual practice. The law is beginning to sanction divorce by mutual consent. Everyone knows that it has always done so in practice (and increasingly as time has gone by), but only recently has it begun to do so in theory.

2. *Vacillation with respect to migratory divorce.* American divorce litigation is confused and complicated by the fact that it is handled by 48 different state jurisdictions and several territorial jurisdictions. Although all of these grant absolute divorce, the circumstances and conditions under which they grant it differ greatly. The result has been, as everyone knows, to allow people to escape the more severe legal restrictions of conservative states by going to more liberal states for divorces. A state has jurisdiction over divorce if the plaintiff is domiciled there. Competition for the divorce business has led some states to lower the residence requirements to a few weeks or months; for example, six weeks: Nevada (1934), Virgin Islands (1944 and 1953), and Idaho (1947); sixty days: Arkansas (1947) and Wyoming (1945); ninety days: Florida (1943). This, plus the increasing ease of travel and mobility of the American people, has made migratory divorce easier, though it remains true that such divorces account for

---

[1] Joseph K. Folsom, *The Family and Democratic Society,* New York, John Wiley & Sons, Inc., 1943, p. 515.

only a small portion (something around 6 per cent) of the total.[2] The determination of the validity of these migratory divorces and the adjustment of the consequent rights and obligations of the divorced parties and their dependents have led to an enormous amount of confused litigation and a great outpouring of legal literature.

The legal theory is that, by the full faith and credit clause of the Constitution, a divorce granted in one state must be recognized by the other states, provided the state in question has jurisdiction—that is, provided the plaintiff is a resident of the state when the action is initiated. By a legal fiction, however, this theory is not applied in practice, so that out-of-state or migratory divorces, which in theory are impossible, nevertheless occur. Divorces are regularly granted by states really lacking jurisdiction, and these divorces are treated as valid.

The basis for the legal fiction lies in the ambiguity of the notion of domicile, on which jurisdiction depends.

Domicile in this country has lost much of the stability it possessed in earlier times. . . People are in the habit of changing their homes frequently from state to state. In many cases they have homes in several states. Again, married women are permitted to have domiciles different from their husbands'. Under present conditions, therefore, it is frequently difficult, if not impossible, to ascertain where the domicile of a person is.[3]

The legal definition is subjective: a bona fide domicile is a place which the person *regards* as his home and where he *intends* to stay more or less indefinitely. But a subjective definition cannot be applied in practice consistently unless it is transformed into an objective one—that is, unless certain ascertainable criteria are admitted as proof of the subjective state of mind. The states in fact lay down the requirement that a person must *reside* in the state for *a certain length of time* before he can initiate divorce action there. This is not what the ordinary person, the Supreme Court, or our legal philosophers mean by domicile, because they are thinking of intentions. A man who takes a

[2] No one knows how many out-of-state divorces are granted in the United States, because in theory no such divorces occur. A rough estimate made by the writer for the year 1950 places the proportion at 6.4 per cent. Of course in those states having severe divorce laws, a much larger proportion of the residents go elsewhere for their divorces. In the case of New York, for example, more of its citizens get divorces out of the state than inside it. See PAUL H. JACOBSON, "Marital Dissolutions in New York State in Relation to Their Trend in the United States," *Milbank Memorial Fund Quarterly,* 28:25-42 (January, 1950).

[3] Ernest G. Lorenzen, "Extraterritorial Divorce—Williams v. North Carolina II," *Yale Law Journal,* 54:805 (December, 1944).

vacation from his New York job and leaves his apartment in New York for six weeks to go to Reno, secures a divorce, and comes back to his job and his apartment in New York has had no intention of establishing a residence, a legal domicile, in Nevada. He simply went there to get a divorce by a legal fiction—a fiction kindly connived at by the state of Nevada itself. In statements of theory by the courts, a state to which the party "has moved immediately prior to the divorce and from which he removes immediately afterwards is uniformly held not to be the domicile of the party in question." [4] Yet this is exactly what most persons getting out-of-state divorces do. Presumably, then, if the law practiced its theory, it would treat nearly all such divorces as void. But it does no such thing. The courts continue to grind out divorces for out-of-state applicants, the persons who obtain these decrees practically never get prosecuted, and when the validity of the divorce is challenged, the courts in other states often refuse to reopen the case out of respect for the doctrines of estoppel and *res judicata*.

Most divorces in the United States (about 95 per cent) are the result of mutual agreement. This does not mean that both parties want the divorce, but simply that neither will try seriously to compel the other party to stay married. As a result, after the divorce is granted neither one is likely to challenge the decree, and usually no one else is interested in doing so. This means that in the great majority of cases an out-of-state decree can serve without penalty as a basis for subsequent conduct, such as remarriage. But suppose somebody does challenge the decree later, will the courts then treat it as void? In case of remarriage, will they recognize the first spouse as the legitimate heir in preference to the second one? Will they refuse to admit the "void" divorce as a valid defense in suits for alienation of affection? The answer seems to be no. "Oddly enough, it is only in the case of a prosecution for bigamy that one can be certain that such results will follow, and prosecutions for bigamy after anything which resembles an effort to obtain a divorce are so rare that, for practical purposes, they may be and are ignored." [5]

The law rationalizes its unwillingness to treat a "void" divorce as void by two devices. First, it invokes the doctrine of estoppel when both parties have appeared in action and have not contested the court's

[4] Fowler V. Harper, "The Myth of the Void Divorce," *Law and Contemporary Problems,* 2:338 (June, 1935).
[5] Ibid. p. 339.

jurisdiction. Each is, by his participation in the "void" divorce, estopped from subsequently questioning the jurisdiction of the court that granted it. Second, the law invokes the doctrine of *res judicata*. Even if the person has fought the action and has not remarried, he may nevertheless be forbidden to question the validity of the divorce. "It is simply not true that a divorce rendered in a state to which both parties resorted solely for the purpose of obtaining the decree is without legal effect. On the contrary, it has the precise effect which the parties desire." [6]

Of course if the defendant spouse does not enter the action or accept service in any way, he or she may bring suit in the state of real domicile either for another divorce or for a settlement of property and custody, but it seems virtually impossible, by direct attack on the out-of-state decree, to re-establish the marriage.

The use of legal fiction to accomplish out-of-state divorces has obviously led to suggestions of reform. Proposals have been made to have domicile federally defined for purposes of divorce, all states thus being similar in this respect. On May 6, 1953, the United States Senate passed a bill attempting to confine divorce jurisdiction to the last state in which the parties were domiciled together as husband and wife.[7] The idea has been put forward that intrastate divorces should be handled by federal rather than state courts, and that these courts should have the power to determine the facts of domicile and thus decide which state's laws should govern the action. In the meantime, the volume of interstate divorces is tending to increase. They represent a convenient means of escape from the rigid laws of divorce in some states.

3. *The drive to supplement adversary procedures with administrative arrangements in divorce cases.* Recognizing that the old adversary theory of divorce not only is breaking down in practice but also fails to fit the facts of modern life, many individuals and states are working to reorganize the handling of divorce cases. One measure being taken in this direction is the establishment of special family courts to deal with family litigation. In these courts preside judges and referees specially selected for their ability to deal with family problems, and the court is furnished with trained family counselors, social

[6] Ibid. p. 341.
[7] For a description and critique of this bill, see the article by William D. Ferguson in *Cornell Law Quarterly*, 39:148-53 (Fall, 1953).

investigators, and psychiatric consultants. An effort is thus being made to acquaint the court with the real facts of the cases that come before it, so that matters will not be decided on the basis of purely legal technicalities and fictions.[8] In addition, the legal-aid societies that have been growing in number and scope are also of help in straightening out divorce tangles. These and other social agencies help not so much with reference to the main issue of divorce as in the ancillary judgments with respect to alimony and custody. Doubtless as the law loses its adherence to an outworn theory of divorce as a matter of conflict, guilt, and punishment, this humanizing tendency will continue.[9]

4. *The increasing role of the separation agreement.* Although on its way, the modification of the litigious process in divorce has not gone very far yet. In the meantime it is interesting that couples appear to be placing more and more reliance upon the separation agreement to settle their property and custody problems in connection with divorce.

The emphasis on an adversary determination of questions of guilt and innocence (usually completely unrelated to the real marital difficulty) and the absence in most parts of the country of any judicial machinery capable of surveying a total marital picture have resulted in a situation where the court rules on the technicalities of the divorce while the essential questions are settled by the parties extra-judicially, usually by negotiating and entering into a contract known as a separation agreement.[10]

Ordinarily the court tends to accept the terms of the agreement, without really examining their merits in the particular case. Since the agreement is almost invariably worked out by the two lawyers in the case, it is in a sense the lawyers who are serving as the fact-finders, mediators, counselors, and lawmakers in cases of divorce. Thus the ponderous formality of the law has resulted in a certain abdication,

[8] In Michigan, the Wayne County Circuit Court, which has jurisdiction in divorce matters, has since 1929 had attached to it the office of "Friend of the Court," the function of which is to ascertain the facts and bring in evidence of aid to the court. See Edward Pokorny, "Observations by a 'Friend of the Court,' " *Law and Contemporary Problems,* 10:778-89 (Summer, 1944).

[9] Paul W. Alexander: "Let's Get the Embattled Spouses out of the Trenches," *Law and Contemporary Problems,* 18:98-106 (Winter, 1953); and John S. Bradway, "Family Dissolution—Limits of the Present Litigious Method," *Selected Essays on Family Law,* Brooklyn, The Foundation Press, Inc., 1950, pp. 881-96.

[10] Harriet F. Pilpel and Theodora S. Zavin, "Separation Agreements: Their Function and Future," *Law and Contemporary Problems,* 18:33 (Winter, 1953).

the people who want divorces taking things into their own and their lawyers' hands and working out agreements which somehow get the job done.

THE DIVORCE RATE

The divorce rate in the United States has experienced a long rise. It jumped up sharply after World War I, fell back slightly in the early 'twenties, dropped noticeably during the depression, then rose sharply again in connection with World War II. A peak was reached in 1946, after which the rate declined noticeably. In 1951 the rate stood slightly lower than in 1942. There is evidence of a saturation point being reached. (See Table 1. In this table the divorces are not related to the marriages in the same year, but to marriages occurring in the previous ten years. That is to say, the table shows the number of divorces per 100 marriages occurring each year on the average in the ten years previous to the year in question. This ratio is taken

TABLE 1. The Divorce Rate * (per 100 marriages)

Year	Rate	Year	Rate	Year	Rate
1881	5.1	1905	9.6	1929	17.3
1882	5.3	1906	9.9	1930	16.3
1883	5.4	1907	10.1	1931	15.9
1884	5.3	1908	9.8	1932	14.0
1885	5.2	1909	9.9	1933	14.2
1886	5.6	1910	10.0	1934	17.8
1887	5.9	1911	10.5	1935	18.8
1888	6.0	1912	10.8	1936	20.1
1889	6.5	1913	10.2	1937	21.0
1890	6.6	1914	11.0	1938	20.1
1891	6.9	1915	11.1	1939	20.4
1892	6.9	1916	11.9	1940	21.2
1893	6.9	1917	12.5	1941	22.7
1894	6.8	1918	11.7	1942	23.7
1895	7.2	1919	14.0	1943	25.0
1896	7.5	1920	16.5	1944	27.0
1897	7.7	1921	15.0	1945	33.5
1898	8.0	1922	13.7	1946	40.1
1899	8.5	1923	15.0	1947	30.0
1900	9.0	1924	15.3	1948	24.4
1901	9.7	1925	15.4	1949	22.4
1902	9.5	1926	16.0	1950	22.1
1903	9.8	1927	16.8	1951	21.5
1904	9.7	1928	17.1		

* The figures are derived from data contained in the releases of the Bureau of the Census and the National Office of Vital Statistics.

because most divorces represent the breakup of marriages that were formed during the preceding ten years.)

OTHER WAYS OF DISSOLVING A MARRIAGE

Divorce is not the only way of dissolving a marriage. Other legal ways are by annulment and by formal separation. Nonlegal ways include desertion and informal separation. From an adjustment point of view these other ways of dissolving a marriage raise as many problems as divorce, for their effects on the mates and their children are in many ways more complex and more serious than those that divorce creates.

The number of desertions occurring each year is perhaps half the number of divorces. Since the average number of children affected by desertion is greater than the number affected by divorce, this means that the total impact of desertion on the American family is sizable. In the 1950 census there were 1,169,000 wives who were separated from their husbands. (In addition there were 839,000 wives whose husbands were absent from the home but not separated.) This almost equaled the number of divorced women in the population (1,373,000). Those reported as separated in the census probably included deserted wives as well as women who were legally or informally separated, but in any case it appears that desertion and separation taken together probably account for as many marital dissolutions as divorce does. In thinking of family breakdown, people give a disproportionate amount of attention to divorce because it is a legal process, is better measured, and catches the popular imagination; but it must always be remembered that divorce represents only half the problem of marital dissolution.

In the United States as a whole, annulments constitute only a small proportion of legal dissolutions. In 1946 they represented only 3.5 per cent of the total. But according to Jacobson, they were much more important in California and New York:

Thus in California, annulments constituted somewhat more than one ninth of all legal marriage dissolutions in 1948. In New York they were an even larger proportion of the total; almost one quarter of the marital dissolutions in 1940, and since 1946 almost one third. In at least five counties in New York, the number of annulments now exceeds the number of absolute divorces.[11]

[11] Jacobson, op. cit. pp. 35-7.

New York State has this high annulment rate because it grants divorce only for adultery but gives annulments for any one of eight different grounds, many of which are ill defined. The Roman Catholic influence in the state is clear.

DIVORCE AND THE CHILD

The most serious aspect of divorce concerns the child, particularly in our culture. Forty-two per cent of the divorces and annulments granted in 1948 were to couples with children. The average number of children per divorced couple with children was 1.8. In other words, about 313,000 children under age 21 were involved in the 421,000 absolute decrees granted in 1948.[12] (This figure of course does not include children in homes broken by separation and desertion.)

There are several features of our family system that make the problem of the divorce child peculiarly difficult. First, because of our pattern of low fertility and high geographical and social mobility, the effective family unit is small in size and extremely isolated from other kinsmen. Second, because of our urban economy, the nuclear family has remarkably few functions and activities in common and consequently must depend heavily on sheer sentiment to hold it together. Third, our family organization is extremely democratic and permissive, with a minimum of fixed patterns to serve as guides in domestic conduct. As a result of these features, the parent-child relation tends to be at once emotionally close but conflictful, so that any tension between the parents tends also to involve the child. Furthermore, when the marriage is broken, the household is usually broken up too. There is no stable milieu wider than the small family to which the child can remain attached, as there is in many cultures. There is no relative who can immediately substitute for a missing parent.

Both parents are entitled to feel they have an equal claim upon the child, which sets the stage for conflict over custody in divorce cases. Although the child's welfare is supposed to be the guide in determining custody, welfare is still too subjective to be determined accurately. One parent, most often the father, is required to support the child, and yet he may live far from him and see him relatively infrequently. The parent who keeps the child most of the time may be forced to work or may enter a second marriage. The child may be shunted back

[12] Metropolitan Life Insurance Co., *Statistical Bulletin,* vol. 31, Feb. 1950, p. 1.

and forth from one parent to the other. In any case, he remains the sole remaining link between the parents and thus is sometimes used as the instrument for the continued expression of antagonism. In sum, the child of divorced parents is placed in a peculiarly anomalous situation laden with potential conflict and insecurity. How well he actually fares, however, depends largely on how intelligently and calmly the parents handle the situation.

The child of divorced parents is in a potentially better situation than the one who has lost one parent through death. He stands the chance of receiving the economic support and affection of both his parents, even though they are divorced. If one or both parents remarry, the child may find a new home better than the old, depending again on how matters are handled. In this connection it is worth noting that the rate of remarriage after divorce is quite high. It seems probable that close to four-fifths of those getting divorced today will eventually remarry, most of them soon after their divorce.

PSYCHIATRIC ASPECTS

Occasionally there is a tendency to regard divorce itself as a mental disorder or at least as an evidence of such disorder. This, however, is merely a sly way of condemning divorce. Since divorce is merely the legal dissolution of a marriage, it may or may not be a result of neurosis in one or both of the parties concerned. Unless the term neurotic is defined loosely, it cannot be used to explain the majority of divorces. Certainly the divorce itself does not constitute evidence of neurosis without independent confirmation. Divorces are in fact so much a part of American folkways and mores that they cannot be regarded as abnormal. Only when divorce occurs two or more times to the same person can it be taken as suggestive of neurosis. Some second marriages work out extremely well, their success being due perhaps in part to experience with the realities of life gained in a first but unsuccessful marriage.

In those cases in which mental disorder appears to be involved, the help of a psychiatrist is of course desirable—not necessarily to save the marriage, for that may be the wrong tack, but possibly to save the individual from another unhappy venture. Sometimes a divorce itself will prove of benefit to such a person, but in other cases it will have little effect upon his mental illness or will exacerbate it.

Divorce does not necessarily end the relationship between the erstwhile married pair. Shreds and vestiges of the former bond remain.

Through alimony payments, through the children, through mutual friends, through continued interest, the relationship tends to live on. The neurotic has much the same difficulty adjusting to the modified relationship that he had in adjusting to the former one. If he needed help in the first instance, he also needs it in the second.

Even if neurosis is not involved, even if divorce is wanted by both parties, the actual dissolution often comes as a crisis. To be sure, the main emotional crisis may have come earlier, when the decision to obtain a divorce was first made. The actual decree, when it comes later, may seem an aftermath. But somewhere along the line the partners are likely to experience the breakup of their marriage as a shock. In our society divorced persons are presented with no socially approved means of adjustment to this crisis such as those available to the bereaved. Instead, they are often faced with hostile or at least uncertain reactions on the part of the community, for divorce is still a negative value among us.

SUMMARY

Divorce offers a peculiar challenge because it raises the problems of conflicting interests in an acute form. Yet the increase of divorce in our society makes it a somewhat normal and regular outcome of matrimony. Even American law, conservative as it may be, is beginning to admit divorce as a matter of mutual agreement and has facilitated the evasion of strict state statutes by refusing to practice its own theory with reference to domicile. Those who give marital advice must meet the issue of divorce with great frequency. One cannot regard it simply as an abnormality suggestive of neurosis. Rather it must be accepted as a normal feature of our popular mores. We are, in effect, returning to the old custom of trial marriage. Our young people get married at a remarkably early age (earlier than in any other industrial nation). They do so knowing full well that if it does not work out a divorce can be obtained, if not in their own state, then in some other state. Many of them do get divorced, and they do so for the most part within a short time after they get married (usually within two or three years). Most of these speedily marry a second time, and most of these unions work out. The custom of divorce is linked with other aspects of our social order and is not likely to change unless the rest of that order also changes.

Topics for further thought:

1. Is the increase in divorce in the United States symptomatic of a disorganized society? Or is it merely an adjustment to other cultural changes?

2. Increasingly large numbers of girls are receiving higher education; increasingly large numbers of women enter the labor market and continue there even after becoming mothers. Discuss the relationship that these two facts have to the high divorce rate.

Selected reading references

Baber, Ray E., *Marriage and the Family,* New York, McGraw-Hill Book Company, 1953.
> A basic and widely used textbook on marriage and the family. Contains especially good chapters on marriage laws and divorce.

Cahen, Alfred, *Statistical Analysis of American Divorce,* New York, Columbia University Press, 1932.
> Classic comparison of divorce law and practice in different states, including corrections for the country as a whole.

Despert, J. Louise, *Children of Divorce,* New York, Doubleday and Company, 1953.
> Actual case studies which show how numerous children have been brought safely through the experience of divorce and how others might have weathered it more successfully had their needs been better understood.

Goode, William J., *After Divorce,* Glencoe, The Free Press, 1956.
> A field survey in the metropolitan Detroit area of adjustment to divorce. Includes analysis of couples' backgrounds, marital conflict, the divorce process, and patterns of readjustment, including remarriage.

Waller, Willard, *The Old Love and the New,* New York, Liveright, 1930.
> Classic, social psychological analysis of the effects of divorce upon the individual, written by one of the most brilliant of American students of the family.

TWO

PREPARATION FOR MARRIAGE

8 THE WISE CHOICE OF A MATE

Ernest W. Burgess

A PERSON makes two great choices in life: one, the selection of a profession or trade; the other, the choice of a mate. When
someone decides on a profession, business, or trade, he usually acts
rationally; he tries to secure all the training and education necessary
or feasible in order to prepare himself for it. When he marries, however, he is likely to behave romantically rather than practically. Some
people still believe that success in marriage is guided by Providence;
to others, the whole procedure appears to be a great gamble. Most
people still regard marriage as a romantic experience through which
a man or woman is mated with his or her affinity. Only a few utilize
science as a guide to the wise choice of a mate. Preparation is necessary for success in marriage in the same serious and thorough way
as for a trade or profession.

In earlier times in many countries marriages were based on pru-
dential considerations. Parents rather than young people arranged
marriages. They limited the union of their children to partners of the
same social class and to those who belonged to the same cultural,
educational, and religious groups. Parents rated economic considerations high; the bridegroom was frequently much older than the
bride. In some countries of the Orient, the young people might not
even see each other before marriage or, at most, for a brief period in
the presence of other members of the two families. In colonial New
England the Puritans arranged the marriages of their children with
more stress on financial considerations than on the personal preferences of the young people. The pioneer situation, however, favored

early emancipation of youth from parental control because of the abundance of free land and the opportunity for setting up a new household.

In modern American society young people have freedom to make their own selection of marriage partners. In the modern manner parents do not impose their preferences or interfere arbitrarily in their children's choice of a mate. Only when the young people are under age, as variously determined by the laws of different states, is it legally necessary for them to secure the consent of their parents to the marriage.

FACTORS AFFECTING THE SELECTION OF A MATE

The change from marriages arranged by parents to those entered into by young people on their own initiative has not increased the stability of marriage. Judging by the increase in the divorce rate, free choice seems to have had the reverse effect. Divorces were practically unknown in the colonial period. Since the Civil War the divorce rate has been steadily rising. In 1954 one divorce occurred for every four marriages. This increase in the instability of marriage cannot, however, be attributed to the fact that marriages are arranged by young people rather than by their parents. Certain long-time factors have made the selection of mates increasingly difficult. The five of greatest importance are urbanization, individualism, the emancipation of women, the secularization of life, and the growing conception of marriage as a companionship.

Urbanization. In 1790, 95 per cent of the population of the United States was rural. Since then, in every decade except one, the proportion of city population in the United States has increased; in 1950 only 36 per cent of the people lived in communities of under 2,500 population. Even more significant has been the growth of urbanization which has accompanied the development of industry. Economic, educational, recreational, and religious activities have been transferred to agencies outside the home. The intimacy and friendliness of the rural neighborhood have been superseded by the formal, impersonal, and disinterested relationships of city life. In the city the primary controls over behavior have broken down in the anonymity and secondary contacts especially of the rooming-house and apartment-house neighborhoods.

Individualism. Living in cities has encouraged the development of individualism; one of the chief manifestations is the self-expression of the individual. The consequent accentuation of the individuality of the members of society promotes the complexity of selecting a mate. In the rural community the occupation, the interests, the ideas and ideals of all were practically the same. In the city these are widely divergent. Another manifestation of individualism is the decrease of control exercised by society over its members. Consequently the person who is dissatisfied with his mate is less inclined to conform to the social controls which would prevent the dissolution of a marriage in the rural areas.

The Emancipation of Women. In the United States the trend throughout the years has been toward greater freedom for women. Increasingly they participate in the economic, social, educational, and political life of the country. This greater freedom, in conjunction with the other factors mentioned, has inclined women more and more against enduring an unsatisfactory marriage; they now seek release when conditions are unsatisfactory. The emancipation of women has also tended to make them more discriminating in selecting a husband.

The Secularization of Life. One aspect of city living has been the trend toward the secularization of life accompanied by a decline in the religious sanction of marriage and the family. In recent generations the role of religion in the family has diminished. Religious observances in the home, such as family prayers and grace at meals, have declined in use. Most marriages are still solemnized by the clergy, but they no longer are protected by as strong religious sanctions as in the past. The stand of certain Protestant churches against divorce has weakened, as indicated by the greater number of marriages of divorced persons performed by ministers. Mate selection takes place to a larger degree than previously outside of the home, the Sunday school, the young people's society, and the church.

Marriage as a Companionship. The trend in the United States has been away from the conception of marriage as a contract sanctioned by law and community pressure toward that of an interpersonal relation expressive of companionship. Marriage as a legal and institutional arrangement was held together by external forces, such as the law, custom, and community opinion; by the authority and superiority of the husband and the subordination and inferiority of the wife; by rigid discipline; and by the sense of duty of husband and wife. Marriage as a companionship is bound together by internal forces, such as affection and comradeship; by consensus based on the equality of husband and wife; by sympathetic understanding; and by the personal happiness realized in the union. The transition from the institutional and authoritarian type of marriage to the companionship and democratic form has often tended to increase the instability of the family. In the long run, however, the realization of the ideal of companionship in marriage should increase its stability.

These five factors—city living, individualism, the emancipation of women, the loss of religious influences, and the growing conception of marriage as a companionship—have all increased the risks involved in making marriage a success. They have made it easier for people to enter into marriage and to abandon a union with which they have become dissatisfied. They have made it more difficult for husbands and wives to become and remain adjusted to each other, particularly if they were not well suited to each other in personality, interests, and ideals. The increase in the divorce rate has demonstrated the bankruptcy of the romantic theory that love at first sight was sufficient guarantee for living happily ever after. The interest is growing in the possibilities of finding a solid foundation for successful marriage in the wise selection of a mate.

FACTORS AFFECTING SUCCESS IN MARRIAGE

How can young men and women improve their chances of a happy marriage by utilizing the knowledge that is now available? Psychological and sociological research has provided new information on the conditions and factors that make for success in marriage. This knowledge can be helpful to young people. Here are five main points that every candidate for marriage ought to consider: (1) the intelligent utilization of dating and courtship, (2) the favorable combination of the social and cultural backgrounds of the couple, (3) their compatibility in personality and maturity, (4) their common interests and values, and (5) the measure of success achieved by them in adjustment during the engagement.

Stages in the Relationship of the Sexes. In American society five stages in the relationship of the sexes finally culminate in marriage. If any one of these is omitted or slighted the chances for a happy marriage may be correspondingly decreased. These five stages in the courtship cycle include dating, keeping company, going steady, private understanding, and engagement.

Dating, a relatively new custom, is one of the great social innovations of our time. It arose, as many changes do, out of a new social situation. Dating came about as a new practice which permitted freer association among the sexes in the new age of the automobile.

In the old-time rural community, selection of a mate was limited to the distance one could travel with a horse and buggy. After World War I the area of selection expanded, both in the city and the country, to the distance one could cover with an automobile. Dating gives young people an opportunity to become acquainted with a large number of persons of the opposite sex before selecting a mate. Pairing can be deferred until the best preliminary choice is made from a wide circle of contacts. Dating also implies that each date is rated in terms of a prospective partner in matrimony. The date, of course, is an end in itself; there may be no further involvement. A person tries a date; if he does not become interested he can decide then and there to stop.

Dating is not utilized wisely if it merely multiplies superficial social contacts. The value of dating for selecting a mate is enhanced to the degree that it enables a couple to determine in a preliminary way whether or not they are compatible in temperament and have similar interests.

Dating is important to the teen-agers as the basis for boy-and-girl friendships. During this time of emotional and social immaturity dating should not pass into pairing too early.

Dating is the prelude to *keeping company*. Keeping company means that a person concentrates his dates on one person, but he is still free to have dates with others. Keeping company is an expression of active preference. A boy or girl can make comparisons before becoming involved in a more serious commitment. Teen-agers should not try to shorten this period.

Keeping company signifies mutual preference which may represent only friendship and not love. *Going steady* indicates a stronger attachment, at least on the part of one. Both have made an agreement that they will limit their society to each other. Going steady should be utilized by the couple as a period of exploration. The couple can find out if they are in love. They can test their temperamental compatibility, the satisfaction of their personality needs, their common interests, and their ideals.

The *private understanding* is a mutual avowal of love by the couple. This development in the relationship is generally kept secret or shared only with close friends. Often at this time the young man and the young woman are introduced to each other's families in order to secure an appraisal from parents and relatives. The function of the period of the private understanding is to permit a further test of the certainty of one's choice before becoming committed to a formal and public engagement. The private understanding may be terminated without the embarrassment that attends a broken engagement.

The *engagement* period is the final test before marriage of the couple's compatibility in personality and temperament, congeniality of interests, and agreement in ideas and ideals. At least one year is the minimum time usually required for this purpose. Of course the sheer passage of time is not important. More significant is the utilization of this period by the couple to resolve any difficulties between them, to make any needed adjustments to each other, and to build a deeper relationship of mutual confiding and common understanding.

Dating, keeping company, going steady, private understanding, and engagement, if utilized intelligently, should contribute greatly to the wise choice of a mate.

Social and Economic Backgrounds. The factors in the social background of the couple that are important in selecting a mate are family relationships, number of friends, membership in organizations, educational level, religious participation, and economic status.

Family relationships are most important in mate selection. When the marriages of the parents of both bride and groom are happy, a high proportion of the marriages of the young people are happy. Conversely, if the marriages of their parents are unhappy, a large percentage of the children's marriages will turn out unhappily. Close attachment to both parents and a corresponding absence of hostility toward them in childhood are associated with a higher than average prospect of success in marriage. When the discipline of the parent has been kindly but firm, the prospect of a child's adjustment in marriage is more promising than in those cases when it has been too severe or too lenient or, worse still, has fluctuated between leniency and severity. Young people who report that their parents gave them sex information—even if it was rather inadequate—are happier in their marriages than those instances when the knowledge of the facts of life came from other sources.

The status of the family in the community and the similarity of the family backgrounds of the young people in terms of socioeconomic status, type of occupation, religious affiliation, and nationality stock are also of great importance in successful marriage.

The *number of friends* of the couple is definitely related to happiness in marriage. The matrimonial risk of the husband is better if before marriage he has several or many men friends and several women friends; that of the future wife is higher if she does not lack men friends and has many women friends. The sociable person appears to be a better marital prospect than the one who has few or no friends.

A person who holds membership in *organizations* or clubs has a higher probability for success in marriage than one who has not been affiliated with social groups. The more the social contacts, the greater the probability of marital happiness.

The higher the amount of formal *education,* the greater the likelihood of adjustment in marriage. For both the future husband and wife a high-school education is better than a grade-school one, college superior to high school. Couples who have a background that includes graduate and professional education in universities provide the highest proportion of successful unions.

The better the record of a person in his *church* and Sunday-school attendance, the higher his chance of making a successful marriage. This is measured by the number of years that he has attended Sunday school, by attending church three or more times a month, and by his activity in church before marriage. Being married by a minister and having the wedding in church or parsonage seem to be associated with marital success. The basic factor here is the degree of religious interest of the person.

From the standpoint of *economic status,* happiness in marriage comes most frequently to people in those occupations that provide a moderate but stable income, that require considerable educational preparation, and that are lacking in mobility. A man with a steady job is a better matrimonial risk. The prospects of good marital adjustment for the wife are increased if she worked before marriage or engaged in civic and social activity, if she was employed at an occupation the same as, or similar to, the one she prefers. The husband with savings at time of marriage is a superior risk.

Young people are inclined to select their mates according to their similiarity in certain of these background interests. They marry within the same social class, at the same or similar level of education, and with others of about the same economic status. Wide differences in cultural background appear to make for unhappy unions. If young people are attracted to each other despite, or perhaps because of,

124 ERNEST W. BURGESS

cultural differences, they should attempt during the process of courtship to find out if they can successfully bridge their divergences so that these will not constitute serious problems in marriage.

Personality and Maturity. Compatibility in temperament and personality is essential to a happy marriage. During dating, keeping company, and even while going steady, young people are likely to be on their best behavior and so do not fully reveal their basic personality characteristics. The intimacy of the period of private understanding and engagement makes it feasible for the couple to find out how well or how poorly they are matched in personality, temperament, and emotional and social maturity.

Certain personality characteristics may be listed in pairs as making for and against happiness in marriage. A person with an optimistic temperament is more likely to be happy than one with a pessimistic temperament. Emotional stability makes for, and emotional instability against, marital adjustment. Submissive tendencies are favorable, while dominating and domineering behavior is unfavorable to success in marriage. A considerate and sympathetic person is a better matrimonial risk than the critical and inconsiderate person. Self-confidence, especially on the part of the husband, is a more desirable characteristic than lack of self-assurance. A person who is emotionally dependent has a better chance for marital happiness than the self-sufficient person, who tends to face trouble alone and to avoid asking advice from others. Evidently, it is most desirable in mate selection for both the young man and the young woman to possess the favorable trait of any of the pairs listed and least desirable for both to have the unfavorable one. The person with the unfavorable trait may raise his chances of marital happiness by selecting a partner with the desirable characteristic. For example, two sympathetic persons are happier in marriage than two critical people; but the union of a critical and a sympathetic person has, on the average, an intermediate state of happiness.

Certain other personality traits have little or no relation to marital happiness. Whether the person is outgoing or withdrawing in his behavior, whether he likes or dislikes the company of other persons, whether he gives or does not give much thought to what impression he makes upon others, whether he finds or does not find it uncomfortable to be "different," whether he is impulsive or deliberate seem immaterial to his chances of success in marriage.

Marriages at too early an age result in a high proportion of unhappy unions. Yet census statistics indicate that the average age for marriage is becoming lower. From the point of view of marital happiness the optimum age for marriage is from 22 to 30 years. Chronological age, of course, is only an index of a person's emotional and social maturity; those are actually the factors to be considered. Too many young people in their early twenties, as well as in their late teens, are still adolescent in their emotional and social development. To be successful in mate selection and marriage, they need to have passed into the adult stage where they are no longer emotionally dependent on their parents or subject to the control of their age group, but able to make their own decisions and to be responsible for their obligations.

Compatibility in temperament and other personality traits is in great measure a question of the degree to which the married couple complement each other in the fulfillment of their personality needs. Persons differ widely in their demand for sympathy, understanding, and encouragement. Whatever their emotional needs may be, their happiness in marriage depends to a considerable degree on the capacity of their mate to satisfy these needs.

Typically in courtship people unconsciously seek either to continue an emotional relationship which was satisfying when they were children in association with their parents, or to establish a satisfactory affectional relationship which they missed when they were children. The boy and girl are successful when they find they can realize this relation in their association with another person. These expressions are often heard: "Our personalities seemed to click," "It seemed we had known each other a long time," and "I feel more at ease with him than with any of the other fellows."

Falling in love is either infatuation or companionship. In infatuation the emphasis is on physical and romantic attraction. This is often called love at first sight. In infatuation, emotional reactions predominate. The pair tend to be isolated from others, to be in a state of high mutual suggestibility, and to be indifferent or hostile to the advice of parents and friends. Unions of this type are frequently between persons of widely different social background and social class. But infatuation in love is blind to the factors that should be considered in selecting a mate. An elopement or other form of hasty marriage is likely soon to be followed by disillusionment and the disruption of the union.

Affection of the companionship type is based on friendship deepening into love. After marriage comradeship is still an important, if not the most important, element. Husbands and wives are in agreement in reporting that companionship is the chief gain that they have obtained from marriage. Modern courtship gives the young people an opportunity to develop and to test the satisfactions which they secure in companionship with each other.

Sexual adjustment in marriage depends largely, first, upon the attitude of the person to it and, second, upon the interaction of two personalities to each other. Persons are more likely to be well adjusted and happy in their marriage if they have received sex instruction from their parents, if their parents had a frank attitude toward early sex curiosity, if they have no disgust or aversion toward sex in their premarital attitudes, if their sexual desires are of equal, or about equal, strength, and if they have not been sexually promiscuous.

Interests and Values. Since companionship is what modern people seek to obtain in marriage the presence or absence of common interests and values is of prime importance in selecting a mate.

During courtship and engagement the couple find out not only what recreational interests they have in common but also the possibility of developing other activities that both can enjoy. If the ways in which they prefer to spend their leisure time differ too greatly the union is likely to be unhappy. The chances for a happy marriage are highest where both enjoy home activities, intermediate when both would rather step out, and lowest where one prefers to stay at home and the other to be on the go.

For a happy union the prospective husband and wife must participate together in a sufficient number of activities that insure companionship. Their mutual activities and interests may be in sports and games, literature, music and art, or religion and a social cause. Sports and games provide mutual enjoyment and a sense of companionship. Literature, music, and art tend to bind the couple together. Religion and interest in the same social causes are particularly binding. Divergences in preferences for spending leisure time may be a source of conflict especially in the last two groups of interest. Differences in religion and politics are known to be destructive of friendship, and this applies with particular force to marriage. If difficulties exist here, they should be resolved during the period of courtship and engagement. A common core of mutual interests and activities leaves room for a certain range of diversity. In fact, such differences may be stimulating to the couple and so increase the satisfaction of the relationship.

A strong desire for children, expressed by both members of the engaged couple, shows a higher association with success in marriage than a mild desire, no desire, or a mild objection. A disagreement in desire between the two is correlated with a high proportion of unhappy unions. This suggests that the couple should come to an agreement if possible before marriage on their wish for children. Contrary to general belief, the engaged young man is only slightly less interested in having children than his fiancée.

Agreement on friends makes for adjustment both in engagement and in marriage. Frequently the engaged couple share the same circle of friends and the same attitudes toward them. In a considerable number of cases, however, each has his own set of friends, and one or both may be critical of the friends of the other. Where there is disagreement the couple should seek to find out if the objections are valid and to determine the standards by which they should retain their old friends and choose new ones. On the basis of this mutual understanding much of the conflict that might otherwise occur may be avoided. In this way there would be more toleration of the old friends of the other and any tendency toward jealousy would be diminished by a sense of greater security in the relationship.

A person who is domestic in his interests and activities is a better matrimonial prospect than one who is not. Domesticity is indicated in many different ways. It is evident, first of all, when a young man or woman places the values of home and family above other considerations. Affections and desire for children is a second index. Interest in gardening and in fixing things up around the house on the part of the man is still another indication. The girl who likes housekeeping, cooking, and sewing will probably make a contented and happy wife.

Couples are more likely to settle down to the enjoyment of married life if both of them prefer to live in a single house rather than in an apartment when they are married and when, even before marriage, they are making plans to buy or to build their own home.

For successful marriage it is important that the couple have the same philosophy of life or at least have discussed their different convictions of what is most worthwhile in life and have arrived at a sympathetic appreciation of the other's point of view. The life values of the two persons should be sufficiently harmonious so that serious difficulties will not develop later. One of the arguments against marriage at an early age is that the ideals and objectives of the person have not yet crystallized and that in the future they may become so widely divergent as to disrupt the union.

Particularly important for mate selection is the career interest of the person. The conception which he has of his role in life, especially in relation to his occupation, is often a decisive selective factor in the choice of a marriage partner. A young minister, for example, wishes for a wife a girl who is idealistic and who has other qualities which will make her a good minister's wife. A rising young businessman desires as a bride a girl with social graces and aspirations. The combination of qualities which each seeks in the other is more complex than these illustrations suggest. What the person may actually desire is a companion with whom he can express the major roles he would like to play in life.

Too often the process of courtship is telescoped into so short a time that the association of the couple before marriage remains on the superficial level. Even where there is a sufficient period of time between first acquaintance and marriage it is often not adequately utilized by the couple to determine the vitality of their common interests, to appraise the significance of divergent points of view, and to arrive at a mutual understanding which will serve as a secure basis for a lifelong companionship.

The Engagement Period. So far the wise choice of a mate has been considered largely as the result of factors over which the couple have little or no control. But to a greater or lesser extent they themselves can influence the outcome. The engagement period is or can be used to improve the probabilities of the happiness of the prospective union. There are five ways in which couples may realize this objective: achieving adjustment in engagement, determination to make marriage a success, adaptability, preparation for marriage, and premarital counseling.

The *adjustment* secured by the couple in engagement is correlated with their adjustment in marriage. Problems in the relationship are generally more easily solved before rather than after marriage. Accordingly, couples should discuss and try to settle the important issues in their relationship, such as children, in-laws, finances, religion, and philosophy of life, before the wedding date. It is a vain hope to expect to reform a mate after the marriage ceremony.

The positive aspect of adjustment during engagement is the building of a companionship to constitute a solid foundation for the marriage relationship. The materials essential for its construction are found in the breadth and depth of love for each other, significant shared experiences, the degree of mutual confiding, and sympathetic understanding.

Other things being equal, success in marriage depends on the degree of the *determination* of the couple to achieve this objective. Not infrequently couples with unfavorable factors in their social backgrounds or in their personality characteristics succeed in marriage because of the additional effort that they are willing to invest in effecting adjustments both in engagement and in marriage. Determination alone, however, is insufficient for this purpose unless both members of the couple are intelligent, are adaptable in attitudes and behavior, and are willing to prepare for marriage and to benefit by premarital and postmarital counseling.

Young women, in general, enter marriage with the realization that they must make adjustments. The great majority of young men have little on no idea that they have any important adjustments to make. The happiness of marriage could be greatly increased if husbands as well as wives realized that they must make adaptations in marriage. There are, of course, great individual differences in *flexibility*. But adaptability is a trait that can be developed. In a society characterized by social change and growing complexity, the flexibility of the person becomes of signal value. A large element in adaptability is the acceptance of the attitude that adjustments in marriage are necessary and desirable. Persons are likely to be good mates if in the discussion and decision upon an issue both are willing to meet the other more than half-way. Flexibility in marriage is increased to the degree that one or both develop sympathetic understanding of divergent attitudes and behavior in the other. Under these conditions the risks involved in marrying a person who in some respects is different from one's self are lessened. In the wise choice of a mate one accepts a life partner as a personality with his own particular combination of traits. Many marriages are wrecked because either the husband or the wife plans to reform the other after marriage. There is an old saying that it never pays to marry a man to reform him.

In increasing numbers young people are requesting courses in *preparation for marriage* as part of their education. This is particularly true of students in colleges and universities, who have demanded the introduction of courses in marriage, sometimes against the opposition of members of the faculty. Courses in preparation for marriage and family living have now been introduced into high schools and to some extent in the elementary schools. Young people are eager to know the results of research on marriage. Many couples devote a considerable portion of the engagement period in reading together books and articles on preparation for marriage.

Most articles on marriage, while of great value, have one serious limitation: they present general knowledge applicable to all couples. What John and Mary, however, wish and need specifically to know are the probable difficulties which *they* will face in their own marriage, what is the best way to prevent them, and, if this is not possible, how to deal with them. In the larger cities *counseling* services are now available which provide this kind of premarital guidance. Sometimes the counselor explains to the couple the crucial difficulties that are likely to arise in their relationship and how they may best avoid or treat them. Or the counselor assists the couple in identifying the problems that exist, perhaps in incipient form, and in stimulating them to find their own solutions.

Young people can greatly reduce the probability of serious difficulties in their marriage if, in the engagement period, they learn the important principle which is common to the fields of physical and mental health: if difficulties arise which do not easily and quickly yield to home treatment, consult a specialist. Many couples in the engagement period adopt the plan that they will settle each day any problem that may arise in marriage. When this program fails they should turn without delay to a marriage counselor for help. Otherwise, any unresolved difficulty, even a seemingly trivial one, may develop into a tension which becomes more difficult and is possible to cure only with expert assistance.

SUMMARY

Throughout this discussion it has been assumed that the problem of selecting a mate would be solved if one found an ideal partner. A person must remember, of course, that it is very important that he himself be a good marital choice. The wise selection of a mate is not completed once a choice is made. On the contrary, it is a process of development in the interaction of the two persons. It begins in dating, it continues through courtship and engagement, and it reaches its culmination in the shared experiences of marriage.

Topics for further thought:

1. Contemporary urban conditions have affected the manner in which marriage partners are selected in our society. Mention the most significant of the conditions and comment upon their relationship to possible marital success and happiness.

2. Describe what you would consider an "unwise" marriage. Why do you think so?

Selected reading references

Burgess, Ernest W., and Wallin, Paul, "Homogamy in Social Characteristics," *American Journal of Sociology*, September, 1943, pp. 109-24.
A research study of the tendency to select as marriage partners persons who have similar social backgrounds.

Christensen, Harold T., *Marriage Analysis,* New York, The Ronald Press Company, 1950.
See Chapter 8, pp. 240-71, for a thorough discussion of mate selection in American society. Includes material on qualities which college students desire in their marriage partners.

Harper, Robert A., *Marriage,* New York, Appleton-Century-Crofts, 1949.
Chapter 3, "Mate Selection: Causes and Effects," contains an able, sociological analysis of the process of choosing the marriage partner.

Hollingshead, August B., "Cultural Factors in the Selection of Marriage Mates," *American Sociological Review,* October, 1950, pp. 619-27.
The most sophisticated study to date of the ways in which selective factors operate to determine who marries whom.

Strauss, Anselm, "The Influence of Parent-Images upon Marital Choice," *American Sociological Review,* October, 1946, pp. 554-9.
Research suggesting that the influence of parents upon the selection of the marriage partner is more complex than that posited by Freud's oedipal theory.

9 THE DIAGNOSIS OF LOVE

Henry A. Bowman

For some years marriage has been changing. The changes apparently involve the way the marriage works out rather than the form, although the instability of modern marriage is relatively new.

Marriage was formerly an association between two people in which the economic, reproductive, protective, and societal aspects were most important, with the personal relationship between husband and wife also important but secondary. Nowadays there is a tendency to consider personal relationships and satisfactions of first importance, with the other aspects of marriage relegated to a secondary position. Marriage is moving from an association of unequals to an association of equals. The husband is no longer the master, the head of the house in the old sense of the term.

The prerequisites for success in marriage formerly were, with the exception of ability to have children, readily observable before the wedding by the prospective spouses, their families, and friends. The man's social status, ambition, economic condition and prospects, conduct and moral standards, and his stability were clearly known. The woman's domestic inclinations and ability and her social behavior were equally apparent. The preparation that either sex needed for marriage was afforded by the family life, home activities, folkways, and mores of the group in which they lived.

Today, with primary emphasis on the personal relationship of husband and wife, the picture has changed. The prerequisites for success in marriage are not readily obvious. They are not measurable in the light of accepted factors. Judgment has become highly individualized.

It rests in large part upon the attitudes, tastes, and emotional responses of the persons concerned. Parents and friends play a minor role. Folkways and mores play a part, but these are changing. Family life and domestic activities do not contribute to the individual's preparation for marriage in the way they formerly did. The old factors that counted in marriage, such as home and family and emphasis on stability, are not now dominant. Increased freedom of individual choice stimulates young people's aspirations, colors their idealism, and influences their judgments without furnishing adequate means for distinguishing between real and counterfeit prerequisites for successful marriage.

With marriage considered primarily a personal relationship between husband and wife, with love considered the first prerequisite for success in that relationship, with nothing to guide a person in the last analysis and in making the final decision except his own judgments of his own responses, how can anyone determine whether or not he has this essential prerequisite?

Can a person tell whether or not he is in love? First, he may analyze himself to determine, if possible, whether or not it is likely that he is prepared to fall in love at all. Second, he may be sure that he understands the differences between love and infatuation. Third, he may examine the contemporary social scene and attempt to determine the degree to which factors in it have influenced his thinking. Fourth, he may analyze himself in the light of certain questions and conditions that may play a part in his decision.

PERSONS UNPREPARED FOR LOVE

Romantic love, the love that prefaces and carries over into marriage, is distinguished from other types of love—filial, parental, brotherly—by the fact that it grows out of an awareness of and response to sex differences. Its focus is a person of opposite sex who is considered an outlet for sexual urges, a stimulator of sexual responses, and an objective of marital aspirations. It leads to a profound and permeating type of sharing found in its most fully developed form only in the marriage relationship. There are persons who are not likely to be in love, in this sense of the term, although they may exhibit some of the superficial, external symptoms or are themselves inclined to place the label of love on their own emotional experiences.

The exceedingly immature person may consider himself deeply in love. He may manifest the stereotyped pattern of behavior, phraseology, letter writing, idealizing. His immaturity suggests that his experience has been so limited, his knowledge of the opposite sex and of marriage so meager, and his attitudes so undeveloped that he is in a state of infatuation rather than in love.

The person who is a victim of a parent fixation—too deeply attached to a parent—cannot readily love anyone else, since he loves only his parent and does that in infantile fashion. He may seem to love someone who resembles the parent or who may become a substitute for his parent. In so doing, however, he merely transfers his love from his parent to the other person; he does not fall in love with the other person.

The narcissistic person, whose love is turned in upon himself so that in a sense he is both subject and object of it, cannot readily love another person. If he seems to do so, it may be only because the other person's attractiveness, devotion, favorable responses, and complimentary remarks are a mirror in which he sees himself reflected.

The person who has a predatory or exploitive attitude toward members of the opposite sex cannot easily experience true love. In such a case the other person is not a love object in the better sense of the term; rather the other person is a means of self-gratification. The person who has never learned to share may fall into a similar category. The person who, because of fear of sex, marriage, or the opposite sex, hesitates to let himself go can hardly share sufficiently to be in love. Yet such a person may exhibit the outward symptoms of love because he is eager to fit into the social pattern.

Anyone who feels inferior, insecure, or unattractive may have a strong desire to love and be loved. Whenever any interest in him is shown by a member of the opposite sex, he hastily concludes that he is in love. Without being fully aware of it, he is afraid that each manifestation of such interest may be the last. This makes his love of a compulsive nature. Hidden deeply within him is a feeling of "I must love somebody, but I am afraid no one will love me." Nearer the surface this becomes "I must love this person." At the surface it becomes "I do love this person."

A person in rebellion against his parents or eager to escape an unpleasant situation may leap to a hasty conclusion that love is the solution to his problem, when actually he is not in condition either to fall in love or to make a judgment about it. A person who has been disappointed in love and soon thereafter transfers his feelings toward the first person to a second person is not thereby in love with the second. Such a person must recover from his unhappy experience before he can fall in love again. His judgments made on the rebound are not likely to be sound.

A person whose leanings toward his own sex are stronger than his leanings toward the other sex can hardly fall in love as a first step toward marriage. Whether such leanings represent retarded emotional development or a full-fledged homosexual fixation, true love of someone of the opposite sex is excluded, at least for the time being.

DIFFERENCE BETWEEN LOVE AND INFATUATION

Love is not a separate entity, existing independently of the personalities involved. It is not something that may suddenly be attached to them or patched upon the pattern of their lives. Love is an attribute of two personalities who bear a relationship one to the other. It is an outgrowth of their association with and appraisal of each other. Every living thing that grows is subject to the influence of time. Love implies a reorientation of each personality with the other as a new focal point. It grows out of association in a variety of circumstances and an estimate of all a person's known characteristics. Infatuation, however, may come suddenly. It is the result of attaching self-generated feelings to another person, of projecting ideals upon him, of oversimplifying the elements in the association of the two persons. It may result from contact in relatively few situations, or even only one. It may be an outgrowth of an estimate based upon only a few of the other party's attributes.

Love tends to produce a feeling of oneness on the part of the couple. They tend to feel identified with each other. A boy or girl who is infatuated tends to think of the other party as a means of self-gratification. Since love tends to produce this "pairness," this oneness, this sense of identification, genuine love is centered upon only one person. It cannot be divided between two persons so that the person loves them simultaneously. If one claims to be in love with two persons he usually is not in love with either and frequently marries a third person not in question at the time the problem of love is raised.

Love tends to give the person who is in love a sense of security and trust when the total situation and the other person's total personality are considered. It does this because when such an appraisal is made the assets outweigh the liabilities. The latter are assimilated into the thinking of the person making the appraisal. Infatuation tends to produce a false sense of security based upon wishful thinking. At times, also, infatuation produces a sense of insecurity that may manifest itself as jealousy.

Since love is other-person-centered, the person in love directs his behavior toward the welfare and happiness of the other party. Their future relationship together is considered in part an opportunity to contribute to the loved one's happiness. Since infatuation tends to be self-centered, the infatuated person often loses his ambition and his interest in the ordinary affairs of life. The infatuated one becomes absorbed in daydreaming about the other party or in contemplation of his own misery at being separated from the one with whom he is infatuated. This self-centeredness often produces a feeling of urgency in connection with getting married and an inclination to set aside or gloss over possible barriers to the wedding. A couple in love may greatly desire marriage, but they are willing to allow sufficient time for preparation. They face and try to solve the problems that may stand in the way of their getting married.

It is impossible to be completely objective and impersonal regarding a loved one. There is always some idealization, more of course in some cases than in others. When a couple are in love, however, the idealization grows out of their relationship and their estimate of each other. When a couple are infatuated with each other the idealization is projected onto the other person.

The path of true love never runs smoothly. There may be some truth in this adage. All couples have their ups and downs during the period that their love is growing. One by one they are solving the problems of adjustment that are inevitable in their relationship. Love, however, is a dynamic, living, growing thing; it is also durable and lasting. When it changes, as it does in some cases, the change is the result of alterations in the personality or behavior of the other person. Infatuation, being the outgrowth of self-generated feelings and attitudes, may change suddenly and without any apparent reason. The one who is infatuated may suddenly feel repulsed by, rather than attracted to, the other, although the latter has not changed.

An expression of affection has more meaning when a couple are in love; this often comes relatively late in their association. A couple who are infatuated may express affection early in their association. Their affection is an end in itself rather than a symbol of what they mean to each other.

CONFUSION BETWEEN LOVE AND INFATUATION

Certain factors in modern society play a part in making it difficult to distinguish between love and infatuation. One is the current over-emphasis upon premarital romance and upon sex appeal. Books, magazines, plays, radio, television, and motion pictures help to keep these emphases alive. Young people are given the impression that the prerequisites for love are largely physical and that they may be recognized shortly after two persons meet. The other qualities that contribute to successful marriage either are not taken into account or are assumed to be identical with those involved in physical appeal. Screen personalities are both a reflection of and a pattern for the particular types of youthful beauty considered to be most highly desirable and against which many potential boy or girl friends, fiancés, and spouses must compete. Young people who cannot distinguish clearly between "reel" life and "real" life assume that, if the superficial aspects of their relationship resemble those of admired stars in the "movies," the great gaps of preparation, experience, and growth will somehow be filled in for them. The demands of dramatization take care of these factors in the motion pictures.

The current world situation is a factor leading some persons to confuse infatuation and love. In the face of this situation many young people have a tendency to be pessimistic about the future. Military service may interrupt a boy's education and may occur at a time when he feels he is at the age for marriage. Thus young couples must choose among three alternatives: (1) marry before the boy enters military service; (2) marry while he is in the service; (3) postpone marriage until he is discharged, perhaps even until he completes his education. The last involves a long delay during which there may be relatively little opportunity for contact and thus for getting better acquainted, while there is ample possibility that the couple may lose interest in each other and drift apart. Thought of this contributes to a sense of insecurity. This, in turn, leads many young people to want to "nail down" their relationship as soon as possible. Hence it is not surprising that some of them leap to the conclusion that any emotional response they have toward each other must be love. If circumstances do not provide the time and opportunity for love to develop, it becomes easy to rationalize and to assume that love can develop in a shorter period and with less acquaintance.

The military situation may play another subtle part in leading young men to confuse infatuation and love. Many young men anticipate military service with regret, dislike, disgust, even fear. A term of service, coming as it does "in the middle of everything," an imposition on a young man's life and involving the upset of his pattern of living, so often unrelated to anything in his civilian life either preceding it or following it, in a sense constitutes a crisis, especially as the young man anticipates it. In times of stress, of crisis, people fall back upon relatively primitive and elemental urges, desires, and behavior. With the typical young man's sexual urge rather prominent in his life anyway, thus making it difficult for him to distinguish between physical appeal and love, this problem is intensified under the stress of crisis produced by the military situation.

LOVE AND RELATIONSHIPS

To Other People. A person is unlikely to fall in love if he has a parent fixation, if he is retarded in his emotional development to the point of preferring the company of members of his own sex, or if he has definite homosexual tendencies. Sometimes girls or boys will say that they are in love, yet at times they prefer the company of some other person of the same sex as themselves rather than the loved one. This makes it doubtful that they are really in love.

The judgments of other people are important. If the loved one is not liked or accepted by friends or family, it may be because the friends and family do not know him well enough. Or it may be because they can appraise him more objectively and without romantic or amorous coloring; therefore, their unfavorable evaluation may be more nearly correct.

If a person has an attitude termed a "temporary permanent" one concerning the love object, this may indicate that true love does not exist. If, for example, a person feels that the other person is at the head of the list at the moment, but is not sure that the other will remain there because each new attractive person is considered a possible competitor, the reorientation of his thinking and the refocusing of his urges have not progressed sufficiently to establish love.

Since true love is other-person-centered and is considered highly private, there is doubt about the love of a person who carelessly and chronically lets intimate details become public property through unrestrained conversation, uncontrolled reading of letters, or conspicuous necking or petting.

To the Loved One. When anyone expresses certainty of being in love yet is hesitant about letting friends or family meet the loved one and is occasionally ashamed of the loved one's manners, language, appearance, or ideas, the presence of true love may be questioned. Moreover, many young people confuse their attitude toward wealth, the excitement generated by expensive gifts, new cars, promises of travel, the prestige of family or position with love. To love someone a person must be able to conceive of the other person and himself as working out a pattern of life that is acceptable to both. To an appreciable degree the other person must fit the concept of the role to be played in marriage by a person of that sex. If, for example, a man conceives of the role of the wife in terms of full-time home-making, child rearing, a complementary relationship between husband and wife, his apparent falling in love with a woman who disliked homemaking, did not want children, insisted upon combining career and marriage would be open to question. In such a case it would be unlikely that he was in love with a total personality. In many instances a girl has a rather clear-cut concept of the husband's role in marriage, thinking of it in terms of support, stability, economic ambition, thoughtfulness and consideration, love of home and children, yet she falls in love with a boy whose characteristics are exactly opposed to the items mentioned. A marriage between two such as these is likely to fail.

Between the Couple. All couples have some conflict at some stage in their relationship. The presence of conflict, as such, is not so important in determining love as the nature of the conflict, the sources from which it rises, its frequency or duration, and the means used to resolve it. The way a couple makes up after a quarrel or difference; the means by which their relationship is re-established, furthered, or blocked; the degree to which they hold grudges; the determination regarding who takes the initiative or who makes concessions; these are all significant. Conflict taking the form of surface skirmishes over inconsequentials is less important than conflict of longer duration over fundamentals, unless the frequency of the spats becomes a problem in itself. In that case the apparent causes are probably only precipitating causes.

Some young persons say they are in love, yet catalogue fault after fault of the other person with the assertion that such faults will not make a difference in marriage or will readily be changed after marriage. In such cases the faults are merely listed; they are not assimilated into the thinking of the person concerned. Hence only a fraction of the other person is the object of love.

In order to determine the presence or absence of love, more is needed than a cross section of the couple's feelings and relationship at a given moment. How they arrived at their present attitudes, feelings, relation to each other is important. The order in which steps in the development of their relationship were taken is significant. Whether a couple's relationship has grown through repeated contacts relatively close together or has grown through infrequent contacts with the intervening periods filled in by the imagination, wishful thinking, and idealizing is an important consideration.

When a couple seem to have common interests that constitute one of the factors drawing them together and making them attractive one to the other, it is important to know when and why these interests developed. They may have been individual interests before association made them common. They may be bona fide outgrowths of the couple's association. They may represent an interest in each other of such nature that each adopts the other's interests. They may represent merely apparently acceptable excuses for being together. They may represent a confusion of interest in each other with interest in each other's interests. In each case there will be a difference in the durability of the interests and in their value as one partial criterion for determining love.

The effect of crisis on the individual's love and the couple's relationship is important. If a crisis tends to draw them more closely together and give them a sense of security in each other's presence and trust, this fact may indicate love. If, however, a crisis seems to drive them apart or if during the crisis each reacts as an isolated person with nothing gained from their mutual love and trust, this may suggest the absence of love.

Without overemphasizing the physical aspects of their relationship, a couple in love tend to have sufficient resources to make their association interesting, stimulating, and satisfying without "external" stimuli. If a couple becomes bored, dissatisfied, "lost," disinterested unless there are external stimuli, such as other people, music, motion pictures, and dancing, to maintain their interest, the presence of love may be questioned.

An individual is an entity, one personality. Yet in different circumstances he may exhibit different traits or play different roles. For example, he reacts in one way when he is ill, in another way when he is well; in one way at work, another at play. He assumes one role with his family, another with friends of his own sex, another with his fiancée. If love grows through association in only one or few types of circumstance, one may wonder whether the boy and girl can know each other's total personality well enough to make the over-all judgments necessary for love to be established.

Love tends to be constant whether the couple are separated or together, because love rests upon a broader base than merely physical presence or physical appeal. If a person seems to be in love when he is with the other person but seems to be less in love when they are separated for a period, it may indicate that when they are together overwhelming physical appeal beclouds judgment and overshadows other considerations, while when they are separated judgment is more objective and the physical element is less intense. If they seem to be more in love when separated than when together, there may be too much idealization during separation, while when they are together a more accurate appraisal of personal traits is possible.

Because of military service or attendance at different colleges or other circumstances making for temporary separations, numerous instances exist in which a couple were apparently in love when they parted, only to find themselves doubtful, seemingly unacquainted, and embarrassed when they were reunited months or years later. In the meantime, however, there had been little or no indication of change. The reason for this feeling is probably that love had not developed before the parting, that during the separation idealization was substituted for personal contact, and that at reunion there was a quick reappraisal of each other against a background of new experience. Hence there was disillusionment.

THE ROLE OF THE COUNSELOR

Finally, only the person himself can determine whether or not he is in love. A simple, numerically scored test cannot give a cut-and-dried answer. A marriage counselor may help define the problem, may offer an opportunity for talking about it, may suggest ways for a person to analyze himself; but a counselor cannot make a final judgment. In some cases the marriage counselor may, in his own thinking, decide that the one seeking advice is probably not in love, but a counselor cannot decide that an individual *is* in love, nor can he help the person much by expressing his judgment.

When a person decides that he is in love and gets married on the basis of his decision, he is taking part in one of the most important processes of his entire life. The decision should never be approached lightly or in ignorance. Young people take it seriously; marriage counselors should do likewise. If a problem is considered serious enough to be brought to a marriage counselor's attention, it is *ipso facto* serious enough to be given careful and sincere attention. The marriage counselor who labels such a problem silly, who laughs at the young person in the throes of puppy love, who gives dogmatic answers to questions about love, and who resorts to such evasions as "It's up to you" or "If you have thought it through and considered all angles, use your own judgment" is not counseling in any accepted sense of the term. Many young people are afraid they will be thought silly. Puppy love can be a trying and painful experience. Dogmatic answers suggest lack of understanding, overconfidence, or moralizing. Evasions add nothing that the hesitant person did not know before he came for a conference.

The marriage counselor may assist the young person in defining the problem and may give assurance that an intelligent solution is possible. He may encourage the young person to wait or to delay a decision, if that seems indicated. If the one seeking advice is trapped in indecision because he is trying to reach a conclusion with insufficient data, he may be encouraged to get more data through experience and contact with the other person, and while doing so, to suspend judgment. The counselor may assure the boy or girl that true love can stand both analysis and the passage of time. If true love is absent, the sooner this fact is discovered, the better.

Topics for further thought:

1. Americans seem to put more faith in romantic love as a basis for enduring marriage than do most other peoples. What are the reasons for this? Is their faith justified, do you think?

2. Is romantic love likely to increase or decrease in significance as women become more equal to men in respect to education and employment?

Selected reading references

Bowman, Henry A., *Marriage for Moderns,* New York, Whittlesey House, 3rd ed., 1954.
    A popular textbook on preparation for marriage. Oriented to the values of upper middle-class, college-educated persons.

Folsom, Joseph K., *The Family and Democratic Society,* New York, John Wiley and Sons, 1943.
    See Chapter 11, pp. 365-408, for an elaborate analysis of love feelings and love interaction.

Magoun, Alexander F., *Love and Marriage,* New York, Harper and Brothers, 1948.
    An extremely provocative approach to the whole problem of marital relationships. Excellent chapter on the nature of love.

Menninger, Karl, *Love Against Hate,* New York, Harcourt, Brace and Company, 1942.
    A noted psychiatrist writes for laymen on the balance of love and hate in the human heart.

Winch, Robert F., *The Modern Family,* New York, Henry Holt and Company, 1952.
    Chapters 12-15 deal with various aspects of heterosexual love. Author introduces his own theory of love deriving from the complementary personality needs of the couple.

10 COURTSHIP AND ENGAGEMENT

Evelyn M. Duvall

THERE was a time when a young man interested in a young woman walked her home from church and met her father. Father had a talk with the man which was based on two questions: "What are your intentions?" and "What are your prospects?" The first question was designed to ward off the men who were out for only a good time. The father wanted to make sure that anyone hanging around his daughter had ultimate intentions of marriage. This careful supervision saved many girls from "the fate worse than death" in times past.

The second question was designed to find out the young man's visible assets: how many acres of land he owned or would fall heir to, whether he had a house or the prospects of one, and how he planned to earn a living that would support the girl in the manner to which she had become accustomed. Parents were responsible for seeing that a girl's husband-to-be would be a good provider. This was essential in the days when women were entirely dependent on their menfolk for economic security. When Grandma made her bed she had to lie in it, even though it was a hard one.

Grandpa had some practical purposes in mind when he made his selection, too. Though he might have been attracted by a shapely figure or a slim ankle, when he came to the place where he announced serious intentions, he made sure that the girl could cook. "Can she bake a cherry pie, Billy Boy, Billy Boy?" was a serious question in the days that preceded the corner delicatessen, the commercial foods companies, and the ubiquitous restaurant. A man needed a woman around the house to cook, sew, garden, can, and lay her hand to the hundred and one home industries that produced just about everything the family needed to keep going.

Today courtship is much less frequently subject to parental approval, is conducted far more casually, and is burdened with many fewer practical considerations. For marriage itself is contracted not so much for the mutual economic dependence of man and woman as it for purposes of companionship.

DATING

Today's teen-age couples go out together just for the fun of it. This pairing off for an evening's entertainment at the motion pictures, a dance, a game, or a party is called dating. Dating is distinguished from courtship in the older sense in that there is no commitment of either girl or boy for the future; there is relatively little parental evaluation of the young man's eligibility; and the young people themselves choose each other more in terms of desirability for the occasion.

The young person who rates as a date is one who ranks high in dating desirability in the particular group. The tendency is for high-ranking girls to date the high-ranking boys in any given community or campus.[1] The rivalry tends to be keen, and the rating assigned by the group is often mercilessly without regard for such factors as stability, character, and real worth of the person. Rating by the group is done in bull sessions, around cokes after parties, and over malted milks at odd hours. The more important factors are (1) physical attractiveness [2] ("He is so handsome"; "She is cute-looking"), (2) personality factors (vivacity, friendliness, social poise), (3) reputation among others ("They think she is swell"; "He was a big shot at camp last summer"), (4) participation in activities ("He is captain of the team"; "She was president of the Glee Club last term"), (5) social status ("He is a big fraternity man"; "She is one of the Ritzys, you know").

In any given community, except those where the ratio between the sexes is skewed, there is usually a considerable number of both boys and girls who do not date.[3] This is often a source of distress and

[1] See Reuben Hill's revision of Willard Waller's *The Family: A Dynamic Interpretation*, New York, Dryden Press, 1951, pp. 150-55.

[2] Arnold Green and Stuart Loomis, "The Pattern of Mental Conflict in a Typical State University," *Journal of Abnormal and Social Psychology,* July 1947, pp. 342-55.

[3] The Purdue University Opinion Panel for Young People reports that 48 per cent of the boys and 39 per cent of the girls 12-20 years of age in their

anxiety to the nondaters, who may feel that something is wrong with them if they do not get dates. Sometimes the lack is covered up consciously or unconsciously by devotion to home duties, absorption in school, work responsibilities, attention to a hobby, or development of a talent. There are situations where special interests or budding genius keeps the youths so busy that he has literally no time for dates. This seems to be far less frequent than the use of a preoccupation as a rationalization for not dating.

Boys and girls who get the dates in most groups are those who have three qualifications. The first qualification is that they "rate" (they enjoy a favorable place in the dating hierarchy assigned by the rest of the crowd). The standards for rating vary considerably from group to group. The country-club set in most towns has different standards and values from the across-the-tracks group or the Sunday-school crowd. A young person who rates high in one neighborhood may move to another and find himself rated quite differently. Rating standards differ within a set from time to time. The changing standards [4] among teen-age boys who begin by expressing their preference for the nice, well-mannered, quiet-spoken girl may end a few years later by preferring the daredevil, active, vivacious girl. Later still other standards appear and disappear as the young people mature and ready themselves for marriage.

The second qualification for dating popularity is related to social and emotional maturity. Here, too, wide variations exist among young people. Chronological age is not a reliable gauge of the emotional maturity of a boy or a girl, or even of his or her physiological age. Maturing sex interests, feelings, and concepts of self in a sex role *follow* physical maturation.[5] Thus an early-maturing girl of twelve may have already begun to date while her late-maturing neighbor of sixteen has not even started to date.

Boys mature later than girls. It is not unusual for two-thirds of the eighth-grade girl graduates to be already into their pubertal cycle while two-thirds of the boys in the same age-grade have not yet begun

national sample seldom have dates. H. H. Remmers and C. G. Hackett, *Let's Listen to Youth,* Chicago, Science Research Associates, 1950, 49 pp.

[4] Caroline Tryon, "Evaluation of Adolescent Personality by Adolescents," *Society for Research in Child Development,* Vol. IV, No. 4, National Research Council, 1939.

[5] Calvin Stone and Roger Barker, "The Attitudes and Interests of Pre-menarcheal and Post-menarcheal Girls," *Pedagogical Seminary and Journal of Genetic Psychology,* LIV, March 1939, pp. 27-71.

their maturation.[6] This is why girls at this age tend to be taller and heavier than the boys. It also explains why girls through junior-high and high school tend to be in advance of the boys in social interests. On the whole, girls are ready for dating, dancing, and courtship before the boys of their own age group. In the average high-school community the girls must launch the parties, plan the dances, and teach the boys to dance. This is sometimes hard on the boys, who are forced into social situations for which they are not quite ready developmentally. And it is not always easy for girls to take so much of the initiative in boy-girl affairs. But it has a sound basis in developmental fact and must be accepted as one of the realities of the early dating situation.

The third qualification for dating is a measure of social competence.[7] It is the socially skilled who date most readily. The boys and girls who possess ability in conversation, skill in dancing and in the more common sports such as swimming, skating, and tennis, musical competency, and poise in a restaurant, on the dance floor, and in each other's homes get dates most easily. Behind these special skills lie the social poise and maturity that are characterized by such qualities as a genuine friendliness and liking for others, the ability to make other people of both sexes and various ages feel comfortable, and the relegating of selfish ego interests to second place in preference to the common interests and loyalties of the group.

Social competence keeps dates from falling into the stolid patterns of a motion picture, a soft drink, and home again. Couples with initiative and originality practice a give and take of hospitality in a variety of dating patterns. Picnics, hobby interests, whole group activities, "smart" dates, and dates at home offer a wide variety of dating experience planned by either the boy, the girl or both together.

Schools and community agencies such as YMCAs, YWCAs, church youth groups, scouts, settlements, and other social clubs can do much to assist young people to meet each other and to gain poise and social skill. Attention to such needs for social development appears to be imperative from the recent surveys of high-school populations which reveal that less than half of the boys and girls are dating regularly.

[6] Lois Hayden Meek, et al., *The Personal-Social Development of Boys and Girls with Implications for Secondary Education,* New York, Progressive Education Association, 1940, p. 35.

[7] For a fuller development of this point see Evelyn Millis Duvall, *Facts of Life and Love,* New York, Association Press, 1950, Chaps. 5, 6, 7, 8.

Too often dances and parties for teen-age youth are poorly planned, with too few mixers and too little competent guidance to assure adequate social opportunities. Consequently even in schools that do provide some such social affairs, only the more socially expert attend, and those youths who most need the learning experience are left out.

Social affairs which promote social development are planned to elicit wide participation of all potentially interested youth. Active working committees that have real responsibility for specific details of the occasion are helpful. A few of the more frequently recommended activities are picnics, skating, folk games, and interest groups, which allow boys and girls to be near each other, sharing in the fun, without too long intervals in which they are required to maintain a high level of social competence. In contrast, ballroom dancing requires a girl and boy to keep up an interesting conversation, observe the elaborate courtesies of the dance floor, execute the intricacies of the dance, and move in step with the music all at the same time—a combination often overwhelming to the beginner, the shy boy, or the inexperienced girl. This is one reason why stag lines become stagnant and why so many girls do not brave the affair at all.

Families can help by providing their children with graduated social experiences from childhood on into young man- and young womanhood. Having friends in for meals or for overnight, keeping an open house where the crowd can congregate after an affair, going to camp, doing things together with other family and neighborhood groups all help. The socially active family rarely produces a permanently socially handicapped youth. Nonparticipating young people often come from relatively isolated families with few opportunities for meaningful social contacts through childhood.

Dating is a learned skill that is acquired, as are all learnings, through the actual process of the activity itself. A person learns by doing in his friendships as in anything else.

Now that parental supervision of courting young people is rarely heavily restrictive, the responsibility for the relationship lies increasingly with the young people themselves. The many varieties of background of young people in the average American community complicate the setting and keeping of common standards of dating behavior. Some young people are called "fast." They go in for petting, thrills, and excitement. Others are known as "slow." They are dull, uninteresting, or kill-joys to the fast set and salt of the earth to others. Finding other young people who share one's values and standards is often a difficult task, especially when the young person himself or herself has not clearly defined his or her own position in the confused and changing patterns of moral conduct.[8]

Dating is sometimes a touch-and-go affair, with a different partner every date or so, on a quite superficial plane. Other couples date with each other to the point where they are recognized as going steady by the rest of the set.

GOING STEADY

A couple is said to go steady when the others of the social group expect them to appear together at social affairs and when varying degrees of possessiveness are felt by the couple toward each other. Among the college set a couple may go steady for many reasons. They

1. Mutually prefer each other to others who might be dated at the time.

2. Are in love; caught in emotional involvements that make being together a highly desirable end.

3. Cling to each other for social reasons. She can be sure of a date; he does not risk being stood up if they are going steady.

4. Are thrust into going steady by group expectations and demands. After a date or two together the others hang back and expect the two to date only each other. This is particularly pronounced in some schools and colleges. Often the custom is regretted by men and women alike but, once established on a campus, is hard to break.

5. Go steady because it is cheaper and easier than "playing the field." It costs less money and time to go together time after time than it would to impress a new date every time. Couples accustomed to each other can do simple things together that neither would dare suggest to a newly acquired companion.

6. Establish the fact of their social success by hanging onto the fraternity pin or the other symbols of having acquired a steady of high rating in the competitive hierarchy of dating. In order to date at all on some campuses a girl must hold a steady or a series of steadies. Before letting anyone go she must be sure of her ability to attract a man of at least the same dating ranking, or she loses ground socially.

7. Go steady preliminary to getting engaged and being married. Mutual exploration of each other's tastes, habits, values, backgrounds, ambitions, fears, and hopes can be done without the interference of intruding competitors. As interest in each other deepens, the steady date readies itself for the understanding that precedes engagement.

[8] See the section on "Changes in Courtship Patterns," in Evelyn Duvall and Reuben Hill, *When You Marry,* New York, Association Press, and Boston, D. C. Heath and Co., 1953 revision, pp. 79-80.

It is not infrequent to find young people of junior-high and high-school age going steady with each other. Many adults and some young persons are concerned over this tendency to go steady so early. Going steady too soon provides less opportunity for knowing the many other eligible young people of the other sex who might be dated were it not for the possessive restriction of the going-steady relationship. Going steady too soon limits the scope of self-understanding. Different people call forth different responses in a person. Various friends draw forth a variety of responses, feelings, and roles. One boy may make a girl feel roguish and coquettish, another make her feel quiet and subdued; one may make her feel maternal, while another may make her feel like a little girl enjoying the protection of a big father-figure. It is possible that in the process of growing up both a girl and a boy should have the opportunities of playing many of these emotional roles with each other, in order that they may learn from experience the kinds of boys and girls that there are and achieve a deeper understanding of their own emotional repertoire, from which they may more intelligently choose the partner who will be most harmonious.

Still another problem of going steady too soon is that of an uneven commitment of the couple to each other. One of the pair may take the relationship seriously, while the other sees himself or herself much less seriously involved. This problem becomes acute when the less involved partner wishes to withdraw and is able to do so only by hurting the other and feeling a burden of guilt himself. This has been known to be so serious that couples poorly suited to each other have been precipitated into marriage simply because the courage for breaking off with a clinging "steady" has been lacking.

Breaking off with a steady can be a difficult and uncomfortable procedure. Loosening the hold of an unpromising relationship is bound to involve some hurt and often is full of heartache and anguish for one or both of the pair. Recognizing these factors, the initiator of the break will do well to choose a method that will soften the blow for both. There are several procedures to consider. The first is the sudden complete severance of the relationship. The steady who was so reliable one day just is not there the next. If the woman is the initiator of the break she fails to answer his telephone calls, she is "out" when he drops by, she is "busy" when he does catch up with her, she begins to appear at social affairs with other girls or boys. The male aggressor stops calling, asks for no further dates, and soon is out with another woman. This method has the advantage of being quick, easy, and effective. Its disadvantages are that it causes the one who is being sloughed off needless pain and bewilderment, which in turn boomerang on the more active member of the pair in feelings of guilt and fear of being faced with his or her duplicity.

The other extreme is the long agonizing discussion of such questions as "How washed up are we?" "Why don't you love me as you used to?"; and the unanswerable questions: "What has happened? What did I do? Why can't we be friends again?" These scenes are apt to be extremely uncomfortable to both the man and the woman. The raking over of dead embers of a love rarely causes them to burst into flame again or brings much insight into what has happened and what the break means.

A middle ground is that of easing off. Couples who have gone steady on dates three and four times a week begin to taper off to once or twice a week. Their ardor in expressing affection cools. Possessiveness begins to dwindle. One may suggest to the other double dates with mutual friends; or the attractiveness of another companion may be called to the other's attention. Some understanding and acceptance of the impending break helps each to release the other and to redefine the relationship on a more casual plane. Basic to the success of this procedure is a realization of the place of dating and going steady in final mate selection and its particular function in weeding out incompatible and uncongenial prospective mates. Before a couple become engaged they should have mutually established the fact of their ability to please each other, feel comfortable with each other, and be the kind of people who are sufficiently compatible to build a lasting and satisfactory union.

Going steady has as its chief values that of allowing opportunities mutually to explore each other as two whole persons and of facilitating the selection of promising mates. It is not unlikely that patterns established during this stage of courtship carry over into engagement, very much as engagement adjustments preview the marital adjustments yet to be.[9]

THE ENGAGEMENT

A couple become engaged when they have a mutual understanding of intention to marry. Some high-school and college engagements are

[9] See especially Ernest Burgess and Paul Wallin, "Predicting Adjustment in Marriage from Adjustment in Engagement," *American Journal of Sociology,* 49, 1944, pp. 324-30; and their full report, *Engagement and Marriage,* Philadelphia, J. B. Lippincott, 1953.

little more than formalized "steadies." A boy gives his pin to a girl much as a prospector stakes out a claim, which holds others off while he explores its possibilities. A girl sometimes accepts an engagement ring that means little more than a symbol of her being able to catch a highly desirable man in the competitive race for social recognition. She may wear the ring for very much the same reason that others wear a Phi Beta Kappa key—as a mark of achievement.

People more often think of engagement as a prelude to marriage. The engagement period has several recognized functions that are important for the success of the marriage. One of these functions is to place the couple as a pair in the eyes of their friends and families. The parents get used to the idea of the serious involvement of their son or daughter. Friends invite the couple as a pair. The crowd the couple go with may shift to those others who are engaged and looking ahead to marriage rather than just playing around. A "we" feeling develops within the couple in which each is increasingly included in the other's plans, supported by the recognition and acceptance of the engagement by the others round about.

The engagement period further provides the couple with the time and the privacy for becoming basically and understandingly acquainted with each other. Sharing past experiences, relating the important and the trivial episodes in their life histories and how they felt about them, within the permissiveness and encouragement possible with the affianced, are highly significant ways of getting through to each other. Such insights, understandings, and sympathies are imperative for two people who are to share a life together as mutually loving companions.

Sharing the present is another important function of the engagement period. Not only the good times, but also the troubles, the disappointments, the dreams, and the ambitions of each of the pair can be shared to the advantage of the total relationship. Learning to talk freely and frankly about things which may be cloaked with reticence in more casual contacts is a powerful cement in the pair unity. Working together in common interests and purposes weaves a bond that has promising durability and strength.

Establishing patterns of mutual giving and receiving of affection is a vital part of engagement. Society encourages more freedom and privacy for the engaged couple than is approved for less seriously committed couples. So each couple is left to find its own best ways of loving and being loved. Couples should approach marriage ready for the full intimacy of the marriage relationship. How best to achieve that full union of man and woman both physically and emotionally is a highly disputed question today.[10] There are some sophisticated young people and adults who argue for complete sexual exploration before marriage. They point to the importance of sex compatibility and imply that premarital experience allows the couple to discover whether or not they are physically satisfying to each other. Much of the research on this subject indicates premarital sex experience is *not* conducive to good marital adjustment. The psychic atmosphere of the premarital relationship is not at all that of the married pair. Elements of fear, anxiety over exposure, guilt, suspicion, and jealousy occur frequently enough in cases of premarital exploration to indicate that many, many couples simply cannot get this far away from what people in general will stand for.

Furthermore, many very happy marriages do not achieve satisfactory sexual adjustment until some time after the marriage was first consummated.[11] Most couples must learn to orient themselves to each other sexually, so that each achieves satisfaction and gives to the other the degree of pleasure that makes for a satisfying union. For most people the indications are that these specific accomplishments are best learned *after* marriage, when the sense of belonging, permanence, and social approval support the process of mutual accommodation.[12]

What degree of intimacy is wise for an engaged couple? Surely there is no argument that the extreme reserve and prudery of the Victorian era are not conducive to wholesome, happy marriages today. The engaged couple can safely be encouraged to express their affection in many ways not allowed their strait-laced ancestors. The good-night kiss, the enthusiastic embrace, the caressing and fondling

[10] Note the extensive research reported by Alfred Kinsey, et al., in their *Sexual Behavior in the Human Male,* Philadelphia, Saunders, 1948, and *Sexual Behavior in the Human Female,* Philadelphia, Saunders, 1953; as well as the widespread discussion of their findings throughout the popular and professional presses through the years since the appearance of the first report.

[11] Judson Landis, "Adjustment after Marriage," *Marriage and Family Living,* May 1947, pp. 32-4.

[12] Lewis Terman and others in their *Psychological Factors in Marital Happiness,* New York, McGraw-Hill, 1938, report, "in general those husbands and wives who were either virgins at marriage or had had intercourse only with each other tend to have higher mean happiness scores (in marriage) than the other groups" (with premarital experience with others than spouse), p. 329. For a detailed analysis of other research studies of the effect of sexual behavior upon the person, see S. M. Duvall, *Men, Women, and Morals,* New York, Association Press, 1952.

that lovers find pleasure in have won a degree of social approval and encouragement unknown a few generations ago. At the same time there can be reassurance that the full physical experience can wait, and that petting and fondling that arouse sex excitement in either or both of the pair may be postponed in favor of the tender, lighter caresses which before and after marriage convey a depth and beauty of affection that is highly conducive to stability of the relationship.

Engagement may be seen as a period of planning ahead for the marriage that is to be. Before marriage many of the marriage plans can be discussed most fruitfully.[13] Questions such as, shall the wife work? and for how long? and on what basis? can far more easily be faced before than after marriage. Other questions are relevant and important for consideration before the actual contingencies arise. Can they live on the man's earnings? Will some help from parents be acceptable? Is his further education worth sacrificing for? Who will hold the purse strings? Will there be an attempt to live always within the income, or is some indebtedness justified? The attitude of the couple about becoming parents is significant. Do they agree on the number of children they want to try to have? Is there a comfortable consensus on the way the children shall be cared for, disciplined, trained, and introduced to life? The way each feels about his and the other's family is important. In-law troubles rank high in complaints of newlyweds. Emotional dependencies and immaturities are better faced before than after marriage. Some understanding of the place of the members of the extended families in the partnership is helpful. What constitutes a good time, attitudes toward friends, recreation and social participation are another whole area for consideration and understanding that is well undertaken before the marriage takes place. The balance of power, who shall be boss, and when, can be explored both verbally and in behavior to the great advantage of the settling down of the partners into comfortable patterns of mutually desirable dominance and submission.

SUMMARY

Courtship and engagement can be seen as somewhat similar to the casting and rehearsals for the real drama of marriage. Potential mates

[13] Read particularly, S. M. Duvall, *Before You Marry: 101 Questions to Ask Yourself,* New York, Association Press, 1949, as well as any of the marriage texts appearing in recent years that deal competently with these questions. See Selected reading references for a starter listing.

are cast and recast in the complex of modern dating, going steady, and getting engaged. Mutual adjustments and planning before marriage establish patterns carried over into the permanent relationship. It is not surprising to learn that the longer the period of acquaintance and engagement, the more stable and happy the marriage.[14] Conversely, the hastier the marriage, the sooner the divorce.

Courtship and engagement today are not at all the rigid, formalized, supervised affairs they once were. Today's young people must accept responsibility for making them the kind of relationships that are conducive to personal fulfillment and marital stability.

Topics for further thought:

1. Describe the pattern of modern courtship, mentioning in particular what you consider its most significant features. Do you think it is important that this kind of behavior should be "patterned"? Why? Explain fully your idea.

2. Do you believe there is greater chance for a marriage to be successful if it has been preceded by a formal engagement period? Explain your answer.

Selected reading references

Blood, Robert O. Jr., "Uniformities and Diversities in Campus Dating Preferences," *Marriage and Family Living,* February, 1956, pp. 37-45.

Though the author's conclusions are rather similar to those of Lowrie, indicated below, his data appear to support Waller's theory about equally well.

Kirkpatrick, Clifford, and Caplow, Theodore, "Courtship in a Group of Minnesota Students," *American Journal of Sociology,* September, 1945, pp. 114-25.

[14] Ernest Burgess and Leonard Cottrell, *Predicting Success or Failure in Marriage,* New York, Prentice-Hall, 1939, p. 167; Lewis Terman and others, *Psychological Factors in Marital Happiness,* New York, McGraw-Hill, 1938, p. 198; and Harvey Locke, *Predicting Adjustment in Marriage,* New York, Henry Holt, 1951, pp. 91-6.

Sophisticated research on the emotional content of the love affairs of college students. Adds to the complexity of the controversy surrounding Waller's competitive-exploitative theory.

Lowrie, Samuel H., "Dating Theories and Student Responses," *American Sociological Review*, June, 1951, pp. 335-40.
Report of research stresses the positive, educational aspects of dating and courtship.

Nimkoff, Meyer F., and Wood, Arthur L., "Courtship and Personality," *American Journal of Sociology*, January, 1948, pp. 263-9.
Considers dating and courtship as a pleasant trial-and-error process resulting in considerable insight into the opposite sex partner.

Waller, Willard, and Hill, Reuben, *The Family: A Dynamic Interpretation*, New York, The Dryden Press, 1951.
Chapters 8-12 include a theory of dating, courtship, and engagement which stresses bargaining and exploitation between men and women. Has aroused considerable controversy, resulting in research such as that of Blood and Lowrie cited above.

Bibliography

Bowman, Henry, *Marriage for Moderns*, New York, Whittlesey House, second edition, 1948, Chap. 8.

Burgess, Ernest, and Locke, Harvey, *The Family: From Institution to Companionship*, New York, American Book Co., 1945, Chaps. 12, 13, 14, 15.

Burgess, Ernest, and Wallin, Paul, *Engagement and Marriage*, Philadelphia, J. B. Lippincott, 1953, 819 pp.

Cavan, Ruth, *The American Family*, New York, Crowell, 1953, Chap. 13, "Courtship and Engagement," pp. 330-66.

Christensen, Harold, "Dating Behavior as Evaluated by High School Students," *American Journal of Sociology*, May 1952, pp. 580-86.

Connor, Ruth, and Hall, Edith, "The Dating Behavior of College Freshmen and Sophomores," *Journal of Home Economics*, April 1952, pp. 278-81.

Cuber, John, "Changing Courtship and Marriage Customs," *The Annals of the American Academy of Political and Social Science*, September 1943, pp. 30-8.

Duvall, Evelyn Millis, *Facts of Life and Love,* New York, Association Press, 1950, 360 pp.

Duvall, Evelyn, and Hill, Reuben, *When You Marry,* Boston, D. C. Heath, revised edition, 1953, Chaps. 3, 4, 5.

Duvall, Sylvanus, *Before You Marry: 101 Questions to Ask Yourself,* New York, Association Press, 1949, 171 pp.

Folsom, Joseph, *The Family and Democratic Society,* New York, Wiley, 1943, Chap. 16.

Kirkpatrick, Clifford, and Caplow, Theodore, "Emotional Trends in the Courtship Experience of College Students as Expressed by Graphs with Some Observations on Methodological Implications," *American Sociological Review,* October 1945, pp. 619-26.

Koos, Earl Lomon, *Marriage,* New York, Henry Holt, 1953, Chaps. 6, 7.

Landis, Judson, and Landis, Mary, *Building a Successful Marriage,* New York, Prentice-Hall, 1948, Chaps. 4, 8.

Locke, Harvey, *Predicting Adjustment in Marriage,* New York, Henry Holt, 1951, Chap. 5, "Courtship and Engagement," pp. 86-105.

Magoun, F. Alexander, *Love and Marriage,* New York, Harper, 1948, Chaps. 6, 7.

Merrill, Francis, *Courtship and Marriage,* New York, Sloane, 1949, Part I, "Courtship," pp. 3-107.

Nimkoff, Meyer, *Marriage and the Family,* New York, Houghton Mifflin, 1947, Chap. 12, "Courtship," pp. 365-98.

Taylor, Donald, "Courtship as a Social Institution in the United States, 1930 to 1945," *Social Forces,* October 1946, pp. 65-9.

Waller, Willard, and Hill, Reuben, *The Family: A Dynamic Interpretation,* New York, Dryden, 1951, Chaps. 10, 12.

Winch, Robert, *The Modern Family,* New York, Henry Holt, 1952, Chap. 16.

Wolford, Opal Powell, "How Early Background Affects Dating Behavior," *Journal of Home Economics,* November 1948, pp. 505-6.

11 PREMARITAL SEX RELATIONSHIPS

Anna O. Stephens (revised by Morris Fishbein)

THE premarital period may include three merging stages. First, acquaintance or friendship extends through adolescence, but may exist indeterminately for those who do not marry and for the married person and members of the opposite sex other than the mate. During the second stage, courtship, the boy or girl is definitely seeking a mate. This stage usually leads to and ends in the third period, engagement. The engagement stage begins when a boy and girl have definitely committed themselves to each other by promises to marry— with or without the accompaniment of fraternity pins, rings, parties, or formal announcements. The engagement period terminates at the wedding. Because of unforeseen complications such as change of interest, physical disability, family responsibilities, or economic problems some engagements may be broken.

FRIENDSHIP

During early adolescence boys and girls seem to prefer gatherings of groups rather than dates with one person. Their personal contacts more often include roughhousing than intimacy. While ordinarily these youngsters are assumed to be harmlessly engaged in getting acquainted, all such contacts make possible the arousal of more specific sex interest. The early adolescent is physiologically capable of mature sex experience without the accompanying maturity of judgment. Because of a variety of psychological and environmental factors, adolescent boys and girls may indulge in sex play, intensive petting, and ultimately in intercourse.

Encouragement should be given to boys and girls to meet in groups where adequate facilities for play make friendship possible without leading to sexual intimacy. This sort of relationship progresses to the more personal relationship of courtship easily and naturally and paves the way for ease in dealing with persons of the opposite sex in personal, business, and social relationships throughout life.

COURTSHIP

Courtship, which may occur at any period of life, is most common during middle or later adolescence. Physiological maturity and the ability to have sexual intercourse develop, however, in early adolescence. Added to these factors is the discouragement of marriage until education has been completed and social and economic maturity have been reached, usually not until early adult life. This long time must be passed by adolescents in the almost constant presence of the opposite sex, with opportunities for intimacy increasing as freedom increases. Adolescents are subjected on all sides to advertising, music, motion pictures, and literature which place emphasis on sex appeal and glamour as highly desirable factors in personal charm. Since the adolescents are inadequately informed about the significance of these sex attitudes and contacts, many young people find it difficult, if not impossible, to maintain the ideals of society regarding the importance of preserving chastity until marriage. An early marriage may solve some of these problems, but others often appear which may be even greater than those already resolved.

PETTING

The adolescent is especially interested in being popular in his or her own group, often promoting this popularity by a grown-up appearance. Family standards, physical well-being, and personal ideals may be sacrificed to obtain the much-sought popularity. Petting is considered to be mature behavior, and is often tried for this reason. Like the reckless driving of the car, this exploration may lead to serious difficulties before the much-desired maturity has been achieved by the slow natural process of continuing growth and development. Once started, petting easily becomes practically the only form of entertainment on a date for many young people.

Webster states that to pet is "to fondle, to caress." Henry A. Bowman, in *Marriage for Moderns,* defines petting as follows: ". . . physical contact for pleasure which is an end in itself, arising from sexual desire in one or both parties but stopping short of coitus, and of such nature that in one or both there is produced an increased sexual sensitivity and response, a stirring up of sexually colored emotions, and an increased tension that can be relieved immediately only by coitus or some substitute therefor." In the absence of relief, the tension has a tendency to persist for some time. The physical contact with which petting deals usually takes the form mentioned by Webster—caressing and fondling. Such caressing and fondling is normally part of the love-making that precedes sexual intercourse in married life. Petting helps to create sexual desire and to make physiological preparation for the completion of the sex act. When unmarried young people pet without understanding this biological effect, they may unexpectedly find themselves so stimulated that it is difficult for them to stop short of coitus. What is commonly called heavy petting usually means caressing of the more intimate parts of the body such as the breasts and the thighs. Young people who indulge in heavy petting often reach a sexual climax or orgasm as a result of this manual contact rather than by coitus.

Many adolescent girls begin petting at the request of their boy friends for various reasons. They believe that it may be the only way to insure future dates, that they owe it to the boy as evidence of their appreciation of a pleasant evening, or that it will show that they are grown up. Only after the practice is well established do they learn its real physiological significance. Then it is difficult to establish a new pattern of behavior unless both the environment and the boy friend are also new. The young boy may begin petting because he thinks the girl expects it of him or that she will be impressed with his maturity. In many instances he recognizes the sex urge before he begins to pet or at least much earlier in the process than the girl does. Believing that the girl shares his sexual stimulation, he assumes that her reasons for continuing the process are the same as his. As petting becomes more intimate the girl may be bewildered by his ardor and insistence upon coitus, while he is confused by her resistance or her surprise at his intentions. The result is often unhappy for both. Whether coitus results sooner than one or both had wished or intended, whether friendship is disrupted by misunderstanding over the matter, or whether petting is discontinued after physical desires have been aroused and the friendship is difficult to re-establish on any other basis, the situation is undesirable. Young people from junior-high-school age on need to have a thorough understanding of the physiological implications of petting.

Robert L. Dickinson, the author of *Human Sex Anatomy,* has contributed to an understanding of this problem of petting and continence. His examination dwells chiefly on the physiological functioning of the sex organs with a frank discussion of male and female urges. Not only are the physiological factors revealed, but also the standard conventions and the new approaches and possible solutions to the problems engendered by these conventions.

DATING CONDUCT

Persons of different social, educational, and cultural backgrounds have different ideals and standards. The same standards should apply when selecting friends of the opposite sex as when choosing those of one's own sex. Among friends of the same sex it is usual to find more or less similar cultural background and experience. Friends of the opposite sex should be chosen from this same group. Boys and girls reared in the same home will usually have similar ideals and standards. It is reasonable to find one's dates among the brothers or sisters of one's friends or among the friends of one's brothers or sisters, so that wide cultural differences will not complicate the relationship.

Since the temptation to make petting a major part of courtship inevitably arises, young people who wish to avoid its hazards, assisted by those who advise them, should be resourceful in planning interesting ways of spending their time together. A generation or two ago, adults, children, and young people alike found their recreation in their homes. Many young people now find that homes, their own or their friends', are the center of their lives. Yet homes cannot fully meet the need of providing interest and recreation. Many young people are employed away from home. Many homes are so small, so crowded with other activities, or so inhospitable to the enthusiasm of youth that young people find it difficult to spend their leisure at home.

The young people themselves need to understand that marriage is based primarily on friendship and a deep underlying unity of spirit of which sexual relationships are an expression rather than a cause. They need to see the great importance of being able to do many things together for pleasure before sharing sex experience. If opportunity for some of the more popular activities is provided at a time and place and for a price that is convenient to the young couple, they may be helped to postpone petting as an indoor sport. The average community has limited facilities at the disposal of young people. They can attend motion pictures, many of which are sexually stimulating; go to public eating places, which are expensive; go to church, which is usually limited to certain hours on Sunday; or walk in the park, which is either dark and cold or warm and moonlit, neither of which conditions can be long endured by the average couple without problems arising. A few communities have bowling alleys enough to provide for an extremely small per cent of their population and these are usually assigned to certain organizations at the hours that the dating couple would wish to use them. Then, of course, young people can visit libraries and museums, but even adults do not find these really exciting for long; besides, they are usually closed evenings when young people are dating.

Anyone who watches young people skiing, skating, playing tennis, picnicking, making candy, and playing records together knows that young couples are eager for shared experiences in many fields of activity. The community is not without obligation to provide more adequately for these needs. Whether the school, the clubs, the church, or some independent organization will be the first to attempt to meet the need will depend on the people who make up the particular community. These group activities will help to diminish the sex urge that might often follow an erotic motion picture or an especially stimulating dance. The simple urge to eat may forestall any difficult situation, especially if there is a convenient place to eat where friends can be met.

Young people need to decide upon a standard of conduct ahead of time. Many young people, having their emotions aroused by petting, are suddenly faced with the question of how far they shall go. In such situations, time is lacking for a coolheaded decision. This decision must be made in the peace and quiet of one's own room before the temptation arises. Each young person should ask himself: Where do I stand on the matter of chastity? What is ideal marriage? Does it permit premarital sex relations? If it comes to the point of deciding between premarital sex relations or losing the friend I've been dating, do I still plan to maintain my standards? Shall I go all out for virginity, or do I admit extenuating circumstances? Once this decision has been made and is so clear cut that the boy or girl is convinced in his own mind of the ideal he holds and the price he is willing to pay for that ideal, the whole problem is simplified. Having decided that marriage is worth waiting for, the problem becomes how to handle courtship so as to avoid or reduce the temptation to compromise this ideal. As friendship leads on to courtship and as affection develops during courtship the emphasis in this growing relationship should be placed on shared experiences other than the physical. Later on physical intimacy develops readily on the firm basis of this enduring friendship. When emphasis is placed on the physical early in the relationship it becomes increasingly hard to distinguish between love and infatuation, so that an unhappy marriage is more likely to result. Excess petting that constantly stimulates sexual desire may lead a couple to marry prematurely, before either party is ready to assume the responsibilities of marriage and a home. Dating time spent in working and playing together and in exploring one another's interests and abilities is never time wasted.

The custom of blind dating raises special problems. While love at first sight may be possible, the blind date that turns out to be a bore at first sight, or at least after the first hour, is much more probable. The situation is then likely to deteriorate into a petting party. This hazard can be reduced somewhat by insisting that all blind dates be double dates. This is especially important in the case of girls going out with strange men. If a girl insists that the other girl in the foursome be one whom she knows and who shares her ideals and standards of conduct, she can avoid the difficult position of being the only dissenter at a heavy petting party. Two girls who stick together in their opposition to conduct of which they do not approve can usually win.

ENGAGEMENT

As courtship leads to the definite selection of one person as the object of affection and as the prospective mate, the relationship of the young couple will naturally increase in intimacy. During courtship the partner selected for one or a series of dates may be dropped as soon as a more interesting partner is available. Even couples who go steady at a rather early stage in their acquaintance may later break up. In this respect the engaged couple are quite different. Engagement signifies a mutual pledge and the occupation of one's interest with the betrothed alone. The period of engagement, be it short or long, is filled with definite preparation for marriage. The young couple during this period are engrossed in plans for everything from the size of their anticipated family, whether the wife shall be employed, how money matters shall be handled, and what church they shall attend, to such remote events as where they wish to live when they retire, or where they will travel if they ever can afford to travel.

Since affection is the basis of this new relationship, this affection may be expressed not only by candy and flowers but by petting. If chastity until marriage is a valid standard, the amount of petting that is desirable during engagement will vary under different circumstances. In general these circumstances include the length of time the couple must wait until marriage can take place, the ease with which either party becomes sexually aroused, the amount of time that is spent together, the frequency of seeing each other, the privacy from interruptions, and the readiness of each for marriage. If by early training (or lack of it) either party is hesitant about entering into the marriage relationship, surely the expression of affection during the engagement period should awaken desire sufficiently to make the sexual relations of marriage seem a natural and right next step. If, however, the couple are physically fully ready for marriage, physical contacts may have to be limited severely during the engagement in order that they be not too strongly tempted to disregard the idea of continence before marriage. This is especially so if the marriage is to be postponed for some time. Many couples, as they approach their wedding date, will find that the temptation for them to consummate their relationship before their wedding becomes strong. If each understands the problem of the other they may help one another to avoid the situations that make the temptation real and vivid. Determination on the part of one or both may be needed to find ways of doing things together and at the same time of avoiding complete intimacy. So many activities which demand physical activity can be done together or with other people or at least permit a lighted room and a certain degree of independent activity that a couple who really desire to avoid sexual intercourse can usually do so. The couple must have adequate information and understanding of the physical factors involved. Many girls and some men even today do not understand the relationship of petting to sexual desire. This understanding must be clear if the couple is to handle their problem intelligently.

SUMMARY

Each young person must decide what his standard of conduct is to be. Young people need to be prepared by sex education for the problems associated with physical maturity before they are called upon to make a decision in a particular situation about whether or not to relinquish their chastity. This can be done only by the co-operation of all the resources of community life in providing straightforward education, instructions, student counseling, premarital advice, and adequate opportunities for recreation. Attention must be given to the needs of youth during the periods usually occupied with heterosexual group acquaintances and growing friendships among individuals as well as during courtship and engagement. Common interests and mutual participation in work and play must be stressed as a basis for the later development of affection and its natural expression by physical means. Since the too early development of the habit of stimulating sex desire by petting or other physical means may impair happiness in marriage, young people should find other means of enjoyment of one another in their usual daily contacts and dates until such time as marriage is seriously contemplated. The avoidance of sex-stimulating activities as petting should not be accomplished by threat or fear but by concentration on the positive elements in friendship developed through work and play together. In the present state of our social organization, adequate opportunities for such work and play together are not provided in most communities. Adults and young people alike should bend every effort to find new and better ways of meeting the recreational needs of youth in order that our society may continue to develop toward a higher plane of moral and spiritual life. The problems of young people who are engaged and contemplating marriage are related to the experience of each, the length of time until marriage will take place, the frequency with which they see one another, and the degree to which their affection for one another has developed. They may be helped to limit the degree of intimacy desirable for them by encouragement to put first emphasis on the solving of other problems related to their anticipated marriage, such as finances, religion, and similar subjects, and to limit the expression of affection to such petting as does not bring undue temptation to either.

Topics for further thought:

1. Discuss the favorable and unfavorable aspects of the independence and freedom given unmarried couples in their "dating" as a consequence of the relaxation of parental controls and the disappearance of the system of chaperonage.

2. What major controls do you think a society should continue to impose on the premarital behavior of young people? Explain your answer.

Selected reading references

Bromley, Dorothy D., and Britten, Florence H., *Youth and Sex: A Study of 1300 College Students,* New York, Harper and Brothers, 1938. An excellent, though not widely publicized, study of the sexual experiences of college students. Demonstrates forcefully the inadequacy of simply classifying students into those who have had sexual experience and those who have not.

Kinsey, Alfred C., Pomeroy, Wardell B., and Martin, Clyde E., *Sexual Behavior in the Human Male,* Philadelphia, W. B. Saunders Company, 1948. Along with its companion volume on the female, the most exhaustive study of human sex behavior yet produced. Careful, detailed interviews with 5300 men document the widespread and varied nature of premarital sex behavior.

Kinsey, Alfred C., Pomeroy, Wardell B., Martin, Clyde E., and Gebhard, Paul H., *Sexual Behavior in the Human Female,* Philadelphia, W. B. Saunders Company, 1953. Companion volume to the reference cited above. Interviews with 5940 women indicate a considerable increase, particularly over the decade of the 1920's, in the proportion of women becoming involved in premarital intercourse.

Murdock, George P., Woodward, Luther E., and Bolman, Frederick, "Sexual Behavior, What is Acceptable?" reprinted from *Journal of Social Hygiene,* 1950, pp. 1-31, in Landis, Judson T., and Landis, Mary G., *Readings in Marriage and the Family,* New York, Prentice-Hall, 1952. Presents the varying views of an anthropologist, a mental hygienist, and a professor of philosophy.

Stokes, Walter R., and Mace, David M., "Premarital Sexual Behavior," *Marriage and Family Living,* August, 1953, pp. 234-49. A discussion of the issues involved in premarital sexual behavior sponsored by the American Association of Marriage Counselors, Inc.

12 PREMARITAL PHYSICAL EXAMINATION

Morris Fishbein

ALTHOUGH most of our states, perhaps forty, three territories, and parts of Canada now require a medical certificate before
granting a license to marry, these legal controls are concerned primarily with the prevention of the spread of venereal disease. A comprehensive and proper premarital examination as regards fitness for
marriage goes far beyond this limitation. The laws that have been
passed since 1910 vary, for the most part, in different states. In
Alabama, North Dakota, Oregon, and Wisconsin, a medical certificate
of freedom from venereal disease was all that was at first required.
In New York and Pennsylvania applicants for marriage licenses had
to state under oath that they were free from venereal disease and
tuberculosis. The Connecticut law passed in 1935 required that a
blood test for syphilis be made and that both applicants have a physical examination. These laws have been amended but freedom from
syphilis as shown by a suitable blood test, such as the Kahn, Wasser-
mann, or Eagle test, is still the very minimum requirement. Certainly
freedom from gonorrhea as determined by a microscopic examination
of secretions should be demanded. Fortunately modern methods of
diagnosing and treating these conditions make diagnosis more accurate than it used to be and treatment more effective and of much
shorter duration. The available records indicate that less than 1 per
cent of applicants for marriage are found now to have a positive blood
test for syphilis.

PREMARITAL EXAMINATION OF A MAN

The examination of a man regarding his fitness for marriage should be a comprehensive physical examination, at least as thorough as that required for taking out a life-insurance policy. The doctor should inquire about his birth and any complications that may indicate the necessity for study of the Rh factor (see page 347). Certain diseases run in families—for example, diabetes, blood disorders, and some disturbances of the nervous system. The candidate for marriage should be aware of such possibilities. Occasionally a boy is found at birth to have a rupture (hernia) in the groin or in the center line of the abdomen near the navel or umbilicus. Sometimes the testicles or male sex glands do not come down during childhood into the scrotum. Such undescended testicles may lose their power to develop sperm cells capable of producing progeny. Many young men need reassurance about the possible effects of illnesses or accidents they have had. Many are worried about having practiced masturbation in childhood or adolescence. Rarely indeed has this almost universal habit interfered with the ability to have sexual intercourse or to produce impregnation. In recent years good tests of male fertility and sterility have been developed. Perhaps such a study is desirable before marriage rather than years later, when failure to have a child may have produced worries, suspicions, recriminations, or other difficulties interfering with the happiness of marriage. By proper questioning the physician may detect unusual attachment of the young man to his mother, to other members of the family, or to friends; he may discover insufficient habits of cleanliness or other difficulties wherein a suggestion or hint may prevent future sorrow.

A good physical examination should include a study of vision, hearing, the throat, the heart, the blood pressure, a record of abdominal distress or persistent indigestion, an x-ray of the chest, the presence of allergies and skin disorders, ringworm of the scalp or feet or groin, rheumatic disease, examination of the blood for anemia or failure to clot, examination of the urine for albumin, sugar, or blood. The doctor should test a few reflexes which reveal the integrity of the nervous system. A basal metabolic test may indicate deficiency or excess action of the thyroid gland. Overweight or underweight may lead to suggestions for the diet.

Finally the premarital examination should give the doctor an opportunity to inquire into the sexual experiences of the applicant and to answer questions about habits of intercourse, its frequency, the proper approach to physical marriage, the prevention of conception, or whatever the doctor as a marriage counselor may consider desirable. A medical education may make the physician thoroughly competent as a doctor and yet not qualify him as a good marital counselor. The young man who consults the doctor wants adequate authoritative information. This should be given in a dignified manner without cynicism or disillusionment or any hint that will lead to fears or mental stresses.

PREMARITAL EXAMINATION OF A WOMAN

The girl who comes to the doctor for a premarital examination requires the same careful check-up as the young man—and more. Her history or record should be just as meticulously investigated and recorded as that of her prospective husband. She needs the same examinations of the integrity and functions of the eyes, ears, skin, nervous system, heart, circulation, breathing, and elimination. The physical examination should include study of the lungs with an x-ray of the chest, determination of the glandular action and of the weight. An added factor is of course the menstrual history: the age of onset, regularity, freedom from pain, excessive or scanty menstruation, and worries about it. Psychosomatic studies have shown how little many know about this function in relation to marriage, how much it affects successful marriage, and how often dysmenorrhea, or painful menstruation, is dependent on mental attitudes. She should be questioned about infectious and venereal diseases. She will have questions about masturbation, effects of sex play in courtship, or even premarital sexual intercourse. The answers to such questions require the utmost tact and dignity on the part of the doctor.

The examination of the woman before marriage concerns first her fitness, her readiness, and her understanding of sexual intercourse. The evolution of our culture has placed considerable value on virginity. Actually a large percentage of women reach marriage without the physical sign of virginity, the untorn hymen. The hymen is a thin double fold of mucous membrane which partially obstructs and narrows the opening into the vagina. Some books, both fictional and nonfictional, have made so much of the brutality, the pain, or mental horror of the first intercourse with the breaking of the hymen that many girls dread it. Sometimes a mother whose own experience has been unsatisfactory has by suggestion intensified unwarranted fears in her daughter. The hymen, if present, is torn with the first sexual experience and there may be momentary pain. Most girls need time for adjustment to the physical side of marriage. They may need to be reminded of the innumerable women who have had the experience without too much pain and who have accepted it as normal.

In a few cases women have had distress which suitable examination and preparation for coitus could have avoided. The examination made by the doctor, with a nurse or other woman in attendance, will involve inspection for the presence or absence of the hymen, its thickness or fragility, the presence or absence of inflammations or leukorrhea, the possible infection by ringworm or trichomonas which have been unnoted or concealed. The doctor usually avoids unnecessary injury to the hymen in such examinations.

Leukorrhea is an excessive flow of moisture from the vagina. If there is infection, the material is thick, white, and odorous. If there is only excessive flow resulting from inflammation or congestion, treatment may be helpful. Itching or burning with a discharge is a symptom of something wrong and must be studied, properly diagnosed, and treated.

The physician can determine from the menstrual record much about the structures involved in childbirth such as the ovaries, tubes, and uterus. He may learn more by feeling the size and position of these structures. If there has been venereal infection, the symptoms may lead to various further studies, including the use of the x-ray.

About 14 per cent of couples seem to be unable to have children. Nearly half of these can be helped by diagnosis of the cause and by medical aid. Injuries, infections, inflammations, surgical operations, abnormalities of structure, either congenital or resulting from growth, glandular imbalance, or other physiologic factors, may be detected during premarital examination. Suitable treatment when possible may prevent sterility.

Nowadays children grow up in good health and there seldom seems to be need for pelvic examinations of teen-age girls. Such examinations, however, if made on entrance into college or even late in high school, would help to establish wholesome attitudes about the genital organs. The procedure should be free from any suggestion of impropriety. Abnormalities when found may be corrected early.

Dr. Lovett Dewees made 650 premarital examinations of women in a middle-class suburban practice. The study showed that 59 per cent had a hymen and were what the scientists call anatomical virgins.

About 30 per cent had had some experience of coitus or sexual intercourse. About 10 per cent, though without sexual experience, had a relaxed or elastic hymen with adequate opening. In 3 per cent there were tumors, cysts, or other abnormalities of the sexual outlet requiring surgery.

More than 20 per cent of the women examined had the uterus or womb with its larger upper end leaning toward the back instead of toward the front. The condition is called retroversion. This does not ordinarily interfere with coitus or childbirth, but it is one of the most important reasons for a premarital pelvic examination, and surgical correction may be required before childbirth.

About 35 per cent had some degree of redness or abnormal color or texture of the tissue covering the cervix—the neck with the opening of the uterus into the vagina. This can be inspected and felt by the physician. Two-thirds of the women with redness of the cervix had an excess amount of moisture in the vagina or leukorrhea. If a thick fluid obstructs the opening of the uterus, there may be sterility.

QUESTIONS ABOUT CONTRACEPTION

Both men and women during premarital examination are likely to ask about the possibility of having children—fertility or sterility—and about the prevention of conception. Many young women think this is the chief purpose of the premarital interview. They ask, "Will the use of contraceptives lessen fertility?" The answer, justified by scientific evidence, is that the proper use of contraceptives does not lessen fertility. Permanent devices installed in the uterus are dangerous; they produce irritations and inflammations and should not be used and particularly should never be installed before marriage.

PREPARATION FOR INTERCOURSE

Few young men need instruction or medical attention during the premarital interview to enable them to have sexual intercourse after marriage. They need to be enlightened about the desirability of a gradual seductive approach accompanied by manifestations of love. They should have information, if needed, about cleanliness. They may be given instruction with diagrams on the relationship of male and female structures in intercourse.

Dr. Dewees found that 10 per cent of the women without previous sex experience needed some weeks of preparation before marriage. Rarely a small surgical incision of the hymen was required, with stretching after the incision. Many young women fear their vaginas are too small to receive the male organ but only rarely is anything more than simple reassurance about their normality necessary. At least 10 per cent of women have elasticity of the hymen with adequate relaxation; these will have no difficulty in coitus. Eighty per cent of women may have mild momentary pain with the first intercourse. They may choose to have the opening stretched in the doctor's office by the use of suitable instruments and a local anesthetic, or they may wish to use suitable devices at home as prescribed by the doctor with adequate instruction. Instruction by the doctor about postures and procedures used in coitus is helpful in avoiding difficulties.

The recent widespread adoption of the vaginal occlusive diaphragm for the prevention of conception makes necessary an understanding by the woman of the nature and structure of her sexual organs if she is to use this method of contraception. Few physicians recommend the use of the contraceptive vaginal diaphragm before the first intercourse, preferring to leave contraception to the devices employed by the man, to the selection of the safe period, or to the contraceptive jelly during the early months of marriage. Many physicians are so convinced of the importance of bearing children early in marriage that they avoid discussions of contraception as a part of the premarital examination.

SUMMARY

The premarital examination required by law is employed principally to control such venereal diseases as syphilis and gonorrhea. Premarital physical examination provides the opportunity for a complete survey of the health and physical condition of the prospective bride and groom. In the man a study of the normality of the sex organs, heart, lungs, blood pressure, and glandular constitution is stressed. With the woman, special attention is paid to the organs concerned in childbirth as well.

One of the chief values of the premarital examination is to answer questions and relieve doubts which may produce marital stresses and sexual incompatibility or failure.

Decisions about information on various methods of contraception, the time of employment, and methods of use must be left to the individual physician in his relationship to the particular patient.

Topics for further thought:

1. What kind of health examinations do you think our society should require of all persons before marriage? Explain your answer.

2. Study the program of the Planned Parenthood League of America. What are the arguments for and against such a program?

Selected reading references

Blood, Robert O. Jr., *Anticipating Your Marriage,* Glencoe, The Free Press, 1955.
Chapter 7 includes a discussion on "Getting Help before Marriage," which deals with the physical examination and the securing of information.

Cuber, John F., *Marriage Counseling Practice,* New York, Appleton-Century-Crofts, 1948.
A somewhat technical treatise on marriage counseling which indicates the need for couples to prepare carefully and completely for the marriage relationship.

Kavinoky, Nadina R., "The Gynecologist as Marriage Counselor," *Marriage and Family Living,* Spring, 1950, pp. 44-5, 50.
Describes the role of the medical specialist in helping to prepare women physically and emotionally for marriage.

Levine, Lena, *The Doctor Talks with the Bride and Groom* (pamphlet), New York, Planned Parenthood Federation of America, Inc., 1950.
Places the premarital examination in the broader context of healthy preparation for the sexual aspects of marriage.

Mudd, Emily H., *The Practice of Marriage Counseling,* New York, Association Press, 1951.
Describes, among other things, the kind of premarital counseling done at the Marriage Council of Philadelphia, Emily Mudd is the author of Chapter 19, "Women's Adjustment to Marriage," in this book.

THREE

THE MARRIAGE

13 THE WEDDING AND HONEYMOON

Ada Hart Arlitt

W EDDINGS may be categorized into six types: the secret wedding, the elopement, the simple home wedding, the large home wedding, the simple church wedding, and the large church wedding. In all types of weddings except the secret wedding and the elopement there is a steadily heightened emotional tone leading up to and through the festivities which precede the wedding to the wedding itself. This is true of the family, their friends, and the engaged couple. The result is an emotional tone favorable to marital adjustments. After the ceremony the parents and friends are ready to release the couple from adolescence and to welcome them into the young married group. For the couple the high tension of the parties and the final ceremony is ready to change over into the physiological and psychological states which accompany love, including sex. The bride has been the center of attention which she knows will terminate adolescence for her and for the groom. Having been the center of the stage, which is the desire of all normal adolescents, she should now be willing to relinquish this position.

All her social group and the surrounding social groups have been notified of the wedding. Both families have obviously approved to such an extent that the wedding has proceeded publicly. Society approves and, with the proper notices in the papers, the parties, and the ceremony, has given its final sanction.

The guests have had a part in setting the stage for a successful marriage, as most of them have contributed presents with which the couple will set up housekeeping. They have had a part in the entire procedure from the announcement of the engagement to the actual starting of the couple's home. Naturally, then, they will co-operate in making this marriage a success. Even if the wedding is a small one to which the only the family is invited, these attitudes and adjustments are still present.

THE SECRET WEDDING

The secret wedding has only one advantage; it eliminates the cost of the simplest home wedding. Its disadvantages far outweigh the saving of time and money. Both in their relationships with family and friends and in their relationship with each other, the secretly married couple suffer for the absence of public attendance and approval of their wedding. The relatives and friends who have been deceived and whose generosity has been frustrated may carry actual dislike for the couple and a conscious or unconscious desire to see the marriage fail. This is as true of the immediate family as it is of its friends. Socially the marriage is off to a poor start, even if it is announced within a few days after it occurs. If it is not announced for several months, only a few men of extraordinary good will can fail to suspect an element of shotgun technique in the marriage. If this is complicated by the birth of a child within a few months after the marriage is announced the child carries a definite stigma and society will accept the child and its parents only if the families on both sides stand back of them wholeheartedly.

Emotionally the situation may be even worse. The whole wedding procedure has been surreptitious and therefore associated in the minds of both partners with the fear which accompanies concealment. Fear inhibits love and produces throughout the entire physiological organism conditions that make normal sex adjustments impossible. The irritation that arises is likely to be directed by the couple against each other. The emotional pattern is one of fear and anger, not love. The first adjustments are the most important. Only in very rare instances indeed will these be good. There is little excuse for a secret wedding and none whatsoever if it is announced immediately after it occurs.

ELOPEMENT

An elopement is also a poor method of starting married life. It is rarely based on a long engagement discussed with and approved by both families. It is often a result of a sudden whim or an escape, by one or both partners, from something which should be faced before they marry. When the couple have decided that they prefer to save the cost of a simple home wedding they should nevertheless have the

backing of the family on both sides and have the immediate family—
that is, mother, father, sister, and brothers on both sides—attend.
On the whole elopements are not successful. Statistics show they result in many more divorces than do marriages entered into in the
usual fashion with a church or home wedding.

THE SIMPLE HOME WEDDING

In the simple home wedding the ceremony may be performed by
any legal authority who is a friend of the family or, more frequently,
by a minister. Psychologically the latter is the wiser plan, as the church
and the state are concerned with the adjustment of the couple. With
the success of marriage as uncertain as it is today, the more social
pressure that can be brought to bear to keep it together, the better.

For a simple home wedding without bridesmaids the cost to the
bride's family should not be more than that shown in Table 2.

TABLE 2. Bridal Expenses

Item	Summer	Winter
Decorations	$ 25.00	$100.00
Dress and veil	50.00	75.00
Trousseau	300.00	300.00
Linens	200.00	200.00
Present (bride to groom)	10.00	10.00
TOTAL	$585.00	$685.00

The major expenses of this type of wedding are the trousseau and
linens which present-day custom states are to be the gifts of the
bride's family. The refreshments, if they are supplied, should not
cost more than fifteen dollars, since at a wedding of this sort cham-
pagne is not provided and a caterer is not employed. This type of
wedding has every advantage and few disadvantages, since the expense
for the groom is equally light: an engagement ring ($200); a wed-
ding ring ($20); present for the bride ($20); and fee for the minister ($15)—total of ($255). The change from summer to winter
makes no difference in the groom's expenses. Every psychological
need except that for display has been met. Both parents of bride
and groom have come and shown their approval. The bride has appeared in the traditional bride's clothing, complete with veil, so that
her husband can remember her at her loveliest for the rest of her
life. The too great excitement of complicated church weddings has

been avoided and the couple have saved sufficient funds to set up housekeeping in a more normal way.

THE SIMPLE CHURCH WEDDING

The expenses for a simple church wedding for an average family are shown in Table 3.

In recent years many stores have added special departments for prospective brides. The services which these offer should be approached with caution, since their cost, including photographs, may be double the amount given here for a simple home wedding.

It is hardly necessary to point out the general effect of overexpenditure. The parents are left with so many bills to pay that they cannot easily help the couple in their normal plans. The groom has been put to an enormous expense. Unless he has saved a great deal he enters married life with a crippled financial status. The wife may have to work for several years in order to save enough to meet emergencies. Instead of entering married life relaxed, both are worried. Weddings of this type are the result of a general tendency in society today to increase possessions at the expense of spiritual growth. There can be little if any advantage in such increase in complications, except that they make the bride feel that she has had as good a wedding as any in her set and better than most.

For families of large incomes and grooms who are well on their way toward financial success, these expenditures present no problem, but very few couples are so well situated financially.

THE LARGE HOME OR CHURCH WEDDING

The large home wedding and the large church wedding are so far beyond the means of the average family that tables of expenses for these are not included here. Under modern conditions of living, large, expensive weddings occur rarely. Psychologically, economically, and sociologically, the disadvantages far outweigh the benefits from such lavish displays.

PSYCHOLOGICAL ASPECTS OF THE WEDDING

The psychological state that immediately precedes weddings other than sudden elopements should be kept in mind. For at least twenty-four hours before the actual wedding takes place there is a mounting tension in both men and women, but it appears to be higher in women. The girl begins to worry about the marriage and finally comes to the conclusion that the man is a stranger and that she does not wish the

TABLE 3. Expenses for a Simple Church Wedding

Bride	Summer	Winter
Bridesmaids' flowers (3)	$ 30.00	$75.00
Decorations	100.00	150.00
Gifts to bridesmaids	30.00	30.00
Sexton	10.00	10.00
Invitations and/or announcements	85.00	85.00
Photographs	100.00	100.00
Rehearsal dinner	50.00	50.00
Organist	25.00	25.00
Breakfast or reception	350.00	350.00
Dress and veil	70.00	150.00
Trousseau	300.00	300.00
Linens	200.00	200.00
Present (bride to groom)	30.00	30.00
Groom's ring (if double-ring ceremony)	25.00	25.00
TOTAL	$1405.00	$1580.00

Groom	Summer	Winter
Bride's bouquet	$ 15.00	$ 25.00
Corsage for groom's mother	10.00	10.00
Corsage for bride's mother	10.00	10.00
License	2.00	2.00
Engagement ring	200.00	200.00
Wedding ring	25.00	25.00
Present for bride	100.00	100.00
Fee for minister	25.00	25.00
Flowers for ushers	10.00	20.00
Dinner for ushers	25.00	25.00
Presents for ushers	7.50	7.50
Suit—rented	10.00	10.00
Honeymoon	200.00	200.00
TOTAL	$639.50	$659.50

Bridesmaid	Summer	Winter
Dress	$35.00	$ 50.00
Sandals	6.00	6.00
Hat or garland	4.00	15.00
Showers for bride	50.00	50.00
TOTAL	$95.00	$121.00

marriage to go on. This tension may be so strong that at the last minute she will elope with someone else as an escape. Such elopements are doomed to failure. Generally the groom is in the same state and at the dinner which occurs before the wedding he may drink too much and the ushers must see him home and put him to bed. He wakes up just about in time to dress and to rush to be married. The girl has no such easy way out and must fight her fears.

Many brides have described their fears, including the final one, in very much the same language. When they enter the church and look at the groom they feel that he is a complete stranger. This feeling increases as they go up the aisle. When the groom speaks the fear may be dispelled. For some it is dispelled only when at the end of the ceremony the groom kisses the bride.

Emotional disturbances of every kind are less for home weddings than they are for church weddings. They apparently increase with the size of the church, but in every one of the brides interviewed some fear did develop.

Other things being equal, the simpler the festivities, the better. The bride and the groom are already somewhat tired from the festivities preceding the wedding, and the longer they stay with their friends in a state of high emotional tension, the less they will have to give to the wedding night.

In many cases the number of parties given for the bride and groom and the complexities of the wedding itself, together with the reception which follows it, produce such fatigue in the bride and groom that the marriage may not be consummated for as much as forty-eight hours after the wedding. There are many instances in which twelve hours' sleep is necessary to relieve exhaustion before any emotion other than irritation can arise.

THE HONEYMOON

The choice of the place for the honeymoon should have been made in advance of the wedding and in the light of the financial position of the groom. He has not only to take care of all the expenses incurred during the honeymoon but also to have a sufficient reserve to meet the expenses incident to establishing a home and supporting a family.

No one should accompany the bridal couple under any conditions. The presence of a third person, no matter how loving and considerate, is sufficient to bring about a state of frustration in both bride and groom. It may easily become a source of serious quarrels. Relatives and friends should not surprise the bride and groom with visits during the honeymoon for the same reason. To go where there are a number of friends who will entertain for the couple is equally unfortunate. The purpose of the honeymoon is to provide a period of adjustment to marriage and not to provide an occasion for further entertainment and further follow-up by the family. The simpler the honeymoon, the more provision should be made for many activities of an interesting sort in which the couple may engage. Anyone who has had a long train trip—say, three days—with a good friend in the same compartment or space will remember that the first day was interesting enough but that by the end of the third day the friendship was strained or even terminated. No doubt married couples think they wish to see each other all day long without any special activities planned, but this is far from the case. No one is fascinating enough to provide a source of stimulation and interest for twenty-four hours a day for ten consecutive days.

Camping trips on which the couple constantly need to adjust to a changing environment, motor trips which are not too long and too wearing, places where there are sports in which the couple are mutually interested, or a city with motion pictures, theaters, museums, and parks, if the couple have sufficient funds to finance the expenses, are all good choices. Long train trips are not.

During the honeymoon certain psychological states will be present of which it is well to take account. They should be met before they produce lasting conflicts. One writer has pointed out that these are the desire to tell the beloved everything about one's self, a willingness to promise anything, and a desire to possess completely. Each of these must be watched carefully. It is always interesting to talk about one's self, and this is usually more common in brides than in grooms. Nothing is more boring than a person about whom one knows everything. While the bride and groom know each other very well, or they should not have been married, some things should be left for them to discover about each other for many years to come.

If the material talked about is in the nature of a too full confession, it is likely to produce shock effects from which they may not recover. If the couple are adult, and they should be, then each has fallen in love with someone else before the final engagement and marriage. Unless what has occurred during the preceding experience is of so serious a nature that it should have been told before marriage, then to give names, places, dates, and the blow-by-blow description of what has gone on when one was previously involved is simply to make

clear and vivid images in the mind of the confessee which may interfere with all later marital adjustments. If a couple who have been
happily married fifteen years or more are asked if they had ever been
in love with anyone other than the wife or husband, the answer will
be that they fell in love only once and were never in the least interested in anyone other than the person to whom they are now married. All previous experiences are forgotten rapidly unless they are
told in detail. If they are so told the partner in marriage will not let
them be forgotten and they become inhibitory in their effects.

Plans of the bride and groom should not be so inflexible as to make
an early pregnancy feared. The effect of fear on sex relations is too
well known to need discussion here. Tension because of sex maladjustments during the honeymoon period may never be overcome.
Many authorities tend to minimize the role played by sex in marriage, but it must be kept in mind that marriage is primarily a sex
relationship. The end of the honeymoon should find the couple
physically and psychologically adjusted to such an extent that they
are ready to undertake a lifetime of living and working together.

If the honeymoon is not satisfactory to the bride a number of
things may happen. All girls carry into marriage a species of imaginary
playmate whom they bring out for their own satisfaction whenever
life is not sufficiently interesting or rewarding. For brevity's sake this
imaginary playmate may be called the fantasy lover. The fantasy lover
is usually someone whom the girl might have married but did not.
She brings him out and tells herself that life would have been entirely different had he been her choice for a life mate. If the honeymoon is dull he may be brought out at once, and in the process of
telling her husband everything she may make the imaginary playmate
too real and too vivid to herself and to him. Even if he is never discussed with her husband she may make her adjustment to the imaginary lover rather than to her husband and never thereafter adjust
to married life. Most marriages are made permanent or lost in the first
two or three months. Many are lost through the failure of the honeymoon to satisfy psychological and physical needs. Brides should recognize the presence of the imaginary lover as a fantasy. Husbands should
never be made aware of the device which their wives are using for an
escape from dullness and frustration.

The second attitude, a willingness to promise anything, should
also be watched. No promise of any kind should be made during the
engagement period or the honeymoon unless it can be kept completely
and without reservation. At this point many married couples lose

confidence in each other; for if promises are made and then not kept the marriage partner feels his mate to be untruthful and unreliable, two conditions on the basis of which no good marriage can be set up.

Complete possession is frustrating to both. All adults need a sense of freedom, but not too much freedom. They wish to be loved, cherished and needed, but also to feel that they can function in the normal life pattern without being pulled back by strings. This is somewhat more true of men than of women. The young man who told his wife that she might bow to any man she had known before her marriage but that she was not to stop to speak to him on the street or to let him buy her an ice-cream soda is a case in point.

The girl who continued to accept luncheon dates when her husband was busy and dinner dates when he was out of town was misusing any freedom which her husband had allowed her and should have been held to strict account for her behavior. Still worse was the girl who while still on her honeymoon insisted on having time to write to the men who had rushed her before marriage.

Finally the honeymoon may simply be dull. All marriages are characterized by periods which in a learning curve would be called plateaus; namely, periods which are somewhat dull and boring and in which the marriage seems to have come to a standstill. The first of these may occur during the honeymoon, which is much earlier than they tend to appear in an average marriage. A bride and groom who have some months of adjustment behind them do not find it difficult to pass through a plateau when it occurs. There is no such background of the habit patterns required in normal living to help the honeymooning bride and groom through a period of dullness and frustration.

If there is the least chance of a plateau occurring it is far better for the bride and groom not to take a trip but to move into their new home and spend their time together making it ready for pleasant living. Such work is never dull, and there is not time enough for a plateau to develop. Any disagreements which they might have about where articles shall be placed and who shall plan what arrangement of which room are forgotten in the first rush of affection and in the joy of being together.

It should be made clear that large issues are not the ones that often cause the most serious difficulty. It is the sudden quarrel about unimportant matters, followed by a series of such quarrels, which makes the marital adjustment poor. Every quarrel results in pain. Pain inhibits the setting up of habits which make being together enjoyable, just as it inhibits the setting up of all other habits. Every quarrel sets a brick in the wall between the people who engage in it. Every quarrel produces blocking and frustration. It also makes the person with whom one quarrels a stimulus to fighting rather than to the activity concerned with love-making. The age for quarreling is nine to eleven, not adulthood. It is to be hoped that such disagreements as exist will be met by other techniques, and the honeymoon is the time to establish these.

A busy, active, constructive honeymoon which results in joy in companionship and constructive work and thinking together sends the marriage more happily and more permanently on its way. The sooner the couple adjust to the circumstances that are to surround their first year or more of married life, the more stable the foundation for permanent adjustment.

Topics for further thought:

1. Participation in some kind of a ceremony in the presence of witnesses has customarily been expected of people getting married. Explain why this is regarded as important and desirable by society.

2. Comment upon the personal value of a honeymoon to the newly married couple.

Selected reading references

Arlitt, Ada H., *Family Relationships,* New York, McGraw-Hill, 1942.
A basic textbook on family relationships for college students.

Duvall, Evelyn, and Hill, Reuben, *When You Marry,* Boston, Heath, 1953.

Hollingshead, August B., "Marital Status and Wedding Behavior," *Marriage and Family Living,* November, 1952, pp. 308-11.
Courtship and wedding behavior are analyzed in terms of whether either the husband or wife or both have been married before.

Hsu, Francis, L. K., "Chinese and American Marriage Practices," from *Americans and Chinese,* New York, Henry Schuman, 1953, as reprinted in Sussman, Marvin B., *Sourcebook in Marriage and the Family,* Cambridge, Houghton Mifflin Company, 1955, pp. 8-12.
A comparison of certain aspects of Chinese and American marriage and family practices. Helps to place American practices in broader perspective.

14 ANATOMY AND PHYSIOLOGY OF THE SEX ORGANS

Robert L. Dickinson

MATING is an activity in which instruction can foster needed skills and forestall grievous blunders. This holds particularly true for the physical relationship. Failure in this area, due to physical or emotional difficulties or to lack of skill, is a leading cause of divorce. For every occupation save one, examination for physical fitness is the rule. That one is the most vital and worth while of all—marriage and parenthood—and for it, someday, routine preliminary examination will come to pass, through custom, into code.

The first step in insuring a satisfactory physical adjustment is to examine attitudes toward sexual response. Next comes a search for physical factors making for distress in intercourse or for frigidity. These disabilities are found in about one-sixth of the maladjustments, with some analyses reporting them in one-half or more of all complaints from unhappy wives and husbands. Yet such discords are largely or wholly preventable.

The physiology of sexual intercourse is simple. With affection and eagerness, a cylindrical passage, elastic and lubricated, receives an organ with taper point and tender cover in a quickening rhythm inciting to mutual ecstasy. Nothing would appear less complicated for two persons who have never been indoctrinated with shames or repulsions and who are free from fears of conception, infection, or detection. With the anatomical normalities that are usual, happy accord thus hangs on preamble and timing, on gentleness and consideration. And a certain amount of information about each other's anatomy.

Understanding of this anatomy is only possible through description accompanied by diagrams or pictures in which the names of the parts are in those medical terms—mostly euphonious—that often lack equivalents in everyday English.

THE FEMALE GENITALIA

Description. The flexible channel, the vulvovaginal canal, slants upward and backward to the womb, the uterus, the rounded mouth of which, the cervix, dips into it at right angles. From each upper corner of the flattened pear-shaped uterus (Fig. 2) the thin, expanding Fallopian tube runs out to the ovary, to bring down an egg each month for more than thirty years. The widened top of the vagina is the space where the male organ, the penis, deposits millions of sperms, in order that some may ascend through uterus and tube to reach the egg, the ovum. The female sex organs are divided into two groups: those external parts making up the vulva, and the internal parts comprising the vagina, the uterus that nests the ovum and grows the baby, and the tubes that loop around the hanging ovary—with the hymen standing between the two groups. In Figure 2 the front half of the uterus and of one tube and ovary are cut away to show interiors. The ovum can be seen about to leave its follicle and enter the trap of the outreaching fringes of the tube. Closure of the Fallopian tube at the inner end, or adhesion of the mobile fringes, produces about a third of sterilities.

The portal of entry, the vulva, is closed in a lengthwise cleft between two rounded, tapering cushions covered with fine hair, called the outer or larger lips or labia majora. Above where they broaden and join is the pubic area, at the base of the abdomen, with its crosswise hillock named the mons, covered with its hair shield of triangular shape. As these outer labia are drawn apart there appears an arched recess an inch in depth and two in length known as the vestibule. The vestibule is lined with smooth mucous membrane kept moist by a pair of glands called the vulvovaginal glands. The ducts of these glands open just outside the hymen and furnish abundant lubrication during sex excitement in order to facilitate entry. The vestibule supplies the funnel of access for the douche tube and the menstrual tampon, for the cervix cap in control of conception and the penis during sexual intercourse. On the inner aspects of the larger labia, on each side of the archway, the inner or lesser lips or labia converge above as hanging skin folds. They vary markedly at times in size, shape, surface, and projection. They meet over the top of the clitoris to form its cover, called, as in the male, the foreskin or prepuce. The clitoris, not unlike a miniature penis without its water passage, is the external center of erotic sensation. Its rounded end, the glans, is endowed with closely packed nerve ends. This tip is about the size of a pea, or a quarter inch across. It has no visible shaft and may enlarge and harden and darken in erection, but erection is relatively infrequent. Erectility, as a somewhat tense filling of veins, is found more often in the little sausage-shaped bulbs on each side of the vestibule and in the veins of the walls of the vagina, high up laterally, both shown in Figure 2. Under the prepuce the trifling white material is not secretion but shed surface cells.

On the real wall of the vestibule, under the overhang of the clitoris, is a tiny slit, the meatus, the opening of the urethra, exit channel from the bladder. The meatus has two tiny pockets, the second favorite resorts of the gonorrhea germ. Below this is seen the slight projection of the crescent of the hymen as puckered pink foldings of delicate mucous membrane, thinner and softer than the lower eyelid, and hiding the entrance to the vagina. In the virgin the hymen admits the owner's full forefinger or is an inch in diameter deployed. This is ample for douche tube or commercial tampon, provided the sensitiveness is lessened or lost by douching or gentle placement. The hymen is easily rendered elastic by careful repeated stretching, so that there is rarely reason for cutting or notching or for forcible dilation by the doctor preceding marriage.

The back rim of the vestibule fully drawn open is a thin cross fold of skin (unless there has been some damage in childbirth) with the name of fourchette. An inch farther to the rear, set back in the groove between the buttocks, lies the anus, the opening from the bowel, with its radiating folds.

In the drawing of the midsection of the body (Fig. 1) the bones are the solid sacrum that continues the spinal column down to its hinged little tip, the coccyx, and the narrow strip of the front part of the girdle of the bony pelvis, the symphysis, from which hangs the clitoris. Across this opening or outlet in the bones stretches a remarkable supporting structure called the pelvic floor. In the standing posture it holds up all the interior organs. Yet it has three gaps that must close themselves securely and automatically except for the times of the four escapes, namely, the voiding of urine and bowel contents, the slow trickle of blood and mucus during the menstrual days, and

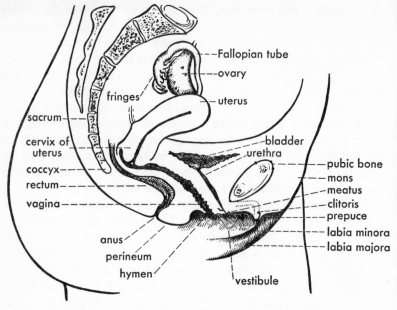

Figure 1. FEMALE ORGANS: MIDSECTION VIEW

finally the escape of the baby after a long softening and enlarging process.

This mechanism is concerned in voluntary and involuntary activities and particularly in the climax and the throb of sex relations. The main element of this structure is muscular, in edge-to-edge loops or slings in thin layers, called the levator group, together with the accompanying sheaths and connective tissues and some filling pads of fat. The whole resembles, in form and thickness, one's two hands held with interlacing fingers, palms upward, curved cupwise. The vaginal entry has a thin muscle loop of its own, but this is feeble compared with the twin circle, the anal double sphincter. It is the sweep of the levators, in a loop like four thin fingers, along the sides and rear of the lower vagina, and with front attachments, that keeps the vagina a flattened passage. The loop can resist entrance either by voluntary contraction or involuntary cramp. The upper and much wider half of the vaginal tube, its front and rear walls in contact (accounting for the expanded appearance in Fig. 2), is an elastic bag around the projecting lower tip of the uterus. The dotted upright side lines show the passage stretched as during intercourse. Moreover,

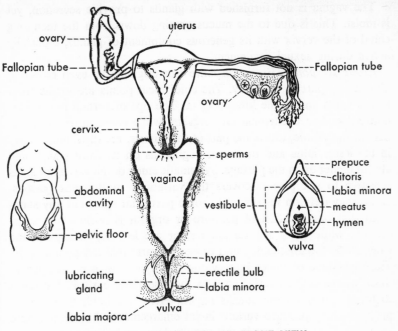

Figure 2. FEMALE ORGANS: FRONT VIEW

In the center diagram sperms are shown in the vagina near the cervix and also in the uterus. In the cross-sectioned ovary and Fallopian tube at the right an ovum is represented as about to leave the ovary. (For a discussion of ovulation and conception see Chapter 26.)

it is important to remember that the uterus is so suspended by India-rubber-like bands called ligaments that it (with the bladder) can readily move up and away or aside with each to-and-fro thrust of the penis. This synthetic resiliency of Nature is so well distributed for happy mating that the short six inches of the vulvovaginal receptacle readily accommodate the long six inches of the penetrant. The anterior vaginal wall is about two and one half inches long, the posterior three and one half, while from hymen to outside of the larger labia averages one and one half inches.

In a certain number of women orgasm is accompanied by rhythmic contraction and relaxation of these muscular bands looping around the lower vagina, and this has been labeled the acme of real orgasm. The most intense climax, however, may lack such activity. This limitation to one special form of reaction is an excellent example of the dogmatic definitions that often appear in sex literature.

The vagina is not furnished with glands to provide secretion, yet is moist. This is due to the mucus coming down from the inch-long canal of the cervix with its generous equipment of glands, especially active during sexual excitement.

Erotic Response. Erotic response can originate or even center in almost any part of the body. The chief focal points are in the front of the vulva and in the lower vagina. The tips of certain nerve ends that respond in excitement and orgasm, while concentrated in numbers in the visible, touchable part of the clitoris, are distributed freely in the lesser labia and the lower vagina, as on its front wall, while absent higher up in the passage. Systematic study of the variety of areas sensitive to sex play discovers the variations in different persons. Habit may develop restriction to some particular spot, but any statement that one location of pleasure or orgasm is normal and satisfactory, while other regions are not or are less so, belongs in the category of the unscientific and causes unwarranted disappointments. The avoidance of finger play within the hymen before marriage in those whose active ovaries awaken them sexually early in life tends to fix attention on the clitoris region. Here any habit of rhythmic pressures may produce various labial enlargements that demonstrate which nerve ends answer in this person. It is the husband's technique to discover such area and rhythm of self-relief in order to insure mutual timings. Long repeating of friction on the clitoris tends no more to enlarge this organ than the same practice enlarges the penis. Size has little relation to function in either. There are steady averages in genital anatomies, but there are also variants, all within satisfactory activity. However, the injuries of labor, not properly stitched, and some relaxed tissues may defeat felicity until repaired. A small vulva of the persistent juvenile type may require special massage before marriage. All these and the easily freed adhesions of the prepuce are remediable when diagnosed at the premarital physical examination.

Menstruation. Each month from the age of 13 to nearly 50 the uterus prepares its lining to nest an egg. When a fertilized ovum does not come down out of the tube the top layers of this thin mucous membrane are shed in minute fragments in an ooze of blood and mucus for 4 or 5 days, to the amount of 2 to 4 ounces or up to half a cupful, as an average. Although 28 days is the commonest type of repeat, the cycle may run between 23 and 36, but even with those who consider themselves regular a range of 8 days is found. The period of fertility may last 35 years or so; even with four children and absence of periods during full nursing, there may well be 400 menstruations. The beginning and ending of the function may show irregular intervals, and fertility is at times low at the start and usually so toward the change of life. Illness, anxiety, travel, and excessive tiredness may upset the timing.

Ovulation. At the start of the monthly cycle the tiny master gland at the base of the brain, the pituitary, sends chemical orders along the blood stream (the hormone estrogen) to the ovary. Hence, of the 25,000 potential ova ready, one outstrips the others, to ripen, by the midmonth, into a speck in the clear dewdrop on the surface of that olive-shaped organ. A spurt tosses it into the egg trap made by the seizing fringes of the tube (Fig. 2). This occurs about 14 days before the next period is due, ranging from the ninth to the sixteenth day of the cycle, counting from the first day of the period, but illness or strain may affect the orderly procedure, so that verily no day of the whole series is an impossible one for the egg to be fertilized. Thus, within the outer end of the tube a pin-point target is up for about one day, while a barrage of sperms may attack for some two days, with a single cell allowed to penetrate. Then the empty pocket whence came the ovum fills with blood and proceeds to manufacture a chemical (another hormone, progestin) which stirs the uterine lining to prepare itself to nest the egg. Developing on its travel inward, down the maze of tubal channels, the egg pauses to select its site within the week of the start and, if sound, has nearly nine chances out of ten of producing a living child. The defectives Nature rejects, and thus one-third to one-half of the interruptions of pregnancy are spontaneous endings. Intercourse for conception is therefore timed by studying some months of intervals to find when this fourteenth day occurs, and covers it by sperm deliveries on the tenth, twelfth, and fourteenth days. The idea that orgasm produces ovulation is only true of a few animals, nor does orgasm bear any proven relation to successful conception. Twins occur about once in eight births from the release of two ova, with fraternal twins often unlike, or from a single ovum with the twins identical.

The second function of the ovary is the giving out of the hormone that develops bodily sex characteristics and sex forms, and its activity persists after it no longer produces ova and after menstruation ceases. See pages 358-9.

THE MALE GENITALIA

The parts related to reproduction and sex play in man and those filtering water and waste products from the body conjoin and interlock (Figs. 3 and 4). From the bladder, the reservoir for urine, its

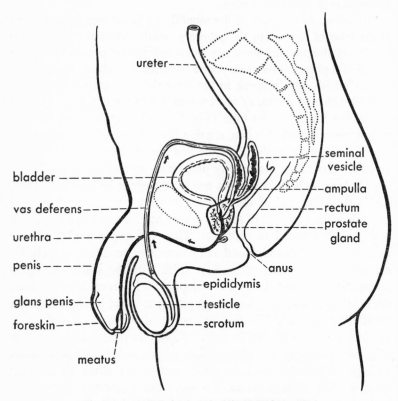

ureter

seminal vesicle

bladder

ampulla

vas deferens

rectum

urethra

prostate gland

penis

anus

glans penis

epididymis

testicle

foreskin

scrotum

meatus

Figure 3. MALE ORGANS: MIDSECTION VIEW

Arrows indicate route of sperms from the testicle through the vas deferens and the urethra.

outlet, called the urethra, is seen distended and terminating at the opening in the tip of the penis, the meatus, whence both urine and semen are delivered. Glands along this tubing lubricate it and secrete the clear mucus at its outlet in erotic excitement. In the diagram, the testicle on the right, hanging in the rear of the penis, is shown with its sac of flexible skin, the scrotum, while on the left the two-inch twin oval is opened up to suggest its compartments of micro-scopic tubings. This gland is the factory for the male cells, the sperms or spermatozoa, as well as for the male sex hormone or activator of maleness in body forms and sex urges. Its annex, the epididymis, is the finishing shop and also a part of the storage space for these cells.

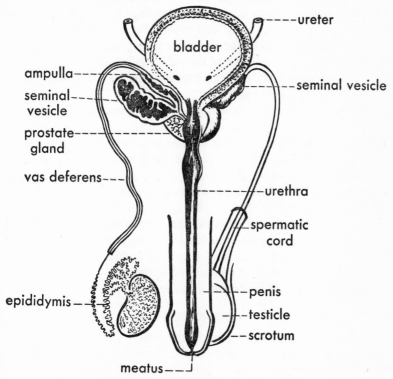

Figure 4. MALE ORGANS: FRONT VIEW

Up from each of the latter organs a pipe line rises through the spermatic cord with its many tortuous veins. This is the vas, with a pin-sized channel and strong muscular layers that shunt the minute product, hour by hour, upward through the groin into the body. Then the vas runs round behind the bladder to its base, to end in an elongated expansion, the ampulla, which forms the chief storage space for sperms. This reservoir, not yet commonly recognized as such, is one and a half inches long and has a fine nozzle leading into the upper urethra, the ejaculatory duct. Close to the ampulla, and the size of a flattened testicle, lies a laboratory, the seminal vesicle, for producing mucus which, with that of the prostate, forms the teaspoonful of fluid which sweeps the sperms along at ejaculation and initiates and activates their swimming vigor. Its outlet joins that of the ampulla as it penetrates the prostate, the solid gland like a big horse chesnut beneath the bladder and circling its outlet. Such crowding activity helps carry these rotating, whip-tailed tadpoles through the uterus to their destination, the rendezvous with the ovum in the outer end of the Fallopian tube (Fig. 2). The ampulla holds four to six rations, each of the earlier deliveries containing from two to six hundred million sperm cells—cells so diminutive that it takes two to span a thin hair.

The penis is here shown relaxed, with its somewhat conical top, the glans, protected by the foreskin, or prepuce, the thin, elastic cover which is wholly or partly absent in those who have been circumcised. The white substance found under the foreskin is made up of shed cells. When the penis is quiescent, its length, along the upper surface, averages some four inches in the white adult, with a range of variation, while its diameter is about one and a quarter inches. When it is erect, recent figures (curiously enough, the only considerable series of observations on this pivotal problem) give the average measurement on the upper border as six and a quarter inches, starting from its base, with the tissues there compressed against the bone. The largest grouping of diameters is one and a half inches.

INTERCOURSE

At the climax of the sex act in the male—that is, at orgasm—ejaculation drives out in spurts the three elements that make up the total half to one teaspoonful (less than most suppose)—first the sperms, then the prostatic secretion and that of the seminal vesicle, to mix together in what old English dubbed the seed and is now labeled semen. In ten to twenty minutes after deposit in the upper vagina the whirling crisscross of sperms begins to penetrate mucus on and within the cervix, the rate of drive seen under the microscope being an inch in eight minutes. Therefore, to study conditions favorable or unfavorable to conception, one step is to draw by a long dropping tube from within the channel some of the mucus for the doctor to view through the high-power lens.

The duration at the act of sex intercourse varies widely with individual desire and skill, but series of reports show averages running from two to five minutes intromission, with an average for orgasm of fifteen seconds, or a quarter minute—an oblivion too intense for any count until our statistical era—and with the same wide range in ability to repeat at long or short intervals.

No bodily function of human beings compares with sex intercourse for far-reaching effects from a single act, or for manifold implications based on total time of action. New life or no life hangs on seconds. The sum of the average activity of a twelvemonth—exclusive of foreplay—runs only to few hours—less than the dark of one day, and the span of climax adds up to half an hour a year.

For frequency of intercourse the average in certain series of studies among American white adults runs above twice a week. The range covers gaps of days and weeks and months at one end and coitus daily or oftener at the other—any of these with good health accompanying the practice. There is no standard or normal because of this wide difference in endowment and capacity among individuals, the variant habits and mores at different economic and social levels, the diversity of welcome between the partners, and decline at older ages. Erection in boys from babyhood and orgasm long before ejaculation culminate in adolescence in masturbation. Self-relief is nearly or quite universal in the male, and in some degree in the female. In both sexes homosexual play is the substitute or deviation most concealed but only infrequently leading to permanent addiction. The great disparity lies in the male's biological power and urgency and frequency as compared with that of the woman, with her education in reactions of shame and fear and the risks of pregnancy. The facing of actuality, sane sex education, and knowledge of techniques and protection can, in time, bring better balance and happy adjustment.

Posture during intercourse has its basis in the anatomy of the biped, together with the distribution of the special nerve endings. The method commonest in our culture is with the wife reclining and the husband above. (His weight is carried on elbows or hands.) This attitude may be reversed for her to regulate pressures, rhythms, or duration. Avoidance of abdominal pressure, as in pregnancy, may foster rear entry. Side-by-side positions favor prolongation. Across the lap permits casual affection. In any of these the closeness that yields clitoris seizure and excursion by the two pubic areas is a consideration, whenever this is the main focus of feeling. Variety and adaptation in techniques and adventure in environment belong to all loving contacts.

THE HYMEN

The doctor, in examining a prospective bride two weeks or more before the wedding bears in mind the shapes and measurements given in the preceding pages. He knows how husbands and wives adapt to each other. In the case of the patient who has previously borne children with proper care, the vulvovaginal entrance readily admits his two examining fingers in their thin rubber gloves, or even three. With the wife who has not had a child but has had regular satisfactory intercourse, two fingers enter full length without discomfort, owing to the recurrent stretch and massage of happy marriage. With the virgin he finds an opening about one inch in diameter that admits two joints of the lubricated gloved forefinger. Secondly, he finds a sharp edge. Lastly, tenderness. There are many variants, but this is the most usual record for anatomical virginity.

These three criteria call for clear understanding of modifications. More crises or curiosities have developed regarding the hymen than any other part of the body. This little crescent is susceptible of progressive elastic distensibility under certain circumstances without loss of continuity of edge and with quick resumption of its puckered form. The use of the douche and the narrow menstrual tampon remove tenderness and favor dilatability. A doctor's careful local treatments needed for the virgin with inflammation of the cervix (comparable to her sore throat in frequency and innocency) does stretch the circle somewhat. Petting to orgasm may develop the practice of finger entry within the hymen. With all such instances the digital examination or calibration with a cone gives the clue and tells the degree of further stretching required to forestall any pain or unnecessary damage on the wedding night. A familiar myth is the still-accredited tale of girls born without hymens or girls whose hymens have been ruptured in athletics or accidents. The writer recorded premarital dimensions for several decades but never found a case of a hymen broken by a picket fence or a bicycle.

For the tight hymen the doctor advises one of three treatments. The first is adapted to almost any girl or woman. Gradual finger stretch by the patient herself, begun in the hot bath or following a douche to render surfaces insensitive, is repeated with good lubrication and painlessly for one to two weeks or thereabouts, according to the results—attainment of her three-finger entry without surface break or notch or irritation. Dilators are sometimes suggested, such as graded test tubes or the rubber forms available. The penis as a dilator after marriage is a possible but somewhat clumsy device, with its thickness of one and one half inches to enter a one-inch thin membrane. Office dilation is often recommended, especially when the wedding is but a couple of days from the consultation. Although the local anesthetic renders this painless, raw surfaces result and the husband's active honeymoon attentions irritate them further. This is timing as poor as the old standard first-night rape for the sake of the red evidence. Actual cutting is needed only with the unusually thick hymen, the one that resembles the whole bridge between the thumb and fore-finger. Moreover, this is no real operation but merely scissor snips for notches, two or three, not more than an eighth or quarter of an inch deep. Deplorable words have been applied to these tiny injuries, even in the writings of counselors. The stock terms are rupture, break-ing, tearing, and hemorrhage. Dilation or dilatation should be the title and procedure, and absence of tenderness the test of its need. The partitioned hymen is a rarity, and the closed hymen, discovered when menstrual fluid is retained at puberty, still more so.

THE VAGINA

The vagina varies in form and depth, but its elastic character in the upper parts, combined with the free displaceability of the organs previously described, yields fewer problems among the married. One woman in five may have some degree of backward tip of the uterus and thus a shorter passage. In the absence of inflammation or swelling or other symptoms this retroversion or retroflexion need not be classed as a disorder to be treated or operated upon. Forward bend of the uterus may also shorten the passage, especially if it is part of defective local development or infantilism. Unless the walls are really basically short, regular intercourse does the stretching, the point of the penis by-passing the cervix into the upper pocket of the vagina. The S-shaped pessary that holds a backward displaced uterus in place is out of the way of the penis. As to the lower vaginal canal, the loop of muscles described may, through spasm that is involuntary or through fear or refusal or pain from inflammation, hamper entry. The athletic woman may have thick muscles hereabouts, but excite-ment relaxes these. And in some there is definite throbbing. The lack of nerve ends in the upper vagina keeps deep thrusting from being painful, except in the presence of swellings or infections. After the change of life some shrinking of the walls may be found in the wives neglected, and the lining tends to grow thin and pale in any case. Happily, glandular products may restore the hormone balance so well that the lining returns to previous receptive stages.

THE BONY PELVIS

The compartment holding or supporting all these organs is the circle of bone between the sockets of the hip joints, built to let humans stand upright. This rigidity pays one penalty. The baby must make a roundabout exit through a curved passage of irregular form, long behind, short in front, with entry or exit occasionally twisted. The doctor, at the premarital examination, can spot any definite deformity or narrowing of the interior of the bones. Late in pregnancy pictures by x-ray yield clear measurements which show just how much room there is for the child's head to pass, molded as it will be from ball shape to egg shape by the pressures of the contractions of the uterus.

THE ANATOMY OF STERILITY

One marriage in eight or ten is infertile, however steadily the couple may try for years. Early search for reasons and special skills in relief are rather recent. The average wait before consulting a doctor is two or three years, yet the average start of a pregnancy, in the absence of birth control, is three or four months. Even when under way, in about a tenth of pregnancies Nature may reject defectives or ill health of the mother may bring interruption—in conditions often curable. All barren marriages used to be blamed on the wife and in some cultures barrenness was ample reason for divorce. Indeed, consent of childless husbands to be examined dates back but a few decades, with the initial general American openmindedness. Because a man possessed full vigor in sex relations he was certain he was fertile. Now, however, examination begins with the husband because over a third of failures are traceable to him, while, with a given couple, among the usual two or more reasons for delay or impossibility of conception, some of the responsibility is likely to be his. Also, it is simpler to discover male than female factors.

Sperm meets egg. When both are sound and the way is clear and the timing is right, male cells travel through bristle-sized channels upward from the testicles and, when deposited at the mouth of the womb, travel outward from its cavern through tubes of somewhat similar caliber, in order that one cell may enter the ovum to start a new life. Closure of either of these canals accounts for a large part of sterility—indeed in woman for about a third of her share. Whether the obstruction be in epididymis or vas or in Fallopian tube, these blockades constitute the most difficult—or the incurable—set of conditions to attempt to conquer.

The sperm-forming tissues must turn out good product. Full-sized testicles may be disqualified by old infections, as from gonorrhea or other inflammations or from a complication of mumps. The commonest male fault is the finding of the following defects in the spermatozoa, either singly or in combination: the shapes may be defective or show immaturity or deformity; the activity may be sluggish or entirely absent; the numbers may be small or, with full quantity of ejaculate, there may be no sperms at all. Judgment concerning quality of sperms and sperm counts are new accomplishments, for of old any lively swing across the field under the microscope was supposed to guarantee fertility. Now numbers and forms are counted, swarming is studied hour after hour. Soon after intercourse, a drop of mucus is sucked out of the canal above the mouth of the womb by a long dropping tube and is studied with a microscope. In a few puzzling cases a speck can be nipped out of the testicle to make the final decision on good or bad machinery in that workshop.

The fault may be with the ovary. Monthly ripening of eggs may fail from poor health, lack of some one hormone as from thyroid incompetence, or a vitamin deficiency. Inflammation can imprison ova. The tubes are often offenders. Their flaring fringes may be glued together by inflammation or their branching inner gullies cemented. This follows some hard labors or fevered convalescences, or may be due to inexpert abortion operations or to gonorrhea or other inflammations, such as a neighboring appendicitis perhaps not acute enough for operation. A number of such closures yield to persuasive air pressure applied through the uterine cavity, but few operations for reopening or reimplanting closed tubes succeed.

To grow the egg the uterus must be of adult development. Its linings undergo striking changes every few days between the menstrual periods by chemical blood orders called hormones. The ovum, when fertilized, comes into the flat cavern and hunts about for a spot for attachment. For the sperms to have reached that ovum from the vagina the canal of the cervix must not be pinhole size at either end of that important inch. Nor may this canal be clogged by viscid mucus or unhealthy discharge, though such catarrh is not uncommonly encountered. Fibroid or ovarian tumors may call for removal.

Lack of erection sufficient to prevent entry into the vagina for the deposit of the sperms is rare. Still more so is the lack of descent of the testicles in fetal life into the scrotum. The opening of exit—the meatus—along under the base of the penis is a curiosity. Such also is a closed hymen, discovered by the distress of banked-up blood in a postponed start of menustration. The absence of uterus or ovaries is revealed by absent periods. When a vagina is missing it may be fabricated, and best by inward push and stretch of a pocket into the double-walled partition found between urethra and rectum. This is far simpler than dissecting a cavity in this partition with a lining that is borrowed from some near-by surface.

When the husband has no sperms at all or they persist in poor quality after careful treatment, adoption of a child is recommended. If this is refused, one means remains that is sought by thousands of couples these days. At the time of ovulation, into the mouth of the womb or at its mouth a slender tube places a little sperm from a donor selected with all care. His identity is never known to the couple or theirs to him. His health and heredity, his mind and race and religion, even his resemblance, are taken into account. This is called artificial insemination. With the expert and conscientious specialist success is reported in three out of four to four out of five fertile women, say within three months of three trials each, with some at once and a few over longer time. The birth is in charge of a different, uninformed doctor, who can therefore sign the birth certificate. Thus the baby belongs and time banishes memory of the method of its conception.

In this matter of sterility there is hope that in some not too distant future incurables will be discovered early. This will be when the custom of adequate examination prevails, and at a time preferably before the wedding day is chosen, and still better before the engagement is announced.

Topics for further thought:

1. Artificial insemination of human beings is a relatively new practice. What arguments can be used for and against it when one considers family stability and personal happiness?

2. Is it likely that personal happiness might be more assured if the unmarried are informed about the physical aspects of marriage before being allowed to get married? Explain your answer.

Selected reading references

Butterfield, Oliver, *Sexual Harmony in Marriage,* New York, Emerson Books, 1953.
    A simple, factual, and practical guide to the sexual aspects of marriage.

Ellis, Havelock, *Psychology of Sex,* New York, The New American Library, 1954.
    Chapters 1 and 2 of this classic treatment cover the biological aspects of sex and sexuality.

Exner, M. J., *The Sexual Side of Marriage,* New York, W. W. Norton and Company, 1932.
    A competent treatment by a capable physician.

Kelly, G. Lombard, *Sex Manual,* Augusta, Ga., Southern Medical Supply Company, 1950.
    Chapters 2 and 3 deal with the reproductive systems of male and female. Diagrams supplemented by simple, forceful explanation.

Van de Velde, Theodore, H., *Ideal Marriage,* New York, Random House, 1930.
    One of the most comprehensive works dealing with the sexual aspects of marriage. By a famous Dutch physician.

15 TECHNIQUE OF MARRIAGE RELATIONS

G. Lombard Kelly

Men and women both have been supplied with organs intended to make sexual intercourse mutually enjoyable. Especially sensitive microscopic nerve endings are present in the head of the penis and of the clitoris, and in the areas near these centers. Stimulation of these end organs under optimum conditions will result in that intense consummation of love, the climax of sexual feeling technically known as the orgasm. When this occurs there are rhythmic involuntary contractions in the muscles of the male causing ejaculation of semen from the urethra. The rhythmic throbbing contraction and relaxation that take place in some women have helped to give rise to the false belief that a woman also ejaculates during her orgasm.

There is a flow of mucus just at the vaginal orifice, but this occurs during sexual excitement preceding the act of coitus. The purpose is to lubricate the vulva in order to facilitate the entrance of the penis, or intromission. The amount of this flow varies considerably in different women. In a few it is so abundant that it wets the inner side of the thighs; in others it is so scant that some artificial lubricant must be used to make introduction easy, though none compares with the mucus for lack of greasiness or stickiness or stain. In addition to the mucus provided by the glands within the vulva close to the vaginal orifice a considerable amount is derived from the glands in the neck of the womb, pouring out freely during sexual excitement, thus lubricating the interior of the vagina, which itself rarely has mucus glands of its own.

Since the male organ is normally dry, easy introduction requires that the vulva provide adequate lubrication or that a lubricant be used. This may be applied by either partner. Artificial lubricants include vaseline, surgical lubricating jelly (which is preferable), and a number of jellies and creams advertised for "feminine hygiene"— which means contraception when injected into the vagina.

THE FIRST SEXUAL ACT

The ease of the first entrance will depend on absence of disproportion between the two partners. If the opening of the hymen is of average virgin size, unstretched as preamble to marriage, it cannot admit the penis. Days of gradual, gentle, painless stretching with fingers or smooth conical dilator by the bride-to-be (or the new husband) can be depended on in almost all instances to avoid the enlargement done by the doctor. Hymens that are elastic enough to permit entry without discomfort have been described previously (page 198).

The bridegroom should be the personification of tenderness. The bride should be courted and petted to the state of active passion, and any fears she might have should be allayed. The first embrace to be completed will depend on her being fit for response after recovery of the fatigue from the usual wedding and also on knowledge of each other's readiness. Her climax may come at once or soon, but many wives—particularly in the upper educational and social levels—are found to require weeks or months or longer to develop capacity for full and spontaneous orgasm.

Meanwhile the husband searches and finds out what counts with her. She wants darkness or dim illumination, where he likes light. She rouses to endearments in the beginning of the caresses but must have absolute silence to concentrate on climax. She has times and seasons of awakening, such as before and after the period. There are signs he learns or teaches her to tell. Patience pays large dividends.

A bridegroom who is selfish and cares only for his own satisfaction will certainly offend and disappoint a sensitive bride. If the woman is not quite apt and does not reach a climax easily she may remain in an unsatisfied state, with a resultant congestion of her generative organs and an unrelieved nervous tension. If this one-sided kind of marital act is persistent, the wife may tire of the disappointments and the nervous tension and turn against the act entirely. In short, the husband who does not take the necessary steps to make his relations with his wife mutually enjoyable and satisfactory may eventually ruin his marriage.

Fortunately it is no longer necessary in the large majority of cases for wives to remain frigid. Psychological and glandular treatment may be helpful provided that the husband does not suffer from premature ejaculation (which can often be successfully treated by application of a local anesthetic ointment).

SEAT OF FEMININE SENSATION

The fact that the orgasm in woman is felt chiefly in the clitoris does not mean that this organ is by any means the only part of her body capable of erotic feeling. The dilation of the vaginal orifice by the erect penis gives the average woman the most voluptuous sensation; the penetration of the erect organ to its full length into the vagina accentuates this pleasurable feeling. The breasts are erogenous zones to a great degree, and most women can be highly excited by proper attention to them before or during coitus. It is possible to fondle them in many positions of intercourse. In the face-to-face position, with the woman sitting on the man's lap, it is easy to fondle or kiss them alternately. Some women are excited by such foreplay as the deep and prolonged kiss or biting the neck or lobes of the ears or finger play in various areas of the skin surface, such as the inner thigh or the breasts, but the goal is always the same: stimulation of the genital area, preferably by the erect penis, toward the end point of sexual orgasm. Some authors lay chief stress on what they call the vaginal orgasm. They may go so far as to claim that any woman, no matter how passionate, who fails to attain a climax by the vaginal rhythmic thrusting, but requires massage of the clitoris to reach this release, does not compass real orgasm and is in some degree frigid.

Proponents of the vaginal orgasm, who claim that the clitoris is predominant in children and adolescents but that the vagina takes over completely in grown women, are adherents of the Freudian school. Their claim that every woman who does not have a vaginal orgasm and perceptible contractions of the sphincter muscle at the orifice during orgasm is frigid simply does not conform to the vast array of statistics to the contrary. Possibly 10 or 15 per cent of women require the sensation of the erect penis in the vagina during orgasm.

The notion that fluid secretion from one or another set of glands produces orgasm by squirting through ducts has been handed down from generation to generation. Actually orgasm occurs without ejaculation in boys who produce full and repeated orgasm by masturbation well before puberty.

POSITIONS IN SEXUAL INTERCOURSE

The important variations of posture in this ultimate intimacy between husband and wife, together with the advantages of each, are as follows:

. *Man-Above Position.* At the first approach the woman assumes a recumbent attitude and the man stretches out above her. This combination has been called the instinctive, the habitual, and the normal, because it has been the standard for Western cultures and theological prescription as well. Under the most favorable circumstances the woman lies flat on her back, spreads her thighs until there is room between her knees for those of the man, flexes her legs slightly on her thighs, and assumes as relaxed an attitude as her mental state will permit. In this position complete intromission, with proper contact of the penis with the clitoris, is possible.

In this position the man will ordinarily lie between the woman's thighs, but he can place one or both of his outside of hers. This is a satisfactory variation in prolonged intercourse. If the woman holds her thighs close together after entrance it is claimed that a small penis is kept erect by pressure of the feminine parts; also that a long penis will not enter too deeply and cause pain.

Woman-Above Position. This position may be accomplished by rolling over from the one just described, but this requires considerable care to prevent withdrawal of the penis. Experienced couples accomplish it by having the man lie flat on his back while the woman kneels over him and settles backward upon his middle. She then straightens out her legs and lies full length, with her thighs between or outside those of her partner. At first the man will have to guide the penis into the vagina, but later the woman will be able to feel the end of the penis with her vulva and envelop it as she settles backward and downward.

This position has at least two distinct advantages. It enables the woman to adjust herself to the penis in such a way that full contact with the clitoris and other most responsive areas is obtained and kept. In addition the woman has complete freedom of movement and can seek her own satisfaction in an abandon of motion that would be impossible with the weight of the man's body pressing on hers. This position is usually advised when the woman is considerably shorter or lighter than the man, but it is an excellent variation for couples with builds that are not disproportionate.

While in the woman-above position the woman can rise to a sitting posture by bringing her thighs up alongside the man's body, at the same time he can flex his thighs and support the woman's back. The clitoris gains excellent contact with the penis itself and its base in this way, but there is a tendency for the penis to penetrate too deeply and cause some discomfort. This is sometimes called the astride position. Its principal value is as an adjuvant to sex play.

The partner above, man or woman, should seldom lie dead-weight on the other, but should support the weight of the body by resting on the elbows. Only the weight of the hips should be imposed on the one beneath. The connubial bliss of many a small or medium-sized woman has been marred by the thoughtlessness of a heavy partner lying dead-weight upon her. In the woman-above position the same unpleasant experience could befall a small or medium-sized man with a partner considerably heavier.

Lateral or Side Position. The act of coitus may begin in this position, in which the man and woman lie on their sides facing each other. The woman places her upper thigh over the upper thigh of her partner in order to give him freedom of entry. This position may be attained by turning on the sides from either the man-above or woman-above postures. It is recommended by some during advanced pregnancy and also when the couple like to fall asleep after completion of the act with the organs still in contact.

Rear-Entry Position. The man and the woman may both lie on their right or left sides, with the woman's back against the front of the man's body. The man will have to lie well behind the woman's buttocks for good intromission, but for him this position is quite satisfactory. For the woman this posture is deficient in that the penis, entering from the rear, is "upside down" in the vagina and does not touch the clitoris. The man can easily reach the clitoris with his fingers and by stroking it during the progress of coitus can bring about simultaneous orgasm. This position is recommended during pregnancy and in any condition in which it would not be wise for the man to place his weight upon his companion's abdomen.

In the other rear-entry position the woman assumes the kneeling posture or even the knee-chest position. The man kneels behind her and after intromission is able to caress his partner's breasts or her clitoris. The penis does not come into contact with the clitoris in this posture, and unless the woman can reach the climax from strong passion it will likely be necessary to fondle the clitoris to bring her to the orgasm. This position has been advised during pregnancy, but it is easier for both when lying on their sides as described in the preceding paragraph.

Sedentary Positions. With the man using an armless chair the woman sits across his lap, intromission taking place as she settles down on him. The woman can get perfect contact of the clitoris with the penis and the cushion above it in this position, especially if she arches her back a little and leans forward on her partner and produces the desired sweep to and fro. The man does not have so much freedom of movement by this method but he has all that is necessary. When a chair is used, the height must be suitable for the woman, so that she can support her weight on her feet and take the active part when she desires. This posture is quite comfortable for both participants and it is thoroughly effective. When desired the man can massage the clitoris satisfactorily.

Standing Position. When there is not too great a disproportion between the heights of the man and the woman it is quite possible to bring about entrance with the partners facing each other while standing. It is necessary, of course, for the man to have a good erection and for the woman to place her feet apart and open her thighs.

The positions described are fundamental ones. Some authors describe many postures, with some claim for true variation. I once purchased a small, highly touted book which describes scores of positions, differing as slightly as bending the knee of one leg. This, of course, approaches the absurd. Conceivably male and female gymnasts might effect sexual union in a wide variety of postures, even while standing on their heads. There is a distinct difference between body positions during coitus (that is, the actual relation of one body to the other) and where the two bodies may be (as being in bed, across bed or table, sitting on a chair or standing up). Since a person has only one front and one back and can only lie, sit, stand, or kneel, the fundamental possibilities in this regard are definitely limited.

The clitoris is located an inch to an inch and a half from and above the vaginal orifice. It hangs on the front of the pubic bone, suspended by a ligament or band which allows an excursion, as it is swept by pressure or stroked, to the extent of an inch or two or three, in that type of action upon it which procures the climax. And its neighboring parts have much the same reaction, as shown by the enlargements of the labia in those women who are given to a habit of friction for self-relief. During intercourse, with the man in a somewhat high position compared with that assumed when fully within, the upper surface of the penis can glide back and forth against the clitoris and the labial folds, in normal rhythms, to secure the explosion of feeling. With complete burying of the penis within the vulvovaginal canal that cushion of flesh at the base of the penis that is covered with hair, called the mons, with his pubic bone underneath it, makes the to-and-fro pressures, the clitoris being effectively caught between the two structures for the caress. The circular muscle at the vaginal entrance can be contracted voluntarily by some women, and husbands may ask them to do it for its voluptuous effect.

With the majority of couples each partner can learn to detect the signs of approaching climax in the other and with the exercise of control attain the state of orgasm together. If the woman is unduly slow the man can caress her clitoris gently with the rhythm of intercourse until she arrives with him. It is easy to insert the middle finger into the upper crevice of the vulva, even when the penis is deeply in place. It is true that some women cannot reach orgasm in normal intercourse, no matter how long or how vigorously continued, but many such women can reach a climax once or more by patient massage of the clitoris. As time passes, quicker response occurs until no finger play is needed, in many instances. Unfortunately, there are still other women who cannot reach a climax under any circumstances, while some women are satisfied with excitement alone.

To reach a climax, intercourse is not always necessary. There are imaginative women who can attain orgasm by mental stimulation, either by thoughts of attractive men or by being in their presence. These are, of course, exceptional.

FREQUENCY OF SEXUAL INTERCOURSE

How often may sexual intercourse be practiced with satisfaction and without immediate and eventual harm to one or both individuals? The consensus seems to center on twice a week for normally healthy persons, although many factors may alter this general average upward or downward.

Some of the most important items bearing upon frequency of intercourse are health, degree of mutual happiness obtained in the act, temperament, and age. Naturally, illness or poor health will militate against sex desire and also against the ability to indulge in it. It is assumed that men as a rule reach a satisfying climax, but this is by no means true of women. A woman who is not satisfied may be willing to repeat the act after a shorter interval than if her needs had been amply taken care of. If consistently disappointed, however, she may eventually turn against intercourse and refuse any longer to be left hanging in the air.

Many women are thwarted in their ardent desires to achieve sexual satisfaction because of premature ejaculation of the husband. Women as a rule are slower than men in preparation for the climax of sexual excitement, requiring often ten, fifteen, or more minutes to reach the orgasm. In his book, *Sexual Behavior in the Human Male*, Kinsey states, "For perhaps three quarters of all males, orgasm is reached within two minutes after the initiation of the sexual relation, and for a not inconsiderable number of males the climax may be reached within less than a minute or even within ten or twenty seconds after coital entrance." The writer regards this estimate as too high, but his researches on premature ejaculation and its treatment with an anesthetic ointment applied to the head of the penis, carried on now for eight years, attest to the great frequency of the failing as well as to the large number of broken marriages that result when it is not corrected by proper treatment.

Since age is accompanied by degenerative changes it can be expected that a gradual slowing up of sexual expression will take place. This does not mean that many men fail to remain virile to advanced age, but frequency of intercourse will lessen appreciably in nearly every case. In many women after the childbearing years there is an accentuation of desire to such an extent that they may crave sexual union more often than their husbands. One of the principal reasons for this, as a rule, is cessation of the fear of becoming pregnant.

Minor factors influencing frequency of intercourse are mode of life, climate, diet, mental or nervous strain, and worry, as well as general attitude toward sexual matters. Some of these factors may at times cease to be minor and greatly affect sexual desire or performance. Exhaustion from overwork or from much worrying is a strong inhibitory factor. Inhibition in sex matters as a result of repressive upbringing may affect sensitive women to the point of sexual frigidity.

Sexual intercourse is not too frequent if it does not produce any undesirable aftereffects in either partner. Some individuals are far more passionate than others, and husband and wife may vary widely in this respect. In such cases a mutual agreement based on love and common sense is essential. It is possible for either partner to arouse desire in the other by fondling the appropriate organs. In each act, however, the complete satisfaction of both must be striven for and attained if at all possible.

Sexual excesses may not cause immediate damage, but the eventual result may prove disastrous to a happy union. The act may become commonplace, and interest may be lost. Excess on the part of one partner may turn the other's affection away and ruin a marriage that restraint could have preserved.

Recent researches covering thousands of marriages show a variation of frequency from the so-called sexual athletes who have intercourse regularly once or more a day to others who have sexual union once or twice a year. Couples between twenty and forty years of age were found to have sexual relations about twelve times a month, or about every second or third day. The extremes in this group were from once a day to once a week.

Frequency of intercourse is considerably greater in newly married couples than in those married for a period of years. It can be safely assumed that normal persons can determine without difficulty how often they desire complete intimacy with each other. They are not likely to go wrong if each act is an expression of love to the point of mutual orgasm and entire satisfaction. The quality of the embrace is more important than the intervals between repetitions of it. And sex play short of orgasm has its place, where both enjoy it.

MASCULINE SEX HYGIENE

A man may well wash his penis every day with soap and warm water, dry it with a cloth or absorbent paper, and even powder with a good grade of scented talcum. In the uncircumcised this will prevent the accumulation of white, bready material that tends to form beneath the foreskin after a few days. This secretion, known as smegma, has an objectionable odor. The warm, moist incubator underneath a long foreskin may foster development of germs of venereal disease. The occasional person who has a long foreskin with a small opening that hinders or prevents complete retraction (skinning) may develop accumulation of smegma calling for circumcision.

Young boys occasionally suffer from an annoying inflammatory condition around the head of the penis and just back of it. This is readily amenable to treatment with soap and water, followed by drying and application of talcum powder. Ointments, such as vaseline, can be used, but the dry powder treatment is quicker and better.

FEMININE SEX HYGIENE

The woman who requires it should have either a fountain syringe with a vaginal nozzle (long, slightly curved) or a large vaginal bulb syringe. In some women a douche is advisable after each menstrual period. The natural secretions from the cervix present in the vagina and the whitish cells of the shed lining have a characteristic odor. In some women odor is not perceptible, while in others it is objectionable. A certain amount of caressing or fondling of the female genitals is part and parcel of normal sex play, and while mucus of excitement is odorless as a rule, in other cases it does have odor.

The douche material may be warm water. Many proprietary products are widely advertised for use in maintaining feminine hygiene, but under this label most are intended for contraception, however ineffective. Such products are too expensive for use as cleansing agents, and for this purpose they are not better than good soap and water or vinegar, two tablespoons to the quart, as this latter matches the normal slight acidity of the vagina.

Many women, if indeed not all of them, show more or less of this whitish secretion derived from the slight steady shedding of the surface layers of the passage, just as the skin is constantly invisibly peeling its surface cells. If this is considerable it may appear at the vulva or after intercourse. If a man withdraws temporarily, as in play of one kind or another, and sees a little leukorrhea, it might seem to him a discharge. Cleansing the external parts, the vulva, with soap and water should be done daily.

There are few expressions of gratitude that come to medical advisers or other marriage counselors that are more keen and enduring than those which are the outcome of perfected—or corrected—adjustment of the interlocking spiritual, mental, and physical act of love between husband and wife.

Topics for further thought:

1. Research has indicated that techniques involved in foreplay and in sexual intercourse vary by socioeconomic and educational levels. What implications does this situation have for young husbands and wives in their initial sex contacts in marriage? What implications does it have for definitions of what is "right" and "wrong" in the sex relations of married couples?

2. The notion of a fairly common tendency toward frigidity in women is prevalent in the U.S. Yet ability to derive satisfaction from intercourse often increases with length of time married and sometimes makes a definite upsurge after the menopause. What does this suggest about the relative influence of biological and social factors in producing sexual inadequacy? Discuss.

Selected reading references

Butterfield, Oliver, *Sexual Harmony in Marriage,* New York, Emerson Books, 1953.
 A simple, factual, and practical guide to the sexual aspects of marriage.

Groves, Ernest R., Groves, Gladys H., and Groves, Catherine, *Sex Fulfillment in Marriage,* New York, Emerson Books, 1943.
 The title of the book accurately reflects its content. By three members of one of the pioneering families in family life education.

Hamilton, Gilbert V., *A Research in Marriage,* New York, Boni, 1929.
 One of the first research efforts to deal with sex problems in this country. By a practising psychiatrist. Sexual histories from a select group of probably neurotic patients.

Kelly, G. Lombard, *Sex Manual,* Augusta, Ga., Southern Medical Supply Company, 1950.
 Chapters 14-16 present a detailed and candid account of the techniques of marital relations.

Van de Velde, Theodore H., *Ideal Marriage,* New York, Random House, 1930.
 One of the most comprehensive works dealing with the sexual aspects of marriage. By a famous Dutch physician.

16 SEXUAL ADJUSTMENT IN MARRIAGE

O. Spurgeon English

Nearly everyone agrees that people need to know much more about sexual adjustment in marriage. Such difficulty is by no means the only cause of divorce and separation. Yet the increasing separation and divorce rates, as well as the increased amount of extra-marital sexual indulgence, are an indication that many married couples are not finding sexual compatibility and happiness. Some authorities blame the woman and her lack of interest in sex and her failure to have any response in feeling to the sexual advances of the male. Others say the man is chiefly responsible because of his inadequacy as a lover. Conservative estimates report that less than half of all marriages show sexual compatibility. Less conservative ones indicate that not one marriage in ten has a satisfactory sexual relationship.

FAULTY ATTITUDES TOWARD SEX

Today's woman, by reason both of biological endowment and social training, seems less disposed to physical response. But the father of the daughter today is conditioning somebody's wife of tomorrow. The American man is rare who is not doing his best to discourage the development of any sexual interest his daughter might have toward men of her age and class. Not only can the man be indicted as an inadequate lover with his new wife, but he is also working to perpetuate what he complains most bitterly about—that is, the sexual frigidity of the American woman.

The woman complains that her husband never shows any interest in her or any tenderness toward her unless he desires sexual relations.

He is unappreciative of her daily activities. When he does desire sexual relations he does not take time enough to excite her through caresses, kisses, and endearments. When intercourse begins he is not enough interested in the position assumed, the timing and technique of bringing his wife to orgasm, or in his verbal appreciation of her as a love partner to make her happy.

The man in turn complains that his wife is never interested in sex relations, or cannot be made interested often enough, or is not appreciative enough of his advances. Or in sex relations she is physically inactive, emotionally unresponsive, takes too long to come to orgasm, or has no orgasm at all. She may even be critical of him as low, bestial, brutal, lustful, unaesthetic, ungentlemanly, or lacking the proper appreciation of her in wanting to have intercourse with her.

Millions of married couples want to love and appreciate each other, and they are able to do so in every other way, but they disapprove of each other in sexual relationships which potentially hold the greatest joy for each of them.

Why is the sexual situation so faulty at present? The difficulty seems to begin in childhood when the mind is being formed. Adults have so much fear of the sexual impulse—far more fear than is warranted. There are two basic urges in mankind—sensual gratification and aggression. The former is no more dangerous to society than the latter; in fact, less so. Yet aggressive impulses are not feared as the sexual impulses are. Fighting is discouraged among children, but it is not taboo. In fact, sports and games are encouraged and even open fistic encounters among boys are regarded as desirable to the child's development. Even murder, while condemned, can be discussed with children and they are allowed to see it in the motion pictures and the comics and hear about it on the radio, but that same child must not hear of sex. Is sex more powerful or more malicious to man's welfare than aggression? No. Yet sexual activity—the only means of complete physical expression of love—is tabooed and punished from the earliest days onward. It is assumed one has the power to control aggression but that he cannot control his sexual desires.

Now the fact is that humans have not controlled their aggressive impulses. But they are at least wise enough to admit they have them. Various agencies are working at modifying the aggressions—racial, religious, industrial, and political. This is progress, and people must be equally progressive in the realm of sexuality. A person must admit he has sexual impulses and needs, that they have a purpose, that they can be misused, but that they can also be controlled and used constructively. In fact, people have not begun to tap the reservoir of value that lies in more wholesome and satisfying body relationships. This is true not only between man and wife but also between mother and child and even father and child. People have been made afraid and ashamed to be close to one another and enjoy one another. Until this great handicap in our thinking is overcome it is doubtful that aggressive and destructive forces can ever be brought under satisfactory control.

THE INFANT AND ITS MOTHER

The infant likes to be close to the mother—to enjoy the warmth and touch of her body and to nurse from her breast. This is all-satisfying and gives him a sense of well-being. It is the forerunner of happiness, tolerance, magnanimity, gentleness, and generosity. Even when the child has given up the breast for other foods he will want to snuggle up to the mother in a gradually diminishing amount for several years. In fact, this desire hits a minimum only around the age of ten, to break forth afresh at puberty, but now directed, instead of toward the parent, toward a member of the opposite sex of his own age. This is the rhythm of life; this is psychosexual development. It needs guidance and fostering rather than the taboo, criticism, and silence which has prevailed for so long. As the child leaves the nursing period and goes through toilet training he need not be made ashamed of these functions in order to have the training completed. Co-operation in these as well as other social obligations can be achieved without invoking shame, anxiety, and criticism. This is most important because love is made with the organs associated with excretion. Put morbid emotional attitudes around the excretory organs and you have involved the organs of love. True love is expressed with the eyes, the lips, the hands, and with a clothed embrace, but in marriage the ultimate expression of love must be with the unclothed body and a union of the genital organs. If the latter are regarded as shameful, disgusting, or otherwise unaesthetic, the sexual union can never be an act of happiness or beauty for that person. The man who said, "I cannot think of anything more horrible and revolting than a man on top of a woman in sexual intercourse," expresses a lurking feeling common to most humans, even in the minds of some of those who feel themselves most sophisticated about sexual relations. It is inconsistent twaddle for adults to talk about the beauty and sanctity of the marriage relationship (mean-

ing the sexual relation in marriage) if they have not given the child
some glimpse of this possibility during his formative years.

During or soon after his toilet-training period the child is going to
meet two critical episodes of his sexual development. These are when
he begins to ask questions pertaining to the human sexual relation and
when he discovers that he can obtain pleasure from touching his
own body, particularly the genital region. It is a wise and well-adjusted
parent who can answer his child's questions calmly, sensibly, factually,
and stick to what the child wants to know. It is inherent in adults to
feel that knowing will do the child harm or that "his mind is too weak
to integrate such strong stuff," or "with his lack of judgment he will
surely misuse it." The answer to these attitudes is that knowing will
not do him harm, sex is not a bad or dangerous thing to absorb (it
is only the adults who have come to think so), and any lack of
judgment he has about using sex knowledge should be neutralized
by some positive useful philosophy about when and how sexual expression is acceptable and desirable. As for touching himself for
pleasure, this offers no serious threat to health, morals, or aesthetic
standards. It is a natural phenomenon, necessary to awaken the genital
area to a capacity for sensation and pleasure, and it never produces
any problem in the child who is on good terms with his parents and
has playmates and wholesome interests for his age. Around the age
of three the child of either sex is likely to pass through a stage of
frequently touching the genitals. Nothing need be done about this except to keep the child occupied and happy and it will pass. Occasional
manipulation of the genitals for pleasure may and probably will occur
up to marriage, carried on in privacy. The chief concern of the parent
should be that the child have no guilt or fear over the activity and
that he or she be so interested in his work, play, and social activity
that he does not fall back upon his own body too frequently as a
source of satisfaction. The good life is a useful, creative, and loving
life, and overpreoccupation with unnecessary burdens of guilt defeats
the avowed purposes of religious wholeness.

SEXUALITY IN THE CHILD

The acceptance and tolerance of manifestations of sexuality in the
young child is most important. Let no one erroneously assume that
sexual activity does not begin this early in the human being. At this
time the basic attitudes toward sexual feeling and functioning are established. If children are made to feel fear or shame or even if their

interest has never been allowed to gravitate toward sex, then we allow to develop one of the most difficult conditions a physician has to treat or any husband or wife to change or any counselor to modify. Moreover, once the parent has failed to play his role adequately in this early period of attitude building—if he has been too severe or has ignored the subject—the child is likely never to turn back to the parent and take a trusting attitude toward him on this subject. He falls prey to the misinformation and to the gutter information and values of the "crowd" who perpetuate the very thing which needs changing. The morbidly curious or even the uninformed child between the ages of five and fourteen who has not been given the wholesome truth about sex from his parents is likely to gather much of the worst and little, if any, of the best about the subject during these years.

SEX ADJUSTMENT AT PUBERTY

At puberty a new situation prevails. The sexual glands become active, sending their hormonal secretions throughout the body and adding a greater impetus to the general desire for body contact and release of sexual energy through the orgasm. In addition to this activity there is a social factor at work also. Adults push the young people of both sexes together in order that they may gain poise and find mates, while motion pictures, television, and magazines heighten imagination and fantasy surrounding sex.

In general the adult attitude toward sex at this age of the child is no wiser than before. Parents and children are generally farther apart at this age than ever and more self-conscious with each other about the subject of sex. Many parents delay discussions of sex until the teens, when the child supposedly needs it. By this time both parties are so embarrassed that neither can carry on a satisfactory conversation on the subject. So the talk is indefinitely postponed or tried unsuccessfully and ends in a sense of futility for both. Without parental guidance the child has to struggle with his sex desires himself. He may be in conflict about masturbation; in any case, he has to undergo more of what is called repression—pushing the dangerous subject out of consciousness by various means. Some of these phenomena of repression are quite healthy and valuable. The young person unable to gratify his love needs directly may become an exceptionally good student, athlete, musician, actor or actress, or inventor. But others less well motivated can become overpreoccupied with religion, using it not as a means of a fuller, more meaningful life but as an escape from the realities of life. Or they may take flight from life through day-dreaming in which they achieve exceptional merit and imagine so much love and prestige that they do not have to resort to home and family life for emotional satisfaction. In fact, they often look upon the home with its day-to-day physical problems in which body needs are so much concerned (eating, sleeping, bathing, elimination, sex, illness) as unaesthetic, uninteresting, and unworthy of the interest and enthusiasm of a remarkable person like themselves. Or, never having been taught that they must play a part in these activities with pleasure, they retain a childish attitude which, put into words, would be something like this: "Well, those things are for Mother or Father to do or for the servants to do but not for me; I should be allowed to be a privileged character and remain aloof from these crass realities. I shall enjoy only the clean, well-ordered, already arranged, neat, gay, glamorous things of life, but nothing which has to do with the body, dirt, or that which requires persistent effort or painful thinking."

The majority of parents have two or more of the following attitudes which interfere with the developing of their children into emotionally mature young adults. They fear that their adolescent child will have sexual experience and become morbidly unhappy over it; that he or she will have it and be a party to an unwanted pregnancy; that he will be a participant in the sexual relation and be found out and suffer some degree of social condemnation; that he will have the experience and contract a venereal disease; or that he will have some pleasurable experience the parent himself has missed. Now most of these are definite matters of concern and should be faced and discussed as such rather than remain unverbalized barriers which spoil the friendship and value of closeness in the important years of adolescence. Millions of parents and their adolescent children are on bad terms all during this important period just because the parent is frightened and suspicious and does not understand why he is distrustful, suspicious of, and restrictive toward the child.

It would seem to be a mistake to try to train children to go through adolescence without conflict about sex or without sexual desire. To attempt this leads to a suppression of the sexual impulses; fantasy results, as do exaggerated discussions and in some cases excessive petting. In order to have enough sexual desire to be reasonably normal during the adult years it is inevitable that the adolescent have sexual desire. Moreover, having it is not necessarily painful or unpleasant or dangerous. It is healthy and human. It should be accepted and parents must assume the responsibility of making such good friends of the children that they will control it reasonably well if they are shown why they should. It is a sad commentary on many intelligent parents that they never seem to think of using a positive education in connection with sex by telling the child the facts and then asking him to adapt himself to conventional standards and live up to a certain ideal of behavior in the setting of a full social existence. The formula would look like this: Facts of sexuality, plus personal social ideals, plus a well-balanced work and recreational program equal morally good, happy, and responsible citizens. In contrast to this: No facts of sexuality, plus no personal or social ideal, plus a restricted and empty work and recreational life (out of the parent's fear of the child's coming into contact with temptation) equal unhappiness, inefficiency, poor marital adjustment, neurosis, and personality defects contributing to alcoholism, delinquency, psychosis, and suicide.

Few people today realize the long history of the development of the sexual emotions. They are present at birth and have to be integrated into the rest of the personality during the whole period of growth from infancy to the day of marriage—and even thereafter. Anyone who assumes that the sexual emotions can be ignored for a lifetime and that they will start functioning satisfactorily on the day the marriage ceremony is read is truly mistaken. This historical perspective of individual sexual development, as it struggles to unfold in an unsympathetic world, when applied to any married person will give some indication of whether he can make love pleasurably with his body or not. The love emotions (including the physical expression of them) must be in some continuous interaction with other people who are receptive. Through late childhood and adolescence some, though not all, of the physical must be withheld until marriage. This takes continuous wise and kind counseling—not rejection. But it is also true that there are few people after marriage who do not need counsel. In the best marriages, where sexual adjustment is harmonious, the partners accept the fact that they need to help each other to derive the most pleasure from their contacts together. They need to guide and advise each other upon how the satisfaction of each can be obtained.

SEXUAL ADJUSTMENT IN THE NEWLY MARRIED

Each newly married couple should realize that a good sexual adjustment is necessary to a happy life. It is more than a luxury to be accepted if present but ignored if absent. For each married couple there are years of hard work, responsibility, and at times a variable amount of hardship and suffering ahead. To neutralize the adverse effect of life's conflicts and struggles upon the mind a man and woman should do everything they can to find what happiness they can enjoy with each other. They need close communion and sympathy, which are much easier to achieve if they can give each other the ecstatic happiness of frequent sexual relations. Pleasure begets gratitude, and the thoughtfulness which makes one capable of giving pleasure begets respect and love. Such a state of mind existing between man and wife is worth working for, but it *does* have to be worked for. There is probably no young couple so well adjusted sexually that they will not have to keep working to retain that adjustment. They must feel free to talk about their sexual desires and feel free to say when and how each derives the greatest pleasure. Here is where one partner must avoid the dangerous attitude of seeming to have, from some obscure source, an innate knowledge of what is proper, aesthetic, or good. For instance, one of the partners may want to have intercourse in the daytime or early in the evening, but the other feels that sex relations take place only late at night in bed, the last thing before going to sleep. Actually they can take place any time, any place, if mutual happiness is the goal. One of the partners may want a position other than the usual one of the man lying on top of the woman, between her thighs. Naturally that position is acceptable which makes the partners happy. The woman may like the man to caress her a great deal so that she may become aroused before the act begins, yet the man is impatient of caresses, perhaps regards caressing the woman's breast as childish. He should realize that when he fails to please her he runs the risk that in some way sooner or later she will fail to please him. Less common than the kissing of the breast is the desire to kiss other parts of the body before the act begins. The wife may desire this when it does not appeal to the man. In either case the thing for each to remember is that no laws prescribe what is good or bad for those who, loving each other, want to bring happiness to each other. They should avoid getting blocked by a feeling of "It isn't done," "Nice people don't do it," or even the more smug statement, "I may not be able to say who condemns it, but I have an instinct for decency and I know it isn't right." Such convictions in matters of sexual activity preclude mutual adjustment and are unfortunate.

If a young married couple have a good sexual adjustment to begin with they must take care not to disturb it through selfishness in behavior. For instance, the husband should continue to be tender and affectionate during his wife's menstruation. He should be thoughtful and willing to endure abstinence graciously during illness, the last month of pregnancy, and the first few weeks after the birth of a child. The wife should be considerate in her demands if the husband is overtired from work, but in her defense it be must pointed out that the husband should not continuously be too tired. If such is the case, he is either in the wrong job or working too hard. Or it may be that he is organically ill or is suffering from a neurosis in which chronic fatigue is one of the symptoms.

Neither partner should be averse to giving the other orgasm manually should they desire it in any situation where normal relations are temporarily not possible. In short, plain human consideration on the part of two reasonably well-adjusted people should keep a good adjustment working. The importance of consideration cannot be overemphasized, however, as many people let a good adjustment deteriorate through carelessness, thoughtlessness, and laziness until counseling on the part of an expert and much hard work on their own part have to be done to get things in order again.

THE NEED FOR OPEN-MINDEDNESS

There is a great tendency for the person with a difficulty in sexual adjustment to avoid facing it and doing something about it. There are many reasons for this. Having been brought up to think of sex as a shameful, dirty, unbecoming aspect of one's behavior, he is reticent to discuss it. Never having dealt with sex openly, he feels justified in keeping it a personal matter and therefore hidden from others. Since in the popular mind the capacity for sexual enjoyment also connotes vigor and strength of a kind, the one who is unable to function adequately would like to keep his weakness hidden. It stands as an evidence of imperfection, and he finds it hard and sometimes impossible to face any imperfection in himself. For example, a wife says, "John, I feel I might obtain orgasm if you could retain erection a little longer." Instead of replying, "Well, I wonder how that might be accomplished. Is there any source of help for that?"—instead of seeking out that help—he feels criticized, is wounded, pouts, withdraws, will not admit he may be at fault, and insists upon continuing the present pattern, disregarding his wife's lack of pleasure. Or the husband might say, "Jane, I feel you don't give any thought to physical lovemaking.

You make yourself very busy with other things, all of which are important, but you ignore my recurring need of enjoying your body and your enjoying mine." Instead of accepting this as a helpful suggestion and thinking about its truth and why it is so, she feels criticized, cries, defends herself, says her work is not appreciated and that he is just a nasty man with a low, sexy mind.

Before marriage husbands and wives feel they are marrying the cleverest, the wisest, the most agreeable, co-operative person in the world, but find after marriage how hard it is to believe that the person they married ever says anything helpful or worth heeding. So the first plea to husbands and wives with a problem in sexual adjustment is to have an open mind, some degree of humility, and a continuous conviction that the other may be helpful if listened to. If the one with the greater problem could just admit he has a problem and humbly ask for and use the help of the partner, many difficulties in sexual adjustment could be solved by the husband and wife themselves. Each could act as counselor for the other. For example, the common problem of disinterest or frigidity of mild degree in the woman is best described, tersely, by one husband as follows: "I can never get my wife to be interested in enjoying herself sexually with me unless I take her away from home for a few days on a holiday." The fact that she can enjoy sex away from home indicates that her frigidity is not too deep. If such a woman would realize that such a state of affairs is not good and say to her husband, "What do you think I can do about it?" then he could say something as follows: "Be less absorbed in cleaning the house and having everything in such perfect order all the time. Give some thought to what I would like from you rather than being constantly prepared for some unexpected visitor who never arrives. Relax and read a little romantic literature once in a while. Change your idea of how a decent married woman behaves and be a little sexy and seductive with me and see if my appreciation doesn't repay you for the effort you make." A woman, to profit by this, would have to have more respect for her husband and his needs than for her parents' values which made her the way she is, but that capacity for learning new attitudes and values constitutes the means and practically always the *only* means of improving sexual adjustment. Happiness in physical love is a gift which husband and wife give each other. A few people give it easily and naturally all their lives, but they are exceptions. Most couples have to keep trying to improve upon it as they grow older. Generally people improve on their ability to do things as they get older, but in love-making in marriage the common trend is more toward deterioration in the love relation.

For the husband who is deficient in precoital tenderness, affection, and caresses, and comes to ejaculation too soon, the very acceptance of the defect itself and making a resolution to do something about it are the first steps toward remedying the condition. Certainly he *can* control the affection, tenderness, and caressing. If he will do this and endeavor to be more considerate of his wife's needs in between the times of intercourse, he should achieve a better love relationship for both.

The preceding remarks may be too optimistic about what can be done by husband and wife themselves in improving their sexual relations. But it is hoped they are not. More and more people are becoming enlightened on the fact that difficulties in sexual adjustment are rarely due to organic disease or hereditary defects. They are practically always developmental defects in the personality and remediable to the degree that people are willing to work on themselves to correct wrong habits in thinking and feeling. In any case it is better to be optimistic than pessimistic in what people may accomplish with a little information and encouragement.

There are definite differences in the personality make-up of men and women. For instance, while practically all men are sexually aroused by the female body dressed or undressed, very few women are aroused sexually by sight of the male body clothed or unclothed. Similarly, men respond to pictures, stories, jokes, and exotic clothing, while women seem to respond only somewhat to a romantic movie, chivalrous attention, and even to touch itself. Preliminary courtship seems to mean much to women and little if anything to men. Women want and value home, affection, and children to a higher degree than men. Men are more interested in adventure, conquest, and success. Women are much less likely to be troubled by sexual urges when alone than men. Men are intrigued by the more tangible aspects of sex, such as burlesque shows, musical comedy, and pin-up girls, while their equivalents do not excite women.

Husbands and wives, then, knowing these variations, should try to understand their mates better and try to compensate for these differences. A husband should be more affectionate and attentive to his wife all of the time and woo her more gradually to the point of intercourse. He should understand additionally that kissing, caressing, and sex play should be used to arouse his wife to the point of sexual excitement and that this will make sex relations more enjoyable. He should not ignore or neglect this thoughout his marriage. (An exception to this might pertain if his wife, over a period of time, proved to be completely frigid and requested that love-making, to which she could not respond and which she found unpleasant, should be discontinued.)

The average wife, on the other hand, should try to realize that her husband has greater sexual spontaneity and a more frequent urge for sexual relations than she and be willing to participate in intercourse somewhat more frequently than she might feel to be ideal. The husband should bear in mind that out of all the women (nearly six thousand) studied by Kinsey, one third said they responded by orgasm only a small part of the time, another third responded more or less than half of the time, and the final third responded a major part of the time. Only a few equaled or surpassed the male in the desire for frequency or capacity for pleasure. Each partner of the marriage, therefore, must try to meet the other half way to improve the quality of their sexual relations and neither can set as a goal the idea that orgasm in the woman shall always take place. Such an ideal is unrealistic and may cause dissatisfaction or self-reproach in both partners. Much more mutual happiness is possible, if these differences are borne in mind and a more realistic and attainable ideal is strived for. Trying to make the partner act and feel like oneself can be a disillusioning endeavor.

It would seem that the quality of sexual happiness has improved between men and women over the past few decades, measured in terms of physiological response and mutual understanding, but there is farther to go in this direction and knowledge, patience, and understanding of the sexual nature of the opposite sex offer the best hope of bringing about this improvement.

THE USE OF PHYSICIAN OR MARRIAGE COUNSELOR

Those husbands and wives who in spite of information and good will cannot help each other should visit a marriage counselor without delay. Once a problem is known to exist, the longer seeking help is postponed, the harder it is going to be to eradicate it. This is partly due to the fact that bad attitudes tend to get fixed and rigid, but also because good will—that is, patience and friendliness—in both husband and wife is so necessary to effect a change. Hence a couple should not wait until these important qualities have become dissipated in either or both partners.

Since it is so hard for husbands and wives to help each other with these problems the solution is made easier by consulting a third person who has had some training in the science of human relations and who can impart the necessary information, appeal for new attitudes, encourage and give approval for accomplishment, and act as referee when questions arise about which one of the partners should defer to the other. The same rule cannot be applied to every couple, since in some marriages the woman will need more consideration than average or in another marriage the husband will need more tolerance and understanding than average. While in marriage complete partnership and equality in giving each his own way should be the usual goal, there is no getting around the fact that some marital partners have more to give than others, and this may be either the man or the woman.

When counsel is sought it should be of the best quality available. Many people take their marital problems to a friend or some advertised adviser, and this is dangerous. It is an unusual occurrence to find a friend with the objectivity to be helpful. More physicians are receiving training in their medical-school courses or after for helping with these problems. Within the last ten years many cities have set up marriage-counseling organizations with people especially trained for helping with marriage problems. The Planned Parenthood Federation is taking a greater interest in marriage counseling, and a committee has worked out optimum standards for those who work in this field. A counselor, whether he be physician or layman, must have as much experience with life as possible, be as unprejudiced as possible toward either sex, not to mention being unprejudiced in regard to race, religion, political belief, and sexual expression in any form or under any condition. He or she should preferably be married, although this is not the most important qualification. He should be optimistic and be able to expect and *get* the best from people; in other words, be good at inspiring, encouraging, and getting people to work together as well as being an expert analyst on what is wrong. So, after choosing a counselor in whom they have confidence, a couple should work as hard as they would in class, or at a golf or tennis lesson. Surely marital harmony is worth as much time, effort, and practice as are put into learning a new sport or hobby. This may seem an undignified comparison, but the fact is that people are less likely to exercise their mental and emotional muscles than they are their physical muscles.

THE USE OF A PSYCHIATRIST

Some individuals will be unresponsive to ordinary counseling. As might be inferred, these are cases with a much more profound personality disturbance. The psychopathology is so marked, so unconscious, or requires the combination of so much time and so much skillful handling to effect a change that the services of a psychiatrist are needed. One such type is that in which there is so much love of self that the patient finds it extremely hard, if not impossible, to think of anyone's feelings but his own. He has been starved of love as a child and hence has none to give anyone else. He has been given neither warmth nor affection nor had any example of it shown him. So during his period of growth he has had to give whatever love he possessed to himself. He knows no other way of behaving—when he hears of someone showing altruism or devotion he feels that such a person is a sap, a sucker. Women of this type are calculating and frigid, are determined to be kept, waited on, served by men, without giving anything in return. Such men feel women are out to exploit them, and they reflect this feeling in their every conversation. They feel that tenderness and affection are silly. They have a conviction that there is nothing that cannot be bought with money, if one has enough. Both sexes are relatively uninterested in children. A man and woman of this type, each one needing so much and disinclined to give, usually avoid each other and hence usually pair off in marriage with a type of mate who can give them more.

These people are referred to in psychiatric terms as narcissistic. They are often attractive and glib and hide their emptiness behind an articulate expression of their good intentions and a statement of what they feel they deserve. Their explanations usually sound sensible until the other partner has been heard. Then their emptiness, coldness, and inability to give become apparent. Their sex problem may be simply stated. The woman may be "just frigid" or the man "just unable to maintain erection." But this one symptom can harbor beneath the surface a lifetime of coldness, self-centeredness, stubbornness, ungenerosity, irritability, criticism, and lack of social interest which will take two to three years of continuous psychiatric treatment to modify, and which may not be modifiable at all. The woman will never feel any vaginal warmth or pleasure until she learns to be warm and friendly to all. The man will never be able to have and hold an erection until he has modified the character traits enumerated. If this can be accomplished at all it can be done best by two to three years with a Freudian psychoanalyst. Some of these people cannot be changed even with such intensive treatment. After a three to six months' trial treatment this may become clear and the couple should be told the outlook and the decision left to them on whether they continue living together or not. There is already so much separation and divorce that any counselor is reluctant to suggest more. Yet it must be kept in mind that living in an atmosphere of affection, including physical affection, is necessary to the health and well-being of most people. If it is reasonably certain that the patient cannot change and the continued emotional and sexual coldness is going to be detrimental to the other partner, the counselor owes it to both parties to make the situation as regards the future as clear as possible. A physician would not expose a man or woman to live with a spouse with active tuberculosis without warning of the danger. The same holds for sexual and emotional frigidity.

Akin to this narcissistic type and almost a variant of it is the man or woman who is really in love with his or her own sex. These people are latent homosexuals or, psychologically at least, bisexual in nature. They, too, have little love to give to the opposite sex. What is not being used up in loving themselves goes over to their own sex. These cases are serious and require a great deal of strenuous psychologic study. They must come to understand the nature of their delayed emotional development and learn to love in a more altruistic way. It can be seen that if love is not in the mind it does not find its expression through the genital organs. There are women who envy the man his role in life and his sexual organs and psychologically refuse to submit to him or to feel or show any pleasure his sexual organ might give them. There are men who envy the woman her role and who refuse psychologically to play the male role. They do not wish to give a woman an orgasm, children, a home, or any of the things a woman receives from a man. They want to be the recipients of these things themselves. If this unconscious psychologic constellation is strong enough it is surely going to interfere with the man's ability as a lover.

There are some men and women who, deep within them, just cannot get over a feeling of sin or wickedness connected with sex or a fear that they will be hurt, punished, or have to suffer in some terrible way for sex pleasure. Naturally the changing of these attitudes takes considerable work with a psychiatrist.

Sexual maladjustments vary in severity, depending on the severity of the personality disturbance behind them. They are all too numerous.

Preventive treatment comes through better sex education, as counselors can never treat the large number of cases individually. Fortunately the younger clergy are taking an active interest in better personality adjustment, including the sexual adjustment. This will help to neutralize the strong sense of sin and guilt so long associated with sex. More education for marriage is needed in the high school and college, including teaching about the sexual side of marriage adjustment.

Topics for further thought:

1. The kind of sexual adjustment an individual makes in marriage is believed to be a reflection of his early training and home life. Discuss this idea, explaining what parents might do in order to prepare their children for the sexual aspects of marriage.

2. Many married couples do not have mutually satisfying sexual relations. In your opinion does this fact constitute a threat to the family institution or is it merely a matter of personal unhappiness and maladjustment?

Selected reading references

Adams, Clifford, *An Informal Preliminary Report on Some Factors Relating to Sexual Responsiveness of Certain College Wives,* mimeographed, copyright Clifford Adams, 1953.
   Research report on 150 college wives, stressing the interrelatedness between sexual adjustment and general marital adjustment.

Davis, Katharine B., *Factors in the Sex Lives of 2200 Women,* New York, Harper and Brothers, 1929.
   The findings of this study include considerable data on the marital histories of 1000 married women.

Dickinson, Robert L., and Beam, Lura, *One Thousand Marriages,* Baltimore, Williams and Wilkins Company, 1931.
   A classic study of sexual adjustment in marriage.

Stone, Abraham, and Stone, Hannah, *A Marriage Manual,* New York, Simon and Schuster, 1952.
   A popular question-and-answer guide to problems of sex adjust-

ment in marriage. Includes facts of biology, reproduction, family planning, and fertility.

Thomason, Bruce, "Extent of Spousal Agreement on Certain Non-Sexual and Sexual Aspects of Marital Adjustment," *Marriage and Family Living,* November, 1955, pp. 332-7.

A research report indicating that husband and wife tend to agree to a greater degree on behavior pertaining to sexual adjustment than on behavior pertaining to non-sexual adjustment.

17 MEASURING AND PREDICTING MARITAL SUCCESS

Lewis M. Terman

IDENTIFICATION of the factors that make for successful marriage without some kind of criterion of what constitutes marital success is obviously impossible. One criterion is whether the marriage proves to be permanent or is later broken by divorce or separation. This criterion is useful, but it has three shortcomings: it is an all-or-none score and measures only the extreme degree of marital adjustment; it cannot be applied without a wait of several years. The likelihood of ultimate resort to divorce is determined not only by degree of marital dissatisfaction but also by the presence or absence of religious and moral scruples.

THE TEST OF MARITAL HAPPINESS

Early investigators solved the problem by having subjects rate their marriages on a five-point scale: very happy, above average in happiness, average, below average, or definitely unhappy. Hamilton improved the method in a 1929 research project by using a numerical index of marital satisfaction based on the answers to thirteen questions. The more elaborate techniques employed by Burgess and Cottrell and by this writer are merely improvements on that devised by Hamilton.

The test concerned with in this chapter calls for information on fifteen aspects of the marriage:

1. Proportion of outside interest the spouses have in common
2. Rated amount of agreement in each of ten different fields
3. Method of settling disagreements that arise

4. In a list of 40 specific activities respondent
   (a) checks once those he (or she) enjoys doing, and
   (b) checks twice those enjoyed with the spouse
5. Regret of marriage
6. Choice of spouse if life could be lived over
7. Contemplation of separation or divorce
8. Admission or denial of present unhappiness
9. Preference for spending leisure with spouse
10. Gaiety and happiness when spouses are alone together
11. Extent to which the spouse irritates or bores respondent
12. Rated satisfactoriness of the spouse's personality
13. Degree of certainty that no other spouse would have been so satisfactory
14. Subjective rating of happiness of the marriage on a seven-point scale
15. In a list of 38 common faults respondent
    (a) checks once those that the spouse has, and
    (b) checks twice those that have affected the happiness of the marriage

The marital-happiness test in its present form was given in 1940 to 643 members of a gifted group and to their spouses. Their average age at the time was about thirty years. All the gifted subjects in childhood had IQs in the top 1 per cent of the school population and when re-tested for intelligence in 1940 they averaged close to the ninety-ninth percentile of the adult generality. The intelligence scores of their spouses in 1940 averaged considerably lower than those of the gifted subjects themselves but were about on a par with scores of typical college graduates.

The score weights (credits) assigned to the individual items and to the various possible responses to each item were based on experimental work with several sets of tentative weights. Those finally chosen were weights which gave a suitably high correlation of each item with the sum of the remaining scores and which also gave a wide distribution of total scores. The intent was that the test as a whole should have a high degree of internal consistency and thus get at the same general factor of happiness from different angles. That this result was accomplished is demonstrated by the fact that the total scores have a reliability coefficient of .89 for each sex. Moreover, the score distributions which the test yields are much less skewed toward the high end of the scale than the distributions yielded by previous measures of marital adjustment.

The possible range of total scores is from zero to 100, and the scores of the gifted subjects and their spouses extended over almost the entire range. The mean for husbands was 63 and for wives 66. Although this difference is numerically small, it is statistically reliable (critical ratio = 3.8). The difference could mean either that wives on the average tend to be a little better satisfied with their marriage than husbands are, or that wives are more willing to give verbal expression to their satisfactions.

The mean happiness score was almost exactly the same for gifted wives and the wives of gifted husbands, but the mean for gifted husbands was a little below the mean for husbands of gifted wives. In the case of each sex the two distributions were sufficiently alike to justify combining all husbands into a single distribution and all wives into another.

The total score gives a fairly reliable measure of the marital happiness at a given time, but it does not tell how the same person would score on the same test years later. One purpose of the test is to enable an investigator to follow the happiness trends of marriages over an extended period.

It is extremely significant that a test of this kind does not yield a high correlation between the happiness scores of husband and wife. For these subjects the husband-wife correlation was only .52. Marriage is evidently a venture in which the two principals cannot be guaranteed an equal share of the proceeds. A low happiness score on the part of either spouse is predictive of divorce or separation, and the wife's score appears to be somewhat more predictive than the husband's.

The subjects who took the test of marital happiness also answered a number of questions on specific sexual adjustments in their marriage. Information requested from both spouses included usual frequency of intercourse, frequency preferred by the respondent, an estimate of the average duration of intercourse, a rating of the relative passionateness of the spouses, and a rating of how well mated they were sexually. Three additional questions asked the wife for information regarding her experience of the sexual orgasm, the degree of the satisfaction (release) which she obtained from intercourse, and the amount of pleasure and/or pain which she experienced at her first intercourse.

A sex-adjustment score for each subject was computed by assigning weights to the various possible responses to each of the sex items. A response given most often by subjects of high happiness was considered a "good" response and was weighted more heavily than a response less associated with happiness. The maximum sex-adjustment score possible was 23 for husbands and 30 for wives, the higher maximum for wives being due to the fact that more questions were asked of wives than of husbands.

Amazingly close agreement was found between the present group of gifted subjects and the less selected group of 792 couples. There was, in fact, no very significant difference between the two groups. This appears to warrant two conclusions: that the subjects in both groups were probably reporting the facts as accurately as they could; and that intellectually gifted persons are just as normal in their sex adjustments as persons less selected for intelligence and education.

The total score on sex adjustment correlated with marital happiness to the extent of .40 for husbands and .43 for wives. As will be seen presently, the sex-adjustment score is much less predictive of later divorce or separation than is the score on marital happiness.

THE TEST OF MARITAL APTITUDE

The test of marital aptitude described here is the result of several years of search for correlates of marital happiness. Burgess and Cottrell emphasized the importance of factors in the childhood and family background and of facts and circumstances in the immediate background of the marriage. This writer's own data confirm in large part the conclusions of those investigators but suggest that factors of personality and temperament play an even more important role. The test given to the gifted subjects and their spouses included most of the items which Burgess and Cottrell had found predictive and all the items that had shown some evidence of validity in my earlier study. The items fall into three categories, including 117 relating to personality and temperament, 33 to childhood and family background, and 30 to the background of the particular marriage in question. The items in the first two categories can be used with any adult subject, married or single, but those in the third category can be used only with subjects who are married.

The test was given in 1940 not only to the married gifted subjects and their spouses who took the test of marital happiness, but also to 371 gifted subjects who had not yet married. The purpose of the test was disguised by labeling it as a test of personality and temperament.

Consider first the validity of individual items in predicting scores on the happiness test. This was judged by the extent to which the item discriminated between subjects with high happiness scores and subjects with low scores. The high group used for this purpose was composed of 150 couples who had scored high in happiness, and the low group was composed of 150 couples who had scored low. Valid items are those showing a reliable difference between the two groups of a given sex. Table 4 illustrates the method. (Another check on validity was made by comparing the mean happiness score of subjects who gave a particular response with the mean happiness of subjects who gave a different response on the same item. The general principle is the same as in the high-low comparison.)

TABLE 4. Portion of Marital Aptitude Test

Items	Husbands			Wives		
	HIGH	LOW	CR	HIGH	LOW	CR
Do you frequently feel grouchy? Response: No	78%	47%	5.8	81%	61%	3.9
Do you often ignore the feelings of others? Response: No	67	47	3.6	79	64	2.9
Amount of conflict with mother Response: None	52	31	3.7	44	25	3.5

Responses that yielded differences having a critical ratio as high as 2.0 but less than 3.0 were given a score weight of one point; responses yielding a critical ratio of 3.0 but less than 4.0 were given two points; those with critical ratios of 4.0 or higher were given three points. A subject's total score on the test was the sum of the score weights carried by all the responses the subject had made.

Personality and Temperament. There were four sets of items in this category, as follows: 53 items of the type used in the Bernreuter personality inventory; 34 items from the Strong vocational interest test; 16 items on the subject's opinions about the ideal marriage; and self-ratings on 14 traits of personality.

About three-fourths of the 53 items of the Bernreuter type were predictive of happiness. The following carry a score weight of either two or three points for each sex, unless otherwise specified:

Do you daydream frequently?	Credit for No
Do you often feel just miserable?	Credit for No
Are you touchy on various subjects?	Credit for No

Do you often experience periods of loneliness? — Credit for **No**

Do you usually try to avoid arguments? — Credit for **Yes**

One point for men; two points for women. It is apparently more important that women should not be argumentative.

Do you often feel lonesome when you are with other people? — Credit for **No**

Do you try to get your own way even if you have to fight for it? — Credit for **No**

One point for men; two points for women. Such aggressiveness is less objectionable in men than in women.

Do you frequently feel grouchy? — Credit for **No**

Three points for men; two points for women.

Are you frequently burdened by a sense of remorse or regret? — Credit for **No**

Men two points; women one.

Do you lack self-confidence? — Credit for **No**

Men two points; women none. Lack of self-confidence is less serious for women.

Do you worry too long over humiliating experiences? — Credit for **No**

Men two points; women one.

Do your feelings alternate between happiness and sadness without apparent reason? — Credit for **No**

Men two points; women three.

Do you lose your temper easily? — Credit for **No**

One point for men; two points for women. Apparently men are allowed a little more leeway on this trait than are women.

Do you think most religions do about as much harm as good? — Credit for **No**

Two points for men; one point for women.

Is it harder for you to be serene and cheerful than it is for most people? — Credit for **No**

Two points for men; one point for women.

Do you usually feel that you are well dressed and make a good appearance? — Credit for **Yes**

Men three points; women two points. Surprising reversal of what one would expect.

With the opposite sex do you tend to be dominant and have your own way?

No score weight for men; women get two points for the response No. Dominance with the opposite sex is permissible to men but not to women.

There are 19 other items in this list with a weight of one point for one or both sexes.

Only a few of the 34 items from the Strong vocational interest test were predictive of happiness with this group of subjects. Men get one point for liking picnics, Bible study, public speaking, writing letters, conservative people, and women cleverer than themselves. Women get one point for liking picnics, emotional people, Negroes, or old people, teaching children, or contributing to charities. The only weight of two points for men is for liking old people and the only one of two points for women is for liking women cleverer than themselves.

Of 16 items on opinions about what constitutes the ideal marriage, all but one proved to be predictive of happiness in greater or lesser degree. Opinions about which subjects were asked to express themselves concerned such issues as whether the husband should be some years older than the wife, whether the husband should "wear the pants," whether vacations should be taken together, whether marriage should be postponed until income is comfortable, whether the wife should be financially independent of the husband, whether the wife should have a definite budget, whether children should be given religious instruction, importance of the single standard of sex morals, and similar subjects. The fact that so many items in this list were predictive indicates that one's happiness in a marriage is definitely influenced by the attitudes one brings to it.

The traits rated were happiness of temperament, freedom from moodiness, caution vs. impulsiveness, self-confidence, freedom from emotionality, conformity to authority and the conventions, how easy to get on with, enjoyment of social contacts, persistence in accomplishment of ends, integration of life toward a definite goal, inferiority feelings, vanity and egotism, exclusiveness of friendships.

Trait ratings of this kind had not previously been used as indicators of marital aptitude. They proved to be among the best in the entire battery, all but one of them carrying score weights of two to three points for one or both of the sexes.

Childhood and Family Background. Items that are not predictive of happiness for either sex in this group include birth order, number of sibs, number of opposite-sex sibs, report of having experienced a sex shock, amount of petting during the high-school period, and rated attractiveness of the same-sex parent. Items that justify the highest score weights for these subjects include the following:

Rated happiness of childhood, two points to men for "extremely happy"; women two points if "above average."

Childhood punishment, score weight of two points for men and one point for women if there was little or no punishment.

Attitude of parents toward the child's early sex curiosity gets a weight of two points for men if it was described as "frank and encouraging"; no weight for women.

Denial of having experienced any desire to be of the opposite sex gets two points for men and one point for women.

Lack of conflict with the father gets two points for men and one for women. On attachment to father, the husband gets two points if the response was either "very strong" or "none," and the wife one point for either of these responses.

Rated attractiveness of the opposite-sex parent gets a maximum of two points for each sex, the favorable condition being attractiveness rather than the reverse.

High rating on happiness of the parents' marriage carries two points for men and one point for women.

The type of home training (whether strict, firm but not harsh, usually or always had own way, or irregular) gives two points to men and one point to women for any one of the first three conditions.

The following have lower weights in estimating chance of happiness: amount of religious training, history of Sunday-school attendance, church membership, rated adequacy of sex instruction, source of sex information, premarital attitude toward sex, adolescent shyness, preferred parent, and dominance between parents.

Background of the Marriage. Items in this category which showed little or no correlation with marital happiness for these subjects include number of years married, length of engagement, length of time over which the couple kept company, number of persons with whom the subject kept company before marriage, rated resemblance of spouse to respondent's opposite-sex parent, husband's occupation at marriage, outside employment of wife after marriage, ownership of home, height of husband, height of wife (however, one point is given to the husband if he is not 12 or more inches taller than his wife, and one point to the wife if she is less tall than her husband), weight at marriage, change in weight of either spouse since marriage, weight deviation from the average person of the same height, number of social organizations in which the husband holds a membership, whether or not the subject wants children, the wife's present occupation, and the wife's last paid occupation.

Age differences between the spouses give the husband a score weight of one to three points; three if he is 12 or more years older than the wife, two points if he is 3 to 11 years older, and one if he is either 0 to 2 years older or 4 or more years younger. Age difference is less important for the happiness of wives, having a maximum weight of one point if the husband is of the same age, 1 to 8 years older, or younger by 4 years or more.

On age at marriage the husband gets one point for age 23 to 28 and two points for age 29 or over. The wife gets one point if her marriage occurred between the ages 23 to 28 inclusive.

The husband gets one point if the marriage did *not* take place in a civil office, but this item has no weight for wives. If the marriage ceremony was performed by a minister the husband gets one point, but again there is no weight for the wife. It appears that the very circumstances of the marriage ceremony about which brides traditionally are so much concerned are totally unrelated to the marital happiness of wives in this group.

On length of acquaintance before marriage the husband gets one point if the acquaintance was not less than one year, the wife one point if it was not less than six months. Apparently the woman can size up her future spouse more quickly than can the average man.

On number of opposite-sex friends before marriage the wife gets one point for the response "many," the husband one point for the responses "few" or "several."

One of the most heavily weighted items in this section is the subject's report on whether his or her parents favored or disapproved the marriage. The weights here run to three points for the favorable judgment of each parent. Interesting in this connection is the fact that the father's judgment is as predictive as the mother's.

Another predictive item in this list is the respondent's rating of the relative mental ability of the spouses. The husband gets four points if he rates his own ability as equal to or somewhat less than his wife's, two points if he rates his own ability considerably less, and one point if he rates it somewhat greater. Contrary to common opinion, the least favorable condition for the husband is that he should consider himself "very superior" to his wife in mental ability. In the case of the wife it is most favorable for her to judge her own ability to be "considerably less" or "somewhat less" than her husband's. The score weight is three points for each of these responses. The wife gets two points if she says they are "about equal," and one point if she says her own ability is "somewhat greater." The condition least favorable to her happiness is for her to consider her ability "very superior" to that of her husband.

The story changes when one considers the difference between the two spouses in scores on an intelligence test given in 1940. Surprisingly enough, there was only a slight relationship between the happiness score of either spouse and the difference between them in tested intelligence. A score weight of only one point could be given to each, the most favorable condition being a score by the husband somewhat superior to that of his wife.

Unemployment of the husband after marriage is mildly associated with his unhappiness, justifying a score weight of one point if the amount of unemployment represented less than 20 per cent of the period since marriage. The wife, however, gets two points if her husband has experienced no unemployment. Similarly, the husband gets only one point if he has rarely or never changed his position without improving his condition, whereas this circumstance gives the wife two points.

Amount of husband's savings at marriage is relatively unimportant. The husband gets one point for any answer except "none," the wife one point if her husband's savings amounted to $500 or more. Regarding husband's income at marriage, he gets one point for any response except "none," the wife one point for any sum from $200 upward. The income of a couple at the time the test was taken is also of very low predictive value. The husband is given one point if the couple's income is not below $100 or above $500 per month; the wife one point if it is not below $100. This relative unimportance of income and savings is in line with the results of earlier studies.

Size of the community in which the subjects live is not very important, though the husband gets two points if they live in the country. The maximum score for the wife on this item is one point.

An item that shows higher correlation is the subject's rating of his own and his spouse's health. Three points to each spouse for either of the two ratings "perfect" or "superior," and two points to each for the rating "good."

On number of children the husband gets a weight of one point for the response "one" or "none"; the wife gets two points for "none" and one point for "one." Number in excess of one gets no weight for either sex. Both this and earlier studies indicate that in our present culture the relation of marital happiness to presence of offspring is less than it is commonly supposed to be.

Absolute amount of education has no predictive value, but the husband is given one point if his own education is about the same as or less than that of his wife. The wife gets one point if the husband's education is equal to or slightly less than her own, and two points if the husband's education is greater than her own.

Husband's present occupation shows no correlation with his own happiness, but the wife gets one point if her husband belongs to the professional class.

Many of the facts given will seem almost incredible to many readers, but the great majority of them are closely in line with results previously obtained for a less selected group. It seems that many of the current beliefs regarding the importance of this or that factor in the marriage background are based upon nothing more than tradition.

Scores. The maximum possible scores on the three parts of the test are as follows:

	Men	Women
Personality and temperament	118	94
Childhood and family background	37	23
Background of the marriage	38	36

Excluding the third group of items, which can be used only with married subjects, the maximum total for the first two categories is 155 for men and 117 for women.

The reliability of the total marital aptitude score is .86 for men and .82 for women. Its validity is indicated by the fact that it correlates with marital-happiness score to the extent of .62 for men and .55 for women, and by the fact that it predicts later divorce almost as well as college aptitude tests predict college marks.

On the test of marital aptitude, as on the test of marital happiness, the gifted men averaged somewhat below husbands of gifted women, whereas the gifted women and the wives of gifted men had almost identical means. This suggests that if either sex is handicapped for marriage by very superior intelligence it is the man and not the woman (as popular opinion would have it).

THE PREDICTION OF DIVORCE OR SEPARATION

Between 1940 and the end of 1949 there were 104 marriages of gifted subjects that ended in divorce or separation. For most of these subjects, scores as of 1940 were available on marital happiness, sex adjustment, and marital aptitude.

The relative value of these three variables in predicting marital success or failure was estimated by comparing the mean scores of subjects who became divorced or separated by 1949 with the mean of subjects whose marriage remained intact to that date. The results showed that happiness scores and aptitude scores are both predictive of marital failure, and to about the same degree, but that the sex-adjustment scores have considerably less predictive value.

For husbands the happiness scores are somewhat more predictive than the aptitude scores. On two of the variables (happiness and aptitude) wives' scores are more predictive than husbands' scores. Only for one of the three variables (aptitude) is the average of husband-and-wife scores appreciably more predictive than the wife's score alone.

The low predictive value of the sex-adjustment scores suggests that the role of sex, per se, in marital happiness is secondary rather than primary. Couples who are psychologically well mated show a surprising tolerance for the things that are not entirely satisfactory in their sexual relationships. The psychologically ill-mated show no such tolerance, but on the contrary are likely to exaggerate any trifling amount of sexual incompatibility that may be present. Such complaints are often just a convenient peg on which to hang psychological discontent.

THE ROLE OF TEMPERAMENT

Perhaps the most important conclusion suggested by the data reported in this chapter is that one's marital happiness is largely determined by one's all-round happiness of temperament. Happiness of temperament, in the sense here intended, is not to be confused either with Pollyannish or sugary attitudes or with the happy-go-lucky disposition. Its meaning is best defined in terms of the specific responses in the marital-aptitude test which correlate with scores on the marital-happiness test.

This conclusion regarding the role of temperament in marriage is supported not only by the present study but also by results obtained from a less selected group. It seems that there are persons who could live comfortably with any but the most disagreeable mate, and others who would find almost any marriage unbearable. The truth of the latter statement, at least, could be illustrated by the case histories of several subjects who in the course of a few years have gone through three or four marriages and as many divorces.

The role of temperament in marriage is further indicated by the low correlation between the happiness scores of husband and wife. As previously noted, this was only .52 for the present group and only .60 for the less selected group. The correlation could hardly be so low were there not a considerable tendency for each individual to go through life in his own happy or unhappy way. This, of course, is not to say that neither spouse is ever to blame for the unhappiness of the other; such an extreme view would be manifestly absurd.

If the theory here proposed is sound one would expect to find that marital-aptitude scores are correlated not only with later marital adjustment but also with the social and general adjustment in childhood and youth. A check of the aptitude scores against many case-history variables in the gifted group has revealed a number of significant relationships. For example, women who had been rated in 1928 as having "some" or "marked" nervous symptoms averaged 8.5 points lower in the marital-aptitude scores of 1940 than women who in 1928 had not shown such symptoms. The difference is quite reliable (CR = 4.18). Both men and women who had shown "some" or "marked" social maladjustment in 1922 averaged, eighteen years later, 6 points lower in marital aptitude than women whose 1922 ratings on social adjustment were "satisfactory." Men with "satisfactory" social adjustment in 1928 averaged, a dozen years later, 12.6 points higher in marital aptitude than those with "some" or "marked" maladjustment (CR = 4.53). The corresponding difference for women was 8.9 points (CR = 3.00). Men rated "satisfactory" on general adjustment in 1940 averaged 15.8 points higher in the marital-aptitude test taken the same year than men with "some" or "serious" maladjustment (CR = 9.62). The corresponding difference for women was approximately 10 points (CR = 7.00). Checks of this kind were also made on the correlations of case-history data with scores on the marital-happiness test, and with similar results.

SUMMARY

Two tests, then, provide a fairly satisfactory measure of the marital happiness of a husband or wife at a given time, and a rough measure of an individual's aptitude for marriage. The latter, when perfected, has greater potentialities for usefulness than the former because it taps more fundamental aspects of personality and temperament. Happiness in marriage is often ephemeral; aptitude for happiness is an abiding trait.

A shortcoming of the aptitude test is that it measures only the general aptitude of a given person. What is needed is a test that would predict the compatibility of a given couple. There has been a good deal of search for the magical combinations of likes and dislikes, agreements and disagreements, resemblances and differences, that are favorable or unfavorable to marital happiness; unfortunately, few have been found. Terman and Buttenweiser computed tetrachoric correlations between marital happiness and agreement and disagreement of husbands and wives in their replies to some 500 questions relating chiefly to interests, habit patterns, likes, and dislikes. A good many items appeared to be valid measures of compatibility within the group studied; however, when these promising items were tried out with another and larger group few showed much sign of being valid measures of compatibility, although many remained valid as indicators of happy or unhappy temperament in the individual spouse. The search for "good" and "bad" combinations should be continued, but much work will have to be done to go beyond the present general measure of happiness of temperament. Some combinations are better than others with regard to age, education, estimated intelligence, and a few other variables. The problem is to find enough predictive combinations to yield a reliable measure of compatibility.

Finally, there can be no universally valid test of marital happiness, marital aptitude, or marital compatibility. The things that go to make the "good" marriage vary from culture to culture. They are not the same for the Hindu and the Moslem, for the Samoan and the Scot, or for the peasant and the plutocrat of the same nationality and religion. They may differ as between California and South Carolina, Minnesota and Mississippi, Vermont and Virginia. Regional studies should be made for the purpose of analyzing and plotting such differences.

Topics for further thought:

1. In contrast to other authorities the author of this article finds the results of his research suggest "that the role of sex, per se, in marital happiness is secondary rather than primary." Do you think that sex adjustment has been overemphasized in prescriptions for successful marriage? Discuss.

2. The high divorce rate in our society suggests many marriage failures. Is it possible that extensive use of "happiness predictive" tests might reduce the divorce rate? What would you recommend in this connection?

Selected reading references

Burgess, Ernest W., and Cottrell, Leonard S., *Predicting Success or Failure in Marriage,* New York, Prentice-Hall, 1939.
> Report of one of the two pioneer studies that have resulted in the development of marriage prediction scales. Stresses social background factors.

Burgess, Ernest W., and Wallin, Paul, *Engagement and Marriage,* New York, J. B. Lippincott Company, 1953.
> Follow-up study of 1000 engaged and 666 married couples through engagement and the first three to five years of marriage. Validation of marriage prediction tests through testing the same couples before and after marriage.

Ellis, Albert, "The Value of Marriage Prediction Tests," *American Sociological Review,* December, 1948, pp. 710-18.
> A rather critical evaluation of marriage prediction tests, particularly concerning their use in counseling with engaged or about to be married couples.

Locke, Harvey J., *Predicting Adjustment in Marriage: A Comparison of a Divorced and a Happily Married Group,* New York, Henry Holt and Company, 1951.
> Validation of a marriage prediction test through comparison of the responses of couples known to be happily married with those of divorced couples.

Terman, Lewis M., *Psychological Factors in Marital Happiness,* New York, McGraw-Hill Book Company, 1938.

Pioneer study, along with the Burgess-Cottrell reference cited above, in marriage prediction. Stresses psychological or personality factors and includes sex factors.

18 PSYCHOLOGICAL FACTORS IN MARITAL MALADJUSTMENTS

George J. Mohr

In the course of development from infancy to adulthood everyone makes a continuous series of changes and readjustments in personal relationships. This series of changes is characterized by a process of separation from situations that have been secure and satisfying, and of entering into relationships in which some measure of the previous security must be relinquished. Thus, the secure, intra-uterine position of the unborn child is disrupted by birth. He is thrust into an environment that makes new demands upon him. In turn, the nursing infant is soon weaned from breast or bottle and must eat in a more mature fashion. The preschool child must go to school, get along with a bit less of his mother's protective care, and learn to take his place among a group. Similarly, eventually, the protection of a school environment must be relinquished for the more demanding world of active work in our society. Marriage can be regarded as the final step that brings one to the position of adult and parent, in which one is fully responsible for oneself and others.

Each step in this development implies a readiness to meet a new situation that makes greater demand upon the more mature capacities of an individual than did the previous life period. This readiness involves an understanding of the situation to be met and an acceptance of the role to be played in the new situation.

What has just been said places emphasis upon the necessity to emerge from attitudes of too great dependency in order to meet the demands of adult life. A corollary of the basic proposition involved is the necessity to achieve adult attitudes and capacity for relationships in the sexual field. Sexual reactions and the forms they evidence in adult life cannot be separated from the history of the child's emotional life and development. His sexual perspectives in adulthood reflect the history of his interpersonal relationships from infancy on.

EMOTIONAL ATTACHMENT TO THE PARENTS

The initial emotional attachment of any child is to the mother, the source of all comfort and security in infancy. All physical and emotional gratifications stem from the experience the child has in being tenderly cared for by her. The training he undergoes in cleanliness and in habits of eating and sleeping will color his earliest expectations of what is and is not permissible in life. This initial exclusive attachment to the mother is soon modified by the fact that a father begins to play a role in the child's life, a complicating role. While the major relationship between a child and father is that of affection and warm regard, there are many diverse aspects of feeling that color the relationship at various age levels. Children consider the father's presence, in some measure, as a threat to their own exclusive claims to the affection of the mother. Sometimes fathers feel the same way about the children. Fathers are commonly reacted to as threatening; they are big, overwhelming to a very small child, and at times punitive. Normally boys remain quite competitive toward their fathers and inwardly tend to question very much the possibility that they will ever be able to attain his adult, masculine qualities. This competitive attitude of boys later continues to be expressed in the highly competitive relationships between growing boys. The boy who can outdistance, outfight, outswim his mates is accorded the primary position among them.

When a father is able to relate himself to a small son in terms that mean to the boy that the father basically approves of him and accepts him, this tends to bring to the son the assurance that he is a potentially adequate and acceptable person. He can see the possibility that someday he may be a person like his father and expect to assume the responsibilities and prerogatives that go with masculine adulthood. Such a basic attitude is called identification with the father. This identification serves as a psychological platform on which the son may stand as he struggles through the various phases of his development through childhood and adolescence. On the basis of this identification he can project his interest outside himself and beyond the relationships of the family group alone in terms of eventual interest in a man's work, a man's social life, a man's sexual life.

A similar evolution occurs in the basic attitudes of girls. Girls must evolve through an even more complicated series of relationships, the normal end result of which is an identification with the role of the mother as a woman with a corresponding capacity to face a woman's familial, social, and sexual role in life.

The personalities and training attitudes of parents may facilitate the course of development or cause deviations or even serious disturbances in this development. A mother can be too protective, too possessive and encompassing, too directive and domineering to permit a son to develop the necessary certainty about his own masculine capacities. Or a father may be too intimidating, too unaccepting of the son's potential masculinity to permit the boy the development of masculine attitudes and outlook. The result sometimes is, in less serious situations, a young man without sufficient independence of spirit and normal aggression. In more extreme situations the boy may never achieve the capacity for independence in work, social life, and sexual life. The alcoholic, the homosexual, the incompetent, all derive in appreciable measure from disturbances in development of this nature.

Here are some excerpts from actual case histories. The case histories are not to be approached in a spirit of pessimism. Most successful marriages, if scrutinized, would show some or many of the human situations here discussed. Successful marriages are those in which the partners have learned to understand disturbing aspects of their relationship sufficiently to insure the comfortable continuance of family life.

The Mother Attachment A frequent source of failure to achieve good adjustment in marriage is that seen in the life of a young man or woman who remains basically too dependent upon a mother or father. Some mothers refuse to give up their prerogatives as mothers—continue to feel their demands upon the affection and interest of a son or daughter come first, resent the intrusion of an outsider to replace them. In turn, a son or daughter may continue to feel that primarily loyalty is to parents rather than to spouse, may remain too convinced of the wisdom and power of the parent and too dependent to discover that he or she and the spouse constitute a family apart from the parents and are in a position to determine their own way of life, with or without parental sanction.

A young businessman, R. S., sought the advice of a psychiatrist because he had a tendency toward depressive periods that at times severely interfered with his ability to devote himself to his business affairs and periodically he drank to excess. Superficially R.'s marital situation seemed to be satisfactory. Interview with his wife, however, made it clear that he was infantile and demanding toward her. She said: "I have three children, not two." The family continued to live in the home of R.'s widowed mother. The mother presumably remained in the background, but actually all decision and program reflected her judgments and wishes.

R. was the younger of two children, an energetic older sister whom he had always considered an authority having married and moved elsewhere. As a child he was frail; his mother remained solicitous, overprotecting, and maintained a strong guiding hand. The young man grew up, convinced of the high idealism and great wisdom of the mother, to whom he referred all life decisions. His father had been a rather successful and capable businessman but obviously played a secondary role in the family life.

The marital life developed by this man reflected a continuation of his role as a son who looked to women as protecting, maternal persons. His healthy ideas impelled him toward marriage and the establishment of a family. The childish and dependent aspects of his personality determined a great compromise, however—that his family continue to live with his mother. He refused to adopt that independent, active attitude toward his own wife that would make it impossible for her to find in him a "third child."

A situation such as this usually is not well tolerated by either partner in a marriage. This capable young man inwardly rebelled against his position in life. He was surprised to find that his idealization of his mother masked an intense resentment toward her as the person who limited and restricted him. His sense of duty and loyalty to her did not permit him to be aware of this deeper hostility. This conflictful attitude served to make it impossible for him to function freely either as dutiful son or independent man. When he was able to win for himself the permissions his mother was unable or unwilling to grant him, he found it quite possible to arrange a healthier mode of living and a happier marital relationship.

The Father Attachment. This familiar picture of persistence of attachment to a mother on the part of a son has its counterpart in attitudes some young women maintain toward their fathers.

An attractive young woman, H. S., mother of a son and daughter, complained of fatigue, a feeling of inadequacy and discomfort when among her friends. She had lost her previous capacity to work actively at her home tasks and among a group of young women friends who were interested in various club and welfare activities in the lively suburb in which the family lived. She had been married six years. Until recently she had considered her marriage successful, but now she questioned whether her discomforts might not be related to dissatisfactions in her marriage. She expressed affection for her husband. The sexual aspect of their marital life had always been on a wholesome and pleasant basis. Mrs. S., however, indicated a growing disinterest in her husband's physical approaches, and she was critical of him in many ways. She had concluded he was dull and uninspiring, too devoted to his business interests, not socially as active and as "interesting" to others as she thought he should be.

Actually Mr. S. was a personable, pleasant, and capable man. He was head of a small manufacturing firm, successful financially. During the war he devoted long hours to his work, showed much ingenuity and capacity in bringing the wartime production of his plant to a high degree of efficiency, and made a real contribution to the war effort. He was rather a reserved man, friendly with a small group of business associates. While not as socially inclined as his wife, he encouraged her own social activities and took part himself with good grace, but only at times with enthusiasm.

When Mrs. S. spoke of her father her voice kindled with enthusiasm. She described him as a dynamic, energetic, capable person, imaginative, resourceful, very successful in business affairs, inventive, and ingenious. Her father, she felt, was a much bigger personality than her husband. Somewhat pensively she commented on her father's great preoccupation with his affairs that kept him away from home much of the time. Actually she had had relatively little contact with him during her childhood. Her affection and esteem for him, however, were unlimited.

Mrs. S.'s dissatisfactions with her lot and her highly depreciatory attitude toward her husband reflect her appraisal of her father and her expectations and longing as a child toward him. By virtue of his very remoteness, her father could remain the highly idealized being he still represented in the fantasy of the daughter. The nonspectacular, though really adequate, agreeable, and affectionate husband was measured against the image of the ideal father and inevitably found wanting. No matter how effective he may be in reality, no flesh-and-blood husband, with the faults and weaknesses that usual husbands are bound to have, can stand the test of such a comparison.

The childish longings in relation to such an idealized father remained to obstruct the possibility of a realistic appraisal of a husband. For Mrs. S. recognition and acknowledgment of the overemphasized role of this ancient, childhood feeling toward her father permitted a more mature evaluation of her actual life situation and of her relationship to her husband. She found it possible to recapture normal enthusiasm about the everyday affairs of real family and social life and to go ahead effectively in her role as wife and mother.

PERSISTENCE AS A CHILD

The basic persistence of the concept of oneself as son or daughter, rather than as adult man or woman in marriage, reflects itself in many ways.

A successful businessman, J. L. was anxious and uncertain about his work. His discomfort began at a time when he was advanced in his firm and placed in a position of authority over other men. Heretofore he had always been in a secondary position, with a boss over him to whom he could turn for advice and who had ultimate responsibility.

He made no complaints about his marital life, but his wife was somewhat unhappy about their childless state. When questioned about this childlessness J. L. indicated that there were no children because his wife "had not insisted upon it," that early in marriage it seemed quite a responsibility to have children, and now, relatively late, he thought himself and his wife a little too old to begin the rearing of a family. He knew of no physical obstacles to the having of children.

J. was the younger of two sons, reared by a strict and authoritative father. Both boys obeyed him implicitly without thought of ever questioning the father's authority, even when quite grown into manhood. When drafted into military service in World War I, J. L. was recommended for training in the Officer Candidates School. He refused this training, saying he preferred the position of a private rather than that of an officer with responsibilities possibly involving lives of other men. He served through the period of enlistment in a very competent manner, evidenced considerable personal courage in action, but never got beyond noncommissioned officer rating. On return to civilian life he started in a subsidiary position in the firm in which eventually he was promoted to a managerial position.

Throughout life J. L. inwardly considered himself the son who should dutifully carry out the orders of a stronger and wiser father. He refused the authority that goes with the position of a father in rejecting training as an officer—and in avoiding fatherhood in his marriage. When life circumstances made it impossible for him to escape any longer the real responsibilities of a fatherlike person he became psychologically upset and was finally forced to recognize and evaluate the limitations he had imposed upon himself. On gaining an understanding of the nature of his discomfort, he was able to make a good adjustment to the demands of his work situation, but it was a bit too late in life to start the rearing of a family and the rounding out of an otherwise good marital life.

MODIFICATIONS IN ATTITUDES

Time and experience serve to bring about modifications in attitudes toward life situations. This fact is at times overlooked by a partner in marriage.

A 43-year-old attorney, R. B., had concluded he wished a divorce, but he was concerned about the possible effects of family disruption on his only child, a 13-year-old daughter.

R. B. was an only son. His father, successful in law, tended to treat him much as "his boy." Only in recent years had R. decided to pursue an independent career. He severed his professional association with his father and established a new firm. He remained quite close to his own parents, however. He considered his childhood life a happy one, spoke of the great devotion his mother had to home and family, and of her capacity to understand and anticipate his needs and those of his father. R. said that there had been much quarreling and bickering throughout his marriage, but during the last two or three years this had been increasing. His wife was from a family of artistic and literary interests. She had achieved a modest success as a writer of short stories and radio scripts. R. was more impatient than pleased with her success, felt she neglected the home and her child in the service of her outside interests, and constantly compared her attitude toward home and family with that of his mother. Actually the household was a well-conducted and well-regulated one in which, however, the wife made generous use of household help to relieve her of routines.

R. told how he was "madly in love" with his wife at first. He showered her with gifts and affection and did everything to meet her wishes. During their engagement they had a rather serious difference which led to a threat on the part of his fiancée to withdraw from the engagement. He gave in and never risked such a threat again for many years. During recent years, however, he had increasingly resented her "lack of co-operation." While establishing himself independently in his work there was a period of relative stringency; he felt his wife did not go along with him in necessary reduction of expenses. He worked harder and harder, grew short and impatient with his wife. He concluded he was not in love with her any longer, became critical of her person, of her manner, of everything about her. He withdrew from her sexually and felt there was nothing attractive about her in any sense. He toyed with the idea that maybe he would fall in love with someone else, essayed a mild flirtation or two, but soon realized that his dissatisfaction with his wife had nothing to do with the possible attractiveness of other women. Finally, embittered by the innumerable deficiences he apparently found in his wife, he concluded a divorce was in order.

Mrs. B. was taken completely by surprise by the suggestion of divorce, as she had always considered herself fully devoted to her husband. She had been fully aware of his increasing irritability with her, attributed it to overwork and too great preoccupation with his professional affairs, and had been urging him to find time for a holiday away from the demands of his work. She had long been uncomfortable and unhappy but assumed the fault was entirely with her husband.

Here again two intelligent and well-intentioned people almost brought their marriage to dissolution because of inability to see their problem clearly. The initial equilibrium in this marriage was estab-lished by the somewhat too passive and too dependent attitudes of the young husband. Loving and affectionate by nature, he early adopted the attitude that security in love was dependent on con-formity to all wishes and desires of his beloved. It was pretty much a matter of being a good boy so as to risk no rejection or anger, an attitude he held toward his parents as well. Relatively late in life, particularly under the stimulus of his successful independent activities in his profession, he achieved a basically more active attitude and re-acted against his own earlier too-compliant tendencies. The wife, in the meantime, in all good faith, accepted the initial basis of their relationship and assumed a taken-for-granted attitude toward her husband, unaware of the fact that people can and do develop and change as they mature in years. The result was, finally, a "strike" on the part of the husband; after having taught his wife over years of time to expect certain reactions on his part, he rebelled against the very situation he had largely brought about.

It proved not too difficult for each of these people to gain perspec-tive about their marriage and the nature of their difficulties. The real maturity the husband had achieved enabled him, albeit a bit painfully, to recognize the immature, dependent attitude that determined his earlier need to yield in all issues. The wife was truly surprised to dis-cover that she had been much too complacent in her expectations of her husband. It was interesting to note that she was actually stimulated and challenged by the necessity to understand herself and her relationship with her husband.

DEPRECIATING WOMAN'S ROLE

Not infrequently failure on the part of a young woman to cope adequately with marital life is determined by disturbing and deeply implanted attitudes toward sexuality and toward the marital status. Two related pertinent concepts are that sexuality is vulgar or bad and hence forbidden, possibly dangerous, and that a woman's role, particularly in marriage, is a secondary and depreciated one.

This basic depreciation of a woman's role in marriage was a much more emphasized conscious theme in social attitudes toward women a generation ago than it is now. It was a heritage of the Victorian era, in which all sexual interests were considered, at best, bad taste; at worst, sinful. Today, under the emancipating influence of healthier attitudes toward women, toward femininity, and toward the womanly sexual role, the surface manifestations of this attitude have disappeared. In some measure, however, they have gone underground and are represented in the less conscious or unconscious attitudes of many women. Some mothers succeed in transmitting to their daughters attitudes toward sex that make it difficult, if not impossible, for the daughters to accept the sexual marital role as one consistent with self-respect and dignity. At times the sexual role is envisaged not merely as bad, but as brutal, painful, dangerous to physical health; something to be suffered rather than experienced as part of a creative way of life.

Mrs. L., the mother of three daughters, was a conscientious, scrupulous mother. She concerned herself carefully with the rearing of her daughters, with emphasis upon personal cleanliness and strict morals. While her children were quite young the emphasis upon health was extreme; for example, regularity in bowel movement occupied a position of first importance, with ready recourse to enemas or other means of internal "purification" at the slightest provocation. The father in this family was a mild-mannered, good-natured bookkeeper, who provided for the material security of his family but left the rearing of the daughters entirely to the energetic wife and mother.

As the girls matured the mother was insistent that marriage was something to be avoided, sexual behavior to be deplored, and the bearing of children an onerous and distasteful burden to which no daughter of hers should submit. She emphasized the dangers and discomforts of pregnancy and the trials and cares involved in the rearing of children. One devoted all one's time and energy to the rearing of a family with no prospect of thanks, reward, or satisfaction. In view of this, sexual relations had no justification.

The daughters in this family were intelligent and capable. All of them, nevertheless, were sufficiently impressed by the mother's attitudes that none was able to accept the prospect of marriage. Of the three, one, after a period of residence away from home, was able to question the desirability of a life without marriage and sought psychiatric advice. She came to an understanding of the distortions in the mother's attitudes and the effect of these on her own life relationships and eventually she married, armed with understanding which should prevent a repetition of the mistakes in her own rearing in relation to a daughter of her own. The two sisters remained victims of the great limitations imposed by the mother, unmarried, restricted in social outlook, both still preoccupied with problems of physical health in keeping with the mother's great concern in this field.

Without the specific depreciation of the sexual role as discussed above, many girls grow into womanhood with the deep conviction that women are cast in a secondary role in life, and that particularly in marriage a woman's position is a depreciated one. It is a fact that in some societies women may be in the position of chattel rather than in equal partnership in life relations. But even in a society such as our own, where in some respects femininity carries with it special prerogatives, there is still a tendency on the part of some women to feel that the world is essentially a man's world—boys and men can achieve full personal freedom and full expression of their potentialities, while women are thwarted. The result is a tendency to regard homemaking, the bearing and rearing of children as routine, dull, and not a source of gratification as creative work.

Whether or not social attitudes provoke convictions about presumable inferiority of women as compared with men, very early a questioning by both boys and girls about the significance of differences between the sexes is recognizable. A not uncommon conclusion arrived at by very small children is that girls are in some measure deficient. To the small child the lack of an obvious genital organ seems to constitute a deficiency. This is not a theoretical assumption about children. It is something that quite a few children remark upon directly and openly and about which, at times, they need correct information. Often, however, because of anxiety on the part of a child or lack of awareness or prudery on the part of a parent, the whole questioning attitude is repressed. The uncertainty and depreciated evaluation of the little girl remain, however, to color the attitude of both boy and girl.

As might be expected, such attitudes toward the person or the functioning of women are likely to evolve in families in which little girls may be given reason to believe that their brothers are more highly valued by one of the parents. Some parents openly prefer sons to daughters. In such a family a girl may remain convinced that she can never amount to much, or she may possibly strive to become the sort of person the desired son would have been. A certain number of professional women softball players are daughters of fathers who had really hoped to have a son rather than a daughter, a son who should be a fine figure on the baseball field. The daughter attempts to meet the father's hopes and expectations by pinch-hitting, as it were, for the desired son. It does not help them much in their development as girls and women.

A child's greatest need is to be loved and valued by parents as he *is;* this is the key to the possibility of developing dignity and a sense of personal worth. If this self-evaluation is disturbed by the concept that only boys are truly valued by parents, there ensues a never-ending struggle with the proposition that to accept femininity is to accept something inferior.

Many marriages are disturbed by this hidden repudiation of femininity. Resistance to acceptance of the sexual role in marriage, resentment at the demands of household and children, envy of the presumably freer and more rewarding or worth-while activity of the husband disturb the equanimity of many families.

PARTNERSHIP IN MARRIAGE

Any realistic appraisal of the relative positions of man and woman in marriage would allow for the biological fact that men and women are different in their roles; that their differences cannot be gauged on a single scale of values but in terms of complementary functions and activities that make for successful joint living together in marriage. Whenever, by virtue of circumstances or because of pressures depending upon personality peculiarities, one partner is thrust unduly into the role usually carried by the other, a natural equilibrium is disturbed.

This equilibrium, in a healthy marriage, is one in which the wide range of basic needs and desires of both partners is adequately met.

These include the need for love and affection, satisfaction of the more ideal expectations of a respected and beloved partner, material security, social prestige, parenthood, and sexual expression of love. To be sure, the manner and degree to which these needs are met vary widely, and the nature of the equilibrium attained is highly individual for each couple. A marriage may sustain some degree of limitation in both degree and range of satisfactions in the several fields, but it is clear to see from the cases cited above that the possibility of a workable equilibrium can readily be disturbed. This is particularly true when the basic attitudes outlined earlier tend toward a denial of the validity of one's own or one's partner's needs in marriage.

Psychiatrists who have an opportunity to scrutinize the conflicting rational and nonrational attitudes of their patients are able to outline with considerable precision the nature of some of these situations of conflict. Referring back to the attitude on the part of some young women that their role in marriage is secondary, or a depreciated one, one finds with rather astonishing regularity a characteristic sequence of inner reaction and external behavior. Such a young woman, impelled by healthy impulses toward marriage and motherhood, nevertheless unconsciously tends to select as a mate a man who she instinctively feels will not overwhelm her sexually or otherwise, will not dominate or coerce her, and in relation to whom she will feel equal or superior. In actuality, however, such a woman to whom prestige and position mean so much will expect a great deal of her husband, real adequacy if not superiority in all fields, vocational, social, sexual. She will wish him to achieve for her all that she feels she is denied because she is a woman. Having selected as a mate a man whom she considers not too dangerous or threatening, she now senses and resents in him the very deficiencies that enabled her to accept him as a mate. She becomes depreciatory toward him, aggressive and hostile toward him for failing to meet her more unconscious concepts of what a husband should be like.

Many versions of this theme are encountered in real life. If a wife is able to see through the contradictory character of her own expectations she may be able to protect herself from the effects of such a vicious cycle, gain more assurance about the valid aspects of her relationship with her husband, and achieve a workable association in marriage. Similarly, if a husband is able to understand the implications of such an attitude he, too, may be able to do much to promote a healthier equilibrium. It must be remembered that it takes two to create any given life situation. The husband, in the type of marriage discussed here, certainly has made his initial contribution to the difficulty. Those attitudes of unaggressiveness and passivity that made him seem sufficiently nondangerous to the neurotic part of his wife's feeling do exist in him; the question is whether they exist in such degree and operate so automatically as to play into the cycle of fear, depreciation, expectation, and disappointment to which we have referred. He may be able to see that, after all, his apparently domineering and aggressive wife is really dependent upon him and his life success for basic satisfaction as he is dependent upon her. If so, he may surmount his own reactions of resentment and hostility toward his wife, insist on fulfillment of standards of performance he sets up for himself, and in this manner tend to bring about stability in marriage.

PERSISTENCE OF NEUROTIC ATTITUDES

A word must be said about the persistence of psychologically disturbed patterns of behavior in marriage. Deeply implanted attitudes inimical to successful adjustments in marriage disturb or disrupt many marriages in the ways described. These attitudes usually evolve during the course of development of the child toward maturity and are dependent in considerable measure upon the nature of the training and rearing. It should here be emphasized, however, that all too often the nature and the very existence of these disturbing attitudes are not recognized or are explicitly denied by the victims themselves. In personal relationships and in understanding of inner motivations, desires, and strivings, objectivity and rational understanding are achieved with much greater difficulty than in other fields of human inquiry. Many people are never able to approach rational understanding of their own behavior and motivations, although maturing life experience helps in the direction of such understandings.

Medical experience shows, however, that precisely those people who are most disturbed in their marital relationships often fail to learn by their unhappy experiences. A trip to the divorce court is frequently followed by a marriage in which the same marital difficulties are again encountered. One has succeeded in separating oneself from an unhappy situation, but not from the basic attitudes and expectations that made the first marriage an unhappy one and that operate the same way in a second marriage. Perhaps there is little point in the termination of marriage unless there is basic clarity as to the nature of the deficiencies in the relationship. Nothing short of such understanding can offer much in the way of insurance against the possibility of a repeat act in a subsequent marriage. On the other hand, such understanding frequently makes possible the successful continuance of a threatened marriage.

Topics for further thought:

1. Marriage in our society demands that husband and wife play different and distinct roles. Explain how this patterning of marital behavior may be the source of unhappiness to some couples.

2. Why is the married woman in our society frequently thought of as facing a dilemma, whereas the married man does not seem to be in a similar situation?

Selected reading references

English, O. Spurgeon, and Pearson, Gerald H., *Emotional Problems of Living,* New York, W. W. Norton and Company, 1945.
Excellent nontechnical description of the development of normal personality. For well-educated adults.

Flugel, J. C., *The Psychoanalytic Study of the Family,* London, Hogarth Press, 1948.
A comprehensive analytic interpretation of the dynamics of family living.

Hill, Reuben, et al., *Families Under Stress,* New York, Harper and Brothers, 1949.
Analysis of the adjustment of family members to the crises of separation and reunion during World War II.

Levy, John, and Munroe, Ruth, *The Happy Family,* New York, Alfred A. Knopf, 1938.
A fascinating collection of psychiatric insights into the emotional functioning of family members. Especially good discussion of unconscious conflicts in marriage.

Waller, Willard, and Hill, Reuben, *The Family: A Dynamic Interpretation,* New York, The Dryden Press, 1951.
A brilliant analysis of adjustment and maladjustment within the American family.

19 WOMEN'S CONFLICTING VALUES IN RELATION TO MARRIAGE ADJUSTMENT

Emily Hartshorne Mudd

I<small>N</small> the United States, marriage is entered into and succeeds or fails primarily on the basis of the interpersonal relations of the two people who agree to undertake it. Women are concerned with various values which may be conflicting. Conflict is discord manifested in actions, feelings, or effects. Conflict is significant because it is the base of conscious life. Conflicting values can be world-wide, as in contemporary global tension, or they can be local and relate to such simple factors as individual opinions about the use of electric washers or the clothes one wears. All human beings live in conflict and have conflicting values. Variation is evident in the intensity and degree to which a conflict disturbs the activity of an individual person and those with whom he is associated.

Do women as human beings have conflicting values, or is it that men have conflicting values about women? Or is the society in which men and women live responsible for forming and nurturing conflicts? Woman is a complex but oriented organism. She has well-focused needs and goals; she has the desire and ability to attain these goals— goals of physical and mental maturity, the chance to love and be loved, to reproduce her kind, to participate actively in the worth-while work of the world; in other words, to be a person in her own right, to realize creativity in the fullest sense.

Undoubtedly one of the clues to the emotional conflicts or satisfactions of women lies in the religious concepts of any given society. Sophie Drinker points out that the Romans, for instance, expressed their relation to the higher powers in a prayer: *"Sive deus, sive dea* [whether god, whether goddess] . . ." To them, Life Force manifested itself through both male and female. Today the industrial revolution has removed much of the economic value of woman as the producer of products essential for homemaking. The increasing mechanization of life has limited even further woman's own feeling of worth. Actually, the easy availability of the necessary commodities may relieve toil, but it has also removed the importance and much of the skill and uniqueness from the position of mistress of the small apartment. The routine tasks become more or less monotonous drudgery, requiring little ingenuity and utilizing only a fraction of the ability of the average woman. In addition, many college women—handmaidens of higher education, with its emphasis on the intellectual—believe that actual housework and the physical care of children do not utilize their training to the best advantage of society.

Constant improvements in living conditions are in the direction of further mechanization. The home is depicted with even more labor-saving and comfort-giving devices. Rooms may have electrically charged wire to which dust particles will be drawn, thereby eliminating cleaning and much laundering. Homes come in ready-to-order sections, functionally adapted to the changing needs of the family, one section for the bride and groom, which can be varied appropriately for the type adapted to baby. Other sections, suitable for young children, can be traded in later when daughter is dating. Nearing perfection are house-heating devices using solar energy, while attractive prepared foods of all varieties now emerge as T.V. platters, completely ready to serve balanced meals, needing only a few minutes in a hot oven.

These inventions may eliminate labor, but they will not eliminate human feelings, needs, and desires. Do they not merely present women with an even more drastic challenge to understand and develop competence to meet these needs and desires as real and vital essentials of life? A woman will not achieve serenity of the heart and soul by having things done to her and for her. Being a turner of switches, a watcher rather than a participant, does not make for inner satisfaction and feelings of worth.

It is small wonder that in certain instances the attitude of depreciation of the role of wife and mother only, plus the practical difficulties of adequate child care if she has a job away from home, plus the sex discrimination and competition in the job world, plus the often precarious marital adjustment, induce a variety of conflicts in the modern woman. These definitely deter her growth and spiritual development and her feelings of belief in her value as a woman. Ensuing complications, physical, emotional, and practical, are often evident. Foster and Wilson present an illuminating description of some of these problems in *Women after College*. Strecker in *Their Mothers' Sons* shows how the results of these often unresolved conflicts are reaped by the helpless, sometimes hopeless, children of the "American Mom." Lundberg and Farnham, in their controversial book, *Modern Woman: The Lost Sex,* reiterate that the woman of today, rejecting, overprotecting, or dominating her children, is bringing up a race of neurotics. Mead scrutinizes astutely the relationship between women and men in *Male and Female;* de Beauvoir decries the "second sex" in a book of that title; and a somewhat different emphasis is introduced through Ashley-Montagu's controversial volume, *The Natural Superiority of Women* and Doris Bernays' *A Wife is Many Women*. Three recent carefully documented studies furnish new information on women's adjustment to the realities of modern life. Niles Newton highlights woman's response to her biological functions in *Maternal Emotions,* William Goode her difficulties *After Divorce* and Jessie Bernard her potentialities in *Remarriage: A Study of Marriage*. Althea Hottel's thoughtful discussion in *How Fare American Women* and Eleanor Roosevelt's inspiring volume *Ladies of Courage* present perspective for the future.

SITUATIONS OF UNRESOLVED CONFLICTS

The combination of spiritual starvation, mechanization, and dual roles has been overwhelming to some contemporary women who have found it difficult to surmount the barriers to normal activity. Many a woman thus finds herself tossed hither and yon by the pressures of her world, her parents, her job, her husband, her children, or her social milieu, or she charts a stormy course and steers with determination, in spite of combined pressure, toward a beacon, an ideal. Some women try every type of compromise; others exhibit every type of protest. Some ask for too little, denying their value; others demand too much, overasserting their frustrations and feelings of inequality. The results of these conscious and unconscious conflicts propel some women to the physician's office, to the counseling service, to the divorce court, or unhappily to one of the thousands of untrained and unethical advisers who live profitably from the misery of others.

A marriage-counseling office finds discouraging evidence of the practical effect of individual personality growth on marriage and on family life, and so on the community, of situations in which conflicts remain unresolved. So often the conflicts are the result of different expectations that were built up in the childhood of each and in turn were dependent on the cultural conditions of the particular family group, a concept amplified by Buck in *Of Men and Women*. The following cases illustrate situations for which clients, men as well as women, sought help.

1. The situation of Mrs. A shows how the activities of a machine age have changed and in part removed the concept of value from the homemaker. Mrs. A was the "girl back home" when Mr. A, an ambitious, intelligent man in his thirties, married her. She was all his mother had been and more—a good cook, a neat housekeeper, a devoted mother who asked for no more than to perfect her home and dedicate her life to her man. In a large city Mr. A, as a successful businessman, found himself thrown with men whose wives were of a different vintage. Modern equipment, small apartments, and few children left them with the feeling that domestic activities were beneath them and of little value. They were aggressive in their appearance and manner, sophisticated in their glamour, their entertaining, and their lack of household duties, active in clubs and community. Their days, as their husbands', were full of "keeping up with the Joneses" in clothes, cars, schools, entertainments—competition in goals of triviality. Mr. A now had money in plenty. He wanted his wife to take her place with "the other girls" and do him proud. He told her so, at first gently and later accusingly. Helpless, frightened, and confused, Mrs. A clung to her familiar world with tenacity. Mr. A became disgusted, bored, abusive, and resentful in turn. It took him only a short time with the counselor to realize that Mrs. A needed help, reassurance, encouragement, and kindness to learn gradually to try herself and her abilities in a new and strange world, a world which measured success so much in the doing and attached so little importance to the being. Gradually she began to realize that this new effort did not threaten her basic value as homemaker, mate, and mother. And her competence in adjusting herself to her husband's changing needs strengthened when she developed faith in herself as a dynamic unit of society, able to create human relationships.

2. Mrs. B exhibited marked protest against her environment and resented her womanhood. She reconciled herself to her sex by becoming a designer and by attempting to associate with men as professional equals. Having adopted this attitude, she married another designer. Now, however, her impulses as a woman asserted themselves, and she found herself disturbed by the criticism of her friends that a woman could not be successful as a career designer and as a wife. She was not able to resolve this conflict successfully and alternated between being an artist and a wife. Her dilemma was not that she was uncreative in the matter of design, but that her energy was spent in denying the value of womanhood as a creative force. Her *identification with men* in her career injured her spirit as a creative woman.

3. The case of Mrs. C shows in still another way how a woman can become discouraged by her particular social milieu. Mrs. C asked for so little that she reminded the counselor of the proverbial worm. It was the beginning of the turning of this inner worm that led her to seek professional help. Mrs. C had been trained as a teacher. Because she was a woman, marriage was the answer to her desire for children. Because her contacts were limited she married an almost illiterate man who was trying to earn his living as a laborer. Forced to do manual work, she found herself in circumstances for which she was unprepared by temperament, training, and background. One by one she gave up her old interests in a constant struggle to adjust herself. At the age of forty her life was drab and humdrum. Her sole connection with the outside world was a friendship with the wife of a teacher in another state. So after twenty years of marriage she felt herself a failure, and she felt her marriage was a failure too.

In this situation also the criteria held by society in regard to the duties of a married woman were so inimical to the development of Mrs. C's inner life that she did not have the stamina to assert herself. Society so often puts little value on the possible contributions of womanhood, with the result, in Helene Deutsch's words, that "there is hardly a woman in whom the normal psychic conflicts do not result in a pathological distortion, at some point, of the biologic process of motherhood."

4. The case of Mrs. D shows a woman who demanded so much that her marriage relationship become almost unbearable. A librarian by profession, Mrs. D was a woman of great energy and ambition. She married a man who was equally ambitious and gave up her paid position because of the concept held by her and her young husband

that man was the provider and woman's place was in the home. She found housework and the care of three children tedious and not broad enough to give scope to her talents. She attained middle age discontented and bitter. She was dissatisfied with her children who, incidentally, had turned out remarkably well; she did not feel that her husband's outstanding success in business was worth the sacrifice of her own career—a feeling apparently shared, if not verbalized, by many women. She demanded complete devotion and constant attention from her husband. Her unreasonable demands finally drove him to seek distraction elsewhere. Mrs. D's frustration begat a domineering attitude which brought strain and unhappiness to her whole family.

Here again is a woman who did not find sufficient opportunity in her limited conception of her role and whose husband did not know how to help her by attributing equal value to her contribution. What she lacked was more a feeling of the worth-whileness of herself as a person rather than an actual lack of opportunity for the use of potentially constructive energy.

5. Mrs. E was like Mrs. D in her ability and aggressiveness, but her marriage differed in that her husband was neither brilliant nor successful. Mrs. E, therefore, had ample opportunity to contribute within the supposed limits of marriage. She made such good use of her abilities that she became not only the housekeeper but also the sole support of the family. Her husband, thus outdistanced, made little effort to find congenial work and finally gave his affection to a sweet little clinging vine for whom he divorced his wife. During the process of realizing what was happening Mrs. E was precipitated into severe conflict and sought counseling help. She knew that she was contributing more than he as an effective person in their social group, but at the same time she wanted to preserve her family. Her type of conflict was the result of her failure to exert her powers toward the goal of creating a human relationship in which her husband could feel himself as of equal value to her and to their children.

Wherever there are conflicts in marriage which continue over a period of time to cause increasing frustration for one or both partners, almost inevitably there is difficulty in the sexual adjustment of the couple. Either a mutually adequate sexual adjustment is never achieved, or if this experience of loving exchange has been achieved, the completeness and harmony of the relationship lessen and finally may be totally impaired. As D. H. Lawrence puts it, "It was from herself she wanted to be saved, from her own inward anger and resistance—and suddenly—it was gone, the resistance was gone, and she began to melt in a marvelous peace—and further and further rolled the waves of herself away from herself, leaving her, till suddenly—she was gone. She was gone, she was not, and she was born; a woman." Esther Harding contends that "nothing but devotion to a faith in the rightness of one's own nature can release energy, be it sexual or spiritual." When a woman's emotional conflicts are resolved in favor of the naturalness, rightness, and spiritual power of sexual intercourse, then and then only is she freed to give herself, to unite with her man, to achieve the essence of womanhood.

THE ROLES OF WOMEN

Although so far women's conflicting values and cases in which their conflicts have not been resolved have been emphasized, fortunately many women in our times do find satisfactory solutions even within the complexities of the present social order. Such women achieve a degree of comfort, a serenity in being themselves, which in turn brings comfort and serenity to those around them. Usually this finding of themselves as women comes through emotionally satisfying orientation to one or a combination of the three general roles which existing cultural patterns leave open to women. In any one or a combination of these roles such women feel themselves to be of value and are so recognized by others.

Marriage, Motherhood, Aid to Husband. This role satisfies women who feel that their finest contribution can be made through marriage, motherhood, and identification with the creative activities of their man. Who better illustrates this than Emma Wedgwood Darwin, wife of the great scientist Charles Darwin, whose writings on evolution have so revolutionized modern life? Darwin was always physically frail and would, in all probability, have been unable to cope with the complex responsibilities of life and a family—plus creative research—had it not been for the unswerving devotion of this wonderful woman. Mrs. Darwin put at the disposal of her husband an absolute belief and confidence in the things that were vital to him—his researches. She took over the management of his comfortable income, his house and children; she protected her scientist from interruptions and worries that would distract his singleness of purpose; she helped in the preservation of specimens and notes; in addition to all this, she bore him five sons and two daughters. In part, as a result of this devotion, three of these sons have been knighted for outstanding achievement in their own right.

Another illustrator of this role is Madame Pasteur, whose devotion and loyalty to a brilliant and, at that time, an often misunderstood chemist carried her to rural communities, exposed her to ridicule and persecution, put her loyalty to the test through the illness and death from typhoid fever of two of her three children. At all times she accepted the vagaries of a household whose routine revolved around the exotic and untimely events of an experimental laboratory, believing that the hoped-for results of her husband's creative mind merited the means. This great woman found courage even to fortify her own beloved daughter, at the moment of her approaching motherhood, for the continued absence of her young husband who was closeted behind locked doors in her father's laboratory, to tell her that this was part of the life of a great man's wife and daughter—to help her find strength to bear it. Cosima Liszt Wagner summed up this philosophy with the words, "Women are put into the world to help great men."

The majority of American women quite consciously identify themselves with this role, and many, like Mrs. Mamie Eisenhower, Lady Franks, American wife of the British Ambassador and mother of five, Mrs. Grace Richards Conant, wife of Harvard's former president, who later became High Commissioner of Germany, and Mrs. Walter B. Cannon, wife of the famous physiologist, make a striking success of it. As Mrs. Theodore Roosevelt, Jr., puts it, "To be a successful wife is a career in itself, requiring, among other things, the qualities of a diplomat, a businesswoman, a good cook, a trained nurse, a school-teacher, a politician, and a glamour girl. It can be the most utterly rewarding of all careers." The unbelievably capable, intelligent, patient, vital, and withal highly alluring young women of the 1950's serve as continuing representatives of this group. Fashioned by the emergent responsibilities of World War II, they have continued to provide for the needs of their husbands, their homes, their children, and somewhat belatedly their own needs. Together with a G.I. allotment such a wife's job is often the sole family support while the young husband completes his interrupted education. Later as companions and lovers this wife and husband share the care of children, house building, and family financing. All functionally intertwined, Father is equally adept and happy in feeding the baby while Mother mows the grass; and the entire family as a unit invades the supermarket.

It is natural and to be expected that the names of women in this group are seldom known beyond the confines of their families and friends unless their husbands become famous. As a generic type, however, they constitute the large majority of women in this country and are the backbone of our civilization, a fact well recognized in popular song and literature, where they have long been enthroned.

Contributor without Marriage. The second of these roles satisfies women who almost completely sublimate their instinctive biological drives in creative work outside of childbearing. In this group are found the great reformers of the past century, such leaders as the fearless Susan B. Anthony, advocator of equal rights for women; Florence Nightingale, the courageous and indomitable nurse; Dr. Anna Howard Shaw, a great leader in woman suffrage; Jane Addams, the interpreter of the lives of the underprivileged; and Cecilia Beaux, the artist. Nearer the present decade we find Federal Judge Florence Allen, mentioned as a candidate for the Supreme Court of the United States; Dr. Martha Elliott, famed for research in the Children's Bureau and new member of the Harvard Medical School faculty; Katharine McBride, president of Bryn Mawr College; Dr. Florence Seibert, prize-winning researcher in tuberculosis; Malvina Hoffman, illustrious sculptress whose sensitive creations people the Hall of Man at Chicago's Field Museum; Emily Green Balch, winner of the Nobel prize in 1946 for her work toward world peace; and Helen Keller, who, although blind and deaf herself, has contributed so greatly to the betterment of other persons similarly afflicted. These women have each and all left an imprint on social, professional, educational, humanitarian, and personal standards.

Contributor in Addition to Marriage and Motherhood. The third role includes women who contribute through creative work yet earnestly desire wifehood and motherhood, and who in one way or another—with the help of their husbands—succeed in all three. That amazing and unbelievable Englishwoman, Elizabeth Fry, was a leader of this group. At a very early age she consecrated her life to the service of humanity and religion. During all her years she never wavered in her mission on behalf of the miserable and the distressed, in spite of the fact that she reared a large family, eleven children in all. By the time of her death she had spread her propaganda on prison reform through every quarter of Europe.

Madame Marie Curie was the mother of two daughters, coworker and discoverer with her husband of radium, first woman to be given the Nobel prize, and the only person ever to have received the Nobel prize twice. Incidentally, Marie Curie carried on her work after the sudden death of her husband and lived to see her two daughters excel in their own fields, one as a musician and writer, the other as a physicist. The great cinema actress, Marie Dressler, devoted herself through grueling years to an invalid husband, whom she comforted and supported through her professional achievements.

There are many examples among our contemporaries of women who have made outstanding contributions to husbands and children and to the needed work of the world. Queen Elizabeth II has endeared herself not only to England but to the world in her capacity as stateswoman, wife, and mother. The people of the United States take pride in Eleanor Roosevelt, courageous and dedicated worker for human rights; Clare Booth Luce, diplomat; Margaret Sanger, world worker for planned parenthood; Cornelia Otis Skinner, the popular and witty monologist; Pearl Buck, the famous novelist; Millicent Carey MacIntosh, president of Barnard College and mother of five; and Anne Morrow Lindbergh, whose subtle, sensitive, and imaginative writings portray her understanding of human beings. In addition, literally hundreds of women writers, actresses, artists, educators, and government and welfare workers, as well as those who have become successful in the business world, have proved beyond question that women who realize the full potentialities of their womanhood are creating in ways other than in the making of children and homes.

The women mentioned above are able to live creatively and, therefore, satisfactorily within the limits imposed by their environment. They find opportunity to convert their energy and ability into constructive activity. Other women similar to those whose situations were discussed earlier are less fortunate, or less strong or able, or less mature, and so fail in using their energy and ability satisfactorily. The emotional and physical giving and sharing involved in the day-by-day demands of marriage, jobs, or a combination of both are too much for them, and they retreat from the responsibilities of the fulfillment of their womanhood and project their unresolved conflicts on others. This is not their fault but their misfortune.

AFFIRMATION OF WOMANHOOD

Whatever the difficulties, whatever the solution, in every woman there can be found some spark of divine unrest, some residue of the collective consciousness of that past in which women were accepted by their world as contributors of equal value to men in creative power. "No risks," says Lawrence K. Frank, "are great enough to block the human need for aspiration and striving." The clue to this has been suggested by Kurt Lewin, who has shown that there must be in the individual an uninterrupted and free flow between the plane of reality and the plane of unreality, and to "that extent to which the individual's plane of unreality—call it fantasy, imagination, hopes— is restricted, his capacities for dealing with the actual world around him are by so much limited." Is not a realization on the part of men and of other women that all women need this free flow between the real and imaginative, that they are striving to recapture it, one of the most important resolutions of women's conflicting values?

There are now, happily, indications that this affirmation of womanhood, so long held in check, is about to become a creative force again. That new ideals for women are being incorporated into formal education is illustrated by these statements of Katharine McBride, president of Bryn Mawr College: "The student must have a knowledge of fundamentals . . . the perspective that will enable her to live in the midst of change. . . Courses taught as most of ours are taught not only contribute to maturity, it should be noted, they require it." In discussing ways in which the college can be of help to women, Mirra Komarovsky states convincingly, "The touchstone of a liberal education is not its uselessness for a vocation—but its perspective and scope, the range of principles which underlie it, the generality of the relationships which it reveals, the significance of the values it treats." Leading educators believe that such processes will serve women after college as a vitalizing springboard for the complex demands of job, husband, home, and children. In support of this, Kenneth Appel, past president of the American Psychiatric Association and President of the National Academy of Religion and Mental Health, asserted that women are more mature than men in personality attributes that make for civilization.

After school and college the large majority of girls become wives and mothers. During this phase of life miracles of modern medicine and surgery have already removed many of the physical ills which formerly sapped so much of women's strength. The spacing of children, too, has liberated them from the bondage of excessive childbearing. Mothers are now able to regard nature not as an end in itself, but, as all intimate relations with life should be, as a means of spiritual growth through full experience. Among the younger women many can now be found who run their simple homes with grace and capability, who believe in the beneficence of motherhood, the generous qualities of love mutually shared by men and women, and the importance of children as independent human beings.

As society accepts the concept of woman as a potentially mature human being—creative in body, in mind, and in spirit—the conflicting values which women have experienced will tend to disappear. If woman can again be conditioned to have the proper confidence in her capabilities, if she can imaginatively place herself in a creative relation to life, she can then bring to marriage a contribution that only women can bring to it. Of course women will have to compromise and develop competence now as formerly in meeting the exigencies of the times. So will men. So have all human beings through the ages. Conflict that necessitates compromise is a condition of life but is balanced in nature by the principle of co-operation and mutual aid.

Our world—the world of now—with all its difficulties, needs not men *or* women, most certainly not men *against* women, or women *against* men, but rather men *and* women, together shouldering the load and working to lighten it.

Men can encourage women, and women can encourage other women in their search to be of value. Men and women shoulder to shoulder can achieve real partnership, the sharing of two persons of equal value in the enterprise of marriage and of living. Marriage must contain the fundamentals of satisfaction, for marriage forms the nurturing ground for the attitudes and behavior for future citizens.

Topics for further thought:

1. The writer of this chapter says that society is reluctant to accept the concept of woman as a "potentially mature being." Discuss this idea, showing what have been the consequences of this societal attitude as related to husband-wife relationships in the home.

2. How can young boys and girls be trained to regard the position of the wife and mother as an important and desirable one in our society?

Selected reading references

Anshen, Ruth N., *The Family: Its Function and Destiny,* New York, Harper and Brothers, 1949.

An excellent symposium on the family in this and other cultures. See especially Chapter 19, "Sex and Character," by Erich Fromm. This chapter indicates that casting men and women into different social roles is not inevitable even though certain overtones may characterize each sex.

Deutsch, Helene, *Psychology of Women,* 2 vols., New York, Grune and Stratton, 1945.

A comprehensive two-volume work on the emotional functioning of women. A fairly orthodox psychoanalytic treatment that will adequately repay the effort required to master it.

Graduate Education for Women: The Radcliffe Ph.D., Cambridge, Harvard University Press, 1956.

Presents the results of a questionnaire study of the marriages, families, and careers of women who have received the Ph.D. from Radcliffe.

Komarovsky, Mirra, "Functional Analysis of Sex Roles," *American Sociological Review,* August, 1950, pp. 508-16.

Presents a series of generalizations concerning the effects of sex-related training on interpersonal relationships of men and women.

Mead, Margaret, *Male and Female,* New York, William Morrow and Company, 1949.

The product of a noted anthropologist's twenty-five years of study of the nature of sex differences and the ways in which different societies have patterned those differences. Implications for adjustment in modern American society.

20 WORKING WIVES AND MOTHERS

Mirra Komarovsky

THE working wife would hardly have merited a chapter to herself in a textbook published in 1890. In that year only 5 per cent of married women were employed outside the home. In 1957, however, the working wife is no longer a rarity. Some 11,839,000 women combined marriage with gainful employment in 1955.[1] World War II greatly stimulated the employment of wives. After a temporary decline following the war, their employment began to rise again and in 1955 reached a new high of 29.4 per cent of all married women.[2] In that year about 60 per cent of the woman labor force was married, whereas in 1940 only a little more than a third of all women workers were married.[3]

Despite the large number of working wives, home-plus-a-job is still a relatively new pattern of life. Understanding of its problems and discernment of factors that make for success or failure of this way of life are important. The first part of this chapter, then, presents some facts concerning the occupations and earnings of all employed homemakers; the remainder deals with husbands' attitudes and with the other factors that contribute to the success of their marriages.

OCCUPATIONS, EARNINGS, AND AGE

Occupations. Working wives are far from being predominantly career women; 34.8 per cent of them are clerical and sales workers,

---

[1] U.S. Department of Commerce, Bureau of the Census, Current Population Reports, Labor Force, December, 1955, p. 1.
[2] Ibid. p. 1.   [3] Ibid. p. 3.

21.8 per cent factory operatives. The rest are distributed among several occupations as follows: service jobs, 19.1 per cent; professional and technical jobs, 10.5 per cent; proprietory, managerial, and official jobs, 4.6 per cent; farm labor jobs, 7.3 per cent.[4]

By contrast with single working women, wives are more frequently employed in factory jobs and less frequently in clerical and professional occupations. Widowed, divorced, and separated women, many of whom enter the labor market suddenly and without previous training, are heavily concentrated in service jobs.

Another difference in the occupations of married and single women is the greater prevalence of part-time employment among the former. Statistics indicate, however, that not marriage as such but motherhood is associated with part-time jobs. About 37 per cent of employed mothers who had children under 18 years of age worked only part-time in 1950. In the absence of children under 18, employed married women held part-time jobs about as frequently as did single women. The occupations with the largest proportion of part-time workers are farm labor, private household work, and sales work.[5]

Working outside the home is especially difficult for mothers of young children. These mothers are not in the labor force to any great extent, though their employment is increasing. Only 11 per cent of mothers with preschool children were employed in 1948; in 1955 the proportion rose to 16.2 per cent. Mothers whose children are older, 6 to 17 years, are employed more frequently; about a third of them are in the labor force.[6] The proportion of working mothers is especially high among women who are widowed or separated from their husbands. The post-World War II years brought only a small increase in the employment of mothers of young children and a greater increase in the employment of mothers of school children.

The occupational distribution of college women differs greatly from that of the general population. In a sample survey of college women conducted in 1948, 70 per cent of those working were in the professions, mostly teachers; 12 per cent were proprietors, managers, and executives; 16 per cent were in clerical, sales, and other white-collar jobs; and 2 per cent were skilled and unskilled workers.[7]

[4] Ibid. p. 14.

[5] *Women as Workers, a Statistical Guide,* U.S. Department of Labor, Women's Bureau, 1953, p. 81.

[6] Bureau of the Census, op. cit. p. 12.

[7] E. Havermann and P. S. West, *They Went to College,* Harcourt, Brace & Company, 1952, p. 73.

Earnings. The economic motive for seeking employment is apparent from the fact that the proportion of working wives drops as the level of income of the husband rises. According to the Department of Labor, with husbands earning between $1000 and $3000 annually, about a third of the wives worked; only a seventh were employed when husbands earned $6000 or more.[8]

The earnings of married women as distinguished from those of single women are not readily ascertainable. Undoubtedly the average income of the former is lower if for no other reason than the greater frequency of part-time jobs among the married workers. In 1951 the median income of all women workers was $1361, and 67 per cent were earning under $2000 a year. Only ½ of 1 per cent earned $5000 and over during this year.[9]

One characteristic all working wives share with college working wives is this: the women whose husbands earn least are the ones more likely to hold jobs. The husbands of working wives earned less than the husbands of stay-at-home wives. In fact, the combined earnings of husband and wife about equaled the family income of the full-time homemaker. College women tend to work after marriage more frequently than do noncollege women, according to the census figures of 1950.

Although the earnings of women have increased since the prewar year of 1939, they have increased less than the earnings of men. Consequently the gap between the earnings of men and women has widened since 1939, and in 1951 the median income of working women was only about two-fifths that of men.

Age. The increase in the employment of women between 1890 and 1950 did not take place uniformly in all age groups. The most striking increase occurred among older women, those between the ages of 35 and 54. The decade 1940-50 intensified these long-term trends. In 1953 women 35 years and older constituted 56 per cent of all women workers, while before World War II women under 35 years of age predominated in the labor force.[10]

Recent evidence points to some interesting facts concerning married workers. The greatest proportion of working wives are women in their late thirties and early forties, of whom 33.7 per cent were employed in 1955. In the same year only 26.5 per cent of wives under

[8] Women's Bureau, op. cit. p. 84.
[9] Ibid. p. 87.
[10] Ibid. p. 45.

35 were working.[11] It appears that married women are returning to work or beginning to work in middle age, after their childbearing and child-rearing duties have been reduced.

Thus the phrase "working wife" does not designate a uniform pattern of life. Working wives come from various walks of life; some are childless, others are mothers; some work part-time; the occupations and earnings of the husbands vary. They face different problems: the problems of a childless career woman, fearful that her professional success may endanger her marriage, are altogether different from those of the factory-worker mother whose earned dollar is spent for necessities and who returns home after a day's work to a round of washing, cooking, cleaning, and mending.

THE ATTITUDE OF THE HUSBAND

In the absence of children many couples accept as a satisfactory mode of life the wife's combining the duties of home and job. Case studies reveal the crucial importance of the husband's attitude to the success or failure of the employed homemaker. Even if he is sympathetic and co-operative, other circumstances may make her double job too difficult. With lack of moral support, the employed homemaker finds the cost of the combination high.

Studies of successful marriages prove this much: a husband can accept a successful career wife without either resentment or demoralization. All the features of such marriages which allegedly hold so inevitable a threat to the male ego apparently can prove harmless and at times even be turned to his advantage. A husband whose career wife occasionally has to work in the evening of course may be inconvenienced, but he need not suffer the added injury of self-doubt. He need not say, for example, "What kind of a sucker am I to put up with it? What is a wife for if not to share her husband's leisure?" The results of one study showed that the high salary earned by the wife did not break her husband's morale. He accepted her economic partnership before they had children; he accepted her decision to give up her job when the combination of motherhood and job proved too difficult. When the need arose, he adjusted realistically to taking over the full financial support of the family. Another study reported that a magazine writer rushed to the telephone to share with her husband the news of her promotion; she knew that she could count on an

[11] Bureau of the Census, op. cit. p. 1.

appreciative response from him. In other words, it is possible for a man to experience such situations as these without any loss of self-esteem. If a man's ego is not threatened, practical adjustments can be worked out; moreover, the husband is freed to enjoy the economic and other benefits accruing from his wife's occupation. The psychological castration of the husband is not a necessary consequence of his wife's career. Happy adjustments *can* be made. Whether they *will* be made depends upon the norms held by the man and upheld by his milieu regarding the role of women in marriage.

Contrast the man who swelled with pride at a social gathering because, of all the women present, his wife was the only one who was both a mother and a businesswoman, with the man who considered his wife's ambitions to succeed on a job as a perverse evasion of marriage duties. The latter said, "No normal woman whose husband satisfies her would have an interest in an outside occupation." One husband derived pride from having married a successful woman and saw a triumph in the situation. The other husband felt a sense of defeat over his wife's success.

In the "success" case studies such statements as these recurred: "It was understood that I was to continue to work," and "Our families took it as a matter of course that I would not give up my job upon marriage." Now and then, even in these marriages, a wife may tease a husband by saying, "When are you going to retire and let the Mrs. bring home the bacon?" Women friends may marvel at the teacher-mother—"How in the world do you manage?"—but out of her hearing they may assure each other that this or that shortcoming in her children must be due to her career. But by and large throughout the findings of the studies the emancipated views of the husbands were endorsed by friends and associates.

The husband's attitude is not merely a reflection of the mores of his social group; his emotional make-up and the quality of his marriage play an important part in his reaction to his wife's dual efforts. Emotional needs first of all may dictate which of the several current ideologies regarding the woman's role he will adopt, sometimes contrary to the pressures of his milieu. An insecure man may cling to the traditional masculine role. It was this kind of man who, in one study, was reported to have said: "I'd rather turn on the gas than let my wife work." On the other hand and under the guise of emancipated views, a weak man may seek a career woman upon whom he can lean. More complex are the motivations of the weak man who chooses a wife precisely because her strength promises a refuge but who, in his own struggles for self-respect, immediately turns against her because she is not a "real" woman. The emotional make-up of the man operates in other ways, apart from determining the choice of ideologies.

The husbands in the success case studies appeared to be fairly secure and normally aggressive; marriage adjustment seemed to be better than average. Were this not the case, myriads of adjustments to be explored in the relatively novel home-plus-a-job pattern would provide just so many occasions for clashes.

Even when the business-couple arrangement is socially sanctioned, its novelty gives rise to many situations undefined by custom. For example, how much does a wage-earning wife contribute to family support? When every penny is spent on necessities the question of luxuries does not arise. But with couples in a higher-income group, the disposition of the wife's earnings may become a source of conflict. Is she to contribute to family support in proportion to her earnings? Should some allowance be made for the homemaking responsibilities which she retains despite her job? Another example: what does a husband do with himself if a wife is busy and he is free from work? And how does a husband behave with his wife's job associates? The counterpart situations have been long since smoothed by custom.

Well-adjusted personalities and a harmonious marriage cushion the strain of novel situations. This statement is not identical with the widespread conviction that "it all depends upon personality." After all, even an inferiority-ridden male would not be oppressed by his wife's excellence in cooking, and even the most secure man in the world at one time could have been mortified because his wife joined a woman's suffrage group. Similarly, the need to work out almost singlehandedly adaptations to novel situations puts a strain upon the best-adjusted personalities. In a period of great stability, to stress personality and to play down social norms and conditions may be justified. At such times variations in behavior may be attributed to the unique emotional configurations of various personalities. But with norms and conditions changing and becoming diverse, the interplay of social and emotional factors in accounting for differences in behavior must be constantly watched.

The problem of many a young working wife is how to stop being one. With the birth of a child the two-income family increases its expenses at the same time that it reduces its income. When the earnings of the husband are too low for what the couple considers a minimum standard of living, the frustrations of delaying childbearing may be serious.

FACTORS CONTRIBUTING TO THE SUCCESS OF WORKING MOTHERS

Those who combine motherhood with an outside job require a particularly auspicious configuration of circumstances and personalities to guarantee success in both jobs. Imperfections that normally would not threaten the family may disturb the more precarious balance of a pioneering pattern.

Apart from the sympathetic co-operation of the husband certain factors such as these contribute to the success of working mothers: good health, adequate training and work experience before marriage, short and flexible hours on the job, relatively high income which permits household help. Even with these necessary conditions other factors must be considered. For example, mothers satisfied with the all-round effects of their job-holding nevertheless admit that a severe limitation of social life is necessary to guard the time the parents reserve for the children. However, though readily tolerated by some, a curtailment of social life would constitute a severe deprivation for others—for husbands, for instance, whose careers require public and social engagements, and for couples who value an active social life. Added then to the list of conditions making for success is the ability of the working mother to restrict her social activities without a feeling of great loss.

Another factor that contributes to success is a reasonably favorable public opinion. It has been observed that middle-class public opinion in the south or the middle west is less favorable to the employment of mothers than in the east or far west. For example, a mother living in a small southern town returned to teaching when a medical examination of her husband revealed that he was likely to become an invalid. The censure of her friends was so severe because she was working that she wondered whether she had to reveal her husband's impending disability to regain their social status with their friends. Another working mother complained that her neighbors invariably blamed her job for the slightest mishap to her child.

Though a mother may earn enough money to employ a nurse to care for the child, this nurse (or, perhaps in some cases, a relative) sometimes creates additional problems of human relations. There are mothers who, to avoid rivalry and conflict, deliberately choose warm-hearted and reliable persons who easily subordinate themselves to the mother in decisions concerning the child. Other mothers become jealous of the affection the child shows to the nurse. One professional woman confessed: "I hate to admit it but I'm jealous of the baby's nurse and resent any evidence of the baby's attachment to her. I have had a headache all day because of what happened yesterday. The high spot of my day is bathing the baby. I was a few minutes late from work yesterday, and the nurse didn't wait with the bath. I was furious with her and would have fired her at once if she weren't so good with the baby." The headache was caused not merely by the understandable disappointment but by the jealousy which this woman tends to exhibit in all her relations and by still deeper reasons back of the jealousy. The relation of the absentee mother to the nurse is potentially an explosive one. Successful working mothers handle this relationship more happily than the woman just cited; however, a reliable nurse is not a sufficient factor for success.

Even with the best-conceivable family adjustment, the deviant character of the working mother's life creates some problems in her relationship to her children, even if it be only the child's occasional complaint, "Why can't you stay at home like other mothers?" The mother who has no misgivings about her love for the child will be troubled by this question only in so far as it disturbs the child, but she will not magnify this disturbance. "Why aren't you like other mothers?" is a question that might precipitate an attack of guilt and anxiety in some women; others will answer the question by calmly explaining their reasons for working. Similarly, it is all too easy for a guilt-ridden mother to hold herself responsible for every cold, splinter, or bruised knee of the child. She is abetted in this tendency by the general public attitude toward a deviant pattern. Its shortcomings are more visible and the fact of variance provides an obvious explanation of every deficiency. If a daughter rebels the mother's career would be cited as the cause of the rebellion. Similar behavior of a child in a typical family would be attributed to adolescence. It takes a sense of security in a mother to remain objective in the face of inevitable problems in the lives of her children. The quality of a mother's feeling for the child, therefore, is an additional significant factor in the total success picture.

As noted above, relatively short and flexible hours of work, especially for the mother with small children, contribute to the success of the working mother in her adjustment within the family. Mothers who work long hours complain of various disturbances in their relations with young children. For example, one mother said: "I try to pack a lot of bringing-up into the little time my four-year-old boy and I spend together. I am afraid he will think of me as a nagging mother, but I cannot overlook bad manners and other undesirable traits he picks up during the day." Just the opposite feeling was expressed by a mother who felt she was too lenient with her child; she did not wish to mar their brief time together with criticism. Another mother, thoroughly satisfied with the care given her baby by a trusted nurse, felt that she herself was the loser by not being able to enjoy the baby for longer periods of time. The complaint of some full-time housewives who spend too much time with their children to maintain freshness and perspective is here matched by the opposite dissatisfaction. The time the working mother can spend with her children may be too brief for the normal range of shared experiences—criticism, praise, pity, confidence, humor, playfulness, love, anger, dependence, rebellion, or even indifference. To that extent the relationship may lack depth or suffer some distortion.

Mothers who work long hours have to schedule the hours of the day very tightly and must depend upon others. These mothers complain of the sense of pressure on them. Arrangements the mother makes for the day presuppose a perfect co-ordination that cannot always be counted on. The most careful plans run askew if a maid is late, if the child catches a cold, or the mother's job requires some overtime work. The success factor is challenged by problems and complaints when working mothers put in long and nonflexible hours on the job.

The co-operation the husband gives his wife is an important factor in the success of the working mother. How much help in domestic affairs should the housewife secure from her husband? Today, in some young marriages where both are working, the husband has a considerable share in homemaking. For example, a working wife of a veteran completing his graduate studies reports that her husband takes over a number of jobs around the house. She said, "We have worked out a system satisfactory to both of us. The only time it breaks down is when we have visitors—family or friends. When company comes he gets waited on and we, so to speak, quickly sweep all our working arrangements under the rug and out of the sight of the public."

Life in housing developments seems to have weakened the psychological resistances to the emerging patterns of husband-wife cooperation. One young mother said, "My husband is wonderful with the baby. At first he wouldn't do anything around the house that was visible to the neighbors, such as carrying the laundry to the neighborhood machines or washing the windows. Now he thinks nothing of going to the laundry in the evening and talking with the other men while they all are waiting for the wash to get done." Group sanction apparently has given this husband the reassurance he needed so that his male dignity was not threatened by his engaging in "woman's work." Mechanization of housework also may make these tasks more palatable to him—operating a washing machine seems more masculine an act somehow than washing clothes over a washboard.

A wife who returned to teaching because of her husband's poor health and their diminished earnings reports that her husband's greater share in the upbringing of their son has had happy consequences for their family. She said:

> Eventually I hope to be able to stop working, but my job has worked out much better than either of us ever dreamed it could. We have learned to share each other's work. I earn part of our income and my husband helps with Johnny, who adores his father. We share something that, had we not been dividing the responsibility, we never would have experienced. My husband told me that we have stumbled upon some happiness we would possibly never have known had we lived as we originally planned. Even when I stop working my husband will continue to have a big hand in the care of our boy.

Not only changing social conditions of life but also certain intellectual currents have tended to modify the role of the father. The scientific searchlight turned upon childhood in the last few decades has revealed its crucial importance for personality, and this knowledge is being disseminated to increasing numbers of people. More recently groups concerned with family-life education have been campaigning to involve the father in the role of parenthood from the moment of his child's birth. In strata exposed to these influences, many young fathers have accepted the new challenges with great earnestness. In such circles social pressure changed its direction. It is no longer the father who wheels the baby carriage on a Sunday morning who feels apologetic but the one who refuses to do so. One woman told an interviewer in the presence of her husband, "My husband thinks that a father's job doesn't begin until his son is old enough to be taken to a baseball game." Her irony scored a victory, judging from the defensive explanations of her husband. In such circles, men may experience a conflict between their occupational and family interests.

A professional man married to a woman whose professional reputation almost equals his own remarked:

I used to be a militant feminist, but now I envy my father his conventional marriage. I remember that when father returned home in the evening, mother would make us children tiptoe out of his way to allow him to rest. When I come home, not matter how tense and weary, I have to play with the children because I know that their mother and I were both away during the day. My mother could protect my father's rest, surround him with comfort, and adjust herself to his needs. I cannot count on such services from my wife, whose career is just as exacting as mine. She may need to relax when I am in a creative fury, and I may need a "backer upper" just when she wants to tell me some news rather than do all the listening.

Obviously marriages with two such strenuous and absorbing careers present additional problems. A man in a similar marriage situation remarked to his wife, "What both of us need is a good wife." In so far as the pressure to succeed is still heavier upon the male, the man who envied his father may suffer from a double dose of obligations: the undiminished pressure for occupational success and the new expectation of a partnership with his wife in domestic responsibilities.

Even when account is taken of the husband's help in the home— as well as help from children, relatives, and servants—there is no ignoring the fact that the employed homemaker still has to carry the chief burden of home management and a considerable share of the housework. It is not surprising, therefore, that she has less leisure than either the housewife or the unmarried job-holding woman.

SUMMARY

Because even the best-adjusted working wife carries the double load of job and homemaking, she must be all the surer of her values and more efficient about her means. She must realize that the variety of roles now open to women does not mean that every woman must strive to excel in them all. At one and the same time she cannot be the perfect housekeeper, the glamour girl, the most sought-after committee member, the best mother, the most successful careerist. She may have to simplify standards of housekeeping and forego some social activities. She must know *herself* and the needs of her family and strive to achieve the balance that is right for her particular family. Of course there will be days when the most successful working wife will look longingly over her shoulder at the stay-at-home wife. She must remember, though, that there are times in any homemaker's life when she, too, would eagerly change places with the working wife.

Topics for further thought:

1. It is becoming increasingly common for the American woman to combine marriage and motherhood with full-time employment outside her home. Discuss some of the effects which this relatively new pattern of living has upon the members of a family.

2. Is the general pattern of family life changing to adjust to this new triple role of the woman? Will it change even more in the future?

Selected reading references

Gruenberg, Sidonie M., and Krech, Hilda S., *The Many Lives of Modern Woman: A Guide to Happiness in Her Complex Role,* New York, Doubleday and Company, 1952.
Emphasizes the mulitple roles offered to modern women. Written especially for the intelligent woman who wants a home and a career. Positive approach to personal problems and happiness.

Hottel, Althea K., *How Fare American Women?* Washington, D.C., American Council on Education, 1955.
An assessment of the status of American women at the mid-century.

Komarovsky, Mirra, "Cultural Contradictions and Sex Roles," *American Journal of Sociology,* November, 1946, pp. 184-9.
Analyzes the conflicting roles and role expectations of educated American women.

Komarovsky, Mirra, *Women in the Modern World: Their Education and Their Dilemmas,* Boston, Little, Brown and Company, 1953.

A careful appraisal of the inconsistencies in modern women's roles by America's foremost student of the subject.

White, Lynn, Jr., "The Changing Context of Women's Education," *Marriage and Family Living,* November, 1955, pp. 291-5.
A provocative argument for liberal arts education as the kind of education best designed to meet the needs of modern women.

21 HOME MANAGEMENT AND FINANCE

Howard F. Bigelow

Most people marry today, not because they have to in order to live—for many single persons live rich and worth-while lives —but because they expect through marriage to be able to do more of what they want to do. Marriage provides security in personal relations. It provides social status, a base from which to operate in activities outside the home, a place to go for care when sick, for rest and relaxation when well, and for love and companionship and affection. And it is also a place where a lot of necessary work gets done. On the economic side the family provides for the wants of its members.

While of necessity the members of a family group sacrifice some personal freedom for emotional and economic security, at the same time they gain a significant degree of independence of markets and money income by pooling their money and skills and personal possessions and doing for each other many things for which single persons must pay.

Everyone knows that it is impossible for two persons to live more cheaply than one. But it is entirely possible for two people to live together for a much smaller money outlay than they must spend if they live apart. How much better the members of a family will be able to live depends upon the effectiveness with which they manage the family's resources.

THE FAMILY'S RESOURCES

The resources of the family consist of the family's money income from employment and from investments, the skills, abilities, time and energy of its members, equipment and personal possessions which it has available for use in supplementing its purchases in the market, and the community resources available for the use of families of its type.

In taking stock of their resources, families think first of their money incomes. In the first six months of 1956, personal income in the United States reached an all-time high of $323,000,000,000. The average family income was a little more than $6500. Three-quarters of the families had less than this average income. The median family income, of which half the families in the country have more and half have less, was about $4400. Probably the middle 50 per cent of American families had incomes between $3000 and $6500. These estimates of family incomes are before taxes. In the lower-income groups, income and social-security taxes take from 5 to 10 per cent, and in the upper-income levels a much larger proportion of the family incomes.

At the same time at least half the families in the United States own their own homes free and clear or have a substantial equity in them. Two-thirds of the families in the United States own automobiles. There are more radios in use than there are families, though there may be a few families without one. Probably three-quarters of the families own at least part of their furniture and a substantial amount of household equipment. Every family has some sort of clothing inventory. Every member of every family has a more or less extensive list of personal possessions.

A substantial proportion of families, even in the lower-income groups, have some small income from investments, if nothing more than a few war bonds. At least half, and perhaps more, of the gainfully employed are or are becoming eligible for some sort of social-security benefits.

There are few if any families that do not make some use of community resources—schools, churches, parks, highways, police and fire protection, health services of various sorts, or the variety of services provided for servicemen by the Veterans Administration.

Thus resources of the family include much more than a family's money income, though in a market economy such as ours a minimum of money income is fundamental. There is plenty of evidence that successful and happy family living is possible at every income level, except the very lowest, and that too much money, instead of making successful marriage easier, often makes it more difficult. The fundamental problem in family management and finance is to make the best use not only of the family's money income but also of the time and energy and skills of the family members, of their possessions, and of available community resources. From the point of view of the individual family, the best use is that which will enable the members of the family to satisfy as many as possible of their most important wants.

THE FAMILY'S WANTS

Every family wants food, warmth, clothing and shelter, facilities for transportation and communication, and some provision for health, education, and recreation. In addition to these wants, which are satisfied for the most part with material goods, are a number of intangible but equally important wants: security, independence, companionship and affection, social position, the respect of others and self-respect, and even a bit of adventure now and then.

In the satisfaction of wants the material and the immaterial aspects cannot be separated. Some social prestige comes from being able to order an expensive steak in a crowded butcher shop. In a time of housing shortage homeownership gives a much-wanted sense of security. Ownership of an automobile gives freedom of movement. For some people the knowledge that they are well dressed gives a sense of personal security fully as important to them as the respect of others which their clothing commands. Even the affectional side of family living has its economic aspects. Personal relations within the family are often improved if the husband brings home a box of candy now and then or an extra pair of nylons. Flowers on anniversaries mean much to many people. Even husbands who are supposed to be primarily concerned with keeping down expenses appreciate a good-looking new shirt or a new cigarette lighter if it is purchased with money the wife has saved from her share of the family money.

There are three general ways in which families may provide the goods needed to satisfy the wants of their members. They may purchase what they want in the market, they may produce them for their own use, or they may use the facilities, both governmental and nongovernmental, which are available in their community. There is no one way in which all families satisfy any one want. Most families get their own meals, but many families buy their meals outside the home, and most families eat out at least occasionally. Men buy most of their clothing ready-made. Women buy much of theirs, though if they like to sew, or are hard to fit with the current styles, or want better clothing than they can afford to buy ready-made, they may make a good deal of their own clothing. Some families buy the children's clothing as a matter of course, while others are equally matter-of-fact about doing most of the sewing for their children. Most families send their children to public schools, though some religious groups prefer parochial to public education; in some communities excellent private schools do a flourishing business. In metropolitan areas most families live in rented apartments. In smaller communities a substantial majority own their own homes. Similarly, in smaller communities probably four-fifths of the families have at least one family car. In the larger metropolitan centers (with the possible exception of Detroit and Los Angeles) only from one-third to one-half have automobiles, and even the car-owning families depend to a large extent on public transportation.

The quality of living which a family enjoys depends in part on the number of wants satisfied, in part on the ways in which those wants are satisfied, and in part on the balance maintained between different types of wants. Because of the diversity in individual family situations there can be no one best way for all families to work out their problems of management and finance. Instead there are many right ways, and there are also many wrong ways. Each family, therefore, must work out its own problems in its own way, with due regard for the physical and social environment in which its members live, for the resources which the family has available, for the work which its members are called upon to do, and for the special needs and interests of all the family members.

WORK AND MANAGEMENT PLANS

In managing family affairs there is no longer any traditional division of men's work and women's work. World War I, the depression of the 1930's, and World War II have ended the tradition, so far as America is concerned, that the place of women is in the home. If a woman can contribute more to the family by working at home, that is her place. If she can contribute more by working outside and adding to the family's money income, that is what she should do.

However, if wives are to help by working outside for money, husbands can expect to help with the work of the family at home. The eight-hour day and the forty-hour week have left the husband with time to do many things about the house which his wife did of necessity when her husband was employed from seven in the morning till six at night every day in the week.

In the 1920's it was taken for granted that the husband would earn the money and his wife would spend most of it. Now he has time to help with the spending. Especially at the supermarkets men go along to help carry home the week's groceries. During World War II, when husbands were away in the service, wives took over the complete management of the family affairs, including such activities as the payment of taxes and insurance, the supervision of repairs to the house, and the upkeep of the family car.

The problem of management, therefore, is no longer a simple problem of automatic division into men's work and women's work. Instead each family is free to work out for itself the division of work and of management which makes most effective use of the abilities and connections of both the husband and the wife. As the children become old enough they can be given a share in the family responsibilities.

There are a number of typical work-and-management patterns. A family can select the one best suited to its immediate situation and adapt it to its immediate needs, modifying it from time to time to suit changing conditions.

For example: If both husband and wife are employed, both will be helping to earn the money income, both will share in the spending, and both should share in the other work of the household. If the husband only is gainfully employed, the wife will assume a larger responsibility for the work of the household, for much more of the routine planning and management, but she will plan some work and some purchasing for him to do, selecting the sort of thing that he can do best. If the husband is a business executive or a professional man whose work makes heavy demands on his time or takes him often away from home, it may be wise for the wife to take over almost completely the management of family affairs, even if she has to hire some household help to give her the time she needs for purchasing and management. This will leave him only the responsibility of the family's investments and insurance and taxes, which he can handle along with his business or professional activities.

There are similarly a number of ways in which to divide the detailed work and management of the family. One frequently used is for the wife to plan the meals and purchase and prepare the food, shop for her own and the children's clothes, and take care of the details of day-to-day household operation, while her husband sees that the rent is paid, or that the payments are made on the house, and that taxes are paid and the home kept in repair. Usually the husband sees to the upkeep of the car and to the heavy work around the yard, though if his wife likes to work outdoors she may take over the care of the flowers and the kitchen garden. The husband usually manages the family's savings and investments, though if his wife has good business judgment he may consult her about individual investments. Usually the husband takes over the purchase of any articles in which his business connections give him special advantages. If his wife has better money sense than he does and is a good shopper, he may turn over most of the buying to her and put in his time doing more work around the house.

Many families find that it works better to change their division of work from time to time. When the children are small it may be wise for the husband to take over some of the buying and some of the heavier work which his wife did earlier in their married life. Or his wife may prefer to have him take over the care of the children when he is at home and leave her free to get out of the house and do the shopping.

In any case, it is important that each family work out either formally or informally a clearly understood and definite plan for the handling of family affairs. So far as possible it is desirable for each of the members of the family to do what he or she can do and likes to do best. Usually the plan works more smoothly if each member of the family keeps the other informed as to what he is doing and participates in current planning. Usually formal planning sessions are not necessary, though it often helps to sit down and talk over some particular problem. Members even of fairly large families usually know each other well enough so that in their planning they can take each other's preferences into account without formal votes or majority decisions. In fact, some formal family councils which are dominated by one or two strong personalities are actually less democratic in their processes than less formal planning procedures.

TECHNIQUES OF FINANCIAL PLANNING

Many families find that financial planning is one of their most difficult problems. The first step in working out a spending plan for a family is to make a rough plan in general terms, so much for food, so much for clothing, so much for shelter, so much for the family car, and so on, in order to get an idea of what can and what cannot be done with the family's money income. In making this preliminary estimate the family should plan in terms of take-home pay rather than in terms of income before taxes and other deductions. If the family has any considerable amount of business or investment income it must be sure to make adequate allowance for taxes.

Some families like to make a preliminary plan by setting aside a given percentage of the family's income for each of the major divisions of family expenditure. Others find they get a better idea of what they can do with their money if they make their preliminary estimates in dollars and then see what the available dollars will buy.

When the members of the family have a general idea of what can and what cannot be done with the family's income they should work out a detailed spending plan. Since there are a number of expenditures which must be made once a month, many families prefer to work out in detail each month's expenditures. Others prefer to plan the use of their money from payday to payday, as they expect to receive it, planning exactly how they are to spend each pay check.

In making a spending plan, a family must provide both for expenditures, like food and rent and utilities, which must be made each week or each month, and for expenditures which come at longer intervals, like insurance, taxes, vacations, the license for the car, and the winter's fuel. Some families include these occasional expenditures as an integral part of their detailed spending plan, adding them in the months in which they must be met. Other families prefer to make a separate plan for these larger occasional expenditures, setting aside each payday in a special account enough to cover them.

Time is required to make a comprehensive, realistic, and workable spending plan. It cannot be done in an hour between the supper dishes and the evening movies. The things for which a family must spend its money are so many and varied that it seems almost impossible to make a plan without overlooking something. But by working out the plan a little at a time, first planning in detail for expenditures for food, for shelter, for clothing, and so on; then putting the parts of the plan together and finally checking to be sure that there will be money available to make each expenditure when it must be made, any family that can add and subtract can make a usable plan which will enable its members to get more for their money than would be possible with unplanned spending.

Food. For most families food is the largest single item of expenditure. The family's food should be nutritively adequate, though not necessarily elaborate or expensive. In the last few years information about nutrition has become available in simple graphic form. By observing a few simple, easy rules one can plan a nutritively adequate diet for a family and at the same time make plenty of allowance for reasonable food preferences. People can have a nutritively good diet at every income level except the very lowest, although there will always be a few families, even in the upper-income groups, who spend generously for elaborate but nutritively inadequate diets.

Although it is not necessary to spend large amounts of money for food, families with larger incomes ordinarily spend more for food than families of the same size with smaller incomes, but their food expenditures usually take a smaller percentage of the family income. Large families in any given income group usually spend more for food than do small families, but they spend less per person.

The best way to estimate the amount that a family should spend for food is to plan in terms of so many cents per person per day, rather than in terms of a given percentage of the family income. In 1935-6, 40 cents per person per day was the national average. In 1953, food costs were more than double what they were in 1935-6. On that basis a family of four persons in 1953 was doing a good job of feeding the family if it spent not more than 90 cents per person per day, or $25 a week, or $108 a month. A family of two may find it necessary to spend from 10 to 20 cents per person more than the four-person family, since it buys its food in smaller quantities. A larger family, of five or six or more, may be able to save from 10 to 20 per cent over a family of four.

Any family can cut its food costs materially by spending time to save money. It can cut from 10 to 20 per cent and sometimes more from the cash outlay required to provide the family with food by careful buying in self-service supermarkets instead of full-service stores, by buying raw materials and preparing food, baking bread and cakes and pastries, by cooking potatoes, beans, turnips, and cabbage instead of opening cans, by buying low-cost stews and roasts instead of minute steaks and chops, and by growing a garden and doing the family's canning.

Clothing. The provision of clothing for the family involves the purchase of three types of items, those like shirts, ties, and hose, which must be purchased more or less regularly throughout the year, a group of seasonal items which must be purchased in the fall, winter, spring, and summer, and a few major articles—heavy coats, raincoats, and suits—which must be purchased only once in two or three years.

Studies of family expenditures indicate that for any group of families at almost any income level the proportion of the family income spent for clothing is surprisingly uniform. In the early 1950's, families spent about 12 per cent of their income for clothing. Families in the larger cities spent slightly more. Families in the rural areas spent slightly less. These percentages held true for the most part regardless of the size of the family. But while the average expenditures were uniform, variation from the averages on the part of individual families was greater than in almost any other item of family expenditure. In any year in which a family must buy a number of expensive garments its expenditures for clothing will run much above the average. In years when the family is using garments bought a year or more before, the current outlay for clothing will be less than the average.

How the family's clothing expenditures are divided among the different members of the family depends in part upon the income level, in part upon the occupation of the husband, in part on whether or not the wife is working outside the home, and in part on the number and age of the children. Usually when the children are small parents spend more money for their own clothes than they do for the children's, but when the boys and girls are in high school and college, usually the family spends more for the daughter than for her mother, and more for the son than for his father. For this is a time in the lives of the young people when it is highly important for them to feel well dressed.

There are a number of ways in which to plan for clothing expenditures. Some families prefer to make the bulk of their clothing purchases at two or three times during the year, buying a complete outfit of spring clothing just before Easter, some summer things early in June, and their fall clothing in September or October. Other families plan to buy a few new things at the beginning of each season but postpone the purchase of many garments till the end-of-season sales. The family with a regular income frequently finds it easier to spread clothing expenditures along through the year. The family with irregular income may find it easier to outfit the family completely when they have the money available.

There are definite advantages to planning clothing expenditures for two or three years at a time. A family can even cut its clothing expenditures by planning to purchase expensive articles for the husband one year and for the wife the next. Except for the periods when the children are growing rapidly, it is also possible to do the same thing for them, selecting garments that are large enough and of good enough quality to last for two years.

Families purchase a number of garments with the intention of using them for several years. Most women buy street dresses with the idea of wearing them at least two years. Fully as many plan to use them for three years as plan to discard them at the end of one year. This does not mean that they do not buy a new dress every year. Rather they buy a new dress every spring or fall, and they also have a last year's dress to wear shopping and perhaps a dress two years old to wear to the market on rainy days. Similarly there are some indications that men average three quarters of a suit a year. That means they buy a suit every year for three years. The fourth year they buy an overcoat or a topcoat instead. Thus they usually have two or three wearable suits hanging in the closet.

There are a number of ways to keep down the outlay for clothing. Clothing should be bought with the length of time it is to be used definitely in mind. By spending a fifth or a quarter more for a better quality of garment it is possible to get one that will wear twice as long, but if the garment is needed only for a single season it is usually cheaper to buy a quality that will be worn out when it is to be discarded. Substantial savings are possible by buying out of season those articles in which fashion is not too important. It is possible to save by buying one article which can be put to a number of uses, or a few articles which can be combined in a number of ways, rather than by duplicating complete outfits. In families with children, clothing can be passed from one to another, redesigning the garments when necessary. The cost of clothing can be cut substantially by buying materials and making the garments, since materials usually cost only one-third to one-half as much as finished garments of similar quality.

Shelter. The type of housing a family selects should depend largely on what the family wants to do at home. In the war years families had little choice. They had to take what was available in the community and adjust their manner of living to the kind of shelter they could obtain. In ordinary times, however, it is usually possible to choose both the type of shelter and the way to pay for it. If both the husband and wife are employed they may prefer a small, conveniently located apartment which can be kept in order with a minimum of work. If only the husband is employed the family may prefer a larger house in which the wife can do more for her family.

A young couple with small capital may start housekeeping in a couple of light-housekeeping rooms or in a small rented apartment. Then when they have had time to save a little money they can buy some furniture and move to a somewhat larger unfurnished apartment. If they plan to locate permanently in the community they may use part of their savings for furniture and part for a down payment on a house, and use the money they would otherwise save to complete the payments on their home.

The family's choice of a home determines not only the amount that must be paid for the house itself but a number of other expenses as well. If the family rents a completely furnished, heated apartment, the rent includes the payment for fuel, utilities, and the upkeep of the furniture. If it rents an unfurnished house, the type of house, its construction, exposure, and heating plant determine within rather close limits the amount the family must pay for fuel and utilities. The size, design, and construction of the house determine the amount of work necessary to keep it clean, in good order, and in good repair. A large house does not always require more housekeeping than a small one. For in a small house, if the space provided is not quite adequate for all the different things the members of the family do, frequent getting out and putting away of equipment is necessary, while in a large house, with separate space for different activities—a sewing room, a laundry, a rumpus room, and the like—it is possible to walk out and close the door for a time on partly finished tasks. The location of the house determines the amount and type of transportation the family must use and the amount the family will have to pay for transportation to and from work, to stores, to church and school.

It is impossible to make any exact statement about the amount a family should spend for shelter. Usually in the income groups under $5000 or $6000, families with small incomes must spend a larger proportion of their income for shelter than do families with the larger incomes. Larger families usually spend a somewhat smaller proportion of their incomes for shelter than do smaller families, though frequently they get as much or more space per person by living in the older, larger houses. Families in large cities usually spend more for shelter and get less for their money than do families living in smaller communities.

It is usually unwise for a family to spend more than 20 or 25 per cent of its income for the rent of an unfurnished house. A family living in an apartment with everything furnished can expect to pay 35 or 40 per cent of its income for accommodations of similar quality. If the family plans to own a car it should keep payments for shelter to not more than one-sixth of its income. A family ordinarily should not buy a house that costs more than twice its annual income, or three times its present income if it is sure of a steadily increasing income during the period it is planning to live in the house. If a family is paying for its home on the installment plan it must be sure that the payments on the house and provision for taxes, repairs, and insurance do not add up to more than the family is able to pay for rent and set aside regularly for savings.

In deciding whether to rent or buy a home a family must consider the advantages and disadvantages of each method of payment for shelter. Ordinarily, if, over a period of years, the family rents the same kind of shelter it would be willing to own, there is not much difference in the cost. For while the homeowning family does not have to pay rent every month, it must pay taxes, make needed repairs, and either invest substantial amounts from time to time in modernization and improvement or take a substantial loss in the value of its property from depreciation and obsolescence over a number of years. And it must count as part of the cost of owning its home the interest which the money it puts into the home would earn if invested in securities.

When it buys a home the family determines once for all the type, the size, and the cost of its home. The type of shelter cannot be easily adjusted to changes in the family's shelter needs. The family is protected against increases in shelter costs which come with increases in property values, except in so far as these increases affect the cost of repairs and taxes. The cost of the family's housing can be reduced only by sale. Once its home is paid for, however, the family has more flexibility in making expenditures for shelter, for when it is necessary to keep expenditures to a minimum it can postpone improvements and reduce its current outlay to no more than the payment of taxes, insurance, and a minimum of absolutely necessary repairs.

The family that rents its home must make regular payments every month. By moving from time to time it can adapt its shelter to changing family needs and to changes in the family income. It must face the possibility of increases in rents during periods of rising prices and housing shortages. It can adjust its expenditures for shelter downward when prices or incomes decline.

The family that buys its home on the installment plan has some of the advantages of owning and some of the disadvantages of renting. There is no landlord to raise the rent, but the family must make the payments on the property regularly or lose not only a place to live but a substantial part of what it has already paid as well. And it must remember that it has no landlord to make repairs and pay the taxes. It must plan for larger cash outlays while paying for the home than when renting, for it must pay not only the current cost of its shelter but make payments on the principal as well.

Family Car. For the two-thirds of the American families that own one, the family car represents a fourth major expenditure. Before the war car-owning families with incomes up to $5000 or $6000 spent on the average from 10 to 15 per cent of their incomes for automobile ownership and operation. Families that buy a new car every year usually spend from 12 to 15 per cent of their income each year. Families that buy a new car only once in four or five years spend as much as 20 or 25 per cent of their income for a car the year they purchase a new one, but as little as 5 per cent for upkeep and operation the years they "make the old car do."

When a family owns a car there are two types of costs to be met—costs of ownership and costs of operation. Ownership costs continue as long as a family owns a car, whether the family uses it or not. Ordinarily an automobile depreciates in value almost as much if it is not driven at all as if it is driven any reasonable amount. Garage and parking space must be provided. Insurance costs are based on the value of the car and where it is garaged, rather than on the miles it is driven. License and taxes must be paid each year. Operating expenses for gas and oil, for tires and battery, for repairs and servicing depend on how much the car is driven and under what sort of road and weather conditions. Ownership costs are determined when the family buys a car. Operating costs depend on how much the car is used. The more a family drives in a year, the larger will be its total expenditure for the automobile, but the lower will be the cost per mile.

In deciding whether to buy a car, the family must consider the total cost of owning and operating the car. In deciding whether or not to take a particular trip, it needs to consider only the additional cost of the particular use, since the overhead cost of ownership goes on whether the car is used or not.

It costs more to own a new car and more to operate an old one. When new cars are available at moderate prices it may cost less to trade in an old car for a new one every year or two than to buy new tires and pay for a motor overhaul for the old one. When new cars are high in price it may cost less to drive the old car another year or two and pay the extra operating costs. If some of the members of the family can do most of the work on the car the family can get satisfactory transportation at low cost by buying an older car and doing the repair work necessary to keep it in good running order. If the family must pay for all the servicing a newer car may in the course of a year or two actually cost less money.

In deciding whether or not to own a car, a family should consider not only what the car will cost, but what will be the effect of car ownership on other family expenditures. Owning a car may make it possible for the family to live in a less expensive neighborhood and to trade in low-service stores and supermarkets. Sometimes the head of the family can get a better job than would be possible without the car. Owning a car may, however, make the family want to go about more and spend more for other things as well as for the automobile. The decision, therefore, should be based first on the relative cost of living with and without an automobile, and second, on whether the more expensive way of living is worth the extra cost.

Health. Adequate provision for the health of the family involves two types of expenditure—more or less regularly recurring expenditures for minor illness and preventive medical and dental care, and occasional heavy expenses for incapacitating accidents and serious illness which may require hospitalization and surgery or long-continued medical treatment. These occasional heavy expenses are often accompanied by loss of income if the husband is incapacitated, or by extra expenses for additional service if the wife is unable for some time to do her usual work about the house.

The cost of routine care varies from family to family, depending on the size of the family, the ages of its members, their general level of health, any special physical handicaps which may be present, and the types and cost of medical care available in the community. On the basis of their own experience most families are able to estimate closely the cost of routine care, but it is impossible to anticipate either when there will be heavy expenditures for incapacitating accidents or serious illness, or how much the necessary medical and surgical care will cost.

The members of some families seem to have low resistance to disease. Some people work in occupations in which there is more exposure to accidents and illness. Other families seem to be lucky and avoid serious accidents, or have a higher level of health. Often, however, this higher health level is due at least in part to preventive measures. Many families save money in the long run by spending money for regular physical checkups, for the correction of minor difficulties before they become serious, and by the observance of reasonable rules of hygiene. Often the expenditures for medical care may be reduced materially by being sure to provide the family with proper food, comfortable clothing, adequate shelter, and suitable recreation.

Families find that their expenditures for health vary widely from year to year. In the 1920's, 40 per cent of the families in the United States incurred 90 per cent of the total cost of medical care, while the other 60 per cent made only 10 per cent of the expenditures.

A family can provide in advance for a substantial part of the cost of a serious illness or accident by carrying insurance to cover the cost of hospitalization and surgical care. Families can carry health and accident insurance which will provide them with a minimum of income during most of the disability of the wage earner. Insurance can, however, cover only part of the cost. An insurance company will not knowingly provide health and accident insurance paying more than 80 per cent of a person's regular income. Most policies provide for at least a seven-day waiting period before payments begin. In order to keep the cost of hospital insurance within what most families can pay, the number of days of hospital care provided in any one year is limited to what most families find adequate. Insurance for the cost of medical attention is still experimental. While families find that hospital insurance helps in meeting the cost of serious illness, they must expect to provide for a substantial part of the cost out of savings or, if their savings are inadequate, to arrange for credit, and adjust their other expenditures so that they can gradually pay the balance of the cost.

There are two types of hospital insurance now available. One type pays a stated amount per day for each day that an insured member of the family is confined to the hospital. The family pays the hospital bill and is reimbursed by the insurance company when it presents evidence of hospitalization. This type of insurance provides a given number of dollars to apply on the cost of hospital care. The insurance company pays a stated amount per day, regardless of how much the hospital facilities cost. If the patient uses a ward bed which costs less than the per diem payment, the family has the difference to apply on other costs. If the bed costs more, the family pays the difference.

The other type of insurance provides a stated amount of a given type of hospital care. The hospital deals directly with the insurance company, collects what is due under the provisions of the policy, and bills the patient for any services not covered by insurance.

The cost of hospital insurance usually varies with the amount of coverage it provides and whether the insurance is purchased on an individual or a group basis. Usually it is easier for the head of a family to qualify for hospital insurance as a member of a group. Under a group plan he can usually get a given amount of protection at substantially lower cost. A number of industrial group plans now written include provision for continuing the insurance on an individual basis at somewhat higher cost if the head of the family changes his employment. In any case, it is important to learn exactly what any given insurance plan does and does not cover and to observe the terms of the policy carefully so that you will be sure not to be left without insurance when protection is most needed.

Recreation. Recreation is an item for which it is possible to spend almost any amount of money. Some recreational expenditures are for recreation as such—tickets to the theater, sports equipment, memberships in country clubs—while others take the form of additional expenditures for food, clothing, car operation, extra current for the radio or television set, or extras on the grocery bill, such as candy and cigarettes.

Recreation is capable of greater elaboration than almost any other type of expenditure. At the same time, by care in planning, it is possible to have a good time with little if any cash outlay. The family that must keep expenditures to the minimum may entertain simply at home instead of inviting friends to theater or restaurant or night club. If food is indicated they may select meals that do not call for much food, such as Sunday-night suppers. In returning dinner invitations they may serve inexpensive but interesting meals, perhaps with a few extra trimmings, placing the emphasis on attractiveness rather than elaborateness of serving, and on the taste rather than the expensiveness of the food. Much can be added to the significance of anniversaries by such simple devices as candlelight and simple table decorations, with the gift of personal items that would be bought sooner or later but which give added pleasure because they are constant reminders of important days.

Even when a family must keep its money outlay at a minimum it must not neglect adequate provision for suitable recreation, for recreation is an important element in maintaining the family's physical and mental health. If the members of the family have plenty of time and energy at their disposal they can concentrate on the type of activities that require time and effort but little outlay of money. If the family is using all the energy it can safely spend on necessary work its recreation program should provide a maximum amount of relaxation with a minimum expenditure of time and energy, using whatever money the family can afford.

The family should plan its recreation with all its other activities in mind. If the husband is meeting people all day long his recreation may well take the form of quiet evenings reading or listening to the radio. If he is seated at a desk all day he may need physical exercise which he can get from golf, bowling, or tennis, or by working in his garden or at some physically releasing type of hobby. If the wife is kept rather closely at home most of the time her husband should take her out to dinner and the theater occasionally. If both husband and wife are employed and are often away from home they may get the variety they need by entertaining their friends at home. The family's recreation program should not use money which the family cannot afford. But it should provide the release from the current strains of daily living which is necessary to keep the members of the family in good physical and mental health.

PLANNING FOR THE LONG LIFE OF THE FAMILY

If a family is to use the resources at its disposal to provide the richest and most satisfying life for its members it should plan for each particular period in the life of the family with the whole life of the family clearly in mind. This is not so difficult a problem as at first it might seem, for every family passes through a life cycle with a series of clearly defined stages—marriage, the establishment of the family, the birth, schooling, adolescence, maturity, and departure of the children, a few quieter years in later middle life, old age, retirement, and death. Each of these stages brings with it characteristic needs and wants which make varying demands on the family's current money income.

The number of years an individual family spends in each of these stages varies somewhat with the age of the husband and wife at marriage, the number of their children, the intervals between the children's births, and the amount of education with which the children are provided. Even families without children pass through a somewhat similar cycle, which makes changing demands on their incomes as their interests grow and change with the passing years.

Similarly, the swing of the business cycle and other business changes bring changes in the family's income and other resources. Changing business conditions affect the prices a family must pay and the income it receives. They affect the kind, quantity, and quality of goods on sale in the market. They affect opportunities for employment of the family members and for the saving and investment of family funds. Changing business conditions affect the age at which marriage is economically feasible, the size of the family it is wise to rear, the length of the effective earning period of the family members, and the age at which retirement is imperative or financially possible.

Every family will live through several complete swings of business cycles, each one just a little different from all the others. Most families will experience at least one period of pronounced inflation and probably will live part of their lives during periods in which the long-time trend of prices is up and part in periods in which the long-time trend of prices is down.

Because of these concurrent changes in the family life cycle and the business cycle, the family's current income will not necessarily vary proportionately or even directly with the family's changing needs. There may be a few families in which the husband's earnings increase more rapidly during the years when the family is bringing up its children than do the demands upon those earnings. But most families face years in which necessary expenses are larger than the family's current income, years in which the family's income is more than adequate for current needs, and years in which the family, by careful management, is able to live within its income with varying degrees of financial strain.

The establishment of the family involves the investment of considerable money in furniture and other household equipment. This usually is not too difficult to manage, especially if both the husband and the wife are employed. The years in which the children are born bring new expenses at a time when the family must get along without the wife's earnings. Usually the years when the children are in elementary school involve a minimum of financial strain. But during the peak of the life cycle, when the children are in high school and college, only a few families are able to provide everything the members of the family need out of the husband's earnings, or even out of the family's current income, unless several members of the family contribute from their earnings.

ADJUSTMENT TO CHANGING WANTS AND INCOME

There are a number ways by which a family may adjust to the changing demands on its income. Usually at one time or another every family uses all of them. A family may plan in advance for large expenditures, spreading them along over a considerable period, seeing to it that not more than one or two must be made at the same time. This is what a family with a weekly pay check does with its larger monthly bills, when it pays the rent out of one week's check, pays for the utilities out of another, stocks up with staple groceries with the third, and uses most of the fourth week's check for new clothes or for the payment on the family car.

The principle is the same when the family is planning for larger occasional expenditures which are made only once in several years. No family in the lower- or middle-income groups is able to make more than one or two major expenditures out of any one year's income. When the family buys a new car that is the one major expenditure for the year. Next year there will be money for a vacation trip. The year after that it will be possible to redecorate the living room and modernize the kitchen. And the next year the family will want to purchase another car.

A family may provide itself with expensive durable goods by purchasing them in advance of the time they will be needed, when there are not many other demands on the family income. Many families buy and complete the payments on their home early in the life of the family, or buy a new car which they drive for five or six years while the children are in high school or college.

A family may save money for specific expenditures which require a larger outlay than the family can make out of any one year's income. Most families find that several years' savings are necessary to provide for the children's college education. Some families prefer to save their vacation money for two or three years and take an extensive trip rather than to have two or three inexpensive vacations nearer home.

A family may want to make some large expenditure before it has had time to save all the necessary money. If it is sure that it can make the necessary payments it may decide to use its credit. Faced with the necessity of making extensive repairs on their car, a family may decide to turn in the old car and pay for a new one on the installment plan. If there is an acute shortage of furnished apartments a family may find it easier to get suitable shelter by renting an unfurnished house and using their credit to get the furniture they need.

In using credit it is important to distinguish between purchases which will add to the family's expenses and purchases which, once they are paid for, will reduce the family's current outlay. And since there is a great deal of difference in the terms on which credit is available, it is important to know what different kinds of credit cost and to use the type that will let the family buy on credit at the lowest additional cost. It is wise to use credit only when having something now rather than saving first and buying later is worth the additional cost of buying on credit.

A family can reduce the demands on its money income by having the members of the family do more for themselves and by making more use of community resources that do not cost money. A family can cut its food costs by doing more baking and canning. It can cut its clothing costs by making and by making over more garments. It can cut its recreation costs by having good times at home and by using public parks and playgrounds, attending municipal concerts, or getting new books to read from the public library.

And for the inevitable unforeseen and often unforeseeable emergencies and contingencies, like the loss of a job, the opportunity to move to a better job, a chance to make an unusually fortunate purchase or investment, accidents, or unexpected illness, a family can carry insurance of various kinds and can set up a cash reserve for contingencies.

Ordinarily a family finds that it pays to carry insurance against the contingencies in which there is a small chance of a large loss, and to set up cash reserves to cover the contingencies for which the total amount of expenditure varies little from year to year. A family should never neglect to insure its home and furnishings and personal possessions against loss by fire. Usually it is wise to add the additional protection against windstorm and other types of damage which are included in what the insurance man calls extended coverage. Automobile insurance is a necessity. Coverage against loss from fire and theft is inexpensive. Property damage and public liability insurance is required in many states for the protection of others. Collision insurance is more expensive but usually worth having when the car is new.

Already some 85 million people have found it pays to carry hospitalization insurance; an increasing number of families are adding insurance to cover the cost of surgical care. But since bills for routine medical care do not vary much from year to year, most families prefer to pay their doctors' and dentists' bills direct, setting aside a little extra in savings in years when medical expenses are low to use in other years when the family has more than the usual amount of illness. Most families carry some life insurance on one member or more of the family, to provide funds for funeral expenses and something for the family to live on in case of the death of a family member.

Every family needs a substantial cash reserve to draw on in case of any one of a number of contingencies. If possible, the family should have about the equivalent of six months' income in a savings account or invested in government bonds or other easily marketable securities, where it can be got at on short notice. This contingent fund may be used for a number of purposes. If the head of the family loses his job, his unemployment insurance will help to defray some of the family's current expenses when he is not working, but savings are necessary to keep up payments on insurance, a home, the car, and other essential fixed charges. The fund may be drawn on to meet unusually heavy medical expenses. It may make it possible for the family to move to better employment, or to take advantage of an unusual opportunity to buy a new home, or new furniture. In case of serious damage to the automobile, it will provide funds with which to buy a new car. Contingent reserves are to be used. But when funds are withdrawn for these perfectly legitimate uses they should be replaced as soon as possible, so that they will be available for other contingencies.

The management and financing of a family is not an unimportant job to be carried on in spare time. For the way a family manages its affairs has a great deal to do with how well the family lives on the means at its disposal. Nor is it something to work too hard at. There is no value in management for its own sake. The test of success in family management is not the amount of money earned or saved or spent, or the amount of work done by the members of the family, but rather the quality of living the family makes available for its members, not only this year, but every year throughout the long life of the family.

Topics for further thought:

1. Analyze the relationship that societal standards of living have to a family's living within or below its income. As far as the various family members are concerned, are there desirable and undesirable aspects of a family's living above its income?

2. Comment on the suggestion made in this chapter that "if wives are to help by working outside for money, husbands can expect to help with the work of the family at home." What division of labor would you suggest?

Selected reading references

Bigelow, Howard F., *Family Finance,* Philadelphia, J. B. Lippincott Company, 1953.
    Basic guide to management of the family income. Widely used textbook.

Donaldson, Elrin F., *Personal Finance,* New York, The Ronald Press Company, 1956.
    "This book was written to give adequate and practical help to the person who wants to do a better job of managing his personal finances."

Hanson, Arthur W., and Cohen, Jerome B., *Personal Finance,* Homewood, Illinois, Richard D. Irwin, Inc., 1955.
    Discusses in detail many of the problems of finance mentioned in this chapter.

How To Buy Life Insurance No. 62, and *Credit for Consumers* No. 5, New York, Public Affairs Committee.
    Public Affairs pamphlets, simply written, practical discussions for consumers.

Kyrk, Hazel, *The Family in the American Economy,* Chicago, University of Chicago Press, 1953.
    Excellent text on the financial and economic aspects of American family living.

Money Management Library, Chicago, Household Finance Corporation. Set of thirty-nine booklets boxed in four volumes. Deal with: planning expenditures; food; clothing; and home. Nontechnical, designed for the general consumer public.

Thorpe, Alice C., "How Married College Students Manage," *Marriage and Family Living,* November, 1951, pp. 104-5.
A research study which indicates that married students are successfully meeting and solving the management problems that face them.

22 EXTRAMARITAL RELATIONS

Lester W. Dearborn

Among the problems that must be examined as affecting marital success is the question of extramarital relations. By definition, extramarital relations include any sexual relationship outside of marriage. While premarital relations may not necessarily involve the prospect of marriage, they often involve only the intended spouse. After marriage, extramarital relations include illicit behavior by either or both spouses with other persons, married or unmarried.

THE YOUNG ADULT

Larger numbers of young people in this generation are probably freer in their sexual expression than a generation ago. Three controlling fears of the past—fear of detection, infection, and conception—have been minimized by new freedom and knowledge. An important factor is the change in attitude toward supervision of the young. Modern education, which teaches independence and freedom of action for the young, has largely eliminated chaperonage as a social custom. Automobiles make it possible for young people to travel great distances in short times, and so the effectiveness of community supervision is eliminated. The automobile itself offers opportunities for intimacy.

Comparison of present practices with those of 25 years ago is hampered by the little knowledge that was obtainable at that time, and any estimate must be largely a matter of guesswork. Competent investigators reveal that today a relatively high percentage of engaged couples have had a complete sexual relationship before their marriage. Of the engaged couples that this writer has counseled, between 65 and 70 per cent have been having intercourse. These figures do not include heavy petting or intimacies that fall just short of intercourse itself.

A few years ago the writer had an opportunity to interview a group of 18 married women over 45 years of age. Thirteen admitted that they had had sexual intercourse with their husbands before marriage. Together with the admissions of a large number of older wives during counseling, this figure raises doubt that the sex practices of the previous generation differed much from those of young people today.

A study of 4600 unmarried males between the ages of 21 and 28 who underwent psychiatric examination at Army induction centers in World War II reveals that 79.4 per cent had had sexual experience. Approximately 56 per cent of these men had had relations with what they referred to as "nice girls," meaning by this a girl whom the man could introduce to his parents and would consider marrying. The reporting psychiatrists predicted that intercourse with future spouses before marriage might become universal. If investigation were possible, the results might reveal that sexual intercourse with the intended spouse before marriage has been a practice of longer standing and engaged in by larger numbers than ever imagined.

Aside from the premarital relations of engaged couples, however, the sex life of the unmarried adult has always posed a social problem. While celibacy has been the expressed ideal, many find this difficult and others find it impossible to follow. In striving for such an ideal, evidence shows that the resulting nervous tensions, the fears and worries caused by loneliness, and the feelings of insecurity that are the natural corollaries of singleness combined with sexual hunger put such persons in a state of readiness for sexual intimacy.

Most males beyond the age of 30 who are not married are single because they are the sole support of a dependent parent, have some form of family obligation, or have been unreasonably long in becoming vocationally established. Also, they may be among those males who reject marriage; from 10 to 15 per cent of males prefer bachelorhood, but preference for bachelorhood does not necessarily include a preference for celibacy. Whereas a few women may deliberately choose to remain unmarried (particularly those who select a professional career in preference to that of homemaking), many of them are single because of such factors as prolongation of their educational program, overprotective parents, lack of prospective males in their circle, family responsibilities, and a lack of sex drive during those years when an interest in mate selection should be paramount. Some men and women are, because of conditioning or otherwise, homosexual and thus find heterosexual relationships unattractive. Others in practice are bisexual and because of this are not inclined to tie themselves to a permanent relationship. Also there is the single woman who has fallen in love with a married man and, having developed a romantic attachment for a man who is conventionally unobtainable, she prefers to enter into a sexual liaison with him rather than to give him up.

The older a man gets beyond the age of 30, the less concern he seems to have with the possibility of marriage. The woman never seems to give up hope. This may be accounted for in many ways. The need for emotional and physical security and the uncertainty concerning her vocational and social future concern her to a much greater degree than they do the man. Yearning as she does for a home and children and the love and protection of a mate, without them she pictures a dreary future and becomes increasingly anxious to avoid it. As her diminishing prospects of marriage are brought more sharply into focus she finds herself at the same time becoming more than ever conscious of her sexual needs. Personal counselors have for some time been aware of the fact that girls in their late adolescence and early twenties are apt to have much less desire for sexual intercourse than the woman who is eight to ten years older. This fact is substantiated by Kinsey's evidence that the peak of male sexuality is reached somewhere between the sixteenth and twenty-second years and very slowly but steadily declines toward middle age; whereas the sex life of the female evolves so slowly that many women are not aware of any particular drive until they are in their late twenties and early thirties. They reach the peak of desire somewhere between their thirty-fifth and fortieth years. Thus the man's desire for a permanent sexual relationship may be decreasing at the very time when the woman's is radically increased.

Security, a home of her own, and children are much stronger motives in the woman than in the man. With all this she becomes acutely aware that, having passed her thirtieth year, her childbearing years are growing less; while at the same time, whatever a particular male's procreative ability may be and whether or not his chances of fathering children also diminish, certainly the average male does not think of this as a probability. All this, then, leads many a woman as she gets older to decide in desperation to get a man by hook or by crook. Undoubtedly, so far as the woman is concerned, many of such sexual relationships are looked on by her not only as a means of emotional release but also as a device leading to a permanent union. Many refined and educated young women in their late twenties and in their thirties are so forlornly clinging to this hope that they place reliance on tenuous promises despite their better judgment.

This, then, together with the breakdown of social controls, helps to explain why there may be a considerable increase in the number of unmarried people who lay no claim to celibacy. Sex is an appetite that man is predisposed to satisfy, and the stronger the drive, the more insistently he strives to find a means of circumventing a convention that would prevent it. In the male this has always been recognized. While in precept it has rather feebly been denounced, in practice there has been social acceptance. The man will be blamed only if he is caught *flagrante delicto*. The social change is largely in the matter of the woman's behavior. Fears concerning conception, infection, and detection have been greatly reduced. The woman no longer has a fear of being ostracized if a decent regard for the proprieties is observed. It is quite common for friends to dismiss their suspicions of what is going on with a shrug of the shoulders and a none-of-my-business attitude.

There will always be sexual activity among the unmarried, but encouraging it by a laissez-faire attitude is certainly not conducive to a strengthening of marriage and the home.

STUDIES ON POSTMARITAL RELATIONSHIPS

Few published surveys make any pretense at giving statistical information concerning postmarital relationships. While there have been a number of published reports concerning premarital relationships and other types of sexual activity, any account concerning illicit behavior of married people is largely conspicuous by its absence. The author of one leading study frankly admits that there was no attempt to get at postmarital relationships because he feared that in doing so he might lose rapport with his subjects. He did, however, make a study of their desire for such experience. Another study of 100 married men and 100 married women reports that 28 men and 24 women had had illicit sexual intercourse while married to their spouses. An authority who sought to correlate opinion with practice found in the matter of opinion that while about one-fifth of the women agreed there were occasions when the wife might be justified a somewhat larger number sought to justify such an experience on the part of the husband. Then when measuring opinion against practice the investigator found that many who accepted some justification had had no such actual experience in their own marriages, while a number of those whose opinions were negative reported such experience. Any critical opinion from the standpoint of available data would at this time be of little value. At the same time it can be easily understood that in any statistical study it is far easier to get people to commit themselves about other forms of behavior and about their sexual relationships before marriage and in marriage itself than it is to elicit information concerning their present unconventional behavior, especially where such behavior involves serious legal as well as social implications.

The recently published two volumes which have become popularly known as the Kinsey study are, without question, a report on the most comprehensive study of human sex behavior that has yet been made. In these volumes the authors point out that in the discussion of extramarital experiences there is undoubtedly more cover-up than in the disclosure of any other type of sexual activity. While the authors show some doubt about the adequacy of their own figures in coming to any accurate conclusion concerning the number of unfaithful husbands or wives, they feel that on the basis of estimate they have enough information to support the conclusion that about half of the husbands will have intercourse with some woman other than their wives during their married lives. In the volume on the female, they report that about 7 per cent of the married females in their late teens and up to the age of 25 reported such behavior; that from age of 26 to the age of 40 there was a definite increase in the number of such incidents, so that they estimate that about 26 per cent of those who had reached the age of 40 had had or were having such experience by that time. They discovered, however, that after the age of 40 only a few females began, for the first time, to have extramarital coitus. These figures in regard to the female have particular significance because of the already mentioned fact that the woman becomes increasingly aware of her sex needs after the age of 25 and with increasing intensity reaching a peak somewhere between the middle thirties and early forties. In the writer's own marriage-counseling practice he has found an increasing number of wives whose sexual needs are not being satisfied by their husbands, and who are becoming maritally discontented.

It is not uncommon for students in marriage courses to ask such questions as these: Isn't it true that a great many people have extra-marital relations? Isn't it true that most men have extramarital relations? What attitude is the wife to take when she finds her husband has been having relations with another woman? Certainly this subject is of great concern to thousands of our population whose lives are definitely affected by this type of behavior.

Here is an excerpt from a 20-year report of the counseling service of the Massachusetts Society for Social Hygiene, 1934-54, covering 3938 individuals: males, 35 per cent; females, 65 per cent; education: below secondary, 6.6 per cent; having secondary, 31.9 per cent; above secondary, 57.6 per cent; not obtained, 3.9 per cent. About 20 per cent of the married couples who come for counseling report infidelity on the part of one or both partners, generally one, and generally the husband. In a number of cases, however, the wife was the offending partner. In some of these instances there was but a single episode of unfaithfulness, and in many of the others the repeated unfaithfulness has been confined to one partner. Illicit experiences involving a married person incidentally revealed in a conversation on irrelevant matters—for instance, an unmarried woman with a personal problem who reveals a relationship with a married man— would not be included.

The term unfaithfulness refers to sexual intercourse and does not include reported behavior that falls short of intercourse, such as flirtation, petting, or group behavior, such as nude bathing parties or strip poker. Most people who come to a counselor seek to preserve their marriages. Probably a far greater number of couples involved in infidelity are among those who want separation or divorce. Certainly records of divorce proceedings disclose infidelity to be a major cause.

In a study of this kind one becomes overwhelmed with all of the possible avenues of exploration. The personalities of the man, the wife, the paramour, their personal maladjustments with all the contingent factors, similarities and differences in their education, philosophy, religion and depth of religious conviction, parental and sibling affections and hostilities, happy or unhappy home life, vocational and social adjustments—all make such a complicated mosaic as to defy any breakdown into simple patterns for group study. Husbands and wives cannot be classified under specific reasons for illicit relations. The final analysis is a study of the individual case.

Dr. Ernest R. Groves differentiates between acute unfaithfulness and chronic unfaithfulness, defining the first as being an extramarital relationship that has happened but has not become a habit. To this may be added a third classification, quondam unfaithfulness, referring to that situation where the illicit experience has been long past but recently disclosed. The marriages in which the problem is acute or quondam are the ones more likely to be seen by the marriage counselor. In conference that which could be classified as chronic occasionally comes to the attention of the counselor, although often the affair has been so discreetly carried on that the mate has no knowledge of it and consequently it has had little traumatic effect on the marriage itself. It is the single incident or occasionally repeated unfaithfulness or the discovery of an incident which has happened since marriage but now is long past that creates in the spouse a fear for the future, and as their love has not been entirely alienated they seek counsel in the hope that something may be done to save their marriage.

PATTERNS OF CONDUCT

The following lists a few of the sociosexual behavior patterns disclosed in cases of unfaithfulness. Where the husband is the offending partner, he

1. Has marital as well as extramarital relations.
2. Has extramarital relations with no marital relations.
3. Has been unfaithful and yet considers his marriage a success.
4. Complains that his wife's lack of orgasm has made intercourse with her uninteresting.
5. Reports interest in deviated methods of expression or in precoital preparation which are displeasing or uninteresting to the wife.
6. Defends himself on the basis that he has a greater sexual need and capacity and that it would be unfair to the wife to expect her to submit to his frequency.
7. Complains that she fails to meet certain fetishistic needs of his: complete nudity, variety in coital positions, some sadomasochistic ap-

proach, oral stimulation; he seeks a woman who shows reciprocal interests.

Where the wife is the offending partner, she

1. Complains of neglect of her sexual needs on the part of the husband.

2. Complains of him as a lover—he does not show affection, does not compliment her, is abrupt and inconsiderate in his sexual approach; she complains of marriage monotony.

3. Complains of lack of orgasm but feels the husband does little to help her to a climax.

4. Is masochistic and longs for strong and aggressive action on the part of her husband; he fails to comply.

5. Reports an illicit experience and yet reports her marriage a success.

Of course the foregoing are inconclusive and of little value so far as classifying cases is concerned. They are merely excerpts from the original complaint and tend to show that adultery is usually but a symptom of a deeper and more basic problem. Because of this it is extremely difficult to isolate this problem as a subject and to discuss it constructively. One finds oneself tempted to get into personality problems and is immediately conscious of all the neurotic psychiatric implications, the importance of background factors and family conflicts.

Speculatively and for the purpose of oversimplification the following assumptions are made:

1. That in most well-adjusted marriages neither partner is in a state of readiness for illicit experience.

2. That where a state of readiness exists there are both positive and negative factors operating for or against such an experience.

Here is the age-old conflict between duty and desire. While duty sometimes wins, it often comes out second best. With the number of males who are not married and the number of unmarried females most of whom would be married if they could, plus a growing number of unhappy mates, one does not have to go far for the opportunity. In fact, opportunity often comes knocking at the door in the form of a little subtle seduction and some that is not so subtle. The seducer, by the way, is not always the married one or always the older. All that has previously been said about the sex life of the unmarried (this includes the divorced and widowed) becomes part and parcel of this whole problem. One who is in a state of readiness for an illicit experience may find it difficult and may never surrender because of the conflict with his social and religious ideals, but if in doing this he becomes a martyr to righteousness, heaven help the family!

In justifying one's behavior the human being's ability to rationalize is so remarkable that there is no limit to the reasons given. Here are a few of the more common ones:

1. Sexual frustration—difference in intensity of desire, difference in ability to respond, difference in individual love requisites, impotence of husband, frigidity of wife.

2. Lack of ego satisfaction—lack of prestige in the family, no build-up at home, being unfavorably compared to others, conflict with in-laws, inadequate income.

3. Propinquity—there was the opportunity, the excuse; it just happened.

4. Pseudo-romantic love. This refers not to the romantic idea on which the marriage may have been based and which has turned out to be a hoax, although this may be the case, but rather to the romantic idea which causes a man or woman to "fall in love with someone else" and thus implicitly out of love with the spouse.

A composite statement of three cases involving postmarital relations of the husband would read something this: I loved my wife when I married her. We have been getting along very nicely. We have two beautiful children whom I love dearly. My wife is a fine housekeeper and a wonderful mother, but I am in love with this other woman. I can't get her out of my mind."

All three of these husbands deny that their sexual relations with their wives have been satisfactory, but the three wives claim that for them the sex life was very satisfactory up to this time. The husbands are still living with their wives, and each reports that because of the counseling the wife has received she is a better sexual partner and that on the whole the domestic relations have improved, but the wife knows that each is still carrying a torch for the paramour. How long the marriage can continue in this state is anybody's guess. At the beginning each husband talked about divorce and the wife was appalled at the idea, but a woman who has done everything to cooperate and has inventoried her personality traits and tried to make adjustments and has become more active and responsive sexually reaches the limit of her endurance when she finds her husband turning away from a kiss, ignoring the little pleasantries and attentions, and sitting around the house with a bored expression or finding every possible excuse to go out on business.

In these three cases each husband found something more than sexual satisfaction with the other woman, and it is this something to which he is tenaciously clinging—the many little things that are inflationary to his ego. She makes him feel important while his wife has taken him for granted. One thing all three of these men have in common is that each was brought up by a dominant and overprotective mother. In two of these cases the father was reported as lacking in aggressiveness; in the third the father was dominant but in conflict with the mother. In business all three men were successful, but the history of each showed that he tended to withdraw from reality and flee from responsibility in any emotional crisis.

If their marriages do not survive all three of these women are by now better prepared to meet the eventuality, and while their homes will become broken, the attitude of the parents toward the children and the children toward the parents and between the father and mother will be fraught with much less tension than would otherwise be so, for there is such a thing as education for divorce. Where by deed or word the partner's ego has been hurt it is much more difficult to effect a reconciliation than where the problem is merely that of a sexual experience outside of marriage.

Running concurrently with the effort to prepare young people for marriage by providing courses and counseling on successful marriage and family living, there is a similar effort in the direction of re-educating those who have been off to a poor start or have already run into difficulties.

This second effort, like the first, is already paying dividends. Hundreds of couples varying in ages from their early twenties to their late forties, but with the largest group in the age range from twenty-five to thirty-five, are being helped every year by competent counselors to re-evaluate their problems in terms of a better understanding of each other's personalities and needs, of understanding and accepting sex in a more realistic way, in coming to realize that the more we put into a marriage the more we take out, and that spouses are, after all, only human beings with human frailties, and that marriage itself is no panacea for character defects or personality maladjustments. Where there is a will on the part of both there is a way to rebuild their marriage and make it a lasting and satisfactory experience.

Adultery, like poverty, is with us always, but he who helps a couple to make or maintain a happy marriage makes a direct contribution to a reduction of extramarital relations.

Topics for further thought:

1. Our society believes in marital faithfulness. Explain what is involved in this belief and justify it from the point of view of the group.

2. Extramarital relations suggest personal dissatisfaction which in turn implies family instability. Do you think that this kind of personal dissatisfaction reflects societal conditions and situations which the individual translates in his own behavior? Explain your answer.

Selected reading references

Geddes, Donald P., and Curie, Enid (eds.), *About the Kinsey Report,* New York, The New American Library, 1948.
    An evaluation of the Kinsey volume on the human male by eleven experts in the field.

Kinsey, Alfred C., Pomeroy, Wardell B., and Martin, Clyde, *Sexual Behavior in the Human Male,* Philadelphia, W. B. Saunders Company, 1948.
    See Chapter 19, pp. 583-94, for documentation of incidence, frequency, and significance of extramarital intercourse. For further annotation of this volume, see References at end of Chapter 11.

Kinsey, Alfred C., Pomeroy, Wardell B., Martin, Clyde, and Gebhard, Paul H., *Sexual Behavior in the Human Female,* Philadelphia, W. B. Saunders Company, 1953.
    See Chapter 10, pp. 409-45, for findings concerning extramarital intercourse among women. For further annotation of this volume see References at end of Chapter 11.

Levy, John, and Munroe, Ruth, *The Happy Family,* New York, Alfred A. Knopf, 1938.
    Chapter 3, "The Other Woman," analyzes some of the underlying conflicts between husband and wife which may result in extramarital relations. Indicates that such affairs may have varying significance for the marital relationship.

Young, Leontine R., *Out of Wedlock*, New York, McGraw-Hill Book Company, 1954.
Psychoanalytic interpretation of the behavior of women who become unmarried mothers. Analysis of the causes for socially disapproved sex behavior contrasts strongly with the Kinsey interpretations.

23 THE HEALTH AND HYGIENE OF MARRIAGE

Thurman B. Rice

Assume that the choice of the marriage mate has been such that there is a reasonable hope that the partners can carry through their respective roles with at least average success. The excitement of the wedding and the precarious decisions of the honeymoon are recently past, and the happy couple are back home, ready to begin the reality of homemaking.

There is a reasonably adequate income, the housing problem is passably well solved, and there is need to meet the perplexities of everyday life as married couples everywhere must meet them if they are to accomplish the purposes of marriage on an adult level. The health and hygiene of marriage must take the place which until now has been played almost wholly by starry-eyed romance. Actually, a state of health in the marriage relation will enable romance to persist, just as wholesome food will permit health in the usual sense to persist. Romance must be fed with solid food; it cannot long thrive on cake and kisses.

Assume that the couple have married at a time when each was hungry for sexual contact with the beloved one. If such is not the case they should have waited longer, or, failing this, should continue the courtship even though the marriage vows have been said. Healthy young people will find the new privileges extraordinarily pleasing in most cases; the problem is to keep them so. They must learn to use sexual gratification somewhat as they use food, to the end that they may grow in vigor and in appreciation, and thus to accomplish the purposes of sex.

VALUES OF SEXUAL RELATIONS IN MARRIAGE

The purposes of sexual intercourse are three: procreation, self-expression, and security.

1. *Procreation.* If civilization, culture, race, and nation are to be preserved, persons of health, character, and ability must reproduce themselves and furnish the heredity, environment, and training so necessary to the continuation of the species on a high level. This is a duty of those who have good bodies and minds—even more, it is a privilege.

2. *Self-expression.* Something in the nature of men and women makes them desire intimate contact with a loved one of the opposite sex, and with that one to produce and enjoy his or her own offspring. A deep sentiment is involved and must be gratified if the individual is to reap an emotionally rich family life. Just as the healthy person enjoys wholesome food, so does he or she enjoy this family relation and is the better for that enjoyment.

3. *Security.* Men and women are more secure when there is between them a rich sexual relation, and their children share this security. The infancy of the human child is longer than that of any other species of young; he needs his parents until he is fully grown and even beyond that time. Anything, then, which will hold his parents together is a protection to him and to the entire family. The ability of the parents to use sex for such a purpose is of vast importance to all who comprise the family group.

A marriage starts, then, with a couple hungry for sexual contact. But the happy lovers must remember that it will not always be so. They will soon satiate themselves to some extent, at least. Is that, then, the end of love or the beginning of the end? It may well be the death of romance unless there is an understanding of the real purposes of marriage. It is not to be supposed that the institution of marriage was designed merely to furnish safe conditions for intercourse, though obviously that is one of the objectives. There will come a time when even the most ardent man or woman will desire something else—something more. Early in married life the couple must begin to develop other objectives than intercourse. As the years pass these will become more satisfying and precious and will come ultimately to replace the pleasures of sexual union. As a result happiness can continue indefinitely as a reward for wise and meritorious behavior.

An analogy may serve to illustrate this point. Assume that a man is building a new house in which he expects to live. In the beginning he is enormously interested in the digging of the foundation and visits the site twice a day to observe progress. This foundation seems most important—as indeed it is; it even seems most fascinating—as indeed it well may be. Later, as the house progresses, he transfers his interest to the other parts of the building; and finally, upon its completion, he moves into and lives in it with no further thought for the foundation. This is as it should be unless one strangely prefers to live one's whole life in the basement, as so many do—speaking sexually. The basement of the house is important and sexual intercourse, which is the foundation of happy married life, is important, but it is not the whole of the house or of the marriage. Let us hope that the foundation upon which the house or the home is built is utterly sound and secure, as carefully and scientifically constructed as able workmanship can provide, but remember that it is a means to an end rather than an end in itself. Intercourse between two persons deeply in love has many rewards in addition to and exceeding those of physical gratification.

The householder who comes home after an honest day's work has a right to expect an attractive, well-cooked, and nicely served dinner— provided, of course, that his wife is not ill or excessively worn by the day's work. If the food is on the table at six o'clock he will eat, enjoy the food, and then give no more thought to food during the remainder of the evening. If he is still waiting at seven he will be restless; by eight o'clock he will be angry if he is not served; by nine o'clock he will be furious, and probably long before ten he will have gone to the corner restaurant. Sex is much like food in this respect; persons who are not fed at home are tempted—at least—to go elsewhere. Or if the food is on the table at six but consists of a can of salmon, a bottle of milk, and a box of crackers—all of it nourishing but carelessly served—the man of the house is likely to think that his is a poor home and may go elsewhere. The wife whose husband is too lazy or too stupid to try for a bit of glamour is likely to yearn for someone else with a bit more consideration for her feelings. This is not an attempt to justify the implied misconduct associated with this analogy but only to show the attitudes of mind that lead to such misconduct.

NECESSITY FOR CLEANLINESS

What are the actual factors which have a good or a bad effect upon marriage happiness? There is tidiness, for example. It is doubtful if there is anything more destructive to romance than soiled underwear or body odor. They must be guarded against with the utmost care, and yet one must have a smattering of good judgment, too. If the housewife must do her own laundry she may not wish her husband to be overly free with the linen. She may prefer to have him wear his underwear until it is really soiled a bit than to be confronted with a mountain of washing and ironing each week. Possibly her husband would rather have her wear her dainties longer than to have her exhausted with the effort to keep herself as sweet as when she stepped out of her bath. A house, or a wife, or a husband may be so dainty that there is no comfort in living with it, or her, or him. One cannot relax well in a home or with a person who is too nice to get a bit messed up. After all, there is the work of the world to be done, and it is impossible for workers to avoid soil and perspiration entirely. All of this is a matter for adjustment.

Much the same may be said of the matter of personal cleanliness. Surely one cannot compromise with cleanliness, and yet cleanliness is a relative term. A home cannot be managed as would be the surgery operating room in a hospital. There are those who bathe twice or more times a day and others who follow the once-a-week pattern. Certain parts of the body require particular care—the genital area, the feet, the armpits, the hair, and the mouth. Genital odors—if they are not excessive—may be stimulating to some, but in general they are best avoided. Certainly they are objectionable when they can be detected in casual contacts or when one is in the same room with the person from whom they exude. External cleanliness is all that is necessary to prevent such objectionable odors. A cleansing douche is often refreshing, but it is not usually necessary for the prevention of odor. An antiseptic douche will tend to kill the useful bacteria found in the vaginal tract and is best not used. Such a douche is not an adequate contraceptive device and may lead to abnormal discharges which are more offensive than the natural odors of the vaginal tract. Bathing should be adjusted to the sensitivity of the conjugal partner and the convenience of the bathing facilities. Those persons who are so fortunate as to have hot water and a modern bathroom should remember that bathing may be a major operation in a crowded home without modern sanitary conveniences. Clearly in such a home frequent bathing could put a serious strain upon the one bathing and upon those who must live with him or her.

In any consideration of health an evaluation of costs and benefits must be made. It is entirely possible to make such a fuss about matters pertaining to health as to cause health to be lost rather than gained. Just as nothing can be so dangerous as the assurance that one is absolutely safe, so nothing can be so injurious to health as to give to health matters one's entire attention. The couple who work too hard and worry too much attempting to make the home perfect in these matters are likely to be too tired and harassed to enjoy the precious privileges when and if they are attained. Such is far from being a healthful state of affairs. The mother who spends so much time *working for* the children that she has no energy left to *play with* them is not being wise. The father who kills or injures himself in the effort to provide everything for his family is failing to provide them with what they need most—himself. His sacrifice is noble, perhaps, but strangely unappreciated in many instances.

HYGIENE OF THE BEDROOM

The bed and bedroom of a married couple hold an important place in their health and hygiene relations. Arguments are offered for and against the double bed. One sleeps better when he or she is alone, the cover can be better adjusted, there is less danger of transmitting respiratory infections, and there are several other advantages. There are definite disadvantages: the cost is greater, it requires more laundry and more bedroom space. The crux of the matter lies not in such practical considerations, however, but in those emotional and conjugal ones which are the heart and soul of marriage. There are many conveniences and enjoyments in the double bed which cannot be well set down on paper. They lead to a rich warm comradeship which is utterly priceless to many couples who would not wish to be labeled old-fashioned. Young people should give the double bed a try and older couples should make the transition from one twin bed to the other easy and frequent, and as often in one direction as the other. A more effective damper of romance can hardly be imagined than separate rooms for husband and wife, or the practice of having one or the other sleeping with a child. The practice of sleeping in separate rooms or beds so that the number of children can be held down may or may not have the desired results in this respect, and it may or may not lead to interest in another person who is less unattainable.

There are many differences in tastes and there are really good reasons for separation of the beds. Bad breath, body odor, snoring, restlessness, pulling of the covers, differences in sleeping habits, and other peculiarities may make it desirable for the couple to separate themselves in the interest of continued affection. Certainly the beds should be separated when one or the other has a transmissible disease. Sometimes the beds may be set so close together as barely to avoid touching and the advantages of both the single and the double bed pretty largely attained. Whatever the arrangement, it should be the one that gives the least cause for mutual dissatisfaction and the greatest possible opportunity for the unhampered enjoyment of marital rights and privileges.

There are persons who like to indulge in minor vulgarities when under sexual stimulation. They may wish to use words which they would not use at other times, and they may rightly feel that the technical words properly used in a scientific discussion seem stilted and quite out of place in the intimacy of sexual stimulation. All of this is a matter for adjustment. The relation should be neither stilted nor vulgar. It is an intimate contact which calls for words of endearment, for pet names and delicate shades of meaning—for anything, indeed, that will enhance the enjoyment and bring appreciation and happiness to both partners, but in particular to the *other* partner. Cave men may be desirable to cave women, but most women probably prefer to live and make love under more civilized surroundings. A man may wish his wife to be free in her affections, but he will rarely want her to be wanton.

FREQUENCY OF SEXUAL INTERCOURSE

The question of how often intercourse may be indulged or enjoyed is one of that is often asked. Amazingly, many books and pamphlets written to instruct in such matters attempt to answer this question by giving a definite number. Nothing could be more absurd. Individual preference and ability will vary so widely that it is utterly impossible to give a categorical answer. Since the act is good and gives great pleasure; since it is perfectly legitimate in marriage and binds the couple closer together when performed properly, repetition as often as it can be satisfyingly performed should be encouraged. Even writers who profess to great beauty in the act will tend to warn against what they call excessive indulgence. Obviously the determining factor should be one closely related to the desires and the capacities of the couple. Without wishing to be arbitrary in such a personal matter, the following principles are sound:

1. Intercourse should be enjoyed as often as *both* the husband and the wife desire it.

2. It should be an invigorating experience leading to a state of relaxation, satisfaction, or exhilaration which is conducive to sound sleep or peace with the world as determined by the time of day.

3. Due consideration must be given to the matter of childbearing in the determination of frequency and methods to be used.

Within these limits satisfying intercourse in wedlock is of tremendous value to the couple, to the family, and to the stability of society at large. It is impossible to see how one can come to any other conclusion than that—within these restrictions—intercouse is an extremely practical art which should be studied, improved, and finally made perfect.

Nevertheless, it is doubtful if anything could be more disgusting or irritating than a husband—or a wife—who coaxes or demands sexual satisfaction at the most inopportune and embarrassing times, or who wishes to indulge himself or herself at the expense of the other partner. A young husband who observes his bride excessively languid or even exhausted as a result of his demands must surely feel a real sense of shame if he can feel at all. The wife who sees her husband going tired to his work need not be surprised if he is unable to earn the home and the security they need. Excessive childbearing can make of the marriage bed a place of danger and fear; can make the home a place of chaos full of squalling babies and wet, smelly diapers. A wise couple knows how to steer a course between excessive indulgence on the one hand and sexual starvation on the other.

When the husband and wife are rather equally balanced in their sexuality the problem is obviously much easier than when one is hot and the other cold. In the latter instance great tact, patience, and forbearance are needed in the early months of marriage if a satisfactory arrangement is to be expected. Assume—for the sake of variety—that the wife is the more amorous; that she needs more and can enjoy more intercourse than her husband can give to make her thoroughly satisfied with her home and marriage. In such case the husband will do well to play with her as much as he can before beginning the act itself; as soon as she has attained an orgasm he will do well to withdraw and save his energy for the next time, which will come all too soon for his relatively weak powers. At once it will be pointed out by those who still believe in the old-time physiology that he will seriously injure his nervous system by indulging in an incomplete act. Actually the incomplete act is less injurious in such a case than would be overindulgence. If he does not permit himself to get too close to the orgasm it is not injurious at all. Such an arrangement allows many happy acts of love on the part of the husband and a corresponding number of highly satisfying experiences for the wife. The incomplete act—so far as the husband is concerned—is a sort of kiss of affection and endearment at a time when he is perfectly capable of enjoying such, though he would be exhausted by the complete act. The wife of such a considerate man should be grateful and appreciative and should be more than eager to make up to him for any inconvenience the séance may have caused him. By such an arrangement he will not need to wonder whether the eager wife is tempted to make a cuckold of him—a source of considerable additional satisfaction. He will be able to feel a great pride of accomplishment in being able to hold the love of an amorous woman—no small accomplishment! He will be insuring the safety of his home for himself and his children.

It is generally supposed that it is more likely to be the husband who is excessive in his demands. What can a conscientious wife do to take care of such a situation—other than make a martyr of herself? There is indeed much that she can do if she loves the man and wishes to make him happy. Sexual intercourse is exhausting to a wife only when she puts herself into it actively—either positively or negatively. By being utterly passive or nearly so, she can satisfy her husband without tiring herself. At such a time she may well ask him to get along with the project of attaining an ejaculation; she may ask that he cut short the amorous dallying which at other times would be welcome; she may likely need a lubricant; and she may properly ask him to take responsibility for the contraceptive used—if one is used. She should not pity herself and pout about it, but should co-operate to the extent that is necessary for the quick attainment of the relaxation that he may greatly need. How great must be the appreciation of a husband whose wife, observing his unrest, suggests or gladly acquiesces to a short act of intercourse which will ease his tension and permit him to get the sleep which he needs if he is to do the work of the morrow. It is of such things that happiness in marriage is made. Intercourse with a passive wife may not seem exciting, but when it makes a man love the good helpmate by his side and adds to his appreciation of the unselfishness and love she bears him, it serves a purpose which is precious indeed. It is far to be preferred to the arrangement which may make him too susceptible to the charms of the unsatisfied woman he may meet when he is away from home.

DISPARITY OF SEX ORGANS

While the genital organs of most couples are average size and therefore quite compatible, it is entirely possible that there will be some degree of physical disproportion. Such disparity will not necessarily present great difficulty if there is the desire on the part of the two partners to make the attempt to correct the situation by making adjustments. If, for example, the penis is too small to give full satisfaction compensation may be made if the wife will place under her buttocks a pillow or, even better, a few folds of firm, thick blanket which will have the effect of preventing her from sinking down too low in the bed. When the reverse relation is at fault a pillow under the small of the back will turn her pelvis away from her husband in such a way as to avoid too deep entrance. The use of a lubricant such as a surgical or a contraceptive jelly will be of assistance. Investigation by a physician of muscular spasm at the vaginal entrance or search for inflamed or tender areas may be required. By means of different positions of intercourse and other adaptive measures the organs will gradually become more yielding to disproportions.

TIMING IN SEXUAL INTERCOURSE

There may be difficulty in timing. Usually such differences can be overcome by the exercise of some effort on the part of the one partner, or restraint on the part of the other. As a rule it is the husband who tends to come to the climax first. In such case he is likely to ejaculate too early and leave the wife unsatisfied. This can sometimes be corrected by spending more time with sex play before the actual conjugation is attempted, or the husband may cease his movements but leave the penis in the vagina while he caresses the tardy wife. There is a belief that the two orgasms must be simultaneous if the best results are to be obtained. This is not necessary. There are indeed advantages in having the wife reach the climax first. Usually she will not object to a brief continuance after she has attained satisfaction. By this arrangement the one or the other is in full possession of control at all times and can more readily assist the partner in the climax of the act. This is a matter of personal preference and control whether the one or the other method shall be used.

The husband can usually attain satisfaction from the first though he may not be expert in the early months of marriage. The wife, however, may have to learn to relax and to induce the orgasm. Many brides are bitterly disappointed that they are not successful at first. It is not unusual to hear of a young wife who is relatively unsuccessful until after the birth of her first child. This does not mean that she is frigid but only that she is inexperienced. Rarely does the condition continue if the husband is co-operative and skillful and she is willing to relax and to learn. The matter of relaxation is quite important. Young women have been taught to restrain themselves; the muscles of the pelvic region (perineum) are tight and strong. The nervous type of girl may need more rest and sleep than she had been getting in the premarital period; she may need to sit in a warm bath for ten or twenty minutes before attempting intercourse; she must have great love for and reliance in her mate; she needs to have perfect confidence in her contraceptive protection or, even better, to be willing to accept a pregnancy as the natural outcome of the act of copulation. Quite naturally she probably will not wish to become pregnant immediately after marriage, nor will she wish to be submerged by a deluge of children. In such case she can relax only when she is reasonably sure that pregnancy will not ensue. It is rare indeed that a healthy woman with a proper attitude toward marriage will fail to attain success in intercourse if she has a husband whom she loves and respects and who is willing to put the attainment of her success before his own.

Sometimes we hear of women who are so eager to experience an orgasm that they try *too* hard and exhaust themselves in the effort. Hysterical tears and frenzied effort are hardly consistent with the reasonable hope of success in such cases. They may be quite disastrous. Success in this important matter is something that may be requested but not commanded. Rarely is a frontal attack upon the objective successful. One may eagerly *invite* happiness of this sort, but one is not permitted to *demand* it at the cost of tears and sobs. It will not obey such a summons. Women of this sort are *not* frigid—the frigid woman just does not want anything to do with sexual intercourse. The too-eager wife usually needs only to relax and let appreciation for the sexual act develop.

PREVENTION OF CONCEPTION

Methods of contraception relate themselves to the whole matter of marital hygiene. They may constitute an occasional hazard and so need to be discussed in this place. There are women and men who will feel a twinge of conscience in the use of them, as they have been taught that they are somewhat immoral or that they are dangerous in some way. There are couples who hold such a warranted fear of pregnancy that they can in no wise enjoy conjugal relations without them. There are some methods, like the intrauterine stem, which are actually somewhat dangerous to health and should be avoided for that reason; others are ineffectual, like the douche, and by failure lead to a distrust of all such means; and still others are such a nuisance as to be quite disturbing, particularly to the less amorous member of the pair.

The matter of conscience is one for the individual couple and one that would best have been decided *before* marriage. Intercourse has three purposes, not merely the one purpose of procreation. It is argued by some that not even the beasts are so crass as to have intercourse for pleasure only. Well, maybe that is the reason they have remained beasts, while man has developed all of the lovely sentiments and emotions which cluster about the home and have made the human species superior to the cattle of the field. A husband and wife need to be much in each other's arms, while at the same time in this complex world they need to have some control over the number of children they may beget. To practice contraception or not to practice contraception is a matter for the individual couple to decide, and it is to be hoped that they can and do agree on the principle and the methods involved.

As a matter of *danger* there is little to be said except that the use of poisonous douches is obviously wrong. The vaginal mucous membrane will absorb bichloride of mercury, phenol, and other such products, as does the stomach. Irritating douches are a menace. For example, suppose a cresol douche is made up with hard water and the strength is gauged by the color of the mixture. The milky color is really due to the *hardness of the water*. When a wife uses soft water (away from home, perhaps) and the white color does not develop promptly, she is prone to add more cresol and to get a bad burn. Sometimes warm water is not available for a douche. Cold water may be a considerable shock to the organs flushed with blood as they are after intercourse. A stem pessary reaching into the cavity of the uterus obviously may carry infection upward from the vagina.

A method of contraception which is ineffectual may lead to a tremendous family fight if it fails at a crucial time, causing either the husband or wife or both to be much disturbed and possibly to be excessively outspoken on the subject. There is no contraceptive device that is absolutely foolproof. All of them require intelligent use and a certain amount of self-restraint at a time when restraint is not easy to attain. A failure at a crucial time may jeopardize the possibility of confidence in such methods at all subsequent attempts. Couples using contraceptives should remember that in all probability the product of a failure will at a later period be the most precious thing in their lives, and that an occasional failure is nearly always a good thing. It will be fortunate if they remember that he who dances must at least occasionally pay the piper.

By all means the method chosen must be one that puts the burden of bother and responsibility upon the one of the pair who is most anxious to have intercourse. The amorous man who requires his reluctant wife to take all the precautions so that he—the all-important male—may have his enjoyment and then get to sleep is certainly not being wise in looking only after his own pleasure. A more accurate way of destroying the last vestige of passion could hardly be devised. Early in marriage the use of the condom is safer in such a time of inexperience. The method has its many objections but is far preferable to diaphragms, douches, and contraceptive jellies, foams, suppositories, and the like, so long as the wife is relatively uninterested. Even after the wife has become more passionate it would be well if the husband would share with her the trouble, restraint, and annoyance that is inherent in all of these methods.

This is not to urge the use of contraceptives but merely to point out the various possibilities of physical injury or annoyance which may result in injury to the lovely relation that should exist between a husband and wife. Couples will be far happier as a rule and the marriages will be more stable if such a number of children are born as will satisfy the natural parental desires of the individuals concerned. Women with children live longer on the average than those without children. Marriages with children are less likely to end in divorce. Certainly it must be evident that couples with children get tremendous enjoyment out of them and that there is no place in the world so lonely as the old people's home for childless men and women. Men who have something to work for are more likely to succeed in business or in the professions and, in spite of the increased expense of children, amass more wealth on the average than do men without such expensive responsibilities. There is such a thing as being compelled to make good. A man with a family of four or five children has a far more definite incentive than does he who works alone.

INTERCOURSE DURING PREGNANCY

When pregnancy occurs there is much for the wife and the husband—now prospective parents—to learn. They should first go—at once—to the family physician. If they have not made such a connection they should do so at once and stay close to such an adviser during this period—a period of some stress, but also one capable of high and most satisfying idealism. The emotions of two good persons loving each other, legally married, and conscious of the soul-stirring fact of pregnancy are so precious and so complicated that it is utterly impossible to give any conception of them on a printed page. The person who has missed this experience has missed the most exalted experience life has to offer.

What about intercourse during pregnancy? This question has been answered negatively in a categorical way far too many times. One who understands the anatomy and physiology of pregnancy will see in the relation no danger whatever, provided two or three considerations are remembered.

1. Need a loving husband be reminded that he must be very careful and gentle at such a time and that he must under no possibility hurt his wife? It would seem that this is very evident.

2. Intercourse should not be undertaken if abortion or natural labor is evidently likely to happen within the next few weeks. The reason is to be found in the fact that infectious germs might be introduced into the birth canal.

3. If such an act would leave the wife nervous or restless it should be avoided because *nothing* must be permitted to disturb the mother *and child* at such a time if it possibly can be avoided.

It is significant that many wives are unusually passionate during pregnancy. Sometimes it is the only period in their married life when they can have intercourse without fear of pregnancy; sometimes the consciousness of the tremendous role which is being enacted makes the couple more than commonly precious to each other. Pregnancy is—and properly should be—a period of high purpose and unselfish dedication to a great function. Under such a stimulus the prospective parents may well draw nearer to each other in their resolve that, come what will, they will protect, develop, and cherish the child which is developing between them. If refraining from intercourse will enhance this emotion, they should refrain; if indulgence—within the limits mentioned above—has the effect of binding them together more permanently, their own welfare *and* that of the child are served.

INTERCOURSE AMONG THE ELDERLY

What about intercourse as one grows older? Quite naturally the hot fires of youth will abate as the years pass. There are other things in life than passionate love—other things that are even more precious and enduring. The appreciation of these other things should be developed as one becomes more and more mature. Then as the fires of passion grow dimmer there will be other sources of warmth and comfort in the days that would otherwise be cold and lonesome. How foolish is the man who says, "When I get too old to chase a blonde I shall be willing to begin chasing a golf ball!" Or the man who says, "When I grow too old to be interested in a pretty woman I shall be ready to die!" How foolish is the woman past the age of physical attraction in the erogenous sense who tries to look and act as if she were eighteen. It is surprising sometimes that she should succeed so well with her skin and fail so badly with her understanding of life. She, of course, fools no one but herself—if we may suppose that she succeeds in fooling herself.

It will surprise many readers to know that many old couples still are able to enjoy sexual relations—even ardent intercourse—when they are in their seventies and even occasionally beyond. Which ones are they? They are the ones who have been highly successful in such matters in their younger years, the ones who have saved their precious powers and protected them from disease, promiscuity, and abuse. They have not wasted or thrown away their heritage but have developed it and used it to make themselves strong and capable. Many such women greatly enjoy intercourse for long years after the menopause. By having "passed" in the early years of enjoyment they have earned the right to take a postgraduate course in the same subject. What a beautiful picture it is to see an elderly couple supremely happy with life as it is lived by a good old man and a sweet old lady. We can only envy the one who at eighty is able to enjoy the companionship or the memory of the one who has meant more to him or her than any other. Surely this is success in life. It would be better to fail in all else and succeed at home than to succeed in all else and fail at home.

Topics for further thought:

1. Successful sexual adjustment in marriage involves more than physical happiness of the married pair. Discuss some of the fundamental ideological aspects of sexual compatibility.

2. Some of our societal values heavily influence sexual adjustment in marriage. Describe some of the most important of these, explaining their influence on individuals.

Selected reading references

Donahue, Wilma, and Tibbitts, Clark, *Growing in the Older Years,* Ann Arbor, University of Michigan Press, 1951.
A comprehensive analysis of aging and its attendant conditions. Relevant for family life education.

Kelly, G. Lombard, *Sex Manual,* Augusta, Ga., Southern Medical Supply Company, 1950.
See Chapter 17 for an account of the hygiene of marriage.

McGinnis, Esther, "Age is Meant for Living," *Journal of Home Economics,* 1950, as reprinted in Landis, Judson T., and Landis, Mary G., *Readings in Marriage and the Family,* New York, Prentice-Hall, 1952, pp. 430-35.
A constructive approach to the problems created by the increased life expectancy of family members.

Stern, Curt, *Principles of Human Genetics,* San Francisco, W. H. Freeman and Company, 1949.
Contains a valuable and readable account of the operation of the Rh blood factor and its effect upon mother and children.

FOUR

CONCEPTION, PREGNANCY, AND

CHILDBIRTH

24 HEREDITY: FACTS AND FALLACIES

Warren P. Spencer

Heredity is the study of the likenesses and differences between parents and children and the way in which these are transmitted. The bodies of all higher plants and animals, including man, are made up of many cells. In the average man there are about thirty million million red blood cells and in his brain about fourteen thousand million nerve cells. Yet each human being develops from a single fertilized egg cell formed by the union of one sperm and one egg cell. In each cell a small body, generally spherical or oval in shape, the nucleus, contains the material known as chromatin. This substance is the physical basis of heredity. While the human egg cell is much larger than the sperm, this difference in size is due to the cytoplasm, the part of the cell not included in the nucleus. The bulk of the sperm cell is nuclear material. All of the sperm cells, from which the approximately two and one half billion human beings now living in the world have developed, if brought together would form a mass not much larger than an aspirin tablet. Thus all of the physical hereditary material which has gone into the formation of the living members of the human race would form a mass of material approximately the size of two and one half aspirin tablets. This tiny physical bridge carries the total of the hereditary factors from one generation to the next.

Cell Division. The fertilized egg cell contains within its nucleus 48 tiny rod-shaped bodies of chromatin: the chromosomes. The chromosomes occur in pairs, one of each pair contributed by the sperm cell and the other by the egg cell. This cell undergoes many successive divisions, eventually resulting in the myriad cells that make up the adult body. At every cell division each of the 48 chromosomes becomes duplicated; every resulting cell therefore contains a complete set of chromosomes identical to those in the fertilized egg. During development the cytoplasm outside the nucleus of the cells becomes differentiated, resulting in the several tissues and organs of the body. In the ovaries of the female and the testes of the male certain cells, the primary sex cells, undergo a special type of division, resulting in a reduction of the chromosome number to 24. Each sperm or egg cell contains one chromosome of each pair. This is in preparation for the union of the gamete, egg or sperm, with another gamete of the opposite sex to give 48 chromosomes in the nucleus of the fertilized egg or zygote. About half of the hereditary material, therefore, comes from one parent and half from the other parent.

Among the 24 pairs of chromosomes in the male, one pair is different because the two members of the pair are of different size. The larger one is termed an X-chromosome, the smaller one a Y-chromosome. Therefore, at reduction division, half of the sperm cells receive an X and the other half a Y. In the female the corresponding pair of chromosomes are both X-chromosomes. Thus every egg receives an X-chromosome. When a Y-bearing sperm fertilizes an egg, the resulting zygote is XY and therefore male; when an X-bearing sperm unites with an egg, an XX zygote, a female, is formed. The sex of any child is thus determined by the type of sperm cell received from the father. On the basis of this mechanism, about half of the children conceived should be male, the other half female. Of course the sex distribution among the children of a family will be subject to the usual chance fluctuations observed when small samples are involved. Even in large families a certain small proportion of these will be expected to be all of one sex purely by chance.

The Genes. Both the sex chromosomes, the X and Y, and the other 23 pairs, the autosomes, contain the ultimate units of heredity, the genes. The genes are minute bodies arranged in linear order in the chromosomes. As the chromosomes become duplicated at cell division, each gene becomes duplicated. Each gene occupies a definite position, its locus, within the chromosome. As the chromosomes occur in pairs, the genes also occur in pairs. By various methods the number of genes in a single chromosome set, such as occurs in egg or sperm, has been calculated for the fruit fly, *Drosophila,* to be about five thousand to ten thousand. The number of genes in a chromosome set in man is probably of the same order of magnitude.

The gene is a relatively stable unit, which undergoes self-duplication at each cell division. On rare occasions a sudden change occurs in a gene. Such a change is known as a gene mutation. The new form of the gene is known as an allele of the original gene, and generally is stable and capable of reduplicating itself in the new mutated form. A given gene may mutate to more than one type of allele, thus forming a multiple allelic series. As each gene and its alternative types can occupy only one place or locus in a chromosome, only two alleles of a multiple allelic series can be present in a given individual, since the chromosomes and chromosome or gene loci occur in pairs. Furthermore, only one allele of the series can be present in a germ cell where the chromosomes occur singly. Populations of individuals, however, can carry all the members of a highly complex multiple allelic series.

The genes condition the characteristics of an organism. A given gene interacts with the rest of the genetic constitution of the individual and with the environment in the development of a given character. A certain character is not necessarily produced solely by the action of a given gene; but unit character differences are due to the differing effects of a gene and its allele. The gene make-up of an organism is known as its genotype, the expressed characters as the phenotype. Where the two genes of a pair are identical, the individual is said to be homozygous for the gene in question; conversely, an individual containing two different alleles at a certain locus in a pair of chromosomes is termed heterozygous. Any mutant gene which, when present in heterozygous form along with the usual or normal allele, conditions a change from the normal character is known as a dominant. Any mutant allele which must be present in homozygous form to condition the character change from the normal is known as a recessive. Some dominants, however, have a more extreme effect in homozygous than in heterozygous form. Any gene carried on the X- or Y-chromosome is termed sex-linked. The effects of such sex-linked genes may have nothing to do with primary or secondary sexual characters, but their distribution will be correlated with the distribution of the sex-determining chromosomes.

AUTOSOMAL RECESSIVES. Only when a gene is present in alternative forms or alleles in a population or species can its existence be known. The rarer allele or the one that conditions a deviation from normal in character expression is considered the mutant gene. In some cases in which alternative alleles are both present in high frequency it is difficult or impossible to say which is the mutant and which the original gene from which it arose. Where a gene is located on an autosome (a chromosome other than the sex chromosomes) and must be present in homozygous form to have any observable effect, the gene is known as an autosomal recessive. In man autosomal recessives range in effect from those in which the phenotype is an extreme abnormality, lethal at or soon after birth, such as infantile amaurotic idiocy, to those in which the phenotype is probably fully as viable and normal as, though different in quality or quantity from, that produced by the original dominant gene allele. Blue eyes and the inability to taste the chemical phenyl-thio-carbamide (recessives) are examples of such nondeleterious mutant types.

A few other representative samples of human autosomal recessives will illustrate the range of expression of such factors. Ichthyosis fetalis is a disease characterized by greatly thickened and deeply furrowed skin and abnormally shortened neck. The infant dies a few hours after birth. Such genes as this and infantile amaurotic idiocy are recessive lethals and always transmitted by heterozygotes, parents who carry the lethal gene along with the normal dominant gene allele and are themselves normal. Fortunately mutant genes of this type are relatively rare, and there are few matings in which both parents are heterozygous, the necessary condition for the production of an affected infant. Phenylketonuria is inherited as a recessive. Affected persons are idiots or imbeciles, and quantities of phenylpyruvic acid are excreted in the urine. Deaf-mutism is a less serious condition sometimes inherited as a recessive. Alkaptonuria, another recessive, results in a failure to oxidize homogentisic acid, an intermediate product formed in normal protein metabolism. The urine of those with alkaptonuria darkens on standing. Arthritis sometimes develops as a by-product of this recessive. Albinism, in which affected persons lack normal pigment of skin, eyes, and hair and are somewhat less vigorous than normal individuals, is another recessive. Blue eyes and taste deficiency, mentioned above, are clear-cut but innocuous recessives, probably equal in vigor to normal or rather alternative types.

AUTOSOMAL DOMINANTS. An autosomal dominant gene may produce its effect in heterozygous condition. If the gene is fully penetrant —that is, always expressed in heterozygous condition—then it follows that in any family pedigree the phenotypic character never skips a generation. This is in definite contrast to recessives, which usually appear sporadically in pedigrees. The list of known autosomal dominants in man is larger than that of recessives, for any dominant mutant, however rare in the population, will be expressed in those persons who carry it. Here also a series of cases might be arranged according to the degree of abnormality produced. This series, however, will not extend as far toward extremely gross abnormal, semilethal, and lethal types as the recessive series for the obvious reason that such mutants, if they occurred, would immediately be lost. The affected person carrying the mutant gene would be killed off before transmitting it to the next generation.

An example of an autosomal dominant apparently without deleterious effect is white forelock or "blaze," in which a streak or patch of white hair occurs on the head, sharply demarcated from the normal hair. Several dominants are known which affect the skeleton. Examples of these are brachydactyly, short fingers; polydactyly, extra fingers or toes; lobster-claw or split hand; and achondroplastic dwarfism. In the latter condition the trunk is of normal length, but the arms and legs are short.

Several serious diseases of the nervous system are inherited as dominants, in which the abnormal symptoms develop late in life. Such a dominant may appear to skip a generation in its transmission, as some persons carrying the gene may pass it on to the next generation and then die before the onset of the disease. Had these people lived long enough, the dominant abnormality would probably have developed. Creeping paralysis is an example. This condition generally manifests itself in the late fifties or the sixties, long after the normal reproductive period. Such genes, which have their abnormal phenotypic effects late in life, are not selected against in the population, as they are transmitted to the next generation by an individual before they have any lethal or deleterious effect on the individual carrier himself. Huntington's chorea, characterized by progressive mental deterioration, is another such dominant which has its onset in middle age.

The inherited nature of most dominants is relatively easy to determine from their high incidence in family pedigrees and the fact that they do not skip a generation in their manifestation. Where the dominant produces an extreme abnormal effect, either physical or mental, particularly if the effect is present at birth or develops early in life, it would seem preferable for anyone with the condition not to have children and risk passing the gene to them. The chance of any child of such an individual developing the same abnormality is one in two. For a well-expressed dominant with full penetrance, the chance that a normal individual who has a parent showing the abnormality will pass this condition on to offspring is practically nil.

SEX-LINKED RECESSIVES. In the human X-chromosome there is a region that has no homologue in the Y-chromosome. For gene loci in this part of the X there are no corresponding loci in the Y. Certain genes present in this part of the X are known as sex-linked recessives. The gene must be present in both X-chromosomes of the female to produce its characteristic phenotypic expression. However, in the male with only one X-chromosome, the gene, if present in this X, manifests itself, as the Y-chromosome carries no allele at this locus. Thus many more males than females in the population will show such sex-linked recessive characters. Red-green color blindness is an example. With a freqeuncy of about 10 per cent color-blind to 90 per cent normal genes, roughly 10 per cent males and 1 per cent females are color-blind. For other sex-linked recessives the gene frequencies differ and the proportions of affected males and females consequently differ; but there are always more males than females showing the character. The gene for color blindness can be transmitted by a father only to his daughters, while a mother may transmit the gene to either sons or daughters. A color-blind boy always gets the gene from his mother, never from his father. This follows from the fact that his X-chromosome comes from the mother.

Hemophilia, hereditary bleeding, is a sex-linked recessive gene with a low frequency. Only affected males have been identified. Possibly the gene is so rare that homozygous females have not been produced. Possibly the homozygous condition is lethal in females.

Progressive muscular dystrophy of a certain type is inherited as a sex-linked recessive. The affected person shows a progressive degeneration of muscles beginning in the first decade of life. These hopeless cripples die at an early age. There is one chance in two that a normal sister of such an affected male carries this gene. If she marries and has a child there is one chance in eight that the child will be a male with this disease.

SEX-LINKED DOMINANTS. A few sex-linked dominants occur in man. The known sex-linked recessives in man are much more numerous than the sex-linked dominants. These recessives are easily discovered even though a particular recessive is rare, as they show up in any male carrying them. Probably mutant autosomal recessives in man are also more frequent than dominants, but are less often discovered because of their mode of inheritance. One example of a sex-linked dominant is a brownish discoloration of the enamel of the teeth. All the daughters, but none of the sons, of an affected man show the condition, as he passes his X-chromosome to daughters but not to sons.

The Y-chromosome carries a segment which is not represented by a homologous segment in the X. Genes in this segment are passed directly from father to son, and all sons of an affected father will be expected to show the character. One such gene condition is webbed toes. In the pedigree males alone are affected. These exclusively Y-borne genes are much fewer than the sex-linked genes carried in the X-chromosomes.

BLOOD GROUPS. In the human being there are four blood groups or classifications. These types depend on agglutinogens in the red cells and agglutinins in the serum. When incompatible types are mixed in transfusion, the foreign materials cause two reactions: hemolysis, the destruction of red blood cells and the resultant escape of hemoglobin; and agglutination, a joining together or clumping of the red blood cells. To avoid these poor results in blood transfusion, typing of blood has become very important.

The four types of human blood and the groups with which each may be matched for transfusion follow:

Type	May Receive in Transfusion	May Supply for Transfusion
A	A or O	A or AB
B	B or O	B or AB
AB	A, B, AB, or O	AB only
O	O only	All

RH FACTOR. Rh classification, while not related to blood grouping, is increasingly being recorded at the same time as the blood type. It is important not to transfuse Rh-positive blood into the blood of an Rh-negative woman. This is also important to the baby in the event of a future pregnancy.

The Rh factor is a chemical substance found in the red blood cells of most people. The name evolved because of the relation of this substance to a like substance found in the red blood cells of the Rhesus monkeys. If this factor is present, the person is Rh positive, but if the red blood cells do not contain this Rh factor, Rh negativity results. There is nothing basically better or worse about either condition.

When both parents are Rh negative, the woman has nothing to fear in pregnancy. When the father is Rh positive and the mother is Rh negative, an Rh-positive infant may sometimes have a rare type of severe anemia (erythroblastosis fetalis or hemolytic disease of the newborn). Other possible conditions are jaundice and enlargement of the baby's spleen and liver at birth. Parents with this combination of Rh factors, however, should note that complications due to the Rh factor are rare, affecting only about one in every 200 cases. Among the estimated 13 per cent of married couples with this combination, the chances of any difficulty are approximately 1 in 26. The mother can usually plan on having two or more healthy babies with Rh-positive blood before trouble starts.

In the event that the child of the Rh-positive father and the Rh-negative mother is negative, and there is about an even chance of this occurring, then no trouble will ensue. If the unborn baby is positive, however, a reaction is set off when a small amount of Rh substance enters the mother's blood stream. This reaction takes the form of antibodies which are manufactured by the mother's Rh-negative blood to fight off the foreign Rh-positive factor. These antibodies keep up the destructive process upon entering the baby's circulatory system and destroy the baby's Rh-positive red cells.

If blood tests show that a pregnant woman is Rh negative, her husband's blood is also tested. If he proves to be Rh positive, the mother's blood is tested three times during her pregnancy for the presence of antibodies. Often none appear; if they do, they may appear late in pregnancy. Their presence warns the doctor to be ready to deal with the ensuing situation.

If the baby is affected, at birth he receives transfusions of Rh-negative blood, which is unaffected by the antibodies produced by the mother. This corrects his anemia and supplies his organs and tissues with the needed oxygen. While one or two transfusions may be sufficient, if the infant is severely affected a replacement transfusion to draw off and replace all the blood may be necessary.

After an Rh-negative woman has been sensitized and has started to produce antibodies, either by having an Rh-positive blood transfusion or by bearing an Rh-positive child, the condition remains and becomes progressively stronger with each succeeding pregnancy. It is important, therefore, for Rh-negative women of all ages to have transfusions only of Rh-negative blood. Further study in the effects of this Rh factor has revealed that only one of the four Rh-positive types involves the danger of adverse results, but the necessity for extreme caution is not obviated.

NORMAL DIFFERENCES. One might gather from the facts presented that most mutant genes in man are highly deleterious. Certainly many of them are, but these severe hereditary abnormalities have naturally been the first to draw the attention of medical men and those interested in human heredity. Many mutant genes in man condition relatively minor characteristics, some of which should be classed as differences rather than abnormalities. The discovery of more of these character differences, particularly where the mutant gene frequency is high, is one of the major current aims of human geneticists. Such characters will be important in advancing the knowledge of human heredity and eventually will have practical applications in linkage studies involving the more serious inherited human abnormalities.

Many conditions are known to have a hereditary basis, although the exact mode of inheritance is not yet known. Such problems could readily be solved if one were working with plants or other animals, but obviously man is not an experimental animal, at least in so far as the analysis of hereditary differences is concerned. Difficulties of analysis include the fact that some conditions are the resultant of multiple genetic factors, several mutant genes at different loci reacting to induce the condition, and the fact that some apparently identical effects are induced by different genes or even by environmental factors. Genes that modify the action of the principal mutant gene, resulting in irregular expression or even complete suppression of the character, complicate the picture.

The normal alleles are inherited by the same mechanism as the abnormal mutant genes. Fortunately, when the dice of destiny, the genes, were cast, human beings received at least one normal allele at most gene loci. Genetics studies on many organisms, both plant and animal, where controlled breeding experiments were possible over a long period of time, have shown that characters such as bodily vigor, high disease resistance, long life, or excellence in performance of some function useful to man are inherited. Most of these favorable characters have been shown to be the product of the united action of many different gene pairs, so-called quantitative characters. It is reasonable to conclude that favorable characters in man, including many mental, artistic, and creative traits, have a basis in heredity. However, the analysis of the inheritance of such characters lies in the distant future. The uncritical methods and naïve conclusions in studies such as those of the Jukes and Kallikaks are regarded with suspicion by modern students of human genetics. No doubt good and bad heredity were involved, but much more critical methods must be used to establish the mode of inheritance of quantitative mental and physical human characters.

Methods of Study. As man is not an experimental animal the accumulation of data regarding heredity is often difficult and sometimes impossible. Three main methods of study supply most of the information. The first of these to be employed was the careful compilation of family pedigrees involving the transmission of alternative alleles. The second, developed in recent years, has been the statistical study of gene frequencies in populations. This method has been remarkably successful, as it does not rely upon following gene differences through several generations. For many genetic factors it furnishes valuable and accurate data which could not be compiled by the family-pedigree method. The third, studies on identical twins, has added much valuable information on the relative roles of heredity and environment. Identical twins arise by the separation of the product of a single fertilized egg into two units, either at the two-cell or at some later stage. Such twins carry identical chromosome and gene complexes, and consequently differences between members of a pair are due entirely to the environment.

J. B. S. Haldane has reported mutation rates for several human genes. His figures for some human genes follow:

Mutation	Rate
Achondroplasia	1 per 25,000 genes
Hemophilia	1 per 31,250 genes
Retinoblastoma	1 per 71,500 genes
Aniridia	1 per 100,000 to 200,000 genes
Epiloia	1 per 125,000 to 250,000 genes

Most of these studies have been made on the population of Denmark. The highest mutation rate Haldane reports is for achondroplastic dwarfism. Apparently about one normal human gene in twenty-five thousand at this locus mutates to a dominant allele which conditions this phenotype. In a study of the inherited blood disease, thalassemia, J. V. Neel has calculated a mutation rate of about one normal gene in two thousand to the mutant type in an Italian population. These recent studies indicate that even if a human stock could be obtained which carried no deleterious mutant genes, these would soon arise by mutation. The eugenic hope of a race entirely free of defective germ plasm seems to be impossible of attainment.

THE FALLACIES

Hereditary and Environmental Factors. Jean Baptiste Lamarck, a French biologist who lived and wrote in the late eighteenth and early nineteenth centuries, proposed a theory of organic evolution based on the idea that changes which took place in the body of a person through use or disuse of organs or through the effect of various environmental factors would be inherited by the offspring. This idea came to be known as the "inheritance of acquired characters." The concept was accepted by Darwin at least to some extent and by most biologists of the late nineteenth century. Remnants of this theory are still adhered to by many people not conversant with the studies of modern biology. The evidence for this theory is uniformly negative. Changes that take place in the body of a person through environmental influences do not have an effect on the heredity of the offspring. Birthmarks, deformities, mental or physical traits, whether good or bad, are not induced in the child during pregnancy by the experiences of the mother in that period. Alleged effects of this kind are mere coincidences. However, the development, health, and well-being of the fetus may be influenced by the intrauterine environment. The Rh antibody developed in the blood of the mother and acting on the blood of the fetus is a case in point. Presumably the general condition of the expectant mother may influence to some extent the development of the fetus. Such changes have nothing to do with the hereditary mechanism. Syphilis may be transmitted from mother to unborn child, but it is not inherited. To state that it is inherited is a misuse of terms.

The widespread fallacy that nothing can be done if a disease or condition is inherited arises from a misconception of the roles of heredity and environment in the development and control of characters. Throughout life there is a constant interplay of hereditary and environmental factors in the development, growth, and health of the individual. Many characters and conditions having a hereditary basis may be changed, suppressed, or magnified by the manipulation of the environment. The disease diabetes, which at least in many cases has a hereditary basis, may be controlled by the proper use of insulin. Diabetics may lead relatively normal lives and live to a ripe old age. A chief aim of modern medicine is the discovery of environmental factors, including drug treatment and even surgery, which will compensate for hereditary defects. The treatment of the individual, however, does not alter the germ plasm. Acquired characters are not inherited.

RADIATION-INDUCED MUTATIONS

In quite a different category are the changes that may be induced in the germ plasm by radiations from radium, x-rays, and the various radioactive by-products of atomic fission. In 1927 Dr. H. J. Muller demonstrated that x-rays induced germinal mutations in the fruit fly, *Drosophila,* when these flies were subjected to radiation. These observations have been abundantly confirmed by extensive experiments on many other organisms, including mice. Furthermore, it has been shown that the number of mutations induced by radiation is proportional to the dosage, even for extremely low dosages. A current fallacy in this connection is that there is a low tolerance dosage, below which mutations of the germ plasm will not occur. This fallacy ignores the mechanism of mutation. It is of course true that the chance of a mutation being induced in a given germ cell following low dosage exposure is relatively low. In this atomic age every precaution should be taken to keep exposure of individuals and of populations to a minimum. Persons of reproductive age should not have their sex glands subjected even to light dosages of x-rays, radium, or other radioactive agents if this can possibly be avoided. Most mutations induced by these agents are deleterious.

Sex Predetermination. Several methods have been proposed whereby the sex of the human offspring can be predetermined. Experimental studies on rabbits and other laboratory animals have shown that at present these proposed methods are invalid. True, there are more human males than females born. When the records for stillbirths are included there are on the average about 120 male conceptions to 100 female conceptions. The explanation suggested for this fact is that the Y-bearing sperm, possibly because of the smaller size of the Y-chromosome, has a slight advantage over the X-bearing sperm in the fertilization race in which these two types of sperm engage. The time may come, but is not yet here, when some sort of mass sorting of these two types of human sperm, followed by artificial insemination, may make it possible to predetermine the sex of a child.

Sterilization. It has often been suggested that sterilization of the unfit would solve the hereditary problems of mankind. In the case of a well-defined hereditary dominant, marked by gross abnormalities, either mental or physical, sterilization, segregation, or efficient contraception should be advocated. Some of these dominants, however, tend to be self-eliminating through early death of the afflicted persons. Furthermore, Haldane's work on human mutation rates indicates that a eugenic program can never eliminate all defective dominants, although their incidence could be brought down to that determined by mutation rates. At present the chance of transmitting a defective dominant, which is generally one in two, and the seriousness of the abnormality should determine the reproductive behavior of the individual involved.

When the elimination of defective recessive genes is concerned, sterilization or other methods of preventing reproduction of afflicted individuals has relatively little effect on the frequency of the recessive genes in the population and, therefore, on the number of individuals showing the defect in the next generation. This is due to the fact that most of the deleterious genes are carried in heterozygous form, and most such heterozygous carriers cannot now be detected. From the purely personal point of view, however—and in such matters few people place racial welfare above personal happiness—persons in family lines in which recessive abnormalities have appeared would do well by their prospective offspring not to marry blood relations.

Dominant-Recessive Ratios. A fallacy sometimes held by those who have heard a little about Mendelian heredity is that where two parents are heterozygous for a recessive, one-fourth of their children will show the character. Actually, in individual families any ratio might be found between the dominant and recessive characters among the children of two heterozygous parents. In fact, all of the children or none of them may show the recessive character. Likewise, when one parent is heterozygous for a dominant and the other parent does not carry it, there is no assurance that half of the children will show the dominant. All or none of them may show it. Such fluctuations from expected ratios may occur when small samples are taken, and the children in any one family constitute a small sample. Furthermore, it is incorrect to conclude that because two alternative characters appear in a human population in approximately a three-to-one ratio the more frequently occurring character is the dominant, the other the recessive. It may well be that the frequently occurring character is the recessive. The incidence of the alternative characters in the population depends upon the gene frequencies.

A commonly held fallacy is to suppose that characters due to alternative alleles are always invariable in expression. There are many examples known in the heredity of plants and animals where the character expression fluctuates widely under the influence of genetic or environmental modifiers. Many persons carrying the genes conditioning the character may be normal or show the character to only a slight degree. Such persons may, however, transmit the mutant gene.

Race Crossing. Hereditary differences in races and the hereditary effects of race crossing raise difficult questions. Here fact and fallacy intermingle even in the writings of some otherwise competent scientific investigators. Isolated and exceptional cases are used to prove the rule. Prejudice supersedes reason. In spite of many factors operating to bring about miscegenation, there still remain in the world large and more or less contiguous populations that differ from others in a number of obviously inherited traits. To state that one such group differs from another by a few superficial and unimportant hereditary traits would seem to be begging the question. Actually recent studies, which could be carried on objectively on several of the inherited blood factors, have shown definite differences in gene frequencies of the various alleles from racial group to racial group. These studies indicate that probably racial groups do differ widely in the frequencies of many genes.

The factors over which most of the controversy rages—mental ability, physical stamina, emotional balance, and the constituent traits that make up these complexes—are determined intraracially by multiple genetic factors interacting with a large number of environmental variables. Only gross departures from the norm, conditioned by one or a few gene substitutions, have been genetically analyzed. It seems futile, then, in our present state of knowledge to attempt to establish the thesis either of racial superiority or of racial equality. It is no answer to the questions raised to repeat the cliché that fluctuations within a race are greater than fluctuations between races. For the major races of mankind the curves of variation for most physical and mental characters are broadly overlapping. In spite of many published studies purporting to deal with racial comparisons, the data are fragmentary and inconclusive. Where race crossing on a wide scale has occurred, obvious biological disharmonies in the hybrids have not been demonstrated. This does not mean that a careful analysis on a large scale might not demonstrate statistically some disharmony.

In individual cases, in considering marriage between members of two racial groups, the social implications of such matings are likely to far outweigh the biological factors involved. Where no serious social consequences are likely to accrue, racial intermarriage can hardly be condemned on biological grounds. Where social stigmas are still prevalent, two individuals of different races need to consider the security and happiness of offspring in addition to their own inclinations. There seems little doubt that miscegenation will increase in this fast-shrinking world. In any case, the intelligent choice of a mate, sound in mind and body, is the best insurance of success in undertaking the greatest of all biological adventures, marriage and the rearing of a family.

Topics for further thought:

1. Should society through legislation exercise greater control over the process of mate selection? Would the gains for society outweigh possible losses for the individual?

2. What persons should be sterilized? What are your criteria for selection? Comment on the traditional objections to sterilization.

Selected reading references

Herndon, C. Nash, "Medical Genetics and Marriage Counseling," *Marriage and Family Living,* August, 1954, pp. 207-11.
    A brief survey of some of the kinds of problems brought to genetics counselors by married or about-to-be-married persons.

Neugarten, Bernice L., *Your Heredity,* Chicago, Science Research Associates.
    A *Life Adjustment Booklet* designed for boys and girls in high school.

Osborn, Frederick, *Preface to Eugenics,* New York, Harper and Brothers, 1940.
    A basic textbook in the field, by a leading geneticist.

Scheinfeld, Amram, *Men and Women,* New York, Harcourt, Brace and Company, 1944.

Considers the nature and consequences of biological and psychological differences between the sexes. Written for lay persons.

Scheinfeld, Amram, *The New You and Heredity,* Philadelphia, J. B. Lippincott, 1950.

An excellent, non-technical book on human heredity. Answers, to the best of the geneticist's ability, most of the questions usually raised by persons anticipating marriage.

25 OVULATION AND FERTILITY

M. Edward Davis

THE survival of any species depends as much on its ability to reproduce as on an adequate supply of food and a favorable environment. In single-celled animals and lower forms of life, reproduction may be a simple process of fission such as is seen in the one-celled animal Cothurnia, in which the daughter cell, by the simple expedient of fission, separates from the mother cell and floats away to begin life as a new individual; or as in some worms which split in two or more segments, each segment forming a separate worm. Such simple reproductions without sex are obviously not adapted to the more complicated species. Human reproduction involves a carefully synchronized mechanism to allow for the blending of the male and female genetic qualities into an offspring resembling its parents. Male and female germ cells must meet and unite. The resultant fertilized ovum is transported safely to the nesting place where it can continue its development to completion. Human fertility necessitates normal organs, co-ordinated glandular function, and a sound regulatory nervous mechanism.

THE RHYTHM OF REPRODUCTIVE FUNCTION

Periodically in the ovaries of all sexually mature animals follicles containing the ova or eggs begin to ripen. When one or more of these germ cells have become mature their follicles rupture and release them. This periodic event is associated with an intense mating desire in the female. The lowly sow remains quiet and peaceful during the two and a half weeks of each three-week cycle, interested only in eating and sleeping. For a period of three days (estrus) when ripe follicles are present in the ovary, she becomes restless and excitable, seeking out the male and accepting him promptly. The cycles in some animals are short—four or five days in rats and mice—or exceedingly long. The shortest cycle is seen in the hen, which lays an egg once a day, and the longest in the locust, where reproduction occurs once in seventeen years.

In most of the animals the female will accept the male only during those periods when an egg is ripe and ready for rupture. In fact, in a few, such as the cat and the ferret, the sexual act induces the rupture of ripe follicles and the discharge of their eggs. In the human female the reproductive cycles recur at about four-week intervals. Most women usually are not aware that ovulation is taking place or that a ripe follicle is present in the ovary. Probably it makes itself known by certain changes, but these are imperceptible to most women. Rarely, some women will have a twinge of pain in one or the other of the groins or an indefinite sensation of discomfort at the time of rupture of the follicle. This twinge or discomfort has been known as *Mittelschmerz,* the German for pain in the middle of the cycle. Sexual activity is not confined to the short period in the cycle when a ripe follicle is ready to rupture. No unusual sex urge increases the likelihood of fertilization of the mature ovum. Periods of fertility and infertility must be established in each person from physiological data available.

THE ACTIVITY OF THE HUMAN OVARY

The human ovary or the female sex gland has a dual function—to produce ova or eggs for reproduction and to perform as a gland of internal secretion. Reproduction is dependent on both of these roles, for it would be impossible for a fertilized egg to continue its development in the absence of the ovarian hormones.

The activity of the ovary which produces the ova is cyclical in character. Each month in the mature woman a number of primary follicles containing these ova begin to grow in size under the influence of an internal secretion from the pituitary gland. This growth period lasts about two weeks and is culminated by the rapid enlargement of a single follicle, rarely two, for a period of 72 hours. This follicle finally ruptures, catapulting the egg in the direction of the oviduct, or the Fallopian tube. This process of follicle rupture and the discharge of the ripe egg is designated as ovulation.

Theoretically the egg escapes free into the abdomen, but by an ingenious mechanism it is almost invariably directed to the funnel-shaped entrance of the Fallopian tube, which serves as a passageway from the neighborhood of the ovary to the interior of the uterus. (See Fig. 2, p. 191.) This quill-like structure has a special lining consisting of delicate folds and a muscular wall adapted to the transportation of the egg toward the interior of the uterus. At the time of ovulation the Fallopian tubes undergo wavelike contractions, such as are seen in the intestines, designed to move anything within their lumens toward the uterus.

The life of the human ovum is short, probably less than 24 hours if fertilization does not take place. However, if intercourse occurs immediately before or soon after the egg escapes from the follicle, fertilization can take place. Spermatozoa, the male germ cells, are deposited about the cervix or they are forced into the mucus of the cervical canal at the time of copulation. Spermatozoa are equipped with tails which they use for locomotion. They penetrate through the cervical mucus, travel across the lining of the uterus, and seek out the ovum within the Fallopian tube. (See Fig. 2.) If it is still alive one spermatozoon penetrates the outer covering, and its nuclear portion or center unites with that of the egg to accomplish fertilization. The egg can now begin to grow, to divide and subdivide, to produce a normal baby 267 days later. The act of fertilization thus connotes the beginning of a new life.

The fertilized egg is moved slowly down the Fallopian tube, entering the cavity of the uterus at the end of about three days. If its stay in the tube is prolonged beyond this period, its rapid growth will interfere with its movement and it may become attached to the wall of the tube. It may continue to grow in this locality, ultimately giving rise to a condition known as a tubal pregnancy. Normally it enters the uterine cavity, where it remains unattached for three or four days more. At the end of day six or seven, the fertilized egg, now a globular mass of dividing cells, no larger than the head of a pin, attaches itself to the succulent lining of the uterus. It burrows rapidly beneath the surface, producing a minute amount of bleeding, and is covered over by the broken-down, partially digested cells. From this period of implantation its growth will be rapid and spectacular.

SECRETION OF HORMONES AND MENSTRUATION

The ovary, a gland of internal secretion, produces as one of its secretions the estrogenic hormone. This hormone is present in the growing follicle of the ovary and all the cells of the follicle produce it. (This hormone has been found in many body tissues and fluids in different chemical forms and varying concentrations. It is abundant in the placenta or afterbirth during pregnancy, and the placenta probably serves as the chief source of supply.) The estrogenic hormone is known as the female sex hormone because all the feminine attributes depend upon it. Yet it is present in many organs, tissues, and fluids in the male as well as the female. In fact, the urine of the stallion is a rich source of estrogens. Masculinity and femininity are relative terms; male and female sex hormones are present in both the male and the female. In the female, the estrogens predominate; in the male, the male sex hormone or testosterone is normally in greater concentration.

The estrogenic hormone brings about the developmental changes in the girl which begin at puberty and culminate at maturity. Under its influence the feminine figure evolves, the breasts develop, the feminine hair pattern emerges, the external and internal genital organs grow to normal size and shape, and the young girl begins to menstruate. Even the feminine pitch of the voice is dependent on estrogenic hormones.

The menstrual function begins irregularly at first. Then as follicle growth and development in the ovary become cyclical in character it assumes an adult pattern, typical for the individual. The average interval between menstrual periods is 28 to 31 days, but some women have short cycles of 21 to 24 days, and a few have long cycles of 31 to 35 days. Menstrual bleeding at irregular intervals is abnormal in character, and it is usually the result of some hormonal or organic disorder.

It is customary to date the beginning of the typical cycle with the onset of menstruation because the woman is aware of this cataclysmic event. The first day of bleeding is designated as day one of the cycle. In reality the bleeding period belongs to the previous cycle; it represents the destructive phase of what has already taken place. Under the influence of the estrogenic hormone in the growing follicles the endometrium, or the lining of the uterus, begins to grow in thickness. Maximum growth is reached sometime in the middle of the cycle, at which time a follicle in the ovary has reached complete development. Follicle rupture and the discharge of the ovum usually occur somewhere between days 12 and 16 in the average cycle of 28 to 31 days. Ovulation is the result of stimulation of the ovary by another hormone from the pituitary gland. The follicle wall collapses with the escape of the egg, but the cells that make up the wall undergo a sudden spurt in growth, rapidly developing a thick, wavy border of yellow-colored cells about an ever-diminishing central cavity. This structure is known as the corpus luteum, or the yellow body. The lutein or pigment cells that make up the corpus luteum produce the second of the ovarian hormones, progesterone.

The elaboration of progesterone by the yellow body in the ovary is the signal for a rapid change in the development of the lining of the uterus. Under its influence the endometrium now becomes velvety and succulent. The individual glands and cells which comprise it fill up with secretion rich in those nutriments necessary for the early development of the fertilized egg. The interior of the uterine cavity becomes a real nesting place for the reception, attachment, and growth of the developing embryo.

In the event that the egg does not become fertilized, the life of the corpus luteum is 14 or 15 days. As this structure ceases to function progesterone disappears from the circulation, changes in the blood supply of the uterine lining occur, menstruation starts, and the endometrium of the uterus begins to disintegrate. Menstruation is a destructive phenomenon, for it is the outward expression of a process aimed at removing the beautifully developed uterine lining no longer necessary for the fertilized ovum. Each month Nature makes elaborate preparations for the reception of a fertilized egg, but with the exception of one or several times in the woman's lifetime it is doomed to disappointment.

THE PERIOD OF FERTILITY

Fertility is limited to a very short span in the average cycle. It is possible for a normal, healthy couple to fail to conceive after several years of married life. The egg can be fertilized only during a very short period after it leaves the follicle, probably a matter of hours and certainly no longer than a day. Spermatozoa survive a relatively short time in the reproductive tract, although they live for a much longer period under ideal conditions. Spermatozoa in the vagina live no longer than three or four hours, usually less, for the acid secretion within the vagina is inimical to them. The cervical mucus, however, is a favorable environment and they may remain alive in this region for as long as 24 to 36 hours, perhaps longer. In all likelihood the cervical mucus acts as a reservoir for their protection, and groups of germ cells penetrate through the mucus and travel upward toward the Fallopian tubes. If pregnancy is to occur, coitus must take place within 24 hours of ovulation. The fertile period in each cycle when conception can take place can be narrowed down to one or two days.

Time of Ovulation. It is important to determine the time of ovulation. Women who are anxious to conceive must know whether ovulation occurs and the time of its occurrence. Several methods have been devised to determine whether ovulation has taken place in any given cycle, but they have not been practical in detecting the ovulatory period. The physician in the study of a sterile couple may remove a tiny fragment of the uterine lining at the end of the cycle or at the onset of bleeding. The characteristic picture of this tissue will reveal whether progesterone was available in the cycle. Obviously progesterone is indicative of ovulation and the conversion of the ruptured follicle wall into the corpus luteum. He may examine the urine for the presence of pregnandiol, a substance derived from progesterone. The most practical method of following the changes in the ovary, however, is by means of a body basal temperature graph.

Body Temperature Variations. Body temperature variations in healthy individuals are sensitive indicators of physical as well as mental activity, metabolic activity, and other physiologic functions. Muscular work, food taking, or mental excitement tend to raise the level of the temperature. Rest and sound sleep lower it. Typical curves have been set up demonstrating these fluctuations during a 24-hour period under varying conditions. They follow what is known as a diurnal pattern, for the temperatures at night are lower than those recorded during the day, the nights being devoted to rest and the days to activity.

In the healthy male there is no variation in this pattern day after day. In the female, on the other hand, the normal function of the ovaries alters this basic curve. During that period when the follicle is growing in the ovary the daily temperature remains at a rather low level. The rupture of the follicle, the discharge of the ripe egg, and the rapid conversion of the follicle wall into the corpus luteum are associated with a rise in the level of the temperature, following which it reaches a plateau where it remains until the end of the cycle. Twenty-four to 36 hours before the onset of menstruation the temperature drops to the level existing before ovulation. The rise in temperature is due to the elaboration of progesterone by the corpus luteum. In the event that pregnancy ensues there will be no drop in body temperature, for this hormone of gestation will continue to be supplied by the corpus luteum and, later, by the placenta.

The Temperature Graph. One simple method of determining the time of ovulation is by means of a temperature graph (Fig. 5). Theoretically the normal temperature of a healthy individual is 98.6 degrees. Actually, there are always slight variations from this figure. It has been found that woman's temperature is lower during the first part of the menstrual cycle than it is during the last two weeks of

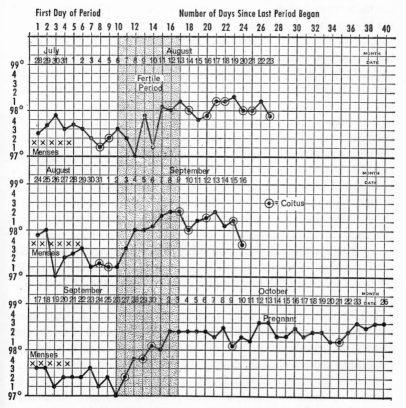

Figure 5. TEMPERATURE GRAPH FOR THREE MENSTRUAL CYCLES

the same cycle, and further, that the shift from the lower level of temperature to the higher occurs about the time of ovulation. Therefore, in many cases it is possible to determine the time of ovulation by keeping a graphic record of each day's temperature. The variation in temperature is slight, only a few fifths of a degree, so it is essential that the temperature be taken with the utmost practical accuracy.

The temperature is to be taken precisely according to a physician's instruction; some doctors wish the temperature taken in the morning, some in the evening; some prefer mouth temperatures, some rectal temperatures. No matter what technique is used, the results will be about the same. One of the best plans is as follows:

1. Take the temperature as instructed by the physician for five minutes by the clock immediately after waking in the morning and before arising, eating, drinking, or smoking. (It is important to take the temperature upon awakening so that it represents a basal reading.)

2. Note the temperature immediately by a dot on the graph. If the temperature so recorded differs markedly from previous readings, and particularly if it is lower than previous readings, shake the thermometer down and reinsert it for an additional five minutes by the clock, and verify the reading before recording it permanently.

If the temperature rises two- or three-fifths of a degree above the previous level and if the rise is not due to a sore throat or some other ailment, it is probable that ovulation is taking place. This is particularly likely if the temperature rise occurs about 14 days before the next period is expected, or if the rise corresponds with a similar rise in the graph of the previous menstrual cycle. In many instances the temperature drops one-fifth or two-fifths of a degree the day before it rises.

If the temperature is taken according to directions and is accurately read, the time of ovulation will be indicated. Intercourse during the 24 hours following the temperature drop or during the 24 hours following the temperature rise offers the best chance for conception.

It is necessary to continue keeping the graph for at least three menstrual cycles before it is of much value. With a graph of two cycles at hand to provide the pattern of the temperature curve it is usually possible to predict when the temperature will shift (ovulation). Sexual abstinence for several days before ovulation allows time for the male to store up matured sperm, and this probably increases the chance of fertilization. Intercourse more than once in 24 hours is unnecessary.

In order to assist the physician in interpreting the graph, it is important to make the following notations:

1. Encircle the temperature dot on the days when intercourse occurs and write A.M. or P.M. as the case may be above the circle.

2. Some women can recognize ovulation by a twinge of pain low on one side of the abdomen, or by a slight drop of vaginal bleeding. If either of these signs appears, make a note of it on the graph.

3. Note any recognized cause for fever on the chart; for example, a cold, grippe, marked indigestion, or even following use of alcohol.

4. Mark the days of menstruation by an X. (It is not necessary to take the temperature during the flow.)

5. Commence a new graph for each cycle, beginning by placing an X at the left of the graph sheet on the line marked (at the top of the graph) First Day of Period.

Body basal temperature record of a woman during a four-month period. She did not wish to become pregnant during July and August, so she refrained from intercourse from the tenth day of the cycle until the eighteenth day. These periods showed the typical rise in temperature associated with ovulation. In September she decided to try for a pregnancy, so she had intercourse on days 11, 13, and 14, during which time the rise in temperature occurred. The subsequent failure of the temperature to drop indicated that she conceived on one of these days.

The body basal temperature curve, an excellent index of fertility, can be used to prevent pregnancy was well as to favor its occurrence. The safest procedure in women who have cycles of average length is to avoid coitus from day 10 until 48 hours after the rise in temperature has reached a plateau. Intercourse can take place from the end of the menses until day 10 and from 48 hours after the rise until the next menstrual period.

Body basal temperature graphs are a great aid to the physician in the study of sterility, menstrual difficulties, and many problems concerning the reproductive organs, so that they are invaluable as a part of a good medical history.

THE MENOPAUSE

The end of the reproductive period, the menopause or the change of life, comes on in the fifth decade in most women. It may occur as early as 40 or as late as 55, but the average is 47 years. The menstrual periods may stop altogether, come at increasingly longer intervals, or become completely irregular. The menstrual irregularity must be carefully evaluated by a physician, for this is the decade when cancer of the uterus occurs most often and menstrual change may mask a developing growth. Fertility of the individual decreases rapidly and ceases entirely with the end of the menstrual function. Many of the irregular bleeding periods are not associated with ovulation. When the menstrual periods have not recurred for six months or longer pregnancy is no longer possible.

It is common gossip that pregnancies can occur during the menopause. Many women have heard about these so-called menopausal babies. They have been ascribed to a sudden spurt of fertility during this period. There is no scientific evidence that such is the case. These pregnancies in the menopausal decade probably occur in spite of rapidly waning fertility. Women are likely to drop the usual birth-control safeguards when they reach the forties and particularly when menstrual periods come at more and more infrequent intervals. Some of these irregular cycles are associated with ovulation, and if coitus is timed so that the ovum becomes fertilized the couple may have a baby to brighten their middle age.

The menopause is associated with a decrease in the ovarian hormones which leads to many physical and functional changes. In most women readjustments take place rapidly so that no serious complications result. In a few, mental and emotional strains may become sufficiently severe to warrant medical treatment.

Topics for further thought:

1. Is an understanding of biological functions so necessary to marriage that study of biology, including growth, maturity, and function of glands, should be required at all levels of education? What materials should be taught at elementary and high-school levels?

2. Are the physical aspects of marriage so important that premarital counseling should be made a function of religious and governmental planning? How might this be done? Are there any disadvantages to government and religious participation in this area?

Selected reading references

Davis, M. Edward, *Natural Child Spacing,* New York, Doubleday, 1953.

Farris, Edmond, "Male Fertility," *Scientific American,* 1950, as reprinted in Sussman, Marvin B., *Sourcebook in Marriage and the Family,* Cambridge, Houghton Mifflin Company, 1955, pp. 134-9.
Analyzes the role of the male in infertility problems. Suggests that the traditional assignment of responsibility for infertility to the female is unwarranted.

Greenberg, Joseph H., "Artificial Insemination," *American Sociological Review,* February, 1951, pp. 86-91.
A study of student attitudes toward two forms of artificial insemination. Some striking differences in attitudes found.

Latz, Leo J., *The Rhythm of Fertility and Sterility in Women,* Chicago, Latz Foundation, 1947.
Discussion of research evidence concerning the periods in the menstrual cycle when conception is possible and impossible. Covers physiological, practical, and ethical questions. Has the approval of the Roman Catholic Church.

Portnoy, Louis, and Saltman, Jules, *Fertility in Marriage,* New York, The New American Library, 1951.
A comprehensive approach to the problem of infertility in marriage. Contains a list of fertility clinics and adoption agencies.

Stone, Abraham, "A World Conference on Human Infertility," *Marriage and Family Living,* August, 1953, pp. 231-3.
An account of the First World Congress on Fertility and Sterility held in New York in 1953. By one of the nation's foremost authorities on the subject.

26 PREPARING FOR A BABY

Janet Fowler Nelson

THERE is no single time or place that is simply and exclusively reserved for consideration of having a baby. From earliest childhood, by the very process of being reared in a family and growing up in a community of families, a young couple have been thoroughly conditioned to the idea of family life. Too often they accept the pattern without further intellectual or emotional examination. They expect to grow up, to get married, to have a baby. "It's the thing to do."

Perhaps there is no other single human experience more rewarding or richer in human values. But the full benefit is achieved only by thoughtful and responsible appreciation of these values. What should be one of the most thoughtful decisions of early married life is often, at best, casual acceptance of an established pattern—a pattern reinforced in today's culture by the oversentimentalization of the mother-baby stereotype. The unreality and sentimentality of much of the escape literature distorts the baby picture as surely as it does love's young dream in a white cottage, complete with rambler roses and the newest in washing machines. Both editorially and advertising-wise, however, there is a hopeful tendency in some of the current women's publications to present a more responsible and realistic picture, as witness the increasing use of professional consultants on magazine staffs.

Ability to understand and weigh the economic and health aspects of childbearing and child rearing, and insight and appreciation of the emotional factors involved, are essential to really responsible parenthood. Dr. O. Spurgeon English, professor of psychiatry at the

Temple University Medical School, remarks: "Parenthood seems to make more demands upon the present-day adult than he is prepared to accept. A study of the needs of infants and children indicates that they must have interest, affection, and time spent with them, which, if given in adequate amounts, conflicts with the tempo of our busy world and the desire for adults to get more out of life for themselves." Baby bookkeeping, therefore, must be written in three columns: psychological values, health factors, and economic need.

PSYCHOLOGICAL VALUES

The psychological values involved in planning to have a baby are vitally important. From the point of view of the baby, the importance of being wanted and loved, of being assured of that element of unearned love which parents give their children and which is such an essential element in their subsequent emotional development, is increasingly recognized. From the parents' point of view, planning to have a baby is itself a measure of their marriage. It certainly requires a high degree of emotional maturity. It is an affirmation of faith. Lawrence K. Frank, writing in the *Journal of Heredity,* states it thus: ". . . planned parenthood is an affirmation—made deliberately and jointly by a man and a woman, who see in childbearing a way of affirming their personal and social values, signifying the importance of love, and courageously projecting those beliefs into the future."

Just as there is increasing emphasis on father participation in the great event, during pregnancy and even in the delivery room itself, so too one cannot emphasize too strongly the imperative of beginning this sharing experience in the planning stage. It would be highly advantageous for everybody concerned to talk not about the pregnant woman but about the pregnant family. The relationship between husband and wife, lines of emotional sensitivity and appreciation and response, should be strengthened not weakened by a new focus on a baby.

A period of initial marital adjustment then, before undertaking a first pregnancy, is almost always desirable. Current statistics indicate that childless marriages are most likely to end in divorce. Such figures have sometimes lent themselves to the argument that having children prevents divorce. Ergo—why worry about early marital adjustment? Have a baby and all will be well. One can as easily argue, of course, that the happy couples have the babies. The others have divorces. There is no argument, however, among psychologists who are concerned with total personality integration and satisfying family relationships. They agree that cold-bloodedly having a baby to trick a recalcitrant husband or wife into a legally more permanent relationship is likely to be a boomerang to the integrity of the marriage relationship itself and downright cruel and devastating to the child. Having a baby is neither an escape from an untenable marriage relationship nor an insurance policy against divorce. It is a fulfillment of a couple's desire to have a home of their own. And it takes time to establish that home. People must have time to work out their own personal adjustments, to establish firmly the Mr.-and-Mrs. relationship, to dig roots of emotional security sufficiently deep to withstand the many adjustments, many of them trivial, some of them more serious, and all of them significant, of pregnancy and early infancy.

Just as the marriage adjustment itself is related to the previous emotional experience of each person as well as to their premarital love relationship, so some of their appreciation and a beginning of their initial acceptance of parenthood go back to their days of courtship and engagement. Similarity of background and interest contributes to successful marriage adjustment. One of the most important of these factors is mutual acceptance of the normal family pattern. From an individual point of view, there must be acceptance of individual masculine and feminine roles.

HEALTH FACTORS

Psychological values, however, are not the only ones to be explored prior to pregnancy, or to marriage itself. Health factors are essentially important. Elsewhere in this book the importance of the premarital examination has been noted. This medical examination of the young wife will have revealed any structural deviations or major organic weaknesses of the heart, lungs, kidneys, or blood. And both husband and wife should have a clear bill of health on venereal infection or such hereditary diseases as tuberculosis. All these factors should be rechecked before a pregnancy is actually embarked on. The chapters on pregnancy and childbirth and on the premarital examination itself indicate the medical implications of these factors; they are merely noted here to reinforce the suggestion that the health of the mother particularly must be recognized as of paramount importance and considered before pregnancy.

Part of the general health picture of the woman is the question of her age at pregnancy. Both psychological and undisputed medical authorities point to the advantage of having children while the parents are young. The best authority teaches that the decade between twenty and thirty in a woman's life is the optimum period for childbearing. This does not mean, however, that with wise and competent medical care women over thirty run undue risk; women have safely borne children toward the end of the childbearing cycle. Neither is childbearing at too young an age to be desired, for it incurs increased risks for both mother and baby. The establishment of nubility, and not just menstruation, is the measure of physical readiness for childbearing.

ECONOMIC NEEDS

"It's not the original cost, it's the upkeep!" This is the common cry of parents. In income brackets from $5000-$10,000 the total cost of bringing up a child to the age of 18 averaged slightly more than $20,000 in 1947; in 1955 the figure was substantially higher. (Of course cash in hand is no more essential here than prepayment of 18 years' rent, but neither is it to be disregarded.) Proportionate to the total income, the cost of bringing up a child is less in lower-income brackets. This is offset, however, by the fact that, statistically speaking, the low-income groups have the largest families. Further, in terms of long-time planning, children not only are economic liabilities in themselves but also constitute a hazard to other members of the family, in terms of availability of housing and similar factors. The much-quoted advertisement is not funny: "Wanted—a place to live by couple with five months' old baby of great sentimental value. Prefer to keep child if possible. Will drown if necessary to get roof over our heads."

The initial cost of having children, however, is not to be lost sight of and is an immediate and practical consideration. Group-hospital and medical-insurance plans have helped to lower the cost of having a baby. Most private physicians are willing to base their fees on the earning capacity of the parents, charging in each case what they are able to pay. Many of them encourage a pay-as-you-go plan during the time before the baby is born, so that the cost is spread over a number of months instead of being paid in a lump sum. Also, excellent maternal-health clinics have been established throughout the country, many operated at state or city expense, which provide medical care at a minimum cost.

Costs for maternity care differ in various parts of the country. In some communities $40 or $50 may cover everything—in others it may cost several hundred dollars. A couple should find out about physician and hospital fees in their community early so they can make whatever plans or arrangements are needed to pay for maternity care.

Careful planning for the necessary day-to-day budget increases—food, clothing, and transportation—as well as the cost of original equipment must be taken into account. Health and medical care for the new baby must be provided for. And parents should figure in the cost of the occasional sitter when they desire an evening out.

THE WIFE'S JOB

One further important and very specific decision which many young couples face at this time is what to do about the wife's job. An over-all philosophy of her relationship to the marriage partnership, in the home and/or on the job, will have been arrived at in many discussions during the engagement period and in the first months of marriage. This is the point, however, where the question ceases to be philosophical and becomes intensely practical.

From an economic point of view, at the same time that initial expense is at its peak, day-to-day income for a shorter or longer time is reduced by the margin of the wife's earnings. These factors must be considered and provided for, budget-wise.

Even more important is the health of the working wife who is pregnant. Many job adjustments can and should be made for her. For instance, at the business or professional level, extensive travel is "out." In industrial occupations, pregnant women should be given lighter and more sedentary work whenever possible. Types of occupations which should be considered undesirable for them include those that require heavy lifting, continuous standing or moving about, reaching, or marked vibration. Hours of work are important, too—no more than eight hours a day or forty-eight hours a week. A forty-hour week is preferable. And in terms of her domestic responsibilities, she needs very practical help. Cynical observers have remarked that working wives work not at one job, but at two. This is never a desirable situation, and during pregnancy it becomes imperative that strain and fatigue be guarded against. Happily this is a very practical area for husbandly co-operation.

The whole question of maternity leaves must also be considered in terms of the job security and economic advantage they offer. Important as these considerations are, an intelligent policy on maternity leaves is equally important to the physical and psychological health of the young mother. The minimum length of leave before delivery is two months. Many doctors are urging that this be increased. Similarly, the minimum leave after childbirth should be two months—or more.

The "or more" is particularly significant from a psychological point of view. The period of adjustment following childbirth is important physically. It is also a highly important period of emotional and marital adjustment. To achieve a sturdy and sound family relationship takes sensitiveness and insight, to be sure. It also takes time. Nor must the baby's psychological needs be neglected. The need and importance of a close mother-child relationship in early infancy is being increasingly recognized by the psychiatrists. Two years, three years, seven years have been variously noted in the literature as the critical, crucial years of a child's emotional development. To the extent that this is related to a woman's job, the decision, mutually arrived at, about just when the mother should resume her occupation is one of the most important a young couple makes. It is quite true that the literal amount of time spent at home is not the single measure—quality of relationship, not quantity, is the concern. Again one suggests the three criteria, this time including the baby: psychological values, health factors, and economic need.

MULTIPLE CHILDREN

All these factors—psychological, health, and economic—are equally, perhaps even more, important with the second or third or fourth pregnancy. They are important in terms of the same practical as well as psychological adjustments which the parents face. But something new has been added: the health, the economic well-being, and the emotional, psychological adjustment of the older child or children must be evaluated.

Spacing. The important factor of time between pregnancies must be considered. Medical research indicates that adequate spacing is important not only to the mother's health or the new baby's, but also to the health of the preceding child. The mother who has a second baby too soon may diminish the adequacy of the health care that she can give the first baby.

In round figures, a two-year interval between births is usually suggested. Dr. Alan Guttmacher of Johns Hopkins University reported a poll of some three thousand physicians whose collective opinion is that "the average medically desirable interval from the termination of one pregnancy to the beginning of the next is 14.1 months, which means a medically desirable interval between babies of 23 months." His report further adds, "With the previous pregnancy terminating in miscarriage, the average physician advises patients to wait six months before trying again."

Costs. From an economic point of view—as in planning the first child—the same factors of initial cost as well as day-to-day budget increases have to be considered. There is, to be sure, some saving in equipment and clothing that can be handed down, but this slight saving will probably be more than compensated for by the fact that parents will have become aware by this time of the general wear and tear of the patter of little feet.

Social and Emotional Development. Important as practical factors of baby budget-making may be, the psychological values for both parents and children inherent in belonging to a large family are numerous. The emotional hazards of being an only child have been frequently discussed. Growing up with older and younger brothers and sisters provides one of the most fertile fields for practical and practicing democracy. The family is the first laboratory in which to develop skills in dealing with difference—difference in age and sex, difference in physical and mental aptitudes and interests, difference in responsibility. The challenge is to avoid developing attitudes of scorn for and exploitation of difference, or the dullness of mediocrity which results from insensitivity to difference. Especially, from the point of view of a democratic society, the importance of being one of a large family lies in learning to appreciate difference and in using it constructively. From the point of view of a child's personal emotional development, it is the original seat of the green-eyed monster—for jealousy of shared affection, of special privilege is universal and perfectly normal. Yet family life carries within its own framework the potential correctives of this particular expression of emotional insecurity. As Dorothy Baruch points out, "Love is the best antidote for jealousy. Where love is rich and plentiful, a person is fortified against pettiness, against envy, against smallness and uncalled-for hurt."

Preoccupied as persons are with the social and emotional development of the child, they often fail to note that the emotional strain on the (over) conscientious parent is considerable. In a day when some parents have become self-conscious and fearful of their personal responsibility for their children's development, it does not ease the situation to have all one's eggs in one basket. Families used to be able to afford at least one black sheep; no one has even that doubtful privilege today. Parents are really less able to evaluate the progress and development of one child than if they have several. They have more time, to be sure, but exclusive preoccupation does not lend itself to objectivity, nor have they within their own family group any practical basis for comparison.

Planning for the New Baby. The relation of children to each other is another consideration. Much of the strength of that relationship, however, will depend on the extent to which they participate in the planning for the arrival of each new brother and sister.

For the very young child there is little in specific overt planning that can be done; the vocabulary range of a two-year-old is itself somewhat limited. Development of attitudes and emotional sensitivity is not limited by verbal expression, however. The exposure method is helpful here. The very young child is not going to resent or question the addition of a baby brother or sister to nearly the same extent if he is used to seeing other people's babies, other people's preoccupation with them if you will, his own mother's pleasure in the arrival of the baby next door. Just as wise parents make a special effort after their own new baby arrives to make sure that their first little fellow feels especially loved and secure, so can the child learn, before the event, that sharing his mother's attention—for an afternoon, say, when together they take over Aunt Mary's youngest—is no fundamental threat to him. At best, however, this is a learning process and it takes time. It is a fortunate child whose parents are sufficiently wise to accept expression of the fear and uncertainty and even hostility that a little fellow feels when baby sister arrives.

Older children, to a degree corresponding to their own physical and emotional development, will actively participate in planning ahead for the new baby's arrival. Having a new baby in one's own family is one of the healthiest and happiest opportunities for sex education. Also, advance familiarity with the actual material adjustments that must be made—provision for sleeping and bathing, for example— removes much of the shock of displacement which is itself a contributory factor to emotional disturbance.

There is, too, for the older child who participates and shares in wanting and welcoming a new baby, sometimes a faint glimmering of giving—of not always being just on the receiving end of unearned love. Conflict and the rough-and-tumble of children growing up together are not eliminated, nor should one wish or expect them to be, but there is something soul-satisfying about viewing the turbulence of normal family life against the fleeting picture of the little girl who, sitting near her father as she uncertainly holds the new baby for the first time, looks up at him and says, "Daddy, now I know what it is to love someone."

Topics for further thought:

1. Discuss factors which you think a couple should take into consideration when deciding the "right" size of their family.

2. Rational parenthood implies that parents want their children, that they love them, and care well for them. Reconcile these ideas with the desertion rate, the divorce rate, and the juvenile-delinquency rate.

Selected reading references

Hare, A. Paul, and Hare, Rachel T., "Classes for Prospective Fathers," *Marriage and Family Living,* August, 1952, pp. 206-7.
Describes a course for prospective fathers given at the Chicago Lying-in Hospital. Includes an analysis of the characteristics of fathers attending the course.

Heardman, Helen, *Natural Childbirth,* Baltimore, Williams and Wilkins Company, 1949.
Exercises for the expectant mother in preparation for so-called "natural childbirth."

Phillips, Marion, *More Than Pregnancy,* New York, Coward-McCann, 1955.
A popular approach to some of the non-medical problems of pregnancy.

Poffenberger, Shirley, Poffenberger, Thomas, and Landis, Judson T., "Intent Toward Conception and the Pregnancy Experience," *American Sociological Review,* October, 1952, pp. 616-20.
Being desirous of pregnancy, indifferent to the possibility, or unwilling for pregnancy were found generally not to be related to

various physical and emotional experiences during the pregnancy period.

Seidman, Theodore R., and Albert, Marvin N., *Becoming a Mother*, New York, David McKay Company, 1956.
A "how to undergo pregnancy with understanding" book written for laymen.

27 PREGNANCY

Edith L. Potter

P REGNANCY constitutes one of the most important events in the married life of any couple. The selection of a mate, the creation of a home, the establishment of a position in the community are most often consciously or unconsciously directed toward the preparation of a suitable environment in which to bear and rear children.

The average couple want to have children and await the knowledge that pregnancy has begun with great eagerness. Most men and women are well aware at the time of marriage of the physiologic processes involved in the conception and bearing of a child. The woman is particularly conscious of and often more keenly looks forward to the possibility of pregnancy than her husband. Within her body cyclic changes are constantly taking place which indicate that she is ready to become a mother.

SIGNS OF PREGNANCY

In a healthy young woman who has been menstruating regularly, the first indication that pregnancy has been initiated is ordinarily a failure to menstruate at the expected time. Soon afterward the breasts begin to grow larger and firmer. Occasionally some disinclination for food and a feeling of nausea on first arising in the morning are experienced.

The physician cannot ordinarily make a diagnosis of pregnancy by examination of the uterus until about two months have elapsed after the last menstrual period. Sooner than this, and usually after about five weeks, one of the pregnancy tests, known as an Aschheim-

Zondek or a Friedman test, will indicate the fact of pregnancy. These tests are based on the fact that parts of the developing ovum produce a hormone which is excreted in the maternal urine. If a small amount of urine containing this hormone is injected into a mouse, a rabbit, or a frog, these animals undergo certain changes which can be easily recognized.

An entirely positive diagnosis cannot be made until pregnancy is sufficiently advanced for the beating of the infant's heart to be audible through the mother's abdominal wall or until x-ray examination discloses the bones of the fetal skeleton. This is generally near the middle of pregnancy.

On rare occasions the development of a uterine or ovarian tumor may simulate pregnancy, and still more infrequently women desirous of bearing children may have all of the symptoms of early pregnancy, even to the abdominal enlargement, without actually being pregnant. This latter condition, known as pseudocyesis, may persist until such time as it is possible to convince the woman that she is not pregnant.

THE PHYSICIAN AND PRENATAL CARE

When any woman suspects that she may be pregnant she should immediately consult a physician. The choice of a doctor is sometimes hard to make, for the average patient has little way of knowing the qualifications of any particular physician. Obstetrics—the branch of medicine dealing with the care of the mother during pregnancy and delivery—is a specialized field and one to which many physicians devote an entire lifetime. Since such persons are specially trained, often having spent many years in a hospital concerned only with this kind of work, they are better equipped to handle emergencies which may arise than is the physician who has not spent time in special training. If the expectant mother lives in a community large enough to support one or more obstetrical specialists she should by all means consult one of them. The family doctor can often recommend such a person, or the names of such doctors can be obtained from the local health department, medical society, or hospital.

The bearing of children is a much safer process now than in years past. One of the most important reasons for the safety of childbearing is the improvement in the care available to women during pregnancy. A woman who consults a physician as soon as she realizes she may be pregnant and remains under his observation until the baby is born will have a much greater chance of having a normal living baby than one who does not see a doctor until late in pregnancy or only when the baby is ready to be born.

Some women have lost their lives during pregnancy because of a condition known as pregnancy toxemia. This disease, if it develops, will be discovered by the physician during the course of his examinations when a woman is being observed regularly. If all women received adequate prenatal care this condition should practically disappear as a cause of death, for only when it progresses unrecognized does it become a serious danger.

When an expectant mother visits the doctor during pregnancy he takes her blood pressure and examines her urine on each occasion. He watches her weight and follows her diet. On her first examination he ordinarily makes a blood test for syphilis. Some women unknowingly acquire this disease and some who believe themselves cured can still transmit it to their unborn children. If the condition is discovered in the first half of pregnancy and treatment is then begun the child will be protected and will almost never be affected.

Most doctors examine the blood of all pregnant women for its Rh status (p. 347). About one out of every seven women is Rh negative. If the husband of such a woman is Rh positive it is possible for the infant to inherit the Rh-positive type of blood possessed by its father. Normally the circulation of the mother and that of the infant never communicate, but in a few instances some of the infant's blood may leak into the mother's blood stream. If this happens the mother may react to the infant's blood cells as she would to bacteria or any other foreign material. Antibodies are produced which can combine with Rh-positive cells and destroy them. This is a protective mechanism which is normal in all people. When such antibodies are formed, however, the infant may be harmed; these antibodies may pass through the placenta into its circulation and may combine with its blood cells and destroy them. Such blood destruction causes anemia and jaundice in the infant. The condition is known as erythroblastosis fetalis, or congenital hemolytic disease. Fortunately it is relatively rare and is found in the children of only one out of every 25 or 30 Rh-negative women. The treatment of the disease is directed toward curing the infant's anemia and relieving its jaundice by means of blood transfusions. The Rh status of the mother's blood is determined before or during pregnancy so that if she is found to be Rh negative the infant may be carefully watched after birth and the earliest signs of the disease detected. With modern methods of treatment about 90 per cent of all children with this disease who are born alive will live and will be entirely well in a few weeks.

Few women need to make any drastic changes in their ordinary mode of life when they become pregnant. Exhausting physical exercise should be avoided, although this is true at all times and not only during pregnancy. Also it is especially important that the diet be adequate in the basic food materials, especially those that are rich in proteins, vitamins, and minerals. Large amounts of starches and sugars should be avoided, for it is important that the gain in weight be not excessive. Many women when they realize they are eating for two indulge in immoderate amounts of food. This is unfortunate not only because overeating may be one of the factors leading to the development of toxemia, but also because the weight put on at this time may be difficult to lose after the termination of pregnancy, and the excessive fat may persist for many years. Many a husband has been sadly disillusioned to find that the slim, graceful girl he married has become the fat, ungainly mother of his children. The weight gain attributable directly to a pregnancy is only about fifteen pounds. The average infant at the time of birth weighs about seven and a half pounds; the bag of waters, the placenta, and the uterus weigh about an equal amount. Any gain in excess of this is ordinarily the result of the deposit of fat in the maternal tissues.

Young mothers are sometimes afraid that they may mark their babies by having unpleasant experiences or by witnessing unusual or distressing events. Such fears are without foundation; there are no nerves connecting the baby to the mother, and no emotion from which the mother suffers can be transmitted to her child. So-called birthmarks are caused by abnormalities in the development of localized parts of the skin and are not related to the mental or emotional state of the mother.

SEXUAL INTERCOURSE DURING PREGNANCY

There is ordinarily no reason why sexual intercourse may not be continued during the early part of pregnancy if the pregnancy is progressing normally. If there have been previous miscarriages avoidance of intercourse during the second and third months, especially near the time when menstruation would have occurred if a pregnancy had not been established, is generally recommended. During the last two months before the expected date of delivery intercourse should be discontinued to avoid the risk of introducing bacteria into the vagina and to avoid the possibility of stimulating the uterus to deliver the baby prematurely. Immediately following the birth of the baby the uterus is susceptible to infection, and bacteria which are present in any part of the birth canal may constitute a possible source of such infection. For this reason nothing, including douches, should be introduced into the vagina during the last few weeks before the expected date of delivery or in the first few weeks after delivery.

THE FORMATION OF THE BABY

When a woman becomes pregnant a marvelous series of events is initiated. The changes that take place in the nine months that elapse between the time the ovum is fertilized by a sperm cell until a fully developed infant is ready to be born are more wonderful and awe-inspiring than any other phenomenon in nature. Two individual cells unite to become one; by growth and division new cells are formed that divide and redivide countless numbers of times in order to produce the gradual differentiation into organs and body forms that results in the creation of a living human being. Each human being is the replica of its thousands of ancestors. Each fertilized egg possesses all the potential qualities with which the father and mother can endow their child; already are determined the infant's sex, the color of its eyes, the shape of its nose, and all of the other characteristics that will become visible only months or years later.

For three or four days the growing ovum moves slowly downward through the Fallopian tube and for another three or four days passes over part of the uterine wall. About the seventh or eighth day it settles near the upper center of the front or back wall of the uterus. During the time of its downward passage it has developed first into a small solid mass of cells and then through rearrangement it has become a single layer of cells surrounding a hollow cavity filled with fluid. In one portion of the wall a small group of cells known as the inner cell mass has remained; in this area the infant will develop; the rest of the wall will grow into the elaborate structure which is known as the afterbirth or placenta. By means of the placenta the infant obtains its food, water, and oxygen and eliminates waste material before birth.

As soon as the hollow ball of cells comes to rest it gradually sinks down into the uterine lining. The wall of the hollow sphere thickens, and on the outer surface small buds appear which rapidly elongate and branch. Quickly the surface of the sphere is covered with small treelike structures. As they grow they penetrate the maternal tissues, dissolving away the uterine cells with which they come in contact. They also dissolve parts of the walls of the blood vessels in their immediate vicinity so that maternal blood leaks out and surrounds all of the branches of these treelike structures.

Inside the branches small blood vessels containing blood cells begin to appear. The ends of the various blood vessels unite and also unite with similar vessels which have been forming on the inner surface of the hollow sphere and in the region of the inner cell mass. When this system is complete a circulation of blood is established which flows from the region where the embryo is forming in the inner cell mass outward over the inner surface of the large cavity and into all of the branching structures growing from the outer surface. A similar set of vessels carries the blood in the reverse direction back to the embryo.

These treelike structures that contain the blood vessels are known as villi; for several weeks they cover all of the outer surface. Gradually part fail to grow and soon become degenerated so that by the middle of pregnancy villi are found attached only to a round area making up about one-fifth of the total surface. The villi in this region continue to become more and more branched; the branches intertwine to form a fairly solid-looking mass shaped something like a pie. By the end of pregnancy this mass has grown to be about an inch thick and eight to ten inches in diameter. It is called the placenta. The part from which the villi have degenerated remains and it, together with the placenta, forms the outer wall of the sac holding the watery fluid by which the infant is surrounded while it is in the uterus. It breaks and the fluid escapes before the baby is born.

Even though the placenta seems a firm, compact structure, enough room is present between the villi to make it possible for maternal blood continuously to bathe their outer surfaces. Blood flows out into the placenta from the arteries of the uterus, circulates between the villi, and returns to the uterine veins. The oxygen and food material that are present in the maternal blood filter through the walls of the villi and enter the infant's blood, which is in the vessels contained within the villi. These substances are then transported to the body of the infant and provide the materials required for growth and development. The infant's waste products are removed by a reversal of the process that supplies it with food. They are carried in the blood of the infant out through the umbilical cord into the villi and from there filter through into the mother's blood and are removed by her organs of excretion. The blood vessels connecting the infant with the placenta are united into a single ropelike structure called the umbilical cord.

Almost all of the organs are produced in a preliminary form in less than four weeks from the time cell division commences. Growth progresses so rapidly that by the end of the first eight weeks practically all organs and all parts of the body can be distinguished. Even the fingers and toes can be made out. From this time until the end of pregnancy the principal change is an increase in size (Fig. 6).

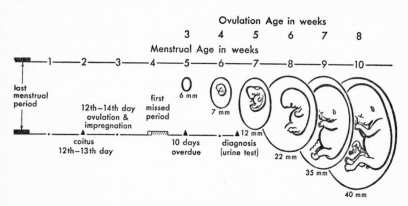

Figure 6. CONCEPTION AND EMBRYO DEVELOPMENT

After the infant has attained an age of about 38 weeks counting from the time of conception, or about 40 weeks counting from the first day of the last menstrual period, it is sufficiently mature to be capable of maintaining a normal existence outside of the mother's body. From 5 to 10 per cent of infants are born between the twenty-eighth and thirty-eighth week of pregnancy. These are premature infants, and in order to survive they must have special care. This is particularly true of the smaller ones.

THE BIRTH OF THE BABY

By the end of pregnancy all of the structures in the lowermost part of the mother's body have become softened and relaxed and are prepared to dilate and permit the passage of the infant. When everything is in readiness the muscles in the uterus begin to contract, and the cervix, which is the lowermost portion of the uterus, gradually grows thinner and the opening enlarges. The muscular contractions generally cause acute discomfort, the amount of pain, however, being variable in different women. The time required for the cervix to open sufficiently to allow the infant's head to pass through is somewhat longer in a first pregnancy than in subsequent pregnancies. Even in a first pregnancy it rarely takes more than 12 to 18 hours.

As soon as the cervix is completely dilated the uterine contractions become stronger and the infant is pushed downward through the cervix and vagina and is expelled from the birth canal. The infant is born! Immediately it opens its mouth and begins to cry. Respiration is established, never to stop as long as life lasts.

Within a few minutes of the birth of the infant the placenta and the membrane making up the wall of the sac within which the infant developed are also expelled from the uterus. These structures are essential to the infant during intrauterine life, but when it is born their function ceases. Since they are expelled after the infant, they are commonly called the afterbirth.

After the birth of the baby and the delivery of the placenta, the uterus contracts down into a firm solid mass that is only a fraction of its size just before the delivery of the infant. The muscles and tissues of the floor of the pelvis also contract and help to hold the uterus up in place. It takes approximately six weeks for the uterus to return to prepregnancy size and for the muscles of the pelvic floor to regain their strength. At the end of that time the processes associated with pregnancy have been terminated and the body starts again on its unceasing cycle of preparing for a new pregnancy.

If hospital facilities are available no woman should consider giving birth to her baby at home. Just as it is no longer considered justifiable to remove an appendix in the farmhouse kitchen, so it is unwise to consider home delivery. In most instances difficulties are not encountered during delivery and both mother and child do well, but one can never be sure in advance that sudden emergencies may not arise. Hemorrhage and infection, the two most important causes of maternal death in addition to toxemia, are much better controlled or prevented in a hospital than they can ever be in a home environment. The infant, too, may be greatly benefited immediately after birth by the facilities available in a well-equipped hospital.

Many women approach the time of delivery with great fear. There is little reason for this in the present day because the great advances that have been made by medical scientists in the knowledge of how to care for women before and during childbirth and the better facilities that are available during the time of birth have greatly diminished the dangers associated with childbearing.

Some doctors believe that fear is at the basis of most of the unpleasant sensations women experience during pregnancy and that it is responsible for most of the pain associated with delivery. To the extent that this is actually true, the expenditure of time and energy in attempting to allay those fears is well justified.

Topics for further thought:

1. Discuss the changes that occur in the role of the man during his wife's pregnancy, pointing out the importance of his adjustment to these new roles.

2. Discuss the psychological and emotional anxieties and fears of expectant parents concerning their unborn child.

Selected reading references

Gilbert, Margaret S., *Biography of the Unborn,* Baltimore, Williams and Wilkins, 1938.
  Excellent little book on the development of the baby before birth. Suitable for use with a variety of age groups.

Guttmacher, Alan F., *Life in the Making,* New York, Viking Press, 1933.
  A noted obstetrician describes the first nine months of life.

Kenyon, Josephine H., *Healthy Babies are Happy Babies,* Boston, Little Brown and Company, 1944.
  Written for mothers and mothers-to-be. Tells them what they may expect from their babies and how they may encourage happy babies.

Rosen, Sidney, "Emotional Factors in Nausea and Vomiting of Pregnancy," *Psychiatric Quarterly,* October, 1955, pp. 621-31.
  Psychiatric insights into a widespread but not well-understood phenomenon.

Zabriskie, Louise, and Eastman, N., *Nurses' Handbook of Obstetrics,* Philadelphia, J. B. Lippincott Company, 1943.
  Semi-technical. Information for prospective parents and the general public as well as for nurses.

28 THE BIRTH OF THE BABY

J. P. Greenhill

SINCE bearing a child is a momentous event in a woman's life there are many details she naturally will want to know to prepare herself for the occasion. This chapter provides information on ways for predicting the date of the birth, preparations for confinement, signs and stages of labor, hospital examinations, the use of drugs, the delivery, and postpartum care.

PREDICTING THE DATE OF BIRTH

It is impossible to predict accurately the day when a baby will arrive. The date, however, can be approximated in a number of ways. One way is to add seven days to the first day of the last menstrual flow and subtract three months. Thus if the last menstrual period began on 10 July, by adding seven days, getting 17 July, and then subtracting three months, the date 17 April is arrived at as the approximate day of the following year labor may be expected. In most cases the confinement will take place within a few days before or after this calculated date.

For a woman having her first baby, another way to calculate the date of birth is to add 22 weeks to the day she first feels the baby move. A woman who has already borne children should add 24 weeks because the second or subsequent babies are felt to move earlier by her than by one who never has had a baby.

If the exact day of conception is known, a woman adds 266 days to this date for the approximate date of confinement. For example, if conception took place on 1 January, counting 266 days from this date makes the approximate date of delivery 24 September.

By repeated examinations a physician can often determine the day of the baby's birth within a few days of its arrival.

PREPARATIONS FOR CONFINEMENT

Since premature delivery—that is, delivery before the expected date of confinement—is not uncommon, it is a good plan to have certain articles ready a few weeks before this time. For a woman who plans to have her baby in a hospital, these articles should consist of two nightgowns, a robe, two pairs of stockings, a pair of slippers, a few handkerchiefs, a toothbrush and tooth paste or powder, a hand mirror, a comb, and a hairbrush. Most hospitals supply the baby's clothes until it is ready to leave. Therefore, the day before the patient expects to depart from the hospital the husband or someone else should bring some clothes for the baby to wear when it leaves the hospital. These should be a shirt, a nightgown or robe, a few diapers, a sweater, a cap, and two blankets. Of course these are only a few of the things which the expectant mother should buy a few weeks before the baby is to arrive.

As newborn babies quickly outgrow their clothes, not much is needed at the time of birth. Nowadays clothes for the baby are made to be comfortable for the child and easy to put on and to take off. They should be of light texture, for in steam-heated houses and apartments babies are generally burdened with too many clothes. The clothes that a newborn baby requires are shirts, dresses, robes, nightgowns, diapers, booties, blankets, sweaters, and a cap.

SIGNS AND STAGES OF LABOR

Labor is the term applied to the process of giving birth. Its onset is usually distinguished by three signs:

1. Rhythmic contractions of the womb, which are felt or defined by the mother as abdominal cramps (labor pains). These may be felt by placing the hand on the abdomen; the latter hardens during a contraction and relaxes when the cramp subsides. At the beginning these cramps are irregular in frequency and intensity; they begin in the back and spread or radiate to the front. At first they occur at infrequent and irregular intervals; later they become more frequent and more regular in time, also stronger and localized in the abdomen. False pains are weak contractions that occur a few days to a few

weeks before actual confinement. They may be distinguished from true labor pains by the fact that they do not increase in frequency, intensity, or duration; they soon subside.

2. The escape of fluid from the vagina. This fluid is not urine. It results from rupture of the bag of waters in which the baby is enveloped. Labor pains usually do not begin until a few hours after this flow or dripping starts, but it is advisable for the woman to go to the hospital after notifying the physician of the flow.

3. A thick, mucous, bloody discharge from the vagina (the show).

Only one of these signs is usually present at first, but one sign is sufficient to warrant notifying the physician. Then the hospital should be informed that the patient is on the way. Ordinarily a number of hours elapses between the beginning of labor and the delivery or birth of the baby, so there is no need for excitement or haste.

Sometimes abnormal symptoms may arise at about the time of confinement, and the physician must be told about them without delay. These symptoms include bleeding from the vagina, a sudden fainting attack, severe and persistent cramps in the abdomen, vomiting, disturbances in vision, and twitching of the muscles. It is a good thing to keep the telephone numbers of the physician, his assistant, and the hospital in a place where they are available without delay.

Labor is divided into three stages known simply as the first, second, and third stages. The first stage is the period of preparation and extends from the beginning of labor until the neck of the uterus is opened up completely. The duration of this stage is generally about twelve hours in primigravidas (women having their first baby) and about seven and a half hours in multiparas (women who have previously borne a child or children). The second stage is the period of expulsion of the baby from the uterus to the outer world. This stage lasts about one hour in primigravidas and from fifteen to thirty minutes in multiparas. The third stage is the period during which the afterbirth separates from the uterus and is expelled from the genital tract; its duration averages about ten minutes. It is difficult to decide on the exact moment when the first stage ends and the second begins, but this is of little consequence. The beginning of the third stage is, of course, easy to determine because it starts immediately after the baby is born. The figures given for the length of each stage are average ones, but there are wide variations. Many labors are much shorter than the average and some last considerably longer. Furthermore, the experienced physician can often shorten the second stage of labor without harm to either the mother or the child.

Since 95 per cent of all confinements are normal, women go through labor in most instances with a minimum of pain and damage. About 5 per cent of labors are abnormal. Some of these abnormalities are definitely preventable; others are not. An experienced physician can deal with complications to the complete satisfaction of both mother and child, but, more important, he possesses the knowledge to prevent trouble and to recognize it early.

HOSPITAL EXAMINATIONS

As soon as possible after labor begins the physician or his assistant should see the patient. In many hospitals an intern greets the patient when she arrives. Regardless of which physician sees the patient early in labor, certain examinations must be made. The patient's temperature and pulse are first taken, generally by a nurse. Then the abdomen is examined by a physician to determine the position in which the baby lies, the frequency and strength of the labor pains, and the presence or absence of twins. If twins are present two distinct heads generally can be felt, especially if one is down low and the other is up high; or two sets of heart tones which are different from each other and different from the mother's pulse can be heard. (Of course, x-ray pictures previously may have revealed the presence of twins or verified an abnormal presentation.)

Position of the Baby. In about 96 per cent of all cases the baby lies in the uterus with its head in the mother's pelvic cavity and its buttocks up near the mother's ribs. These cases are known as head presentations. In about 3 per cent the baby's buttocks, and not its head, lie in the mother's pelvis. These cases are known as breech presentations. In about one half of 1 per cent the baby's body lies crosswise to that of the mother, and such a presentation is termed transverse.

Normal presentations refer to *head presentations,* but not all of these are normal. The most favorable presentation for a baby is that in which the head is in the pelvic cavity in such a way that the face is pointed downward toward the mother's back, and the top of the baby's head (the occiput) is directed upward toward the mother's abdomen. This type of head presentation is known as an occiput anterior (front) position, because the occiput is in the front half of the mother's body. The vast majority of babies are born as occiput anterior presentations, but in many instances the baby's face is pointed upward toward the mother's abdomen at the beginning of labor. Generally the face is turned around spontaneously so that its direction is toward the mother's back, and the baby is delivered normally as an occiput anterior presentation. In some instances, however, the face persists in its upward attitude. This condition is known as persistent occiput posterior, because the occiput remains in the posterior (back) part of the mother's body. These cases sometimes present a great deal of difficulty, but experienced physicians can easily deal with them.

Face and *brow presentations* are uncommon. With the former, delivery is usually spontaneous, but brow presentations must be corrected before delivery can be effected.

A *breech presentation* is abnormal because sometimes it is hazardous for the baby, especially in primigravidas; in multiparas it is seldom troublesome. It can nearly always be detected during the last few weeks of pregnancy and by manipulation can be converted into occiput presentations in many instances. Therefore, the incidence of breech presentations can be reduced by manipulation near the end of pregnancy. This is advantageous because occiput presentations are much less likely to lead to difficulty in labor.

A *transverse presentation* during labor is always abnormal. Whereas the vast majority of babies presenting by the head and also a large proportion of those presenting by the breech can be delivered spontaneously by the mothers or with a little aid, a spontaneous delivery of a full-term child presenting transversely is practically impossible. Therefore, when a transverse presentation is detected, the baby is nearly always delivered by the physician through the vagina as soon as the neck of the uterus is open completely. In cases of transverse presentation the physician delivers the baby's feet first by a procedure known as version (turning) and extraction. Sometimes a Caesarean operation is performed.

Internal Examination. An internal examination follows the abdominal one. Nearly always this is done through the rectum and not through the vagina. Examinations through the rectum require no special aseptic preparations and carry no danger. An experienced physician can obtain practically as much information from a rectal as from a vaginal exploration in most cases. Such an examination will disclose whether the presenting part of the baby is a head (and which type), breech, or other part, how far down the head or other presenting part is, the thickness and size of the opening in the neck of the uterus, whether the bag of waters is intact or ruptured, and other conditions.

Other Preparations. Following this examination, the blood pressure is taken, and a specimen of urine is obtained for examination. If a patient had no prenatal care, the physician will examine the heart and lungs to be certain that they are normal.

Then the patient is prepared by a nurse. First the hairs on the external genital organs are clipped or shaved for cleanliness. If labor is not too far advanced, the nurse will give the patient an enema to clean out the lower bowel in order to avoid the expulsion of feces (bowel contents) and contamination during the birth of the baby.

THE USE OF DRUGS

In a hospital the patient spends the first stage of labor in a labor room, not in the delivery room, where an attempt is made to keep her comfortable. When the pains become fairly strong and regular one or more drugs can be given to relieve them. All must be employed with caution, since large doses of nearly all of them have a serious effect on the baby. Furthermore, the injudicious use of narcotic (sleep-producing) drugs may interfere with labor by prolonging it, by making operative intervention necessary, and by disturbing the third stage of labor, causing hemorrhage. Their unwise use is particularly hazardous because the baby may be born narcotized and will require resuscitation (procedure to restore consciousness). Therefore, drugs must not be given too close to the end of the first stage of labor.

The use of drugs in the first stage of labor is known as analgesia (relief of pain without loss of consciousness). When a general anesthetic is used, such as ether, nitrous oxide, or ethylene, the patient loses consciousness. This is called anesthesia. Most women are given an analgesic in the first stage of labor and many women, especially those delivered in hospitals, receive some anesthetic during the actual birth of the baby. In most hospital cases an inhalation anesthetic is administered in the second stage, a few whiffs during each uterine contraction. This is really analgesia because pain is relieved but consciousness is seldom lost. In many normal cases and in nearly all operative deliveries, however, complete anesthesia is given so that the patient is unconscious for a few minutes to more than an hour. The time varies with the situation presented. During the time of unconsciousness the baby is delivered and lacerations (tears) or incisions are sutured (sewed up).

Some drugs are given during labor not only to relieve the suffering but also to produce a loss of memory. When these drugs are used the women usually have no recollection from the time they take them until a few hours after the birth. Drugs producing amnesia (loss of memory) must be used with great caution. Patients must be watched constantly while they are under the influence of these drugs because some become unruly. Such drugs should not be used if a baby is to be delivered at home.

Spinal anesthesia has a limited field of usefulness because of the chance of producing a minor or a major complication. Because of the possible dangers and complications and of the necessity for trained personnel and special apparatus there is no need to use it for the average woman in labor. Most of the pains of labor, which are quickly forgotten in any event, can be relieved by other selected drugs and anesthetics.

THE DELIVERY

Shortly before the baby is to be born, the woman in labor is moved to the delivery room. Primigravidas are moved soon after the second stage has begun. Multiparas are moved before the end of the first stage because the second stage—that is, the actual birth of the baby—may last only a few minutes. In this room every precaution is taken to maintain as strict asepsis and antisepsis as possible in order to avoid infection.

Nearly all women who have normal deliveries are placed on a narrow bed. The physician stands to one side of the bed, usually on the patient's right side. As the baby's head emerges the physician guides it so as to avoid undue damage to the mother's tissues between the external genital organs and the outer or external part of the rectum. This area is known as the perineum. In most hospital deliveries women are given an anesthetic at this time because the emergence of the baby's head is a painful process.

Very soon after the baby is born the umbilical cord (navel cord), which connects the baby with the afterbirth or placenta, is compressed with two clamps and cut between the clamps. If the baby is very small or if it appears anemic, the cord is not severed until it stops pulsating, which indicates that the baby has received all the blood it can from the afterbirth. One portion of the cord remains attached to the baby and the other to the placenta, which is still in the uterus. The clamp on the baby's end of the cord is replaced by a metal clip or a short piece of tape to compress the blood vessels in the cord and thus to avoid bleeding. Then a 1 per cent solution of silver nitrate or a similar medicament is instilled into the baby's eyes to prevent blindness from gonorrhea. This procedure is an almost universal law.

After birth the painful contractions of the uterus cease suddenly; if the woman is awake she is greatly relieved. However, mild contractions continue until the afterbirth separates from its attachment to the inside of the womb and is forced into the vagina by the uterine contractions. When the physician detects this he pushes down gently on the contracted uterus and the placenta is expelled. If there has been any laceration the wound is repaired.

After the birth of a baby the mother is generally kept in the delivery room or a recovery room for at least thirty minutes to be certain that the uterus remains contracted and that there is no bleeding from it. Then she is taken to her room, where she is watched carefully for a while. If a narcotic is given shortly after the baby is born, it will ensure physical and mental rest and perhaps a few hours of sleep. During the first few hours after delivery it is best to pull down the window shades and to keep everyone out of the room except the nurse. Of course the husband is permitted to see his wife and to talk to her if she is awake on her arrival in her room. However, he should stay only a short time.

The discomfort that most women feel passes a few hours after the baby is born. The multiparas may have afterpains, or painful contractions of the uterus, for 24 to 48 hours, but these are relieved easily by mild drugs. Primiparas seldom have afterpains. On the third or fourth day most women complain of pain and swelling of the breasts. This is caused by the onset of the flow of milk. The discomfort is seldom troublesome and generally disappears after 24 to 48 hours when the baby, by its sucking action, has regulated the amount of milk in the breasts. Babies are generally put to the breast only twice during the first 24 hours, and after this they nurse every 4 hours, except during the night. Breast nursing is beneficial to the mother as well as to the newborn baby.

During the first week the decrease in the size of the uterus is remarkable. Immediately after the baby is born and the afterbirth is expelled, the uterus contracts to a ball-shaped mass the size of a large grapefruit. By the end of the first week this organ has become so small that it can hardly be felt on abdominal examination.

During the first ten days after a baby is born mothers lose about five pounds. The weight loss during delivery is about twelve pounds and consists chiefly of the baby, the afterbirth, and the amniotic fluid, (water), that surrounded the baby.

NATURAL CHILDBIRTH

The term natural childbirth, which is now entrenched in both medical and lay literature, is erroneous. It implies that labor was painless in primitive peoples but this is not so. The leading exponent of so-called natural childbirth, and the one who deserves great credit for his long and persistent efforts to educate physicians and women about the normal processes of labor, is Grantly Dick Read. According to Read, the discomforts of childbirth are largely due to fear and tension. Patients who are prepared for the emotional phases and the muscular work are naturally relaxed and about half of them have no desire for anesthetics or sedatives. Under such conditions the woman goes into labor in a state of exhilaration and animation, which she retains until the cervix (the neck of the womb) is dilated from one to two fifths. At two-fifths dilatation she becomes quieter and a pronounced malar flush develops. At three-fifths dilatation she becomes serious. This is the first emotional menace of labor, and the patient must not be left alone. If she is well cared for, she will carry on and regain considerable confidence before the cervix is four-fifths dilated.

The transition from the first to the second stage is when pain occurs because of the ultimate dilatation of the cervix. Backache occurs in about half the patients. This is the second emotional menace of labor. As the patient passes into the second stage she experiences a sense of relief at being able to help herself. Backache disappears at this point. The third emotional phase occurs when the head reaches the pelvic floor. The patient experiences a terror of anticipation; she will complain of all sorts of things and show a desire to escape.

The fourth emotional menace occurs at the crowning of the head when, unless the outlet of the vulva is elastic and the patient is in full control of herself, she will experience a burning sensation. This usually disappears quickly, and there is almost complete anesthesia of the perineum within 0.5 to 0.75 inch of the vulval margin.

After the head and shoulders are freed, the child is rotated and lies facing the mother. At this stage there is an astonishing transfiguration of a hard-working woman to a mother who suddenly is happy and sits up and waits for the baby to be fully born. The child is handed to the mother as soon as the cord is cut. This stimulates a reflex contraction of the uterus, which is definitely of physiologic value. Twenty minutes is the minimal time permitted for expelling the placenta. The patient experiences a wave of anxiety as the uterus contracts, but the passage of the placenta is a source of great satisfaction.

The following results of physiologic labor made possible by emotional gratification are recorded by Read: (1) confident approach by women to labor, (2) shortened time of all stages, (3) absence of any unbearable discomfort, (4) minimal use of drugs, analgesics, and anesthetics, (5) interference is rarely necessary, (6) no serious pelvic or perineal injury, (7) minimal blood loss and obstetric shock, (8) absence of exhaustion of the mother, (9) sense of achievement and profound happiness, (10) establishment of strong mother-child relationship, (11) breast feeding by choice, (12) uninterrupted progress of the baby, and (13) a desire for more children.

Goodrich and Thoms register their patients for the Read method according to the usual pattern. In addition, they attempt to assess the patient's personality, to reassure her as to her physical condition and to make her feel that the staff of nurses and physicians is taking a real interest in her. On the next visit, she attends a short lecture on the anatomy and physiology of the female genital tract, information about fertilization, fetal growth, and an explanation of signs and symptoms of early pregnancy. She is told about the effects of tension and the relationship of fear to tension and pain. During the next visits, she is taught exercises designed to increase elasticity and tonus of the back, abdominal, and perineal muscles and also breathing and position exercises which aid relaxation. At the first visit in the eighth calendar month she attends a second lecture on the course of labor and will usually return about four more times before delivery. During these visits she attends exercise classes conducted by a nurse supervisor or a nurse midwife. Mistakes are corrected and labor is rehearsed. Breast massage is started for those who intend to nurse their infants.

ROOMING-IN

As Thoms says, rooming-in is the term applied to the hospital arrangement whereby the mother has her newborn baby by her bedside and takes as much care of the baby as she wishes. It is not a new procedure, for in certain European countries it exists in its essentials in many modern hospitals. In our country this natural mother and baby relationship was abandoned in favor of the hospital nursery. This may have disadvantages from a psychological point of view because separation of the newborn infant from its mother may interfere with certain essential psychological needs of both mother and child. The separation of mother and child after delivery may be a frustrating experience for those mothers who want to enjoy their babies. The imposition of a rigid schedule for both does not have proper regard for the newborn's needs and developmental changes nor for the particular stresses of the mother in her adjustment to her new environment.

Under the natural childbirth regimen the husband is encouraged to be with his wife in the early part of labor and after delivery to go to the unit for a brief bedside visit. At this time he may hold the baby after washing his hands and putting on a hospital gown. During the stay at the hospital he may learn diapering and aid in adjusting the baby to feeding. In the rooming-in system the infant is on a demand-feeding or ad lib schedule and to an extent the mother is also, for she is not roused to many of the usual hospital routines. From the obstetrical point of view two things are of interest in a rooming-in system, namely, the fostering of maternal nursing and mother-infant and family relationships.

POSTPARTUM CARE

Nowadays, after an average birth, the mother may return to her home when the baby is six to ten days old. If the mother had no complications during or after the birth she probably is permitted to get out of bed the day after the baby was born and is well able to walk out of the hospital about the sixth day. However, since there is considerable excitement incident to dressing the baby, packing suitcases, saying good-by to the nurses, riding home, meeting neighbors, and so on, in the process of getting home, it is advisable that the patient go to bed as soon as she reaches home and remain there until the following morning. It is best for her to leave the hospital in the afternoon because of the advantage of traveling during the day and because by the time home is reached there are not many waking hours left. Once in the home, the patient should not go into the street until the baby is almost three weeks old.

Probably the most important factor necessary to safeguard a happy household with a newborn baby is a mentally calm and unperturbed mother. This is determined to the largest extent by the health of the baby. The mother must learn to be more or less callous to disturbing influences. Certainly petty inconveniences should not be permitted to interfere with her peace of mind. If there is a nurse at home she, of course, assumes much of the responsibility in the care of the child. Tranquillity of mind and some regularity in feeding the infant will usually guarantee a thriving baby.

During the first week at home visitors should be restricted to two a day besides the immediate family. Tact is necessary to avoid talkative visitors or to limit their stay. Likewise telephone calls should be limited in number and length, especially if at the other end of the wire there is a garrulous individual or one who wants to impart information concerning dreadful occurrences. Visitors who have colds or infections should not be seen and definitely must not be admitted to the baby's room. If the mother herself has a cold she should cover her mouth and nose with a handkerchief or a mouthpiece when nursing or bathing the baby. No medicine should be taken by the mother or given to the baby without the sanction of a physician. Some drugs reach the baby through the breast milk.

For the first few weeks after childbirth a nursing mother should consider herself a convalescent invalid. This does not mean, however, that she should fear doing any kind of housework or lack confidence in her ability to take care of her baby. More consideration must be given to general rules of health than is customary, and the diet should be abundant, varied, and balanced. Throughout the puerperium (the time interval that extends from the birth of the baby until the organs of reproduction return to their normal condition—six to eight weeks) the mother should have an abundance of sleep and, in addition, should rest in a reclining position for definite periods of time in both the morning and afternoon. While resting she should lie on her abdomen for fifteen to twenty minutes, as she did when she was in the hospital.

When nursing the baby the mother may sit up or recline. An extremely important thing to avoid is constant observation of the baby while it is at the breast, for this not only strains the mother's eyes and produces headaches but strains the muscles of the neck and back, which likewise become the seat of pain.

For the woman with a lax abdominal wall a supporting garment is most helpful. Tub baths are best not taken until after the third week, but showers and sponge baths should be taken daily during this time. Walking is helpful, but strenuous exercise, such as playing golf or tennis, swimming, skating, or even driving a car, should be avoided during the puerperal period. Social functions during these weeks should likewise be reduced to a minimum.

If a patient had some disturbance during pregnancy she will need special aftercare. Thus, if a woman had high blood pressure she will have to have repeated blood-pressure readings. If she had a kidney infection her urine will have to be examined every day. These women must be watched not only during their hospital stay but for months and perhaps years afterward. Such follow-up care is important for the patient's future health and certainly for a decision about having more children.

It is customary for a patient to return to her physician at the end of the puerperal period; namely, six to eight weeks after the birth of the baby. At this time the physician will determine, by an abdominal and vaginal examination, whether the reproductive organs have returned to their normal state. Generally this checkup is designated as the "final" examination. This is unfortunate, because the patient regards it as the final contact with her physician until a new pregnancy begins or some disturbance arises. Since some women have complications or abnormalities they develop after childbirth, it is advisable for women to see their obstetrician when the baby is six months old and again when it is a year old. All women should be examined at least once a year, even if they feel entirely well.

RETURN OF MENSTRUATION

The return of menstruation varies in different individuals. In those who do not nurse their babies the flow usually returns at the end of six weeks, while in those who do breast-feed their babies the first menstrual period appears any time after the third month. In some, however, the menses do not return until the baby is weaned. The first period is usually profuse, sometimes enough to cause alarm. At the time of the first period it is best for the woman to keep off her feet as much as possible, but if the flow is too profuse the advice of a physician should be sought.

Topics for further thought:

1. "Natural" childbirth is advocated by many physicians. This is believed to have advantages for both the mother and child. Discuss and evaluate these.

2. The "rooming-in" plan is now used by some hospitals. Discuss the desirable effect of this for both mother and child.

Selected reading references

Dickinson, Robert L., and Belski, *The Birth Atlas,* New York, Maternity Center Association.
Large-scale photographs of the Dickinson models portraying development from the time of conception to the third stage of labor. Suitable for use with a variety of age groups.

Goodrich, F. W., Jr., and Thoms, H., "Clinical Study of Natural Childbirth. Preliminary Report from the Teaching Ward Service," *Am. J. Obst. & Gynec.* **56**:875 (Nov.) 1948.

Marsh, Earle M., "Obstetrical Opportunities for Marriage Counseling," *Marriage and Family Living,* May, 1953, pp. 132-54.
Presents ways in which the physician may aid prospective mothers and fathers through the physical and emotional strains of pregnancy and childbirth.

Read, Grantly D., *Childbirth Without Fear,* 3rd edition, New York, Harper and Brothers, 1953.
"Natural Childbirth" as stated by one of its pioneer developers. Easy reading for lay persons.

——, "Correlation of Physiological and Emotional Phenomena of Labour," *J. Obst. & Gynaec. Brit. Emp.* **53**:55 (Feb.) 1946.

Schultz, Gladys D., and Hill, Lee F., *Your Baby,* Garden City, Doubleday and Company, 1948.
A handbook for parents. Covers the child's development from conception to six years of age.

Strain, Frances B., *Being Born,* New York, D. Appleton-Century Company, 1936.
The story of human reproduction, very simply worded. Suitable for use both with children and adults.

Thoms, H., *Training for Childbirth—A Program of Natural Childbirth with Rooming-in.* New York, McGraw-Hill Book Co., 1950.

29 ABORTIONS

Alan F. Guttmacher

ABORTION is the ending of pregnancy at any time before the fetus or prospective child is large enough to have a fair chance for survival. In terms of length of pregnancy, viability is usually considered the beginning of the seventh month. In terms of size of the infant, the border line between viability and nonviability is two pounds and three ounces. This does not mean that all infants weighing less are foredoomed to death—an occasional infant weighing as little as a pound and three quarters has been known to survive—nor does it mean that all weighing more than two pounds, three ounces are certain to be reared. It simply means that a fetus of this weight has more than an obscure chance for living. When the newborn weighs more than this, it is automatically classified a premature infant rather than an abortion, irrespective of the pregnancy's duration.

The word abortion has an unwholesome, criminal connotation for the uninstructed person. He is accustomed to use the more euphemistic word miscarriage for the spontaneous varieties of early pregnancy interruption, reserving abortion to designate the man-made type. Not so the physician; he uses abortion to designate any previable pregnancy termination. The doctor does differentiate between spontaneous or unintentional abortions and induced abortions, the former occurring from natural causes, the latter being brought about by instrumentation. He also divides induced abortions into therapeutic and illegal. The distinction between these is self-evident.

SPONTANEOUS ABORTION

Spontaneous abortion is frequent. In a series of one thousand consecutive pregnancies among the author's private patients, spontaneous abortion occurred to 98, that is 9.8 per cent. The average frequency of spontaneous abortion among total pregnancies reported by several others was about the same. This figure should be slightly increased to include the patient who aborts so early that she neither needs nor seeks medical assistance. Therefore, the good round figure 10 per cent is probably a more accurate figure for the frequency of spontaneous abortion. This frequency is not affected by the number of pregnancies —it is as likely to happen in the first as the eighth. The incidence of unintentional abortion is greatly increased, however, among women of relatively advanced reproductive age (35 years of age or more), those with histories of previous abortions, and those who required more than six months for the conception to occur. In a series of patients less than 25 years old who conceived in less than three months and who had never aborted, an unintentional abortion rate of 4 per cent was found. In a similar series of women over 35 who took longer than six months to conceive and who had previously aborted a spontaneous abortion rate of 38 per cent was noted.

The time of abortion has been found to be the second month in 30 per cent of the women, the third in 42 per cent, the fourth in 17 per cent, the fifth in 8 per cent, and the sixth month in 3 per cent. Thus, 72 per cent of spontaneous abortions occur before the fourth month of pregnancy begins, the commonest time being 10.8 weeks after the onset of the last menstrual period.

Cases of spontaneous abortion may be divided into two main groups: a major group, in which abortion is the result of random or fortuitous factors, unlikely to repeat in the next pregnancy except by cruel chance; and a much smaller group in which a recurrent factor appears to cause abortion with succeeding pregnancies. Speert, in a recent study, reports 121 instances among 17,490 obstetrical patients of the Presbyterian Hospital in New York who gave the history of three consecutive spontaneous abortions, one case in every 145 pregnancies. In this study Speert demonstrated that in more than 70 per cent of the cases the pregnancy following such a series of consecutive abortions resulted in a term child. Despite the optimistic outlook for the group as a whole, there is the occasional case in which the uterus never seems able to carry a fetus to viability. The use of hormones and vitamins, despite their vogue, seems to exert no influence on a favorable outcome.

What causes spontaneous abortion? The causes are multiple, but by far the most frequent is defective germ plasm. A learned professor explained the concept of defective germ plasm to a distinguished society of obstetricians and gynecologists in this homely fashion. He drew from his vest pockets several unopened pods of garden peas. "Now, gentlemen," he said, "I can present to you a visual example of defective germ plasm. I bought these on the way to this lecture and I dare say in almost every pod we shall find at least one runt placed among the full, large, normal peas." He cracked open two or three pods and, sure enough, in each pod there was a stunted pea among the seven or eight full-grown ones. "This, gentlemen," he said, "is a bad egg; this is defective germ plasm." Bad eggs occur throughout the whole vegetable and animal economy, from the dwarfed, shriveled, rotten plum among the green plums of the plum tree, to the fragmented, deteriorated fertilized egg washed from an oviduct attached to a freshly removed human uterus.

Defective germ plasm may be theoretically due to three different mechanisms: a serious chromosomal abnormality in the egg of the female or the sperm of the male; physicochemical mishap in the complicated reaction of fertilization; or some strictly environmental factor connected with the embedding and early development of the fertilized egg within the lining of the uterus. Perhaps in the third case a normal fertilized egg implants too superficially or too deeply in the lining. Or perhaps the maternal organism supplies inadequate food because of a deficient blood supply to the precise implantation site. Such causes of defective germ plasm are conjectural; when the result, the defective conceptus (fetus, egg membranes, and afterbirth), is examined there is no way to determine which of the several mechanisms was actually involved.

The life history of a typical ten-to-eleven-week abortion caused by defective germ plasm progresses as follows: Pregnancy commences as usual 10 to 14 days after the onset of the menses, but it is likely to be peculiarly free of symptoms. There is the usual failure to menstruate when the menstrual period is due, but breast enlargement is inclined to be minimal. Nausea and vomiting are likely absent or, if present, they too are minimal. The pregnancy continues to progress for three to four weeks; then development ceases and the whole conceptus dies. The patient feels very nonpregnant. Her breasts may even become smaller again, and if there was nausea it is likely to disappear. The dead conceptus is carried without incident for four or five weeks longer, and then a brownish vaginal stain appears. Within 24 to 72 hours some fresh bleeding may commence and soon lower abdominal cramps begin. Clots now pass from the vagina, and later a plum-sized, firm mass—the pregnancy—is expelled. If such is the case, the whole unpleasant episode is over. If bleeding and pain continue, hospital admission may be necessary to carry out curettage (loosening with a tiny hoe from the interior of the uterus the dead and partly fragmented conceptus).

When examined, defective-germ-plasm abortions show varying degrees of imperfection. The fetus or embryo may never have been present at all, and only a thin-walled sac filled with clear fluid is expelled. The English, with their fine sense for our common language, term this degree of imperfection a blighted ovum. At the other end of the scale one may find a normal placenta with intact membranes containing fluid and a dead, well-formed, partially deteriorated embryo. The embryo, however, instead of being firm and slightly transparent, is soft and opaque, with shreds of tissue peeling off.

In contrast to the defective-germ-plasm abortion is the abortion of a perfectly normal conceptus. This normal abortion is commonly a late abortion, usually in the fourth or fifth month. Frequently the first inkling the patient has is the unexpected rupture of the bag of waters. Examination of the aborted specimen reveals a sac containing clear fluid attached at its base to a shaggy chestnut-bur-like placenta (afterbirth). That is, when the placenta is immersed in liquid the normal protrusions from the surface, called villi, stand forth like the spicules of a chestnut bur. Within the sac is a firm, semitransparent, perfectly formed, smooth-skinned embryo.

On the basis of a series of aborted pregnancies examined by two authoritative laboratories, that of the Boston Lying-In Hospital and the Carnegie Embryologic Institute of Johns Hopkins, approximately 70 per cent of all spontaneous abortions are due to defective germ plasm. This means that among spontaneous abortions three or four abnormal, dead ones are expelled to each normal, fresh one in a living or recently dead state.

The next problem is what causes the 30 per cent of abortions that result in the extrusion of completely normal membranes, placenta, and embryo. In such cases some factor within the uterus or without either causes the uterus to contract prematurely and squeeze out its immature contents, or causes the sac of membranes which contains the embryo floating in its protective fluid to rupture. In the latter case the fluid which is constantly being formed drains out continually and after a highly variable time—hours, days, or weeks—the uterus undergoes contractions and expels the whole contents. Many instances remain unexplained, while for others the causes are known. Many people think that physical violence is a common cause for abortion. This is not the case. This writer has been called to the hospital accident room more than once to examine a woman who had been "kicked in the stomach by a gentleman friend." The bruise was there, but the pregnancy remained undisturbed. Once a woman jumped from a cliff to produce abortion. She fractured both legs but delivered a normal child at term. A ballerina at a night club invited the writer to watch her perform when she was four months pregnant. Watching her cavort reinforced faith in the belief that you cannot shake a good egg loose any more than a storm can shake unripe normal fruit from a tree. A careful study recently conducted at a naval hospital compared the abortion rate among wives who remained at the base throughout pregnancy with that of those who traveled about in early pregnancy. The results showed an insignificantly lower abortion rate among those who traveled, whether by automobile, airplane, or train. The reader may question this finding, because he knows someone who aborted while traveling. It is difficult to separate cause from coincidence in medical happenings. Violence or unusual physical exertion may occasionally precipitate the actual expulsive phase in the abortion of a defective, already dead conceptus, but it is extremely rare for unusual physical exertion to initiate the abortion of a normally developing embryo.

If physical activity does not cause the abortion of a normal conceptus, what does? Abnormalities of the reproductive organs may: certain cases of fibroid tumors of the uterus, deep tears of the cervix (mouth of the womb) or scarring from previous operations on the cervix, rarely an incorrect position of the uterus. Multiple pregnancies, twins or triplets, are prone to terminate in abortion. Excessive amniotic fluid within the uterus (hydramnios) is another cause. Severe maternal illness, especially infections such as pneumonia, may bring on abortion. Syphilis, however, does not cause abortion. Untreated, it is likely to cause the birth of a dead, premature infant; properly treated, it results in a normal-term child.

In addition to the causes enumerated are many others about which nothing is known. There is no explanation for a majority of normal-appearing abortions.

An immense amount of misinformation exists regarding abortion. So far as doctors know, there is no proved tendency for abortion to occur particularly at the time of the missed menstrual period. Shock, grief, or fear rarely if ever causes abortion. Fresh paint has no selective action in disturbing an early pregnancy. Stretching, stooping, bending, or pedaling the sewing machine does not unhouse the embryo. Sexual intercourse, in the absence of any abnormality in the woman's reproductive tract, will not bring about abortion. Such iconoclastic statements are hard for many people to accept because they know of a case in which thus and so happened. It must be emphasized again that it is difficult to separate cause from coincidence in medical happenings.

Spontaneous abortion has acquired an unjustifiably dangerous reputation because of its kinship and confusion with its nefarious cousin, illegal abortion. The spontaneous variety almost never invalids and rarely if ever kills, particularly today, with transfusion available to combat blood loss and antibiotics to combat infection.

CARE AND TREATMENT OF ABORTION

As soon as a pregnant woman stains or bleeds she should report to her physician at once. In each one hundred women who commence pregnancy, thirty will stain or bleed at some time before the seventh month. Of the thirty who will stain or bleed, ten will abort and twenty will continue pregnant as though nothing ever happened. The doctor does not know to which group a patient belongs except by the actual outcome; however, he tries to guess from the history and the findings on examination. If the bleeding occurs about the time of the first missed period it may be an abbreviated menses during early pregnancy, a perfectly normal occurrence. Then, too, the bleeding may arise from some abnormality of the cervix, such as inflammation or a polyp (a small tassel-like growth protruding from the mouth of the womb). If, however, the bleeding is significant enough to stain a pad thoroughly in an hour, then abortion is probably threatening. Since the doctor cannot be sure whether it is the 70 per cent germ-plasm variety or the 30 per cent regrettable termination of a normal pregnancy which threatens, he is truly on the horns of a dilemma. He has two problems: first, he does not know whether it is incidental bleeding of little importance or whether abortion impends; second, he does not know whether the abortion is the variety he wants to try to save—the normal-pregnancy type—or whether it is the type he wants to aid in expelling—the defective-germ-plasm variety. Therefore most doctors treat all types of pregnancy bleeding as though each patient were on the verge of aborting a normal conceptus. They argue that if it is insignificant bleeding it will stop anyway and treatment will do no harm; if it is faulty germ plasm no medicines will forestall abortion; but if it is the threatened abortion of a normal embryo treatment may do some good.

Treatment consists of bed rest, the administration of Vitamin E and hormones, body chemicals, either by mouth or by hypodermic. The value of Vitamin E, the substance so important in the proper implantation of the rat embryo, remains more suspected than proved in human pregnancy. Several hormones may be given: progesterone, estrone, and thyroid. Progesterone is a chemical manufactured by the ovary during the first few months and by the placenta (the afterbirth) later. It has a soothing action in preventing the uterus from contracting. Estrone, another placental chemical, is supposed to aid the uterus in the utilization of the progesterone, and it is also supposed to increase the blood supply to the decidua (the lining of the uterus). Thyroid medication stimulates general metabolism, and in so doing tunes up the other glands of internal secretion. The old horse-and-buggy treatment of ice bag and morphine by injection has been displaced by vitamin and hormone combinations.

If the bleeding becomes intense, resulting in the passage of large clots, curettage, the cleaning out of the uterus, is considered mandatory. Sometimes abortion is incomplete—part of the pregnancy tissue is passed and part remains behind in the uterus. If this occurs, curettage must also be performed.

The question of how soon the patient who aborts may attempt pregnancy again is answered differently by different doctors. In reply to a recent questionnaire sent out by the author, 3042 physicians stated their views. The average physician advised his patient to wait 6.6 months before trying again. Some permitted immediate reimpregnation; others required a year to elapse between the abortion and attempted pregnancy.

If the abortion was of the defective-germ-plasm variety there appears to be no reason why immediate reimpregnation should not follow. It is suggested that the patient have a basal metabolism taken so that thyroid can be prescribed if the results of the metabolism indicate a need. If the abortion resulted in the expulsion of a normal conceptus, the patient should be gone over carefully in an effort to elicit the cause. If the cause is found and correction attempted, then the green light can be flashed. If no cause is determined the patient should use contraceptives for about six months in the hope that during this interval the unknown factor will correct itself.

THERAPEUTIC ABORTION

Therapeutic abortion is the legal termination of pregnancy by artificial means before the baby is viable, because some serious health complication of the mother is sufficiently aggravated by continuation of pregnancy to threaten her life or further impair her health. In the United States laws regarding therapeutic abortion vary slightly from one state to the next but in essence are much alike, being patterned after the English Abortion Act of 1860. In substance, abortion can be legally produced only if two physicians who have been in practice for five years or longer and who are in good standing attest in writing that continuation of pregnancy would place in jeopardy the life of the mother. Previously the only conditions believed to merit therapeutic abortion were serious organic diseases of the heart, lungs, or kidneys, or incessant and life-threatening vomiting of early pregnancy. Several years ago the interpretation of jeopardy was broadened to include the mind, so that women who have true depressions, hallucinatory states, and other abnormal mental conditions are now frequently aborted. In many communities further liberalization has occurred so that eugenic indications are included. For example, a woman who produces hemophiliac sons (males with uncontrollable bleeding tendencies) or the pregnant woman who acquires German measles (rubella) during the first twelve weeks of pregnancy is considered a fit candidate for therapeutic abortion. In about 17 per cent of the latter cases the child is born with a very serious abnormality: congenital cataracts of the lens of the eye, a malformed heart, or microcephaly (a form of idiocy in which the head is tiny). The long list of eugenic indications is not well standardized, and the same conditions may be considered grounds for therapeutic abortion by one doctor and rejected by another.

It is difficult to state what proportion of total pregnancies necessitates therapeutic termination. The criteria for interruption are so different from one doctor to the next or one hospital to the next. Most medical authors who have written on this subject feel that an incidence as high as one in every 150 pregnancies is probably justified for teaching institutions with referred problem cases, while in the strictly private hospital the incidence should probably be no higher than one in 250.

Abortion may not be done with the sanction of the law simply because a woman wishes it or because of economic or social factors, no matter how dire. I learned this early in my obstetrical career, when in charge of an obstetrical outpatient clinic. A social agency referred a little twelve-year-old who had been impregnated by her own father. The father had been arrested, tried, and sentenced to the penitentiary. I was young and naïve and greatly outraged at the thought that this little helpless girl must bear her own father's bastard. The Chief of Service agreed to allow abortion if I could get a letter from the state's attorney authorizing it. I tried, I failed, and she bore her father's child.

In England some progress has been made through the famous trial of the Crown vs. Dr. Alec Bourne. A sixteen-year-old unmarried girl was seized and raped by three soldiers. Pregnancy resulted. Dr. Bourne aborted the victim in the public wards of a London hospital, notified the Crown's counsel, and asked to be arrested. A three-day trial followed. His lawyers contended that the law could be construed not only to protect the mother's physical life but her mental and emotional life as well. Courageous Dr. Bourne was acquitted by the jury.

One of the difficulties about the problem of therapeutic abortion is the inequable distribution of the procedure. In borderline cases—and all too frequently in cases that are not even borderline—the patient's prestige and money are very vocal in getting an undesired pregnancy terminated. Far too often a minor difficulty is stretched into a major abnormality for the right person. In order to negate this factor of personal influence many hospitals have set up abortion boards to consider all requests for therapeutic abortion, private and ward. At the Mount Sinai Hospital in New York the chiefs of the five major services—medicine, surgery, pediatrics, neuropsychiatry, and obstetrics-gynecology—make up the board and consider each request for termination of pregnancy very earnestly. The board is privileged to call experts from other departments to help them arrive at a proper decision. If any member of the committee of five opposes the abortion, interruption is disallowed.

Therapeutic abortion is carried out as a vaginal operation if pregnancy is thirteen weeks or less. It is either done in one stage under an anesthetic by dilating the mouth of the womb with instruments and then loosening and scraping out the pregnant contents, or in two stages. In this case the cervix and uterus are first packed tight with gauze, followed 24 hours later by curettage. The operation is done in a hospital under appropriate anesthesia. If the pregnancy is more than three months, most doctors prefer to empty the uterus via the abdominal route. A miniature Caesarean section is done—the abdomen is incised, the front of the uterus cut open, its pregnant contents removed, the womb sewn together again, and finally the abdominal incision repaired.

ILLEGAL ABORTION

Illegal abortion presents one of the most important and yet one of the least studied problems of modern medicine. There are many conjectures but few known facts. This is borne out by a consideration of its incidence. In 1936 the late Dr. Frederick Taussig, in his authoritative book, *Abortion,* concluded that there was one abortion to every 2.5 births in the urban communities of this country and one abortion in every five in the rural areas, yielding a total of 681,600 abortions annually, an abortion rate of 22 per 100 pregnancies. Since the spontaneous abortion rate is approximately 10 per 100, this means that 12 per cent of the total pregnancies in the United States, according to Taussig, are terminated by illegal interference. Stix, in her 1935 study of pregnancy wastage among patients living in the Bronx, reported an illegal abortion rate of 22 per cent, while two years later Wiehl and Berry, in a study of a population sample from the five boroughs of New York City, reported a rate of only 4 per cent. Thus three competent studies show illegal abortion rates varying from 4 to 22 per cent of all pregnancies.

Illegal abortion presents not only medical problems of grave importance but also other problems of equal magnitude. Here are some of the highlights in the realm of medical sociology. Wiehl and Berry reported a high induced-abortion rate for third and fourth pregnancies in women of the low-income group. Taussig wrote: "The vast majority of all abortions, equaling 90 per cent, occur among married women, especially those between 25 and 35 years of age who have had several children. The recent increase in abortion has been primarily in this group." Other investigations conclude that 85 per cent of the women resorting to illegal abortion are married, 12 per cent single, and 3 per cent widowed. Both Stix and Taussig found that the rate among Protestants, Catholics, and Jews was approximately equal. According to the study by Stix, 75 per cent of illegal abortions are induced by persons designated as doctors by the patients, 19 per cent by midwives, and 6 per cent self-induced. Taussig stated that more than 50 per cent are performed by doctors, 20 per cent by midwives, and less than 30 per cent by the patient herself. It is most important for American medicine to admit existence of the problem, a problem that cannot be solved by present prohibitory laws and halfhearted moral censure.

Fisher in 1954 arrived at the conservative estimate of at least 330,000 illegal abortions each year in the United States. He stated that less than one thousand convictions occur annually for this offense. He points out that no other felonious act is as free from punishment as criminal abortion.

The dangers of illegal abortion are twofold, psychic and physical. It is a degrading, soul-searing experience for many women, partly because of the kind of people usually involved in its performance and also because of its clandestine nature. It is an experience that is slow to be forgotten. Then, too, the presence of loved children within a home are constant reminders of the child who could have been and is not. Many a person has deep regrets for the impetuous step she took. In one instance the mother of three sons was persuaded by her husband to have an illegal abortion. Her constant remorse and regret turned a physically happy marriage into virtually an asexual friendship. The physical dangers of illegal abortion are death or infection, the latter ending in sterility by sealing the oviducts closed.

The mathematical likelihood for either danger is in proportion to the skill of the abortionist. Dr. Frederick Taussig observed legalized abortion when he visited Russia before 1935. At this time the Russians claimed a death rate in their hospital abortions of five per 200,000, a much lower figure than in their nonhospitalized abortions. However, Dr. Taussig finally pared down the slightly optimistic-appearing Russian claim to ten deaths per 100,000. This is the best possible figure extant for therapeutic abortions. Since they are done legally far less frequently in the United States than they were in Russia when abortion was within the law, the United States figure even in the hands of the best clinics would probably not equal this.* The real death rate in cases handled by ill-trained, illegal-abortion-performing doctors, or the granny-type midwife, is probably extremely high though any figure

* In the last few years indiscriminate abortion has been legalized for over a billion people, more than a third of the world's human mass. The countries practically allowing abortion on demand are: China, Russia, Japan, Poland, Yugoslavia, and Hungary. Sweden, Denmark, and Norway have mild restrictions.

is a poor guess. The death rate is probably not high in cases handled by the well-trained, big-scale illegal medical abortionist. Many of them have the skill and the physical plant necessary to get good results. No unprejudiced, sound investigation has ever been made in this country or western Europe of the volume, methods, social implications, or results of the large-scale, expert illegal abortionist. Such unbiased research is in order.

Of course the most dangerous variety is the abortion performed by the patient on herself. All varieties of implements are used: hatpins, hairpins, slippery elm sticks, long feathers, or other materials. The most popular is the bougie, a tapered firm rubber tube. Tragically enough, some women who are not even pregnant die from self-induced abortions.

Emmenagogue or abortifacient drugs which are sold by the carload are useless. Both the legitimate and fly-by-night drug houses peddle pills which are supposed "to bring a woman around." These drugs contain ergot and various vegetable compounds, but if the woman is really pregnant, with a normal well-implanted egg, she can swallow them to the point of self-poisoning without effect. If she has a bad egg and is on the verge of a spontaneous abortion the drugs may conceivably bring it about a few hours earlier. If she is not pregnant at all and swallows her twenty black pills with a teaspoonful of water and a glassful of faith it may bring on normal menstruation. The action is through the release of the inhibiting brain censor, fear of pregnancy rather than pregnancy having caused her to fail to menstruate in the first place. The federal government, by virtue of the Pure Food and Drug Act, has launched a campaign against the continued sale of such fake menstrual-producing prescriptions.

Topics for further thought:

1. At various times governments have legalized abortion but none has ever persisted in this attitude. What considerations would make such legislation desirable?

2. What medical discoveries or research would tend to make abortion less frequent?

Selected reading references

Christensen, Harold T., *Marriage Analysis,* New York, Ronald Press, 1950.
See pp. 154-5 and 369-70 for discussions of both the physical and social factors involved in abortion.

Gordon, Edgar S., "Taking Physical Factors into Account," in Becker, Howard, and Hill, Reuben, *Family, Marriage and Parenthood,* Boston, D. C. Heath and Company, 1954.
This chapter includes a discussion of both spontaneous and criminal abortion.

Guttmacher, Alan F., *Therapeutic Abortion in a Large General Hospital.* Surgical Clinics of North America. (In Press) New York Number. To be published in 1957. Saunders, Philadelphia, Pa.

Landis, Paul H., *Making the Most of Marriage,* New York, Appleton-Century-Crofts, 1955.
See pp. 262-5 for a discussion of the hazards of illegal abortion.

Portnoy, Louis, and Saltman, Jules, *Fertility in Marriage,* New York, The New American Library, 1951.
See Chapter 18, "Wasted Pregnancies," for an excellent, non-technical account of the nature of abortion; also treatment for its prevention.

FIVE

THE CHILD IN THE FAMILY

30   THE PHYSICAL GROWTH OF THE CHILD

Wilton M. Krogman

A KNOWLEDGE of how children grow, when they grow, how they increase in size, when they change in proportions, and when they mature will help parents immeasurably in bringing up their children. Study of growth is useful for at least four reasons:

1. As a measure of health progress and nutritional (dietetic) balance. Observation and measurement afford a check on health condition and an assessment of nutritional status. A child whose physical growth shows a uniform, even progress is a healthy and well-nourished child.

2. To ascertain a child's progress with reference to group averages which constitute norms of progress. A child at three years of age, or seven, or thirteen grows at each of these ages at a different rate; he is in a different stage of physical growth. How does his growth at these stages compare with that of other three-year-old boys, or boys of seven or thirteen?

3. To learn as much as possible about hereditary pattern. A knowledge of family background is necessary because heredity plays a part in the growth picture. Some children come from small family lines, others from average, others from tall family lines.

4. To establish each child as an individual. Children do not grow precisely alike; they follow a general pattern but their own growth progress is the measure of their own individuality.

MEASUREMENT OF HEIGHT AND WEIGHT

Height and weight are only two of many measurements employed for a detailed analysis of physical growth. They are, however, two useful measurements which can help parents in checking on the physical growth of their child.

Technically speaking, height and weight are not really simple measurements. Height is made up of head height (from chin to crown), neck length, trunk length, and leg length; it involves, therefore, linear growth in the head, backbone, and leg bones. Weight is made up of bone, muscle, fat, and organs.

A baby's height is its recumbent (lying-down) length. To measure this recumbent length, place the baby on its back with its legs straight, then measure the maximum distance from the top of the head to the sole of the feet, usually at the heels. Be sure the baby lies on a flat, hard surface (table top rather than a mattress or a couch) so that the body will not sag or curve. Use a yardstick alongside the body as the measure, or a cloth or steel tape. If a cloth tape is used, be sure it is stretched or tightened to the same degree each time. As soon as the child stands well, take his vertical (standing-up) height. Place him against a wall and then mark where a level rule on the top of his head intersects the wall. Be sure the rule remains parallel to the floor during the marking. Then, using a yardstick or a tape, measure the distance from the floor to the mark to determine the height.

To measure weight, use ordinary basket scales for small babies and platform scales later on. Be precise in noting the readings—a few ounces one way or another may be very important to the health of the baby.

Measure height and weight as often as the doctor suggests during the first year. After that, every six months until the child reaches six years of age. Thereafter, annually should be enough. Be sure to weigh and take height measurements always at the same time of day. Body weight varies from morning (lighter) to evening (heavier) and persons are "longest" when they first arise.

HEIGHT-WEIGHT TABLES

Tables 5 and 6 should be helpful for checking the baby's or child's measured height and weight. In these tables, the average and the range are shown. Stature (length or height) is in inches; weight, in pounds. For each age the average means the height and weight typical of a boy or girl at birth and at one to eighteen years. The range means the normal range of variation for each dimension at each age. Two of every three boys or girls at a given age will fall within this range. The two

TABLE 5. Height of Girls and Boys (in inches)

Age (in years)	Girls		Boys	
	AVERAGE	RANGE	AVERAGE	RANGE
Birth	22.0	21.0-23.0	22.5	21.5-23.5
1	29.5	28.0-31.0	30.0	28.5-31.5
2	34.0	32.5-35.5	34.5	33.0-36.0
3	38.0	36.5-39.5	38.5	37.0-40.0
4	41.0	39.5-43.5	41.5	40.0-43.0
5	43.5	41.5-45.5	44.0	42.0-46.0
6	46.5	44.5-48.5	46.5	44.5-48.5
7	49.0	47.0-51.0	49.0	47.0-51.0
8	51.0	49.0-53.0	51.0	49.0-53.0
9	53.5	51.5-55.5	53.5	51.5-55.5
10	55.5	53.5-57.5	55.5	53.5-57.5
11	58.0	56.0-60.0	57.5	55.5-59.5
12	61.0	58.5-63.5	60.0	58.0-62.0
13	63.0	60.5-65.5	62.0	60.0-64.0
14	64.0	61.5-66.5	65.0	63.0-67.0
15	65.0	62.5-67.5	67.5	65.5-69.5
16	65.5	63.5-67.5	69.0	67.5-70.5
17	65.5	63.5-67.5	69.5	68.0-71.0
18	66.0	64.0-68.0	69.5	68.0-71.0

TABLE 6. Weight of Girls and Boys (in pounds)

Age in years)	Girls		Boys	
	AVERAGE	RANGE	AVERAGE	RANGE
Birth	7.0	6.0- 8.0	7.5	6.5- 8.5
1	22.0	19.5- 24.5	24.0	21.5- 26.5
2	28.0	25.0- 31.0	30.0	27.0- 33.0
3	33.0	29.0- 37.0	34.0	30.5- 37.5
4	37.5	31.5- 43.5	38.0	34.0- 42.0
5	42.5	36.5- 48.5	43.0	38.0- 48.0
6	48.5	40.5- 56.5	49.0	43.0- 55.0
7	55.0	47.0- 63.0	55.0	48.0- 62.0
8	62.0	52.0- 72.0	62.0	53.0- 71.0
9	70.0	57.0- 83.0	68.5	57.5- 79.5
10	78.0	63.0- 93.0	77.0	64.0- 90.0
11	88.5	72.5-104.5	85.5	69.5-101.5
12	100.5	80.5-120.5	96.0	77.0-115.0
13	111.0	91.0-131.0	106.0	84.0-128.0
14	120.0	100.0-140.0	120.0	98.0-142.0
15	126.5	106.5-146.5	133.0	113.0-153.0
16	131.0	115.0-147.0	142.0	122.0-162.0
17	134.0	118.0-150.0	148.0	128.0-168.0
18	135.0	120.0-150.0	152.0	133.0-171.0

tables will tell two things: (1) the average or mean height or weight at each age; (2) the normal spread or variation around each mean value. If the child varies greatly from the average, it might be wise to consult a doctor regarding his physical growth. The average, however, is not much more than the midpoint of a range of variation. Some children normally will be expected to be below, some above, the average. There are big and small, heavy and light children, just as there are tall and short, heavy and light parents. The problem is only this: when is a growing child too short or too tall, too light or too heavy?

The birth length increases itself by about one half in the first year of life. Boys at birth weigh about 7.5 pounds; girls, 7.0 pounds. At one year they are about 24.0 and 22.0 pounds respectively. Birth weight almost triples in the first year of life.

Table 7 illustrates growth of boys and girls percentage-wise. The percentage is figured as the amount of growth in a given period (for

TABLE 7. Percentage Growth in Height and Weight

Height		Weight	
AGE (in years)	RATE (in per cent)	AGE (in years)	RATE (in per cent)
Birth- 1	50	Birth- 1	200
1- 2	20	1- 2	25-30
3- 4	8	3- 6	12
5- 8	5	7-10	10-11
9-12	3-4 *	11-12	8 *
12-14	4-6	13-15	10-12
14-adult	1-2 until cessation	15-adult	4 until curve levels off

* Girls are about 2 years earlier here; rate may be 1-2 per cent lower for height, 1-2 per cent higher for weight.

example, birth to one year) divided by the size of the dimension at the beginning of the period.

In general boys and girls grow in height and weight much alike until about ten to eleven years of age. Then the girls, on the average, are taller and heavier than boys of the same age. This is true from about ten and a half to thirteen and a half years for height and nine to fourteen and a half years for weight. The weight superiority of the girls begins earlier and lasts longer than their height superiority.

AGE PERIODS IN PHYSICAL GROWTH

Table 8 shows a time schedule for the age periods or phases of physical growth.

TABLE 8. Time Schedule for Periods of Growth

Age Period	Boys	Girls
Infancy	B—1 yr.	B—1 yr.
Newborn	B—2 wks.	B—2 wks.
Infancy, proper	2 wks.-1 yr.	2 wks.-1 yr.
Childhood	1-16 yrs.	1-15 yrs.
Early	1-6 yrs.	1-6 yrs.
Mid	6 to 9-10 yrs.	6 to 9-10 yrs.
Late	9-10 to 13-16 yrs.	9 to 10-12 to 15 yrs.
Puberty	13-14 yrs.	12-13 yrs.
Adolescence	13-14 to 18-20 yrs.	12-13 to 18-20 yrs.
Adulthood	18-20 yrs.+	18-20 yrs.+

This time schedule reveals in itself some of the difficulties of being overly precise about physical and physiological growth changes. It will be noted that childhood, puberty, and adolescence overlap in time. That is because the duration of childhood is established largely on the basis of physical (bodily) growth; the time of puberty is largely a physiological (functional) process; whereas adolescence is really a mixed term—it is part physical growth, part postpubertal adjustment, not only to the physiology of puberty, but (of equal importance) adjustment to the social consequences of heightened sexual functioning and awareness.

PUBERTAL GROWTH

Puberty is a phase of rapid physical growth; as a rule the spurt in stature precedes that in weight. Apart from height and weight, there are other important physical changes. In boys the voice changes and facial hair becomes prominent. In both boys and girls body hair becomes prominent, first in the pubic region, above and to the sides of the external genitalia, and then under the arms. Also in both sexes the sweat glands in the armpits increase in activity just before hair appears there. In girls there is a definite increase in the size and a change in the configuration of the breast. Often in boys there is a slight, temporary enlargement. The most dramatic—perhaps because the most obvious—change in girls is the onset of the menarche (first menstruation).

GROWTH OF THE TEETH

All humans have two sets of teeth, a baby or milk set and a permanent set. The dental formula of the first set is written as 2-1-2. This means, in order, two cutting teeth (incisors), one eyetooth (canine or cuspid), and two grinding teeth (molars). The dental formula of the second set is written as 2-1-2-3. This means, in order, two cutting teeth, one eyetooth, two chopping teeth (premolars or bicuspids), and three grinding teeth. The baby molars are succeeded by the permanent premolars. The three permanent molars have no predecessors in the milk teeth.

The baby teeth erupt (cut the gum) in order and time (in months) as follows: first incisor, 6-8; second incisor, 8-10; canine, 16-20; first molar, 12-16; second molar, 20-30. This order holds for upper and lower, right and left teeth, though lower teeth tend to be a bit earlier.

Table 9 shows the order and time (in years) of eruption of the permanent teeth. The lower permanent teeth erupt earlier than the upper. There is no difference, right and left.

TABLE 9. Eruption Schedule for Permanent Teeth

Tooth	Upper (in years)	Lower (in years)
First incisor	7- 8	6- 7
Second incisor	8- 9	7- 8
Canine	11-12	9-10
First premolar	10-11	10-12
Second premolar	10-12	11-12
First molar	6- 7	6- 7
Second molar	12-13	11-13
Third molar	18+	18+

The foregoing eruption-time schedules are subject to a certain amount of variability. Order may differ a bit, as the upper permanent first (or central) incisor—due to erupt at 7-8 years—may erupt before the upper first permanent molar—due at 6-7 years. A shift in order or a delay of several months is not cause for alarm. Of course, if delay is too long the family physician should consult with the dentist.

DEVELOPMENT OF MOTOR BEHAVIOR

Aldrich and Norval studied the development of the motor pattern of behavior of 215 normal babies in their first year of life. They observed the following twelve traits:

1. Smile: response to an adult or adult voice.
2. Vocal: spontaneous sounds, as "ah."
3. Head control: when child is raised from the lying-down position by his hands the head does not loll.
4. Hand: when toy or other object is grasped.
5. Roll: when baby rolls from back over onto his abdomen.
6. Sit: when baby sits alone for a few minutes.
7. Crawl: when baby moves, by any method, across the floor or in the pen.
8. Prehension: when child uses thumb and forefinger in grasping.
9. Pull up: when baby pulls himself to a standing position.
10. Walk with support: when baby walks, holding onto hand, furniture, or play pen.
11. Stand alone: when baby stands alone for a short while without support.
12. Walk alone: when the baby takes several steps alone.

Not all babies do all these things precisely in the same sequence or at the same time rates; however, the tabulation in Table 10 is substantially correct.

TABLE 10. Sequence of Pattern of Behavior

Traits	Early	Average	Late
	(in months, or tenths thereof)		
Smile	0.3	0.9	1.8
Vocal	0.8	1.7	2.5
Head control	1.8	2.9	4.0
Hand	2.7	4.0	5.2
Roll	3.4	5.0	6.4
Sit	4.2	6.1	7.9
Crawl	5.0	7.3	9.3
Prehension	5.8	8.0	10.1
Pull up	6.3	8.7	10.8
Walk with support	6.8	9.5	12.0
Stand alone	8.0	10.7	13.0
Walk alone	10.0	12.0	13.8

CALORIC NEEDS

From birth to six months, a baby should be fed 100 calories per kilogram (2.20 pounds = one kilogram) of body weight, and from six months to one year, 90 calories per kilogram of body weight. Thereafter, the calories needed per day are shown in Table 11. A

TABLE 11. Daily Caloric Needs

Age (in years)	Calories	Age (in years)	Calories
1-2	840	7- 9	1680
2-3	1000	9-11	1920
3-5	1200	11-12	2160
5-7	1440	12 and up	2400

buffer of about 10 per cent should be added to cover the energy loss of the very active growing child up to about five years and after ten years.

CONCLUSION

The process of growth is as marvelous as it is complex, and it is a privilege to behold it. The general principles presented in this chapter should help in understanding the unfolding developmental progress of the child—especially the relationship of his height and weight to growth, his age periods in growth. Watch the child's growth step by step together with your pediatrician and family doctor.

Topics for further thought:

1. Our society has established certain standards with regard to normal and average male and female physical growth and appearance. Discuss the relationship that attaining these standards has to personality development.

2. Discuss the personality development of physical deviants who are of normal or above normal intelligence.

Selected reading references

Gesell, Arnold, and Ilg, Frances L., *Infant and Child in the Culture of Today,* New York, Harper and Brothers, 1955.
The child's first years in the culture of today. Examines the child's growth in terms of culture and guidance. Includes the child before birth, nursery school, and many other aspects.

Gesell, Arnold, and Ilg, Frances L., *The Child from Five to Ten,* New York, Harper and Brothers, 1955.
A guide to the critical years when the child first goes to school. Treats the development of motor characteristics along with personal hygiene, emotional expression, and the development of interpersonal relationships.

Gesell, Arnold, Ilg, Frances L., and Ames, L., *Youth: The Years from Ten to Sixteen,* New York, Harper and Brothers, 1956.
The latest volume deriving from the work of Gesell and his associates on the physical, social, and emotional growth of children.

Gruenberg, Sidonie M., ed., *The Encyclopedia of Child Care and Guidance,* New York, Doubleday and Company, 1954.
A complete and authoritative guide for all who share their lives with children; with practical information on all aspects of child care and guidance—physical, psychological, educational, emotional, and spiritual.

Neugarten, Bernice L., *How You Grow,* Chicago, Science Research Associates.
A *Junior Life Adjustment Booklet* designed to explain the processes of growth to children in grades six through nine.

31 CHILD DEVELOPMENT

Elizabeth B. Hurlock

THROUGHOUT history children were generally regarded as miniature adults. For that reason attempts were not made to study them or to learn whether or not they might, in one way or another, differ from adults. They were presumed to have thoughts, feelings, emotions, and desires similar to those of adults, only on a more limited scale. These mental states were studied in adults and the results applied without revision to children. Children were treated as adults. They were dressed like their elders and they were expected to behave in accordance with adult standards.

A glance at a young child should be adequate to convince anyone—scientist, parent, or teacher—that the child is not a miniature adult so far as his physical make-up is concerned. His head is proportionally too big for his body; his arms and legs are proportionally too small. His shoulders are narrow and his abdomen bulges; the shoulders of an adult are broad and his abdomen is flat. The eyes of a young child are set in the middle of his face, a position which, if found in an adult face, would produce a grotesque appearance.

The realization that physically the child is not a miniature adult should have raised the question in someone's mind of the possibility of the child's differing from the adult in his mental make-up. In 1633 a Slavic educator, Comenius, published *The School of Infancy,* the first book to help parents in the guidance of their children. This suggested that children were mentally different from adults and, consequently, should not be treated as adults.

With this as an eye-opener, psychologists have investigated and have concluded that children are even more unlike adults in their mental make-up than in physical appearance. The effect of this realization has been a complete revision of the old methods of handling children. Of even greater importance is a reconsideration of what is expected of children. Now they are expected to behave like children and not like adults.

DIFFERENCES IN CHILDREN

No two children are alike, not even identical twins. True, all normal children have two arms, two legs, a trunk, and a head with two eyes, two ears, a nose, and a mouth. But the shape, size, and color of these different features vary in one respect or another in all children. Johnny is a blond; his brother Tommy is a brunet. Mary is short and stocky in build; her sister Alice is tall and willowy.

Identical twins, who can confuse most people, cannot fool their parents or others who know them well. Robert has a small brown mole on his left ear which his twin, Robin, does not have. Jane's eyes are set farther apart than Janice's, and her right eye has a slight brown area in its otherwise blue iris. In mental abilities, differences in identical twins are greater than their physical differences, just as is true of ordinary brothers and sisters.

Children who do not have any blood ties have even greater mental and emotional differences. In a class of thirty pupils the teacher will find thirty different types of mental make-up and thirty different personality patterns. True, some of the pupils will fall into general classifications, such as the bright, the dull, the excitable, or the shy, but within each of the general classifications every child will be a separate and distinct individual.

Differences in children are partly the result of varied environmental influences, but they are largely the outcome of differences in heredity. Although brothers and sisters have the same parents, the germ cells from their parents which have united to produce them have not been identical. No two eggs or two sperms are alike in their chromosome make-up. For that reason the ovum fertilized by the sperm cell that resulted in Mary produced a different child from that produced by the ovum and sperm which united to produce her sister Jane.

The significance is that one can neither expect all children to think and act in the same way, nor hope to get good results if all children are treated as if they were cut from the same pattern. The disciplinary policy that brings good results when applied to one child may build up a sullen, resentful attitude in another.

It is unquestionably much easier to formulate a set of rules for the guidance of children that could be applied to all children with anticipation of equal success. But it simply will not work. Each child must be studied in order to know the characteristics of his individual make-up. Only then will it be possible to direct and guide him in such a manner as to bring out his latent potentialities.

DEVELOPMENT THROUGH MATURATION AND LEARNING

Maturation, the natural unfolding of traits potentially present in the child, is Nature's method of growth. Day after day and week after week throughout the growth period, maturation brings about changes in the individual without any effort on his part. These changes appear at a fairly predictable time for every member of the species.

Everyone knows that a baby's teeth develop as a result of maturation. Rubbing the baby's gums may ease the pain that frequently accompanies teething, but it will not encourage the teeth to grow. Similarly, there is not any known way to delay the cutting of teeth until a time when teething will be more convenient for the baby or the members of his family.

To a boy or girl sexual maturation, or growing up, is a matter of great concern, especially when it is delayed. It is embarrassing to remain childish in appearance when one's classmates look like young men or young women. But what can the child do about it? Absolutely nothing. True, the use of certain hormones may hasten or alter development, but most doctors hesitate to use this artificial method until it is apparent that Nature's work has been completed. Nature will usually take her own time and will not allow for interference in her plan for the child's growing up, regardless of the social problems which delay may bring about.

Learning, in contrast to maturation, means development that takes place as a result of the effort put forth by the learner. From experience the reader knows how difficult it is to memorize a poem, to learn to skate, dance, or play a piano, without putting forth effort in continuous practice. The more correct effort put into learning, the more quickly learning takes place. One cannot count on the aid of Nature as one does in maturation. Learning is entirely up to the individual.

From a common-sense point of view it is unquestionably necessary to discover how much of the child's development can be counted on from Nature and how much remains for the child to acquire through his own efforts. This is not as easy as it may first appear. A person cannot dogmatically say, "I will do this and let Nature do the rest," any more than he can assume that Nature will take over the job if it requires more effort to learn something than the child is willing to put forth. There has never been an instance in which a child has acquired the ability to play the piano through shirking his practice in the hope that the skill would develop of its own accord. A child will grow up without learning, but in the absence of learning many abilities and skills needed for successful living will be completely lacking.

From careful and intensive research on this problem the psychologist has formulated two criteria which may be applied to any physical or mental trait to determine whether its development results from maturation or whether it will have to be learned. The first criterion is *universality*. If all babies start to creep on their hands and knees at approximately the same age and in a similar fashion, in spite of the fact that they come from different home environments where there is little similarity in the methods used by parents in rearing their children, then creeping is obviously not the product of learning but results from maturation.

The second criterion is *suddenness of appearance*. Just before puberty boys and girls are in the gang-conscious stage of development. Their interests are centered in the activities of their friends. The approval and disapproval of their friends are powerful forces in determining their own behavior, and they feel lonely and unhappy when isolated from the gang. Quite suddenly they lose interest in gang activities and begin to prefer isolation to the companionship they formerly craved. This sudden change, with the appearance of a new type of behavior, is characteristic of all behavior that is natural in its development.

. Development, of course, depends upon the interaction of maturation and learning, not upon one alone. The child cannot learn unless the native foundation for learning is present. Nor will maturation alone produce a state of development which is adequate to meet the child's needs as he grows older. Through learning he will have to finish the work started by Nature and polish off the rough edges so that his behavior will conform to present-day standards.

There are two significant conclusions to be drawn from the fact that the child's development results partly from maturation and partly from learning. The first is that the development resulting from learning can be controlled but not the development that comes from maturation. For example, the sequence of steps leading up to walking consists of crawling, creeping, standing, and then walking. It is impossible to eliminate these preliminary stages or even to shift their order. The pattern is set by Nature and is unalterable.

The child's gait, or the way he walks, on the other hand, results from learning. Too small shoes or a too heavy body, for example, may encourage him to toe in to gain better balance. If he is permitted to walk in that fashion, toeing-in will become a habit. Similarly, timidity may cause the child to walk with short, mincing steps. If this kind of gait is unchecked it will become a habit. Gait is controllable. It is possible to develop a gait of one sort or another with directed practice. The longer an unsatisfactory mode of walking is permitted to persist, the harder it will be to change it. But it can be done even as late as the adult years if the individual wants to change his style of walking and is willing to practice until a new habit is learned to replace the old one.

The second significant fact about development is that learning must wait upon maturation. A child cannot learn until he is ready to learn or until the necessary foundation has been laid. The old saying, "You cannot run until you have learned to walk," illustrates this. The child must have the necessary body balance, plus the ability to move by the alternate use of his legs, before he can speed up his walking into a running pace.

There is no known way to speed up maturation so as to produce the necessary state of readiness for learning. Nature's unfolding of the pattern of development for the human being comes about in an orderly fashion and at a pace characteristic of each individual child. In one child, for example, readiness to read may appear at the age of three years, while in another child in the same family readiness to read may be delayed until the age of seven years. And there is nothing that anyone can do to change these speeds of maturation, to slow down one or to accelerate the other.

Trying to interfere with the natural speed of maturation only brings trouble to the child. Any attempt to force a child to learn before he is ready will build up a dislike, on the child's part, for the activity which he finds too difficult for him. Furthermore, it may result in fear of failure, which will militate against successful learning when the state of readiness finally occurs.

Many a child has literally been forced to stand on his feet and walk before his bones, muscles, and nerves have developed to the point where this is possible. No amount of practice in walking will speed up his learning to walk. His frequent falls will intimidate him and will build up so pronounced a feeling of inadequacy that it will actually interfere with his progress in learning to walk when he is ready to walk. Many cases of delayed walking have been traced to attempts on the part of well-meaning parents to speed up their child's walking because Mrs. Jones's or Mrs. Brown's baby was walking at the age of their child.

Putting up barriers to the child's learning when he is ready to learn is also bad. These barriers may result from ignorance on the parents' part concerning the child's readiness, or they may be traceable to parental fear that some harm might come to the child should he attempt to learn. Whatever the cause, the effect on the child is the same. It stifles the child's interest in learning so that, should he be given an opportunity to learn at a later time, he will have little interest in doing so. The result will be slow and halfhearted learning.

THE PATTERN OF DEVELOPMENT

The child's development, from conception to maturity, is neither haphazard nor a matter of chance. Rather it follows a definite, predictable pattern which is similar for all children, regardless of the nationality or socioeconomic status of the family to which they belong. In this pattern of development there is a close interrelationship between physical and mental growth. There is a reciprocal effect of these two, with physical growth in some instances influencing mental, while in other instances the reverse is true.

According to popular belief, the child who develops slowly during the early years of life in some mysterious manner will catch up to the pace of other children of the same age. As a matter of fact, just the reverse is true. The pace of a slow-developing child, as the years of childhood pass, becomes increasingly slower until it is practically at a standstill. Children whose developmental pace is accelerated, on the other hand, continue to grow at a rapid rate throughout the entire developmental period. In other words, development proceeds at the pace at which it started.

Not all aspects of development occur simultaneously. When the child is growing in height, for example, his growth in weight is slowed down. Then, when he begins to take on weight, his height is at a temporary standstill. Similarly, growth in memory ability occurs at one age, growth in imagination at another, and growth in reasoning at still another. Development is thus rhythmic, not regular.

The rate of development differs for different children. It depends upon such factors as the child's level of intelligence, whether the child is a boy or girl, the state of health during the periods when development is normally rapid, his racial heritage, and the presence or absence of environmental barriers. Girls, for example, develop more rapidly than boys and reach their mature level sooner than boys of the same age. Similarly, bright children are ahead of dull children at every age and in every aspect of their development.

Finally, in the normal pattern of growth, not all physical or mental features reach maturity at the same age. The child's brain is mature in size before the internal growth has been completed. The nose is the first facial feature to complete its growth. The hands and feet come next. Unless this is known to the child it will be a source of great concern. Many boys and girls are seriously disturbed about their big noses, hands, and feet, only to discover that in time the rest of their bodies enlarge and thus eliminate the disproportions.

Because growth follows a predictable pattern, with only minor variations from child to child, it is possible to anticipate what a child will be able to do at a given age and to plan accordingly. Educators have planned the curriculum of the school with this knowledge to guide them. They know that most children will be ready to learn to read at a certain age, to do higher mathematics at another age, and to grasp the meaning of historical facts at still another age.

As recent scientific studies have covered almost every aspect of the child's development, it is now possible to furnish parents and teachers with a guide for training children in the form of developmental tasks. A developmental task is one that arises at or about a certain period in the life of the individual. If a child is to make good adjustments and be happy, he must master the developmental tasks for his age. Otherwise, he will lag behind his age-mates and be out of step with what they are doing. Then he will have to try to catch up while they are going ahead to master other developmental tasks.

A few of the important developmental tasks of babyhood are learning to take solid foods, to walk, to control the elimination of body wastes, and to talk. The child must learn the physical skills necessary for ordinary games, learn how to get along with his age-mates, develop the skills of reading, writing, and calculating, learn an appropriate sex role, develop a conscience, and learn a scale of moral values. The developmental tasks of adolescents include making adjustments to their newly developed bodies, achieving emotional independence of parents and other adults, selecting and preparing for a life career, and preparing for marriage and family life.

At each age level certain types of behavior are characteristic of that level of development. For example, spitting out food that does not taste good is a natural protective reaction among animals and human beings. Babies and young children react to disliked food by spitting it out, regardless of where they are and regardless of the fact that, according to present standards of good taste, this is considered to be bad form. The food spitter is behaving in a normal way for his age level. But if he continues to spit out food long past the ages when other children have learned that such behavior is socially unacceptable, then food spitting may be regarded as problem behavior.

In late childhood boys delight in dressing in clothes of sturdy, coarse materials. They shy away from dressy clothes. They are bored with cleanliness and revolt against the use of soap and water, with the excuse that they will only get dirty again. They are careless and slovenly in their dressing and slipshod in the care of their clothing. All of this is traceable to their interest in strenuous play, their desire to be regarded as "regular guys" by their friends, and their desire to cut away from the parental restraints of early childhood.

The careless, slovenly age creates problems for many parents who do not understand that this is merely a phase of growing up and is in no way permanent. The most careless boy, in late childhood, will probably turn into a dandy of the most extreme sort when he becomes adolescent. As he becomes interested in girls the desire to win their approval will motivate him to be as careful about his appearance now as formerly his desire to be regarded as a "good guy" drove him into his careless ways.

Only if behavior that is characteristic of one age level persists into older ages, when in most children it has long since been replaced by behavior of a more mature type, can it be regarded as problem behavior. It is problem behavior because it is infantile in form. The child clings to infantile behavior when he has difficulty in adjusting to more mature levels, or when he discovers that he receives more attention from infantile than from mature behavior.

THE PERIODS OF DEVELOPMENT

Though development is a continuous process, phases or periods occur when there is a shift in emphasis on the type of development that is taking place. This is pronounced enough to justify dividing the childhood span, from conception to maturity, into developmental periods, each with its characteristic form of development.

All children pass through all the developmental stages, but at different rates. Bright children, for example, develop more rapidly than children of average or below-average intelligence. They therefore are accelerated in their development, while below-average children are retarded. Because more children fall in the classification of average than above average or below average, the ages given here refer only to the so-called average child.

Prenatal. The prenatal period extends from the time of conception until the moment of birth. The usual span of time is 270 days or, roughly, nine calendar months. During the prenatal period, there is rapid growth and development. From a microscopically small cell to an individual weighing seven or more pounds and measuring approximately twenty inches in length is tremendous growth in such a short period of time. The development is even more astounding. All parts of the body are differentiated and ready to function several weeks or months before birth.

Newborn. The period of the newborn begins at birth, when the umbilical cord is cut, and lasts for approximately two weeks. This is a time of adjustment in which the infant must get used to breathing, to taking nourishment through his mouth instead of through a cord connecting his body with that of his mother, and to changes in temperature. Like all adjustments, the infant needs time to make them satisfactorily.

During the first week after birth it is not at all unusual for the infant to lose weight and to appear less healthy than he was at birth. Then, during the second week of life, he gradually adjusts himself to the new environment outside of the mother's body. By the end of the period of the newborn, adjustments should be completed.

Infancy is characterized by extreme helplessness. The cause of extreme helplessness is traceable to the fact that the muscles of the infant are so weak that he cannot move his body from the position in which he is placed. The only sounds he can make, should he want help, are cries which sound alike regardless of what is the matter with him.

Without constant care the infant would not be able to survive. Nourishment must be put into his mouth and care taken to prevent his choking when he swallows it. Changes in temperature frequently cause colds which may be fatal. Having become accustomed to an even temperature in the mother's body, it is difficult for the infant to adjust to temperature changes.

While to the casual observer the infant's eyes are fully developed, they do not co-ordinate because of the weakness of the muscles that attach the eyes to the sockets. The result is that everything is seen as a blur. Similarly, the well-developed ear is temporarily clogged by mucus from the prenatal sac. Until this is drained out the infant is practically deaf. Hence, the two most important sense organs, the eyes and ears, are of little value to the infant in adjusting himself to his new environment.

Babyhood. Babyhood, the first two years of life following the two weeks after birth, is a period of decreasing helplessness. This is made possible by a gradual control over the body. The helpless baby, in time, partly through maturation and partly through learning, gains control over his muscles. By the end of babyhood the individual is remarkably independent considering the helpless state that existed just two short years before.

Physical growth is extremely rapid during the first year of life. Its pace then slows down during the second year. An average infant weighs 7 pounds at birth and measures 20 inches in length. At the end of the first year the weight is trebled, or 21 pounds, and the average height is 28 inches. Slowing down of growth in the second year is apparent in the fact that an average 2-year-old weighs 25 pounds and measures 32 inches.

During the middle part of the first year the first tooth erupts. From then until the age of approximately two and a half years baby teeth come in, one at a time, but at a fairly rapid rate, until all 20 have erupted. This makes it possible for the baby to abandon infantile sucking and to substitute chewing and biting. By the end of babyhood the baby can eat much the same food as an adult eats. It is no longer necessary to reduce his food to a sieved or finely chopped form.

Control of the body muscles develops rapidly during the first year. But the dvelopment does not affect all muscles throughout the body simultaneously. Rather it spreads over the body in an orderly pattern from head to foot. This means that the baby can co-ordinate his eyes before he can grasp with his hands, he can hold up his head before he can sit, and he can sit before he can stand or walk.

By the end of babyhood muscle control throughout the entire body is normally so well developed that the baby can be a relatively independent creature. He can take off and put on his clothes, he can feed himself, he can get out the toys he wants and play with them, and he can even run errands or assume simple duties in the home. All of these skills, of course, will not occur spontaneously. They must be learned. But they can be learned only if the baby is given an opportunity to do so.

Speech is one aspect of muscle control. The words used in speech and the combination of words into sentences, however, must be learned. During the second year the baby learns words very rapidly. He thoroughly enjoys talking. He even goes so far as to try to combine his words into sentences. At this age, however, his sentences are usually incomplete and are supplemented by gestures. Being able to talk, even in the limited fashion of a baby, does much to decrease the helplessness that is characteristic of this age.

Early Childhood. Early childhood is, roughly, the preschool age. It extends from the end of babyhood, at the age of two years, to the beginning of school, at the age of six. Physical growth at this time is slow and steady, with a slight growth spurt just before the child's sixth birthday. Because growth is slow the child quickly learns to control his body. It is no longer necessary to make constant adjustments in this control, as was true when growth was more rapid.

Having gained control of his body, the young child now turns his attention to his environment. He is into everything and explores endlessly. What he cannot understand through his own exploratory efforts he questions. During this age every child is normally a living question mark.

Because of his endless exploring, combined with poor judgment that is a logical accompaniment of limited intelligence and even more limited experience, the child needs constant supervision to protect him against harm. His desire to discover what is happening on the street, for example, may cause him to lean dangerously far out of the window. To discover how matches work he may strike a match without taking the necessary precaution of shutting the matchbox first.

Toward the latter part of this developmental stage all normal children begin to crave the companionship of other children. They lose interest in playing alone or in being with adults. But their first social experiences with their contemporaries are not always too satisfactory. Frequently they stand on the side lines and watch other children play or, when they actually try to play with the other children, the usual outcome is a quarrel. In time, and with practice, learning to get along with others will take place.

Late Childhood. Late childhood, which extends from the sixth year until the beginning of sexual maturity, around the age of 12 or 13 years, is often called the gang age. At this time the desire for companionship, which first appeared several years earlier, reaches its peak of intensity. No longer is solitary play satisfactory to the child; he does not derive the enjoyment he formerly did from the companionship of adults. He wants to be with his friends, and his friends are contemporaries of his own sex.

This is the age when antagonism between the sexes is very strong. Boys are contemptuous of girls and girls feel the same way about boys. The influence of the child's gang upon his behavior, his outlook on life, and even upon his morals is very strong. Children think, act, and feel as their friends do. To them, being different is synonymous with being inferior. And this is the source of great emotional tension.

Adolescence. Adolescence, which means to grow to maturity, is a period extending from the beginning of sexual maturing until the age of legal maturity, at 21 years of age. The average child matures sexually at some time between the ages of 12 and 15 years, with girls slightly ahead of boys. During this developmental period the characteristic behavior is so different at different times that it has become customary to subdivide adolescence into preadolescence, early adolescence, and late adolescence.

Preadolescence lasts only for a year or two. During this time the sex organs are growing in size and becoming mature in function, the body rapidly increases in height and weight, and changes in proportions. There is also development of the secondary sex characteristics or physical features which distinguish men from women, such as the growth of hair on the face and body, change of voice and growth of heavy muscles in boys, and, in girls, the development of the breasts and hips, the growth of hair over the sex organs and in the armpits, and the development of subcutaneous fat which produces feminine curves. In girls, preadolescence comes, on the average, between the ages of 12 and 13½ years, and in boys, about a year later. Sexual maturity is generally accompanied by loss of appetite, more or less constant fatigue, indigestion, headaches, skin eruptions, and a tendency to insomnia. While these conditions vary not only in intensity but also in frequency of occurrence, few boys or girls escape their impact.

Marked changes in behavior appear in preadolescence. The childish desire for constant social contacts gives way to a longing for isolation. Boredom, especially in play activities of all sorts, disinclination to work, general restlessness and irritability, moodiness, a critical attitude toward members of the family and former friends, quarrelsomeness, a tendency to be easily offended, sulkiness, lack of self-confidence, excessive daydreaming, and a marked interest in religion and sex are all common at this age. This has been called the negative phase, indicating that it is a period of short duration during which there is an almost complete reversal of behavior.

Early adolescence, which begins with sexual maturity as judged by the first menstruation in girls and by the appearance of pubic hairs and nocturnal emissions in boys, lasts for about three years, from approximately the ages of 13 to 16 years. This is an awkward, shy, self-conscious age, in which the transformation from child to adult has not yet been completed. Owing to the rapid growth that takes place in pre- and early adolescence, the youth temporarily loses control over his body. This results in clumsy, awkward movements which merely serve to increase the self-consciousness that has come from the body changes brought about by sexual maturing.

As a defense against self-consciousness the youth tries to submerge his individuality by dressing and behaving like all his gang. Being different in any way is a source of much mental anguish. The youth feels that it focuses too much attention upon him. Gradually, as he learns to control his newly enlarged body, his self-consciousness decreases. With this comes a new feeling of self-confidence and a recognition of self as a personality.

Late adolescence lasts from about the age of 16 until 21. By the age of 16 years for girls and a year or two later for boys, the youth has gained his mental equilibrium. Instead of trying to submerge his personality into that of the group, the youth now wants to assert himself as an individual. No longer is he willing to be treated as a child. A stubborn, rebellious attitude toward adult authority develops. This grows in intensity until the age of legal maturity is reached and the adolescent is recognized by society as grown-up.

Some of the most common forms of self-assertiveness found in late adolescence are interest in clothes of extreme styles, rebellion against the religious doctrines accepted during childhood, revolt against rules and regulations of the home, the school, and the community, attempts to reform others, with special emphasis on members of the family, radical ideas regarding political matters, constant bickering and arguing with members of the family and friends, and show-off tendencies in dancing, driving cars, and sports.

Late adolescence is the age of romance. Both boys and girls are seriously preoccupied with sex in its every aspect. They are curious about sex matters. This curiosity leads them to talk about, read about, and experiment with sex. They fall in and out of love many times annually. Each romance is accompanied by intense emotions and with a preoccupation that interferes with their other interests and activities. At first the love affairs are more in the form of hero worship of an older individual than of real romance. But after a year or two of hero worship the adolescent falls in love with a contemporary.

Because of idealism fostered by reading romantic stories and seeing romantic movies, the adolescent frequently expects the loved one to have all the attributes, both physical and mental, of a fictitious hero or heroine. With the realization that the loved one is an ordinary mortal, disillusionment follows, and the romance ends in a bitter quarrel. After a few experiences of this sort, which are extremely disturbing emotionally to an adolescent, he gradually adjusts his attitudes to a more realistic level. Then romances become more stable and frequently lead to marriage.

The choice of a life vocation for many adolescents proves to be as great a source of emotional disturbance as are their love affairs. What courses they should take in high school, whether or not they should go to college, what line of work they should train for, what openings there will be for them when they are ready to go to work, how they can go into a line of work that will appeal to them without disappointing their parents who have already planned their future careers for them are all problems that confront adolescents as they approach adulthood.

Today girls as well as boys find the choice of a vocation a disturbing problem. No longer do they assume that their only role will be that of a homemaker. Like their brothers, they plan to have a career, but for them the career must be such that they can combine it with matrimony. Parental opposition to a costly education to fit the girl for the career of her choice, based on the argument that she will abandon her career when she marries, adds a complicating factor to the girl's vocational problems which is rarely present for a boy.

Adolescence, because it is a period of adjustment, is far from the happy, carefree age that most people believe it to be. There is always something to upset and disturb the individual who is passing through this transition from childhood to maturity. If it is not feeling up to par, then it is fear of being laughed at because of a cracking voice or clumsy movements, or, even worse, it is the feeling of utter despair that comes when an all-absorbing love affair has ended in a bitter quarrel.

Much of the moodiness, the rudeness, the lack of interest in members of the family, and the daydreaming of the adolescent may be traced to the fact that he is confused and unhappy. To cover up some of this feeling of insecurity he develops a cocksure attitude of confidence which too often gives others the false impression that all is well. In time the adolescent will, in most instances, make satisfactory adjustments to life, but it will not be until adolescence has passed and adulthood has been reached.

Topics for further thought:

1. All societies demand that their members, to be considered "normal," conform to a general pattern of personality development. This is known as the "basic personality" of the group. One group differs from another in the standards it sets and in the degree of latitude it grants. What is the "basic personality" in American society? How much deviation from this norm is allowed?

2. What changes do you think might tend to lessen the adjustment problems of the adolescent in our society? Discuss the responsibility of the family in this connection.

Selected reading references

Baruch, Dorothy W., *New Ways in Discipline*, New York, McGraw-Hill Book Company, 1949.
    Presents a challenging philosophy of parent-child relations. Encourages the recognition of child's feelings as clues to his behavior.

Breckenridge, Marian E., and Vincent, E. Lee, *Child Development,* Philadelphia, W. B. Saunders Company, 1955.
    A basic textbook on child development. Examines the physical and emotional growth of the child through the school years.

Dunbar, Flanders, *Your Child's Mind and Body,* New York, Random House, 1949.
    Stresses the psychosomatic origin of many children's illnesses. Constructive approach to guiding children's development.

Hurlock, Elizabeth B., *Child Development,* New York, McGraw-Hill Book Company, 1956.
    A more extensive treatment of some of the ideas which the author develops in the present chapter. Third edition of a popular textbook.

Rand, Winifred, Sweeney, Mary, and Vincent, E. Lee, *Growth and Development of the Young Child,* Philadelphia, W. B. Saunders Company, 1946.
    Designed for college students in either child development or education for marriage and family life.

32 ADOPTION: SOME LEGAL AND SOCIAL PROCEDURES

Lee M. Brooks and Evelyn C. Brooks

Cᴇɴᴛʀᴀʟ in today's American family life are companionship and affection. These represent a transition from the old institutional rigidities and authoritarian pressures. More than ever the "good" family is seen as shared experience, freedom and discipline, rights and responsibilities, love and loyalties. Uniquely the adoptive family is this sort of shared experience, one that can rate high because its members have purposefully set about securing the values inherent in the warmth of affectionate companionship.

ADOPTION AND THE ADOPTIVE FAMILY

Adoption is the voluntary acceptance, the transplanting and nurturing of a child of other parents into one's own family circle and kinship. It is not altruism; it is a permanent and complete filial relationship distinct from guardianship or custody, each of these being a temporary legal arrangement for the protection of a child's person or property. Adoption is not foster care, which is a social device whereby, with or without pay, a household provides family life for a homeless child. These provisions may, and often do, lead to adoption.

Who makes up the adoptive family? Many a couple, after waiting and hoping for the birth of a child, refuse to be defeated by their actual or assumed biological incapacity and adopt a child. Others, because of impaired health or questionable heredity, marry with no expectation of having a child of their own blood. Still others, already parents, want to add more children to the family group. Through adoption such people often move into happier marital and family fulfillment. Relatives, stepparents, and fathers of offspring born out of wedlock adopt children. In such homes the motives and adjustments are likely to be different from those of the adoptive family where unknown infants or young children are eagerly sought by a husband and wife who have no blood kinship to the child adopted.

As to the stability of the adoptive family, several widely different investigations emphasize the affection and loyalty, the mutual satisfaction of adopters and children in the family relationship, not only as estimated in subjective testimony, but also as observed by disinterested persons outside the family circle. Social workers who have supervised the placement and watched the developing relationship at close range, as well as researchers with rating scales and other objective measurements, believe that the adoptive family ranks favorably with comparable biological families. Even if this were not so, those who magnify the risks of adoption would do well to compare the adoptive family not with superior biological families but with the alternatives open to adopters and adopted children: childless homes and parentless children. Out of mutual need and purposeful effort can arise a stable and satisfying relationship.

Bound by legal ties after adequate examinations and investigations have been made, the adopted child's position in the family is rightly as irrevocable as though he had been decreed through biological birth for that particular family. He becomes an own child with all filial rights, privileges, and obligations, provided the adoptive parents exercise scrupulous care about rights of inheritance, a matter to be emphasized later. Whenever a child is adopted, parents are adopted too. But for the child adoption is a social type of birth the moment the final decree is granted by the court.

THE VALUES IN ADOPTION

The family is the effective environment for bringing out plus or minus hereditary potentialities that have not developed. Several interesting experiments show an increase of intelligence-test scores in children after their adoption or foster placement in homes of superior opportunity. These favorable results reinforce the belief that the "good" family promotes all-round growth among its members. These results, however, should not mislead anyone into expecting adoption to work a miracle. No investigation yet made has shown an increase in capacity sufficient to allow a child to rise from the bottom to the top of his class in school. That there should be improvement is not surprising. After adoption there may be greater attention to nutrition and other health factors, more stimulating contacts, and perhaps better educational opportunities. There should be added security, responsiveness, and new motivations. Most children fall short of what they might be because the environment fails to call out their full possibilities.

The values in adoption are many for both parent and child, too many to list. For parents they may include: heightened affection and loyalty between mates; the shared joy of guiding growth; a feeling of fraternity with all parents; a deepened concern for all children; an awakening of civic responsibility and a broadening of interests. For the adopted child, as in horicultural grafting, there is a chance for growth and fruitage such as no other experience can assure, especially as one considers the alternatives, the hazards of grudging shelter with relatives or institutional placement.

Children should be in families wherein flows a responsive and wholesome affection that nourishes happy development. However superior physically the provisions of an institution may be for the child, it is lacking with respect to his emotional and social needs. Collective handling does not reach the deeper core of child life to bring out the potentialities. Neither the institution nor boarding home can give the security of spirit that comes from the continuing and concentrated interest of parents with whom the child shares the feeling of identity in a family.

The adoptive home is often a one-child situation, and this it must remain to a large extent so long as there is a scarcity of adoptable children, though there are many good homes with own and adopted children and still others where two or more children have been adopted. Some child-welfare agencies do, however, encourage multiple placements. The only child has been found to rate high in emotional and social development where parents are alert to the need of child companionship and where they provide for the development of skills and sportsmanship through plentiful contacts with playmates and visitors. The presence of brothers and sisters makes for more complete family life but carries no magic for social development. The home with both adopted and own children calls for particularly careful thought and planning to keep sensitive situations at a minimum.

Childhood adjustment in any family and community depends upon parental effort and planning.

SELF-INVENTORY FOR PROSPECTIVE ADOPTERS

Not all people who wish to adopt can expect to do so. Nor should all childless couples be encouraged to adopt. There is the conviction, for instance, that emotional balance and steady affection should outweigh material factors. For sterile couples, if the sterility has a definite psychic basis, its implications and the attitude toward it must be carefully considered. In weighing the matter of age and resources it is to be expected that people in their thirties or early forties who are youthful in spirit, who possess physical and mental health, and the indispensable emotional maturity can satisfy the golden mean requirements. The imperatives of a self-inventory for prospective adopters involving motives, attitudes, and habits would be somewhat as follows:

1. Is our desire to adopt a child but an impulse or is it rooted in earnest purpose?

2. Will the result be mere ego satisfaction or continuous purposeful investment?

3. Do we have a genuine interest in children and youth as humanity's richest heritage?

4. Is our love for each other so sure that a child will bind us even closer without jealousy?

5. Are we willing to undertake twenty years or more of responsibility with many of our former interests displaced by or tributary to the child's welfare?

6. For better or for worse—since adoptions, like other family relationships, carry no guarantee of perfection—will we stand by our adopted child in all circumstances as though he had been our physical offspring?

7. Have we the ability to love the child for himself, whatever his background; to guard ourselves resolutely against the projection of our ambitions on to him; and to guide rather than to mold him—thus encouraging his growth power?

8. Can we grow with him, and share our best with him, without expecting gratitude?

9. Are we developing tolerance, habitual patience, emotional maturity, and the mental flexibility that insures against rut-bound middle age?

10. When our adopted child grows beyond the early need for dependence, will we be ready to let him go, confident that our family life has given him the security indispensable to independence?

SUGGESTIONS FOR REARING THE CHILD

If the answer "yes" can be given to the ten questions set forth, the prospective parents will be well prepared for what is ahead in parent-child relationships. For the rearing of the adoptive child, however, some aspects invite special emphasis.

Study and Guidance. The waiting period after application has been filed can be likened to pregnancy. This is the preparatory period for study—through books, articles, and possibly child-study groups—on physical care, habit training, the mental growth of children, and mental hygiene itself. Thoughtful study and planning are a continuing need for effective parenthood. If they have had no previous experience with children the prospective parents can make an effort to get acquainted with their friends' children, perhaps borrowing them for short periods. They will want to observe receptively a nursery school or play group, for children cannot be understood or managed solely through books.

The actual techniques of physiological baby care are relatively easy to learn. But psychological adjustment, involving emotions, attitudes, and habits in and between parent and child, comes by no formula. It comes only through patient, intelligent, and continuous effort.

Adaptation and adjustment embrace such practical questions as these: Should a fragile piece of furniture be replaced with something sturdier? Are the colors too delicate for rough use? Can a meal hour or a social custom be changed cheerfully? The readiness of the new parents may be partly gauged by their attitude toward necessary changes in terms of joyful anticipation or, on the other hand, of sacrifice.

Guidance and advice concerning problems of child nurture are part of the program of authorized child-placing agencies, which usually continue supervisory contacts with the adoptive home for six months or a year before the final decree is granted.

The Child's Security. The child has undergone one or more separations and changes. Especially he needs the maximum of that which gives self-security. This comes from well-ordered parental care and affection wherein the main ingredients are a steadiness of head and heart, a gentleness of hand and voice. Thus the child grows happily with a strong sense of belonging: *his* parents, *his* home, and *his* possessions; not "smother-loved" into selfishness but guided into socialized selfhood.

As with the physiological needs of the child, household equipment ordinarily is not a great problem. Adoptive parents can, without much difficulty, learn to accommodate house to child: room and toilet facilities; child-size furniture; toys and play space, and other such matters. But adopters, often a little older than other parents, may have to make effortful changes in habit patterns before they are ready to welcome the child they want. His psychological security is paramount.

From the first day he should be thought of as "one of us." If he is thus closely identified with his adoptive family and is told of his adoption as soon as he understands speech, as matter-of-factly as he learns the color of his eyes, he is no more likely than other children to develop mental or social aberrations. The adopted child should not be shielded completely from knowledge of his past but be given strength to face it, to assimilate it through the warmth of constant affection and security. Otherwise there may be unsettling insecurity, even shock and estrangement from his family if unfortunate facts are discovered accidentally.

Growth is the highest good for the individual; mutual growth and trust in the parent-child relationship are the highest good for any family in the universal quest for security.

THE EFFECT OF ADOPTION

As to the effect of adoption, not enough reliable studies of grown people adopted in infancy or early childhood are available. No one can rightly speak with dogmatic assurance. Selection of children and of families for adoption has changed so much in recent years that comparisons are difficult. Many of the changes have taken place because specialists, notably child-welfare workers, have profited from experience in this field. The press may emphasize the fact of adoption in spectacular cases of delinquency or crime, but as any thoughtful person must realize, equally notorious cases occur among people brought up by blood kin or among those reared in orphanages or in those families where there is a breakup in the bases of security. There is no proof or even indication that adoption affects adversely the emotional or social development of adopted persons. The really wanted child, whatever his origin, will have full acceptance, equality, love, and security from those parents who are willing to study, who will accept guidance, and who strive to grow in those mental and spiritual qualities that are commensurate with life's most important privilege.

LEGAL AND SOCIAL SAFEGUARDS

Law and social work are requisites in approved adoption procedures. The courts and social agencies tend to emphasize the interests of the child, and rightly, because he is helpless in the hands of those who are deciding his destiny. He is entitled to all the protecting services available. This discussion, however, will focus attention on the adoptive family as a whole: the relationship within the family triangle with awareness of the interactions of the larger kinship.

Legal action is the unique factor in the adoptive family. Adoption should not be thought of as substitute parenthood, for it *is* parenthood of a distinctive type which requires judicial decision. It must be safeguarded by strict compliance with every detail of the law. Legal records are of special importance. When the child comes to the full understanding of his adoption—and he should be told in the simplest words when he is so young that he grows up with the knowledge—he will be secure in the realization that legal papers prove his family membership. Birth certificates and wills, very specific testamentary directions, are essentials. Many details that seem to the individual adopter unimportant, or even an interference by the state in a private matter, are based on real need when viewed from the perspective of the rights of all the people involved. Whatever his personal opinion, the wise adopter will follow the letter of the law and will make use of all the social aids put at his disposal. The lags in the law, as viewed against social needs, are numerous and even irritating, but advances are being made, especially in recent years. Judicial practices have not always kept pace with the modernizing of the law, but perhaps because of the increasing number of adoptions and the consequent necessity for improvement in procedures, decisions are tending toward more progressive social interpretation.

An increasing number of states require that every adoption shall have the supervision of the Department of Public Welfare, which means that all placements are made either by staff members or by agencies approved by them. In any state the advice of a local welfare official may be sought, or application may be made to a licensed private placing agency or children's home. Proper child placement demands expertness; there are sound reasons why adopters should use the services of a well-qualified near-by agency, preferably one in their own state. Much time and expense may be used up in tracing distant records, gaining consent, or clearing out irregularities that may greatly magnify the risks. Too often adopters who travel some distance for a child are tempted to accept a seemingly promising one without going fully into records and matters of legal procedure. They may hasten the final steps, minimize or circumvent the trial period, or fail to return to procure the final decree without which the adoption is not a fact. The distant agency, however good, is handicapped in its dealings with adopters whom it sees briefly. An agency gives its best services when there is time and opportunity for frequent consultation and full acquaintance with the adopting home.

The social investigation, covering both child and prospective parents, includes interviews, written application, visits to the adopting home, health assurances, and requests for financial and moral references. This is for the protection of the child and is to the advantage of the adopters. The more contacts the agency has with an adopting household, the better its picture of the expectations of the adopters and the fewer the chances for misfits. Because the adopter has a right to know pertinent facts, the careful agency will try to find out as much as possible about the ancestry of the prospective adoptee. The eugenically minded adopted person, when he approaches marriage in later years, will want to compare his questions on heredity with those of his mate-to-be. The results of mental tests and reports on physical condition should not be overlooked. Many agencies have a policy of withholding the identity of a child's natural parents. Some children available for adoption are shadowed by earlier misfortune. Agencies often are willing for the adopters to know general facts about a child's original family even though names are not revealed.

Both the adopting father and mother should have a voice in the decision; acquiescence is not enough. It is the right of the child to be actively wanted, not just accepted, by both parents. Particularly if his early days have been insecure he will need the assurance of steady affection. The small child is more sensitive to the emotional states of his elders than most adults realize. It is unlikely that marriage partners are ready for parenthood if they are not able to agree on the essentials of the choice. They should be prepared for the emergence of unsuspected qualities in themselves and each other. They need not fear, however, that the new experience will detract from their relationship to each other if the decision to adopt and the choice of their child have been reached jointly. Parenthood is invigorating when mature people give themselves freely to it; the adoptive parent misses few of the emotional values. As the personalities of the adopters become enriched and more vital, they not only have more to give in all their relationships, but also their responsiveness to each other is peculiarly heightened by their mutual sharing of emotion as well as by their shared interest in the child.

The Trial Period. A trial period of six months or a year is required by law in many states. During this time the child lives in the adopting family whose name he takes. He is treated as an own child but not yet is the adoption irrevocable, as it is after the final decree. It is always within the province of the judge to require or extend the months of probation, but courts are not always aware of the social implications, for sometimes they can inadvisedly be persuaded to omit or shorten the trial period. From the point of view of court procedure the probation period is an unnecessary prolongation of a case; it means that the decree cannot be granted in the same term of court in which the petition is made, often involving a review of the case by a different judge. The study and experience of child welfare generally point to no less than a year's probation period, whatever the legal minimum.

Many adopters insist that they were as sure at the end of the first week as at the end of the year: This was *the* child for them. For others impatience has meant regrets, even grief. The emotions need intellectual brakes. Like an engagement to marry, the trial period gives the feelings time to get into more normal control. In a year's time the adopters will have begun to have some idea of the labor, expense, and self-control connected wtih parenthood. Twelve months is a long time in the life of a small child during which his physical growth and mental development can be far more accurately gauged than in pre-placement tests. It occasionally happens that even though both child and parents individually are ready for the experience of adoption, they are not suited to each other, are not psychologically fitted to each other's needs. Sometimes, in spite of every precaution, legal difficulties arise which must be cleared, difficulties that would have invalidated the decree had it been granted too early.

Court Proceedings. The laws of every state require court proceedings for adoption. Five requirements or aspects must be emphasized for the welfare of child and family: consent of the child's natural parent or parents; petition by the adopters; decree granted by the proper court; complete, clear, and confidential records; inheritance provisions. The first three have to do with effective implementation in the adoptive process; the last two point particularly to safeguarding the child's future.

CONSENT. One of the most valuable services of the placing agency is its guidance in legal steps. The agency knows the laws as well as the practices and problems of local administration; it will make the necessary contacts with the child's natural parents or other authorized person to secure consent to the adoption. Consent of the proper person in the required form is a fundamental of sound adoption procedure; its importance cannot be overemphasized. When the agency secures consent, a meeting of the adopters and the natural kin is avoided unless the law requires their joint appearance in court. The consent required of natural parents protects their rights by allowing them to express their wishes, but it also terminates their rights and interest in the child. If the natural parents are dead, have forfeited civil rights, are insane or incompetent, or for some other reason are not qualified, another person or agency may be authorized to give consent. A few states permit formal relinquishment of the child to an agency or to the Department of Public Welfare, with the right to consent to adoption as well as for guardianship and custody.

PETITION. The adoption statutes of most states are fairly explicit on the matter of petition, both as to form and court jurisdiction. Here again the assistance of the placing agency is valuable because it is important to make the petition in the proper court, lest the validity of the adoption be questioned later on jurisdictional grounds. Ideally adoption cases are handled in a children's court or family court by a judge experienced in work with children, at a private hearing from which reporters and the public are excluded. More often the petition must be made in a probate or general court before a judge who may not be qualified by training or experience for this highly specialized work and who is under too great pressure of routine cases to give the time that is sometimes needed to authenticate every legal detail. Petition is usually made in the county or district where the petitioners have legal residence, though a few states make the child's residence the determining factor of jurisdiction or allow the latter as an alternative choice. Petition should be made in the manner prescribed and in the court specified, as a protection against any later question.

DECREE. The final decree is granted after the court has filed and acted upon the petition. This is done preferably, as required in the majority of our states, at the end of a six-month or a one-year trial period. A few states grant an interlocutory decree. The decree may be a simple confirmation of the petition or an elaborate court order expressing conditions and requiring the adopters to give the child proper care and treatment. Some decrees are in the form of a contract of which a certified copy is given to the adopters. Commonly decrees specify the name by which the child is to be known.

RECORDS. Records deserve more emphasis than the statutes and courts have given them. Since adoption is an artificial relationship from the legal standpoint—as contrasted with the natural or blood ties which are stubbornly entangled in common and statutory law, and also in judicial usage far beyond the social claims of kinship—it is often necessary to have incontrovertible proof of adoption in order to protect the status and inheritance rights of the adopted person. An increasing number of states require notification by the court to the Bureau of Vital Statistics of every adoption. The child's birth registration is then altered or rewritten, the original record filed and often sealed, and a copy of the new certificate with the adoptive name of the child issued to the adopters. For further protection more and more of our states require that the new birth certificate shall not indicate that the child is adopted or whether he was born outside of marriage. A few states now issue a short form of birth certificate for *all* children in order to avoid singling out those of irregular birth. The adopter has a right to a birth certificate for his child and should request one if it is not provided at the time the adoption takes place. It may be needed for securing admission to school, for working papers, for securing a passport, or even for proof of citizenship. The birth certificate should be in hand as early as possible; there is unnecessary risk in waiting until some specific need arises. Some states require that all records and reports pertaining to an adoption be sealed and subsequently opened only on court order to "parties in action"; other statutes are permissive on this point. Adopters should request this protection in any case.

INHERITANCE. Inheritance rights constitute a most vital consideration. While there are fairly adequate statutes in most of the states to control the mechanics of adoption, there is a lag in the laws and court practices concerning inheritance in some states. Many of the laws dispose of status and inheritance rights by affirming that the adopted child has all the rights of the natural child, and some of the statutes add that these rights shall include inheritance. Yet in the face of such apparently clear statutory protection, court decisions have gone against the adopted child on some technicality which was construed as a flaw in the adoption, even though parents and child had lived together in fullest affection, all measuring up to every filial-parental obligation. In other cases there was no suggestion that the adoption was unsound; only the opinion that when a new statute clashes with an old established precedent, distant blood kin may come before the adopted son or daughter. Most litigation involving adopted persons is caused by disputes over inheritance of property.

New social laws must reckon with traditional attachments to the beliefs and practices of a former day. Until laws become more explicit and court decisions can be depended upon to back them up—as they will do when public opinion makes its mind more vigorously felt—the adopter needs to be particularly watchful. Even though courts are occasionally lenient, showing a fine social understanding, the adopter should see to it that there are no legal loopholes, no flaws in the adoption through failure to comply with some procedural detail. Also, he must specify the child by *name* as his *adopted* child if he wishes the child to be the certain beneficiary of life insurance or the recipient of property through a will or trust fund.

Black and Gray Markets in Babies. Even though increasingly the participation of the Department of Public Welfare is legally required in adoptions, black markets in babies are a continuing problem. Most of them operate solely for profit, with fees that may exceed a thousand dollars for a child who is usually an unknown newborn infant for whom records, reports, and birth certificate are lacking. The prospective adopter should use the services of a licensed, state-controlled organization that is adequately staffed. Never should such an important, far-reaching step as adoption be undertaken under any auspices that countenance a hasty, hush-hush procedure.

Sometimes procedurally questionable, even extralegal placements (gray market, so called) are made without profit by doctors, lawyers, social workers, and others genuinely disturbed over the present adoption situation. These professional people feel, with justification in some instances, that desirable adoptions are being needlessly blocked by inefficiency, understaffing, unrealistically high standards, failure of functionaries to work harmoniously, political preferences that give unfair precedence to applicants with wealth or prestige over better-qualified but less prominent families. A reputable agency or a whole state department may have an obsolete policy or too small a budget for an enlarged job. On the whole, however, Child Welfare Divisions of Public Welfare Departments are expanding their services because of the impetus of the Federal laws and financial aid for children since the middle 1930's. In response to public interest, agencies are showing an increasing sensitiveness to the need for a closer study of bottlenecks in adoptive services.

RECENT TRENDS

Because of the unprecedented increase in the number of children to be cared for and the great demand for adoptable children, some agencies are experimenting with certain innovations and short cuts in an effort to meet the problem squarely and expedite a rather slow process. While exploitive fees have been among the objectionable marks of the bootleg adoption, in order to share the costs with the adopting family reliable agencies increasingly are charging a small fee, a step that seems justified both by financial need and by matter-of-fact public acceptance of a reasonable charge for professional services.

Another experiment, one that considerably increases the number of potential adoptions, has to do with placement age. Some babies are now being taken directly from the hospital to the adopting home, where they are supervised during the study period, with the understanding that if the child proves unsuitable another one will be supplied, and perhaps with a prolonged probation before the final decree. This earlier placement has possibilities of considerable success because it gives to the child the security of attachment to a single home and thus the relationship at an early age more closely approximates that of the biological family. On the other hand, older children are sometimes being placed with families that do not insist on a baby, with especially good results for older adopters. Older children must be chosen and placed with particular skill, since prolonged institutional residence sometimes unfits them for the emotional give and take of family life. A child from a good foster home or from an own home recently broken by divorce or death often makes a good adjustment.

Adoptions are taking place where both the adoptive home and the child are considerably less than superior. This does not mean a deliberate lowering of placement standards but a recognition of the differences in mental capacity and social status that may be satisfied by a careful matching of qualities. Economic condition has proved to be a less reliable criterion for parenthood than emotional factors. Occasionally a child with a slight handicap or an ambiguous legal status is now being offered to a family willing to take the risk.

From war-ravaged countries, transplanted children have been adopted with success comparable to "all-American" adoptions. The legal and procedural details need further clarifying through international agreements if the adoption of foreign children is to be satisfactorily effective for all concerned.

SUMMARY

In adopting a child from proper motives and through approved procedures marriage and family life can be enriched. It has been emphasized that emotional maturity on the part of adopters is of particular importance, that adopting a child amounts to giving it social birth into full and complete family membership, and that there are values as vital and lasting in the adoptive family as in the usual biological family. Children thrive more fully in families than in institutions, for it is family life that nourishes and brings out the flowering of personality. The social and legal aspects, the imperatives of the law with respect to protecting the rights of the adoptive child, are fundamental.

The adoptive family, uniquely democratic, is in keeping with Nature's plan for the continuity of the species. Particularly for the childless couple it has a cosmic as well as a personal meaning. To achieve maximum satisfaction for itself and constructive worth as a democratic function, adoption must be supplied with every safeguard of science and law. The adoptive family has needs that can be met only by community interest and concern for wise placement and the utmost legal security. The success of the adoptive as well as the biological family rests squarely on the parents. Plan, decision, choice—these are the basic steps. Once the child is in the home, whether his advent has been biological or legal, parental functioning is a matter of social and spiritual dedication.

> Thou child of all humanity—
> Thy birth, no choosing didst thou have
> Of time or place or circumstance;
> In darksome cave or atom's dawn,
> By whom or where, or even how.
> Yet in the endless flow thou com'st
> Like others in the cosmic stream.
> Thy home and life are ours in trust,
> God's promise of community.

Topics for further thought:

1. From the point of view of the individual family that wishes to adopt a baby, what are the arguments against obtaining one through the "black" or the "gray" market?

2. In the process of adoption both the child's needs and those of the prospective parents should be met as completely as possible. Discuss these two sets of needs and show how reconciling them may be to the advantage of both.

Selected reading references

Brooks, Lee M., and Brooks, Evelyn C., *Adventuring in Adoption,* Chapel Hill, University of North Carolina Press, 1939.
> A pioneer monograph on adoption as a tool for improving American family life. Realistic and reassuring for prospective adoptive parents.

Cady, Ernest, *We Adopted Three,* New York, William Sloane Associates, 1952.
> An account of a family who found that their adoption of three girls gave them a fresh understanding about children and family life. Includes information about methods of adoption.

Cady, Ernest, and Cady, Frances, *How To Adopt a Child,* New York, William Morrow and Company, 1956.
> Gives practical advice on matters relative to the adoption process.

Kornitzer, Margaret, *Child Adoption in the Modern World,* New York, Philosophical Library, 1952.
> Written in Great Britain, this comprehensive treatment nevertheless applies in large measure to the American scene.

Vincent, Clarke E., "The Adoption Market and the Unwed Mother's Baby," *Marriage and Family Living,* May, 1956, pp. 124-7.
> Considers factors that are important in determining whether the unwed mother places her child for adoption independently or through an agency.

33 REMARRIAGE AND THE STEPCHILD

William Carlson Smith

THE impersonality of our American life tends to place undue strains on marital ties; consequently, a considerable percentage of marriages prove to be unsuccessful. A stepchild in the picture is an additional hazard, and a remarriage becomes an even greater risk than a first marriage.

EXTENT OF REMARRIAGE

Remarriage in the United States is assuming large proportions. Several recent studies make this evident. A study of fourteen states by the Metropolitan Life Insurance Company in 1953 indicates that one-fifth of those wed in 1950 were being married for the second time. Of all grooms who entered wedlock in 1950, 20.1 per cent had been previously married, 14.4 per cent of these were divorced, and 5.7 per cent were widowers. For brides the figures were 21 per cent remarried, and of these 15 per cent had been divorced and 6 per cent widowed.

A sample survey by the Bureau of the Census in April, 1948, indicates that 21.3 per cent of the husbands who had been in their marriages less than two years at the time of the survey were remarried. For wives the percentage was 21.8.

The relative importance of first and subsequent marriages varies considerably according to age. According to the Census survey, among men 14 to 34 years of age, 8 per cent had been married more than once; of those 35 to 54 years, 54 per cent; and for men 55 years and above, 92 per cent. The corresponding figures for women were 14 to 34 years of age, 14 per cent; 35 to 54 years, 66 per cent; and for 55 years and over, 96 per cent.

In recent decades there has been a marked increase in the frequency of remarriage. Wives with more than one marriage to their credit are at present relatively more frequent than at any time in the past fifty years. Among the previously divorced and widowed, the remarried women increased about 17 per cent from 1910 to 1940. Persons in their second or subsequent marriages now constitute a higher percentage of the total of married couples, even though widowhood has actually declined in the younger age groups. While the relative importance of family disruption because of the death of either mate has been decreasing, the increasing frequency of legal dissolutions has more than offset this decline. In the third year of marriage, three and one half times as many unions are dissolved by divorce as by death, and it is only after the fifteenth year of marriage has been reached that the mortality rate outstrips the divorce rate in marital dissolution.

The Census Bureau survey of 1948 shows that three-fourths of those divorced in the five-year period prior to the survey had remarried, while only about three-eighths of those widowed in this same period had remarried. Widowed or divorced women with children tend to remarry more promptly, or not at all, than those who are childless.

That the remarriage rate among divorced persons has reached a high point in recent years may be inferred from the fact brought out in the survey that approximately 5,500,000 married persons obtained divorces in the 1940-46 period, while during these seven years the number of divorced persons who had not remarried increased only by some 500,000. This depicts a trend in which approximately 90 per cent of the divorces end in remarriage.

The recent upswing in the divorce rate has had a decided effect on remarriage. Divorce makes room for more remarriages than death. In widowhood only one of the mates survives to remarry, but in divorce two persons become eligible for remarriage. Since divorce comes earlier than widowhood, divorced persons have good prospects in the matrimonial market.

The chances of remarriage have increased in every age group, but particularly in the range from 25 to 34 years. Since women marry at a younger age than men, most of the divorcees who become eligible for remarriage belong to this young age group. The increase, however, is not restricted merely to these young women, but there has been a striking upswing among the divorced women in all age groups.

Age for age, the divorced have greater chances for remarriage than the widowed, and even greater than the single. In fact, the divorcee of age 30 is the most marrying of all women in her age group. At age 30 she has 94 chances in 100 of eventual marriage, the widow of the same age has 60 chances in 100, while the spinster of 30 has only 48 chances in 100 of entering a marital venture. It is only in the late teens and twenties that the single person has a higher marriage rate than the divorced.

Many women in these upper age brackets are left unmarried as their desirability in courtship bargaining declines. For many it is a choice between remaining unmarried or accepting husbands who do not measure up to their standards.

CHILDREN IN REMARRIAGE

The presence of young children frequently provides an incentive to remarriage. A widowed or divorced father needs a woman's help in caring for his children. Widows and divorcees with children often need breadwinners, but the need is less urgent than in the case of a man, because of the rather common provisions made by widows' pension systems. If several young children are concerned, the need for early remarriage may be urgent.

Children are more likely to be involved in remarriages of the widowed than of the divorced. Widowers are more often left with children than are divorced men. In divorces, children are more often awarded to their mothers than to their fathers. The fact that widowers are more often left with children than not probably is an important factor in their remarriage because of the need for homemakers.

The bulk of divorces come in the early years of marriage, when there are few or no children, while the widowed have, on the average, been married longer and have more children. Hence divorce more often than death separates childless couples in the early years of married life. According to the Census Bureau survey young children were found more often in homes of persons newly remarried than in those of persons who had recently married for the first time. Only about 25 per cent of those married for the first time within two years before the survey had children in their homes under 18 years old, as compared with some 56 per cent for the remarried. This difference is due to the fact that a considerable proportion of the children of remarried persons were the offspring of previous marriages.

The chances of remarriage grow less with advancing age. According to the Metropolitan Life Insurance Company the rates for both marriage and remarriage decrease more rapidly for women than for men, but the divorced person has a brighter prospect of marriage throughout the whole life span than either the widowed or the single.

MATE SELECTION IN REMARRIAGE

When previously married persons remarry, they tend to show preferences for mates in the same previous conjugal categories as their own. Widowers more often choose widows; their next preference is single mates, while they seem to avoid divorcees. The divorced most frequently select single persons, but from the previously married available mates they prefer the divorced persons. Even those who have been both divorced and widowed seem to single out those who, like themselves, have had double experiences.

In a first marriage a man usually chooses a woman who is slightly younger but close to his own age. When he remarries, after the death of his wife or divorce, he tends to select a woman who is considerably younger, particularly if she is single. If he is remarried to a divorcee or widow, she is usually close to his own age group. Frequently single men marry widows or divorcees who are older than themselves.

This tendency of men to select young women, both single and divorcees, works to the disadvantage of women in the same age bracket as the men. Widows are more limited in remarriage choices than widowers. For a widow aged 25, chances for remarriage are best during the second year of her widowhood, but the opportunities decline quite rapidly after the fourth year. After her thirty-fourth year, the widow's chances to remarry are not at all reassuring, while a man has a good chance even after his forty-fourth year. If the middle-aged widow is to win another mate, she must possess unusual qualifications, such as charm, wealth, or social status.

According to Paul H. Jacobson, in a study of the differentials in divorce by duration of marriage and size of family, the 421,000 divorces and annulments granted in 1948 involved about 313,000 children. About two-fifths of the divorced couples had children. In that same year, children were related to more than 50 per cent of the divorces granted to couples married 7 to 23 years. The heavy concentration of annulments and divorces in the early years of married life is responsible for the comparatively low percentage of decrees that involve children. In 1948, more than one half of the decrees were granted to couples married less than seven years. In another connection, Jacobson concludes that there has been a more rapid increase in divorces in families with children than among the childless, and consequently an increasing percentage of children will be affected.

These figures, however, do not indicate the number of children involved in remarriages; they merely give some indication of the number made available for such involvement. Evidence seems to indicate that the remarried widowed have a larger proportion of dependent children than the remarried divorced.

SUCCESS OF REMARRIAGE

Are subsequent marriages more or less successful than first marriages? To that question there is no definite answer, but evidence seems to indicate that remarriages are somewhat more hazardous than first marriages. Undoubtedly the stepchild is a factor in this differential rate. No one knows what percentage of the remarried brought dependent children into their new homes, but with the many thousand children made available for the steprelationship through divorce and bereavement and with the high remarriage rate, particularly among the divorced, a sizable number of children are involved. It may be reasonably assumed that these children played a part in wrecking a considerable number of remarriages.

Undoubtedly the divorced group contains more than its quota of persons unfitted for married life; thus a higher than average rate of failures in their second or subsequent marital ventures may be expected. Since there has been considerable sifting, a high percentage of the poorest marital risks probably do not remarry. Many have learned from the first bitter experience and may bring to the second marriage much more understanding and a greater determination to make a success of the new venture. They are more likely to have passed through the puppy love stage, are less blinded by romanticism, and may be better able to appreciate genuine values. Some remarriages, to be sure, come on the rebound and are based on tenuous bonds. One or the other will remarry hastily in order to show the other that he is not a discard in the matrimonial market. He may impute to a comparative stranger all the qualities he desired in his first mate. Then, when the new spouse cannot measure up to all of these expectations, disillusionment brings him again to the divorce court.

Reliable statistics on the success of remarriage by widows and widowers are not available, but there is some evidence that they have a slightly higher incidence of success than divorced persons. In a high percentage of the homes broken by death, the mates were happily adjusted and fewer twisted personalities are found in this group. Hence they are more marriageable.

There should be more successful remarriages among the widowed than among the divorced because the latter are usually disappointed, disillusioned, embittered. Happiness in a previous marriage, however, may be at times a disadvantage in a subsequent marriage, because there may be a tendency to idealize the deceased spouse. If the new mate cannot measure up to this idealization there may be unfavorable reactions and disillusionment.

In the remarriage of widows and widowers with children, the stepchild problem must be taken into consideration, but probably it will be less troublesome than in the case of the divorced, because many of the children lived in happy homes and were not warped in their development by the dissensions that resulted in divorce. There is, however, the problem of idealization of the departed parent and refusal to accept the substitute parent, who is considered inferior to the real parent.

A remarriage when a stepchild enters into the situation usually has an unequal chance of being as good as the first marriage. This holds true, particularly in the case of the widowed, because death invades all homes, good, bad, and indifferent. Many of these were well integrated and happy homes.

If a mother dies and leaves one or more children, the father needs a housekeeper, but his range of choice is more limited than at the time of his first marriage—prospective wives hesitate about assuming responsibility for someone else's children. Because of this the second wife often comes from a lower social stratum than the first one. This cultural divergence makes it more difficult for husband and wife to adjust to each other. Furthermore, this new mother, who is noticeably inferior to the children's own mother, is not readily accepted by them. A college girl wrote of her home:

At our house we calmly ignored my stepmother. Humble and then defensively antagonistic all at one time, she kept us in hot water with foolish threats of suicide and desertion. I always prayed she'd go ahead and jump in the bayou. Father married her in self-defense to get a house-keeper. Her role was most difficult in a family so self-esteemed. My older sisters treated her "kindly," not "lovingly." We were clannish and she revolted occasionally with loud oaths and much talk of "sassy little angels." We forgot about her in public—few people knew she was in existence. Guests never paid her much attention—she just cooked.

Such a situation was not conducive to harmony between the two spouses. Without the stepchildren the marriage might have been a satisfying one, but with them there was only a slight chance for success.

Undoubtedly the economic factor plays an important part in connection with remarriage. Men have greater earning power and a woman may be willing to assume the responsibilities of stepmother-hood in return for economic security. Widows and divorcees, however, find that children are hindrances to remarriage.

The success of a remarriage usually depends more upon the step-mother than upon the stepfather. She makes closer contacts with the children and consequently is more involved. Her situation, however, is usually the more difficult one. The stereotype of the cruel step-mother sets the stage against her. For a long time the older school-books regaled the children with the Cinderella story and its variations in which the stepmother was always a cruel ogress. The child has heard stories about cruel stepmothers from his elders and even from his playmates. The imprint of this stereotype has been deepened by popu-lar usage of the term stepchild. Anything that seems to be neglected is called a stepchild. Reiteration of this idea does much to maintain the stereotype and hangs more millstones about the neck of the step-mother.

In order to be considered good, a stepmother must really be excep-tional. Because so many children, and adults also, have the idea that the stepmother is usually mean and cruel, her role is a difficult one. Foster mothers do not have to share the undeserved onus that is at-tached to stepmothers. The stepmother has been given such a bad name that it requires a first-rate diplomat to succeed at the job of stepmothering and being a wife in a reconstituted home.

STEPCHILDREN AND MARITAL PROBLEMS

Stepchildren are often responsible for the development of tensions that wreck homes, as the following cases illustrate. A father wrote to a newspaper asking someone to take his nine-year-old boy, who could not live harmoniously with his stepmother, "otherwise we may have our home broken up again."

A widower with a son married a widow with two children. Seven times in seven years the couple separated, largely because of the stepchildren. The boy and his stepmother were at swords' points.

A widower with a daughter remarried, but soon he was granted a divorce because the stepmother was unkind to his daughter. He remarried again and almost immediately the girl began to annoy her new mother. The situation became increasingly tense until the stepmother declared that either she or the girl would have to leave home.

When one wife had difficulties with the stepchildren she left and refused to return to her husband. She stated that one of the stepchildren gave evidence of jealousy whenever she and the father manifested any affection for each other. Consequently they no longer displayed any affection in his presence. This restriction, in her opinion, tended to "pull her husband and herself apart." She realized that the father loved his children and that if she stayed she might disturb their relationship, for which she would then be blamed. She would not consent to remain and try to keep the children, but, on the other hand, she would not demand that they be sent away and thus be separated from their father. She determined to eliminate herself from the volcanic situation.

In some instances, while conflicts over stepchildren do not actually drive anyone out of the home, there may be definite breaks so that a family may live as two separate units under the same roof. In one household the friction between a boy and his stepfather would frequently become so severe that the husband would eat and sleep with his children in one part of the house while the wife and her children would withdraw to themselves.

Sometimes a stepchild resents the presence of a stepparent and sets about deliberately to drive the newcomer out. When a close relationship exists between child and real parent, the situation may be serious. A boy with a father fixation set about to get rid of his stepmother. There was a harmonious relationship between husband and wife, and the stepmother tried to be a good mother to the boy, but he would not accept her. He admitted that she was friendly toward him, but he resented her presence and would not respond. The boy, abetted by his aunt, told falsehoods about his stepmother. He was at least partly successful in his plan, for he was able to develop some strained relationships between his father and his stepmother.

One boy, who was involved in many difficulties, justified his lying, stealing, absconding, insolency, and truancy on the basis of his hatred for his stepmother. He had been greatly attached to his mother, but from the very moment his stepmother entered the house he could not bear the thought of her and deliberately carried out his many acts of misbehavior for the purpose of annoying her and driving her out. He discerned that the more difficulties he created for her the more tense the situation became. He was fond of his father and pleaded with him to have the stepmother go away, never to return.

In one home sharp disagreements developed between the father and stepmother because of the behavior of the boy. At times the father would defend the stepmother when the paternal grandmother would criticize her, but for the most part he was critical of the way she tried to manage his son. The boy became aware of his father's ambivalence toward the stepmother and deliberately created many situations in an attempt to make his father choose between himself and his stepmother. He stated that he would do anything to get rid of her. He complained that she favored her own child but was harsh and demanding with him. The father believed that the stepmother was jealous because the children were fonder of him than of her. The situation became so tense because of the boy that the father said he was a "sucker" for getting married again.

The reconstituted family is often the source of vexatious mental conflicts. One woman who seemingly made a happy remarriage came to be greatly disturbed. Open conflict had not developed between her son and his stepfather, yet since the establishment of her new home the boy had become a delinquent. Should she send the boy away to his own father and thus lose him completely? Should she go on living with the stepfather with whom she was contented, or should she leave her husband and live with the boy? She feared the boy was headed for a life of crime, and if she could be certain that it would be for the boy's own good, she would be willing to leave her husband. But she could not be certain—and the conflict raged within her.

A divorcee with two sons remarried and for some time all went well with the boys and their stepfather. Suddenly, however, one of the boys became rude toward his mother and quarrelsome toward his step-father. The mother, who was doing all in her power to make a good home, was greatly disappointed when the boy and his stepfather quarreled like two children. She was torn between her husband and her two sons. She was fond of her husband, and, were it not for the children, he would be all that she could ask. Since this difficulty had arisen, certain disagreements relative to the boys developed. There had been discussion about sending the boys to their own father, but the mother strenuously opposed that proposal because of the father's instability. She also disapproved the idea of having the boys spend much time with their paternal grandmother because of her overindulgence of them. The boy realized that the conflict with his stepfather was endangering his mother's marriage. He felt guilty about this and said that he would leave home in order to forestall a break.

One woman married a widower because she loved him and was determined to be a good stepmother to his two children. In a comparatively short time, however, the older child became such a disturbing factor that her marriage and family life were in danger of failure. Because of him there was so much dissension that, in her opinion, they had no home—only a house. She became irritable in her relations with her husband. This distressed her greatly, since she had entered the marriage with a keen desire to make it a success. The boy stated that he hated his stepmother and always would hate her because she had taken him away from his grandmother. This attitude on the part of the boy was a disturbing factor in an otherwise happy marriage.

FACTORS IN THE PROBLEM SITUATION

The second marriage is oftentimes a business proposition—a man needs a caretaker for his children while a woman needs a breadwinner. Frequently a widower with children in need of a mother finds a widow with several children in need of a father. This merging of two or more sets of children often jeopardizes family tranquillity. Irritations, tension, and conflict are highly probable when such children are brought together in the intimacy of home life after they have spent several years in widely divergent circumstances. The situation becomes even more complex when there are *her* children, *his* children, and *their* children.

Repeating the words of a marriage ceremony will not all at once fuse two personalities together—they must adjust and grow together. In first marriages the two persons have to make adjustments only to each other and they have at the least almost a full, undisturbed year to themselves for doing so. If a baby arrives in due course of time they have the opportunity to grow up with the child. Unconsciously the child adopts the codes and the values of the home and develops an integrated personality which fits that particular situation. When a widowed or divorced person with a child remarries, the situation is far different. The real parent has had opportunity to become accustomed to the child and has had something to do with training him in accord with his own ideas. The substitute parent, however, usually has had nothing to do with the training and only rarely does he or she know the habits or peculiarities of the child. The new parent must make adjustments not only to the new mate but also to the stepchild. This second personality cannot be ignored and often is the cause of conflicts which wreck the marital venture. In first marriages the two mates may have some constructive conflicts which help in working out satisfactory relationships, but with a stepchild the situation becomes far more complicated and accommodations are less easily made.

Because of the complicating factors connected with remarriage, particularly where there are children, there can rarely be any prolonged period of dating, followed by deliberate courtship and moderately long engagement. A remarriage tends to approach the hasty marriage type, which is correlated with a high divorce rate. In our society, where persons contemplating marriage choose their own mates, courtship is highly important; it affords opportunity for mutual acquaintance and for making adjustments that may have an important bearing on marital happiness. A prospective stepparent and the child, however, all too often have no opportunity for becoming mutually acquainted and come together in a home as total strangers. Serious conflicts may arise because the new parent may have a standard of values far different from those to which the child has been accustomed. In the period since the child lost his parent he may have played a certain rather satisfying role which is disturbed by the coming of the substitute parent who has an entirely different conception of the part that the child should play. These conflicts develop readily when strangers meet in the intimacy of family life, and they teem with possibilities for dissension between husband and wife and may ruin the marriage.

It is no surprise to learn that dissension developed in a home where a man addressed his two stepsons with the words: "Had I known you two when I married your mother, I would have thrown you both into the river. You'd be better off now and not be causing me any worry. You'll never amount to anything, and I'd be doing you a favor now if I dumped you into the river."

Some or many of the habits of a child may be annoying to the new parent, even though there may be no intention of causing difficulty.

Furthermore, the real parent may be utterly unaware of the strain thrown on the new parent.

There are many problems to face when a person knows there will be stepchildren, but the hazards are far greater when a person remarries and fails to tell the new spouse about the previous marriage and children. A girl wrote this about her home:

Friction in the new marriage began the very first year. My father did not tell his second wife about his previous marriage. Two weeks after the wedding he brought home his daughter by his first marriage. This was a most trying situation for the new wife. The girl showed lack of care and the stepmother made clothes for her and tried to help her, but the response was one of disrespect, distrust, jealousy, and sometimes definite hatred.

Five children were born to this second union, and it was not long before they became aware of the difficulties caused by their half sister. They realized that the tension between their parents was due largely to her and, since she was their father's daughter, they tended to blame him for all the family troubles. When the stepdaughter left home the mother thought all would be well, but things had gone too far. The children disliked their father and never forgot the conflicts which had been caused by their half sister.

On several occasions the mother considered separation or divorce but did not carry through because she did not know how she might support the children.

Oftentimes the influence of intermediate caretakers between the breakup of the first home and the establishment of the second one is important. When a wife and mother dies or leaves the home through divorce, the father, who usually must work away from home, makes some provision for care of the children. A housekeeper may be hired. In the lower economic brackets this person is often more or less inadequate. She knows little about children and often cares less; a stepmother who tries to bring order out of chaos encounters difficulties great enough to wreck the marriage upon which she entered hopefully.

If the intermediate caretaker is a grandparent, particularly a grandmother, the situation becomes precarious. The grandmother tends to exercise a pernicious influence over her grandchildren even in so-called normal situations, but where a steprelationship enters the picture, then there is a probability that the perniciousness may be multiplied manyfold. The grandmother is usually overprotective and overindulgent, yielding to every whim of the child. In order to hold the child the grandmother will often use wiles and shower favors on him and will even poison the child's mind against his own parents. In this process the grandmother may develop a feeling of dislike, or even hatred, against the child's mother (her own daughter), a stronger feeling of resentment against her daughter-in-law, but a far stronger feeling against a stepmother who has come in to mother the child in the place of her own deceased daughter. A child who has been pampered by his grandmother is ill prepared for life in a reconstituted home with a stepmother and is a likely source of conflict and disorganization.

When a divorced parent who has custody of the children remarries, the other parent frequently schemes to turn the children against both the stepparent and the ex-mate and thus spoil the new marriage. In one case two divorcees with children had married and the ex-mates of both kept in contact with their children. Such a situation was not conducive to a high degree of harmony in the home.

Within any family there tends to be favoritism when one child receives slightly more attention than the others. In the step-family the setting is ideal for favoritism, be it actual or imputed, to become highly disruptive. A parent is usually more or less partial to his or her own children. The parent may compare his or her own child with the mate's own child, to the disadvantage of the latter. One woman attempted to make her stepson feel inferior to her own son. For instance, she told a visitor that her stepson mispronounced certain words. Then she told her own son to tell the lady how to say the words and then show how the stepson said them.

Particularly serious difficulties may arise in the event the stepchild is defective or has characteristics that make him unattractive. One man accepted two stepsons but was greatly displeased when his wife made plans to bring her blind and mentally retarded daughter home from a state school. The woman was greatly disturbed by the conflict between her desire to allow her husband peace of mind and her duty to help her daughter. The husband contended that his income was insufficient to take on the additional support of the girl. If it were done the other children would suffer. If a stepchild has characteristics superior to those of one's own child, there may also be breakers ahead. One stepmother became jealous of her pretty stepdaughter when she realized that the girl was superior to her own child.

Frequently a stepmother is devoted to her stepchildren until she has a child of her own. Then, apparently, she gives herself completely to her own child and neglects her husband's children. In a situation like this the stepmother is in a precarious position. Even in an unbroken family the first child tends to resent the arrival of a new baby —he can no longer be the center of attention. Even though the parents continue to treat the first child in the customary manner, he will consider that he has been crowded out and is being neglected. What the child believes in such a situation is true for him, and on that basis he reacts. In the split home it is easy for the stepchild to charge his stepmother with neglect. The father, then, may note the pained expression on the face of his child, pity him, and feel resentful toward the inconsiderate stepmother.

Failure to see eye to eye on matters of discipline is a fruitful source of conflict. To be sure, this is found in first marriages but is more likely to develop into bitterness over a stepchild. Often a father will accuse the stepmother of being too severe with his children and overindulgent with her own. Because of favoritism it is difficult to establish a biparental control over a stepchild. A foster child, since he belongs to neither parent, is on a basis of equality and can be controlled more rationally. Frequently a stepchild resents control by the stepparent. He soon becomes aware of the anomalous situation and plays one parent off against the other, a procedure not in the interest of marital harmony.

The age of the stepchild must be taken into consideration. When children are young and helpless enough to feel the need of a mother to love them, pet them, and help them with their little troubles, it is comparatively easy for a stepmother to take a real mother's place in their lives. Oftentimes a child at the age of five, particularly if he has spent some time with an overindulgent grandmother, is difficult for a substitute parent to manage. When children advance in age, and particularly when in their early teens, they tend to become trials to stepparents. When a stepparent comes into the home after the children have grown up and left there is little contact and few opportunities for conflict to arise, except at times over property matters. At times an elderly widower with some property may marry a young "gold digger," and then trouble may come. In many instances the children are glad to have the widowed parent remarry because that provides companionship for the otherwise lonely person. Furthermore, that may avoid the complication of keeping the lonely and restless parent in the home with grandchildren.

Youthfulness of the stepmother is also a factor to be considered. Widowed and divorced men tend to select second wives who are considerably younger than themselves. Oftentimes they are not much older than the stepchildren they are to mother. Sometimes when the stepmother is only a little older than the children she becomes irritable and domineering in an attempt to control the children who are not awed by her youthfulness. In such a situation friction and even intense hostility can readily develop. The lot of the youthful stepmother is often hard.

STEPCHILDREN AND SUCCESSFUL MARRIAGES

Not all marriages that involve stepchildren are necessarily failures; many of them are far better than first marriages. Many enter remarriages carefully and thoughtfully. One stepfather said: "Your own children are sent to you naturally, but for that boy I consciously assumed responsibility and he means a great deal to me."

Many stepmothers have been crowned with success after realizing that they were facing difficult situations and they set about to solve their problems intelligently. William E. Barton writes of the stepmother of Abraham Lincoln, "She transformed the home of the cheerless widower and his two motherless children into a spot of pleasant associations and happy memories." Occasionally a stepmother steps into a difficult situation and does remarkably well with heavy odds against her, with the result that deep bonds of affection develop between her and the stepchildren. This also strengthens the bond between the mates.

A divorced woman remarried and the stepfather treated her son as if he were his own. The boy said his stepfather was wonderful, while he disliked his own father. In another home a boy adored his helpful stepfather. The boy's mother disliked the boy, however, and wanted to get rid of him because his behavior irritated her. She openly rejected the boy from the time of his birth and continually identified him with his father, whom she had divorced. The stepfather was a real asset in the home and served as a buffer between the boy and his mother.

While many marriages involving stepchildren prove to be successful, the number may be increased by taking thought. The children and the stepparent are frequently total strangers to each other. One woman made preparation for entry into the home with a twelve-year-old boy by having the boy live with her for two months before the marriage in an endeavor to become acquainted with him so that she could make good as a stepmother. This was no easy situation, since the boy for some eleven years had lived with an overindulgent grandmother. Even though the new mother did not understand children, she was anxious to learn. On the basis of this attitude she and the boy gradually became pals and he began to turn to her with his questions and problems. When a child feels that he can confide in the stepparent, the rough spots on the road to success have been quite well leveled off. The real parent can do much to prepare the children for a second marriage. One girl wrote thus:

We children were trained by our mother to respect our future step-father, so I cannot give him all the credit for being such an affectionate father. To our mother goes much of the credit for presenting the idea of remarriage in such a sweet way, and we are much better off because of that.

By reason of the stepmother stereotype many women feel a sense of uncertainty and insecurity in assuming the mother role in a recon-stituted family. A woman married a widower who had two children, aged eleven and thirteen. The mother had been dead for three years and the children had lived with their grandmother, who had pampered them. About two months after the marriage the children went home. For some time they were little angels, but soon they began to run wild as they had done at their grandmother's home. The stepmother was nonplused; she did not know what to do with them. She said that since they were not her children she could not discipline them. A social worker with a child-placing agency advised the stepmother to act as if they were her children and just as if she were a real member of the family. In a comparatively short time, with the co-operation of the father, she had the situation under control, and the children accepted the new order. In due course of time the boy joined the Navy while the girl became a Wave, and both of them wrote lovely letters to their stepmother.

Some children think that a stepmother is interested in taking ad-vantage of them, that she is inclined to be a gold digger. One step-mother made it impossible for any such charge to be brought against her when she refused to be made a beneficiary in her husband's insur-ance policy, lest the children be turned against her. She said that if he died she could take care of herself.

Partiality, actual or imputed, is the rock on which many of these marital ventures have been wrecked. To avoid any show of partiality, one stepmother would buy articles comparable, if not exactly alike, for her stepchild and for her own child. Some stepparents do more for their stepchildren than for their own children in order to avoid the accusation of unfairness. One father gave more of his spare time to his stepson than to his own children. The boy would wait for his stepfather to come home and then they would garden, read, walk, or work in their shop together. One girl wrote of her home:

> We never resent correction by our stepfather because he is very just; he does not correct us as much as his own children. It always hurts us when we have to be corrected, not because of resentment, but because we admire him so much that we do not want to displease him.

Disagreement relative to the control of a child can develop friction in any home, but where a stepchild is present it is more difficult to see eye to eye on such matters. When the parent and stepparent discuss matters of discipline and then co-operate in carrying out the program on which they have agreed, the chances for a successful outcome are greatly enhanced.

Now and then any reference to a departed parent in a reconstituted home brings difficulty: it may produce jealousy on the part of the new parent or it may arouse hatred on the part of the children toward the stepparent. One stepmother assumed the care of four children and managed the situation remarkably well. One factor in the situation seemed to be that she and the eldest girl would talk freely about the girl's own mother. Even though she was not present physically, she was a real member of the family and there was no jealousy or tension connected with her.

Frequently a child feels that the new parent has supplanted him in the affections of the real parent. The new parent must exercise care in showing that he or she is not a supplanter but that the child now may be the recipient of the affections of two parents instead of one only. If there is a parent fixation the situation may be sufficiently problematical to call for outside aid. A psychiatrist may be needed to bring a change in the child's attitude to avoid serious difficulty. The child needs to see that this possessiveness of his is extremely selfish and that his real parent needs the affection of the new mate.

Oftentimes a stepparent can see a child's shortcomings more clearly than a fond parent whose intimate association with the child from the very beginning has made him myopic. This does not, however, give the stepparent the privilege of setting about at once to make the child over into a new form according to his or her particular blueprint. A child tends to resent criticism and any attempt by a newcomer to make abrupt changes. Furthermore, a widower often resents this as being a criticism not only of himself but also of his departed mate. More can be done by giving the child the love and understanding of which he has been deprived through the loss of his real parent. If the child's admiration is won through a sympathetic understanding of him in his child's world, more can be done to shape his personality than through an aggressive campaign of reconstruction.

Some women, when faced with the problem of caring for stepchildren, read books on child care and training. Even though they may be bookish in their approach to the children, the willingness to learn and the attitude of open-mindedness lay the foundations for a successful outcome. When the books do not provide the answers, they turn to child-guidance clinics for assistance.

Many stepchildren have been won over when the new parents would share in their interests, problems, and activities. One girl had difficulties in her school work. Her mother said that she was too impatient to help her daughter, "but the stepfather," she declared, "had the patience of a saint." He gave much time to the girl, with the result that she steadily improved and began to like her studies. He was always looking for some new way in which he might help the child. When the mother, with considerable pride, stated that the daughter admired her stepfather and considered him perfect, there was no immediate danger of a rift in that family.

SAFEGUARDS

In popular usage the stepchild suffers from neglect, and in many ways this is all too true. Adopted children, foster children, and orphans sometimes fare better than stepchildren. In the case of adoption, trained social workers investigate prospective foster parents with reference to their social and economic status as well as to their personality qualifications and moral fitness to care for children. Usually a child will be placed for a trial period, during which time the social workers keep a close check before the adoption is finally consummated.

Why should not certain safeguards be thrown about the stepchild? Should there not be some investigation made of prospective stepparents before marriage? In the state of Oregon both persons concerned in a marriage must present medical certificates in order to secure a license. Why should there not be certificates indicating suitability for stepparenthood? Since the stepchild has all the problems of any other child and usually has them in larger dosages, in addition to which he has other problems which grow directly out of the steprelationship, many of the difficulties could probably be avoided or, at any rate, minimized if certain precautionary measures were taken.

Topics for further thought:

1. Remarriage necessitates a double adjustment on the part of the couple, and future happiness is likely to be threatened by their inability to forget the failures of the past. What are some of the most important hazards in remarriage?

2. Remarriage of a parent may have favorable or unfavorable effects on the child. Discuss these in respect to both the older and the younger child.

Selected reading references

Bernard, Jessie, *Remarriage: A Study of Marriage,* New York, The Dryden Press, 1956.
> Comprehensive report of research on people who remarry and issues and cleavages in their families. Evaluates relative success of remarriage, the effect upon children, and trends and implications.

Monahan, Thomas P., "How Stable Are Remarriages?" *American Journal of Sociology,* November, 1952, pp. 280-88.
> A study of marriage records in Iowa and Missouri indicates that remarriages are not as stable as first marriages.

Podolsky, Edward, "The Emotional Problems of the Stepchild," *Mental Hygiene,* January, 1955, pp. 49-53.
> Deals with a range of adjustment problems similar to that contained in the present chapter.

Smith, William C., *The Stepchild,* Chicago, The University of Chicago Press, 1953.
> A comprehensive study of the step-relationship not only in our society but in other cultures as well. Analyzes the position of the stepparent and the stepchild in terms of our culture stereotypes.

34 SEX EDUCATION AND THE CHILD

Charles E. Manwiller

Sex education starts very early in life and includes the entire subject of how men and women get along with each other and what their respective places are in the world. A child learns about sex all through babyhood and childhood; he begins his sex education as soon as he can sense how his parents get along together and how they feel toward their children. In the wholesome family environment, he observes the love and respect of parents for each other, their kindnesses and courtesies, their freedom from fears and embarrassments. This early education by precept and example is more deeply influential than any informal instruction the child may receive. Certainly sex is a lot broader than just the matter of how babies are made. Sex education involves much more than information gleaned from a lecture at school or a serious talk between parent and child.

A normal child begins to get ideas about the things that are connected with sex around the ages of two and a half to about three and a half. At this time of his life he is curious about everything. He asks questions about parts of his body, why boys are shaped differently from girls, why persons do this or that. His sex questions are mixed up with all other "why" questions, because his curiosity is branching out in all directions. Straightforward answers without detailed information will be satisfying to him at this age. He should never be given a wrong impression about sex because this gives him distorted ideas about the subject later on. If he wants to know where babies come from he should be told very simply—this is not the time to give him the whole story of the physical and emotional side of sex relations. If the child's parents answer his questions casually he will turn to them as he grows older and desires more exact information.

Long before the child goes to school he will have acquired from his parents or from relatives, friends, and neighbors basic attitudes toward others, male and female. He will have assimilated his elders' standards of right and wrong, their hypocrisies, frustrations, sexual attitudes, and respect or lack of respect for members of the opposite sex. He will have tasted security or the lack of it in the social world called home.

Every child is entitled to an adequate understanding of the nature of sex. The story of human origin and the development of insight into human relations and a sense of social responsibility should be included in the total pattern of sex education. During the preschool years informal and indirect general education makes for gradual and wholesome development in sex education.

ELEMENTARY-SCHOOL LEVEL

All evidence from research studies on the sexual experiences of youth indicate that (1) an early beginning in sex education is needed; (2) emphasis on broad social implications of sex with regard to long-range individual adjustment is important; (3) social responsibilities associated with sex behavior need to be emphasized; and (4) opportunities for youth to get together in wholesome, happy situations under guidance should be provided by the school.

Every teacher should teach about sex to the extent that his subject or activity contributes to the building of character and to the shaping of ideals. He should provide the facts of life and an understanding of them and help the pupil to adjust socially. In the early grades when both sexes study and play together they are indirectly getting sex instruction by learning to observe others and to accept differences in others without bias. Nature-study classes which include activities involving animals, such as setting hens, rabbits, or guinea pigs, offer wholesome opportunities for learning about sex differences, birth, and care of young. Health-education courses offer valuable opportunities for instruction in the structure, function, and care of the body, in community health, and in personal and social development.

At the elementary-school level children develop life-long habits and attitudes toward personal cleanliness, personal appearance, and care of the body. Teachers must not evade answers to questions about sex. The child is confronted daily with "commercialized" sex on television and radio, in motion pictures and magazines. Sex instruction must be honest, clear, and factual. Personal and social aspects of sex should be emphasized along with the facts of reproduction. If such instruction is deferred until high school, the adolescent's adjustment may be seriously affected by lack of information, misinformation, or superstition.

Attitudes toward sex instruction differ greatly among school systems. In some systems community backing often supports a wholesome program of sex enlightenment. In other systems, however, teachers are forced to hold clandestine discussions with students who seek correct information. An atmosphere of secrecy tends to deepen and distort the natural aspects of sex into forbidden mystery. A child should never be ashamed of sexual truth or made to feel that there is something wrong about it.

Among the schools that take a positive approach to sex instruction, various methods of education have been tried. For the younger children, the approach is made through adults influential in the child's life, such as parents, teachers, clergy, health officials, and welfare workers. Workshops, conferences, courses, and discussion groups provide opportunities for these adults to hear lectures by physicians and psychiatrists, to view motion pictures, and to discuss mutual problems. Some schools offer older children the opportunity to work with nursery-school children. This mutual process helps both age groups in understanding themselves, their friends, their families and their neighbors.

HIGH-SCHOOL LEVEL

During the last quarter of a century, many high-school curriculums have introduced sex instruction under such various titles as human reproduction, the human body, health and growth, life problems, family-life education, human science, human relations, homemaking, social hygiene and health. Emphasis is placed on mental and social hygiene, the biological aspects of sex, family-life adjustments, and normal boy-girl relationships. At first schools leaned toward separate courses for boys and girls. The present trend is to integrate sex education in its widest sense into such subject fields as science, physical education, social studies, and home economics. The single lecture on sex, disease, or morals is poor sex education.

Today's educators differ on the type of instructional approach. Two major methods have evolved through practice: instructional materials are presented as natural parts of other courses in a broad program of education in human relations calling for the co-operation of teachers in various fields; or the material is taught in a special course or courses offered at various maturation levels. The first, the integrated method, is a long-range, co-operative enterprise. The second, the special-course method, is a short-range, emergency type of approach favored during World War II in the hope of meeting problems of sex delinquency, venereal disease, and mental hygiene.

The Integrated Method. The integrated method of sex education may be realized in a comprehensive program extending from kindergarten to the end of high school or it may be confined to the high-school level, where it would be offered by teachers of certain subjects only. Even though wholesome sex education should start in the home, the school should supplement home training in the child's development.

The success of such a program depends on an integration of student-teacher relationship with program presentation. The teacher should know his students, their attitudes, and the best methods for presenting the subject. Students should be grouped according to maturation level, needs, interests, and capacities. The program should be introduced gradually by one teacher and then broadened to include other teachers and subject matter. The practice of outside speakers should be discouraged, for freedom of discussion may be hampered by reticence to speak in front of strangers. The teachers should be well-grounded in biology, physiology, social psychology, and sociology. In discussion, sex should not be forced into any subject area but should be integrated naturally and without undue pressure. A positive and wholesome emphasis is desired, with facts, not preaching, characterizing the instruction. Religious views and ethical differences should not be introduced into the classroom discussion. Personal conferences can handle individual problems, but these should be avoided in the classroom, where the discussion should be impersonal and unemotional.

A brief review of some of the content of various subject-matter fields may indicate the contributions each can make to the integrated method of sex instruction.

Biology—Sex as a biological function; influence of glands on sex behavior; relation of mind to body; development of necessary basic vocabulary; achievement of a scientific attitude toward sex.

Physiology—Structure and function of the sex organs; skeletal and muscular systems; pubertal changes; development of life in the womb; importance of heredity; communicable diseases.

Health and Hygiene—Physical and emotional changes at puberty; sexual development; glands and reproduction; superstitions about sex; self-control; sex and mental well-being; emotional stability; physiology and hygiene of menstruation; masturbation; cleanliness; sex terminology.

Physical Education—Meaning of growing up; physical development; posture and physical fitness; value of clean living; developing self-control; recreation activities: sports, hobbies, clubs.

English—Social aspects of human relations as seen in biographies, novels, plays; marriage customs, personal and family problems, personalities in the family; family norms democratically arrived at; culture patterns; etiquette of social situations.

Social Studies—Manners and customs of social life; place of family in society; marriage laws; eugenics; personalities and roles in the family; effects of the broken home; sex delinquency; the family as a training institution for democracy; social costs of sex misconduct, illegitimacy, prostitution.

Home Economics—Problems in family living; relations between parents and children, men and women, boys and girls; personality development; social conventions; dating; preparation for marriage; normal sex interests; family responsibilities; parental responsibilities; roles of sexes in family life; child care; hygiene of childhood; place of children in the home; sex education of children; family adjustments by and for aged members; importance of cultural values in the home; fostering and building family traditions, ideals, and spiritual values; ways to democratic living in the home.

Teachers planning to work with students in the integrated method of sex education should be encouraged to attend health and human-relations courses. One of these, conducted at the University of Pennsylvania, aimed at the following: (1) to develop teacher awareness of problems in the field of sex and a capacity to think constructively and without embarrassment; (2) to place sex in its biological and socio-psychological setting in the growth of the child to maturity; (3) to orient teachers to agency participation in child and family welfare work; (4) to relate sex education to delinquency, public health, and control of venereal disease; (5) to present problems of teaching and administration related to classroom methods and development of curriculum.

In the extracurricular phase of school work such activities as dancing, music, swimming, hiking, excursions, dramatics, and art contribute to sex education through joint planning of activities by both sexes and the human relationships involved in executing these plans. These are the laboratories for democratic living.

Joint work of schools with agencies and special groups such as child-guidance centers, clinics, nurseries, social-welfare groups, psychiatrists, psychologists, pediatricians, and other specialists can contribute immensely to sex education.

The Special-Course Method. The second method of sex education, the special-course method, has been tried in a number of places but perhaps most extensively in Pittsburgh. The application of this method began in Pittsburgh as an experiment during World War II. At this time, the superintendent of schools called a meeting of representatives of religious groups, the parent-teacher association, the juvenile court, the Allegheny County Medical Association, the child guidance clinic, the Department of Public Health, and the Department of Curriculum Study of the Pittsburgh schools to review the problems of health and sex delinquency. An outline of work was drawn up and later plans for administering it were presented and approved.

The school system took on the major portion of responsibility in administering the instruction. Teachers were carefully selected in each school to conduct the courses. Today segregated classes of twenty to thirty students are organized for six-week sessions in the ninth and twelfth grades. No tests, examinations, assignments, or credits are given, and no visitors are allowed in the classes. At the end of six weeks a physician brings the medical point of view into the classroom and attempts to answer all questions unanswered by the teacher. Students are admitted by parental permit only. To date 97 per cent of the parents have signed permits for the courses.

Students are unanimous in their appreciation of this opportunity for unbiased and complete sex instruction. Much of the success of the program is due to the community support gained by a proper launching and to careful selection of teachers, small classes, an informal approach to the classes, assistance from the medical profession, and the short period of time required for the course.

The special-course approach may be necessary in some school centers before the integrated plan can be operated at the secondary level, since teachers feel the need for additional knowledge and methods of teaching the subject. Perhaps more colleges and universities will offer these opportunities not only to teachers already in service but also to recruits in training who require such orientation.

COLLEGE LEVEL

Colleges and universities are giving increased attention to the problems of home and family living and social hygiene. In addition to short courses in sex education, such special courses as preparation for marriage, family life, parenthood, and prenatal care are being offered with increasing frequency. The need for such courses at the college level is demonstrated by the fact that the majority of young people have received little or no sex education from their parents or in elementary or high school. Most of their knowledge has been derived from books or from contemporaries. Attitudes toward marriage and parenthood developed early in life are not easily changed by one or two college courses or even by the accepted mores of the student-age group, although the latter are more effective than the former in influencing behavior. Frequently the need is not information so much as insight, understanding, and techniques of social control in the relationships with parents, sweethearts, or offspring.

In a study of the sources of sex education conducted at Cornell University with 364 juniors and seniors, it was found that about half had received a major part of their sex instruction directly from their parents. Mothers had assumed more responsibility for the sex education than fathers had; in only 10 per cent of the cases had parents shared this responsibility. Brothers and sisters were sources of sex instruction in only 5 per cent and 8 per cent respectively.

Even though 10 per cent of the college groups checked "both parents" as the source of their own sex information, 70 per cent of the group thought "both parents" should be responsible for the sex education of their children. Such facts, along with a recent public-opinion poll, may well indicate that the public may be more favorably disposed toward sex education in the schools and colleges.

Colleges and universities can do a great deal in instructing young people about better home and family living, better health and human relations, more definite planning for homemaking as a career. Here in an adequate social-hygiene program the students may learn what constitutes good stock and how it can be maintained. Education can point up the meaning of inheritance not only as a moral and social responsibility to society but also in mating to realize the highest ideals of love and personality. Young people can be made to feel pride in their families and to give more serious consideration to prospective mates when they plan to marry.

Topics for further thought:

1. The family, the school, and the church shoulder the responsibility for training the child so that he will become a sexually adjusted adult. Discuss specifically, as well as generally, how this task can be most successfully accomplished by these three institutions.

2. Explain the effects a double standard may have upon the two sexes with reference to ideas and behavior regarding marriage.

Selected reading references

de Schweinitz, Karl, *Growing Up,* New York, The Macmillan Company, 1953.
> An excellent little book for use both by parents and children. Illustrated.

Kirkendall, Lester A., *Helping Children Understand Sex,* Chicago, Science Research Associates.
> A *Better Living Booklet* designed for counselors, teachers, and parents to aid them in working with children.

Kirkendall, Lester A., *Understanding Sex,* Chicago, Science Research Associates.
> A *Life Adjustment Booklet* designed for boys and girls in high school.

Schultz, Gladys D., *It's Time You Knew,* Philadelphia, J. B. Lippincott Company, 1955.
> Brings a mother's interest and understanding to the problems of giving girls the necessary information about the physical and emotional aspects of sex. Stresses how the mind and emotions must be taught to keep pace with a developing body.

Strain, Frances B., *Teen Days,* New York, Appleton-Century Company, 1946.
> Written for young teen-agers from twelve to sixteen years of age. Deals with their problems of sexual and social adjustment.

35 MASTURBATION

Lester W. Dearborn

Since the beginnings of the study of the sex life of man, no other subject has been more frequently discussed, no other practice more roundly condemned and more universally practiced than masturbation. Masturbation is any self-excitation of the genital organs, through manipulation or friction, for the pleasure involved and for the release of tension.

ATTITUDES AND MISCONCEPTIONS

What was the probable origin of the old ideas and taboos regarding masturbation? The knowledge may help to set at rest the feeling that "where there is smoke there must be fire." Many people feel there must have been a reason for the belief that masturbation resulted in harm, or otherwise the impression would not have prevailed.

When people lived in tribes that fought with other tribes, group survival was of paramount importance. The elders of the tribe considered it a social sin to waste sperm by any practice that did not procreate children. The spill of spermatozoa by Onan (which in the past has been erroneously referred to as masturbation) came under tribal interdict. The condemnation did not occur because of the loss of an easily renewable supply of spermatozoa, but rather because of Onan's antisocial attitude in refusing to father offspring.

The attitudes expressed during the twenty-two centuries from Hippocrates to the 1890's bear definite similarities in their obvious ignorance of body structure, causation of disease, lack of objectivity, and almost complete absence of a scientific approach to this subject.

From the 1890's to the beginning of World War I was a period of transition. During this period came a growing interest in psychiatry, the beginnings of the movement for preventive medicine, and an emphasis on the need for a scientific approach to the study of cause and result. While the notion still persisted that masturbation might cause insanity and that it was without doubt a harmful practice, glimpses appear of a more enlightened attitude. Many insisted that the practice might be more widespread and less harmful than had been believed. For the most part, however, these pleadings for an enlightened attitude were greatly overshadowed by the persisting influence of Tissot in France, who blasted the eighteenth-century world by his *Onana, A Treatise on the Diseases Produced by Onanism.* This book is steeped in ignorance and personal bias. Tissot could not be expected to have known the nature of semen or of the male sex hormones. He could, however, have exercised intelligence in the deductions he made from the available facts. Tissot's book went through numerous editions and was translated into several languages. It became the main source book of those who felt impelled to write about the viciousness of "self-abuse." About this time, or in 1763, an anonymous English contemporary published a booklet about tabes dorsalis, or locomotor ataxia, one cause of which he said was "the immoderate loss of so pure a fluid as the semen." Tissot agreed with him and spoke of the preciousness of the seminal fluid, the loss of one ounce of which enfeebled one more than the loss of forty ounces of blood. For these beliefs there was not, of course, the slightest scientific evidence.

Tissot attributed most of the known disorders of his day to the loss of semen; he added a few new ones born of his own observation. He accepted a statement that he had known "simple gonorrhea, dropsy, and consumption to depend on the same cause." The appalling liberties which Tissot took with scientific fact are emphasized best by his contention that sexual relations were apt to cause epileptic fits, the belief being that "coitus is a kind of epilepsy," considering the "orgasm as a convulsive symptom." Such statements, born of the man's imagination, caused immeasurable suffering for generations to follow. One effect credited to masturbation, which has been more persistently believed in than any of the others, is that masturbation caused insanity. As if Tissot had not done enough to cripple man's mind with fear, Rozier, writing fifty years after the seventh edition of Tissot's work, added insanity to Tissot's list. By 1839 the belief that masturbation caused insanity was well rooted.

In 1839 a Dr. M. S. Gove published her work, *Solitary Vice,* in which she quoted the sixth report of the State Lunatic Hospital at Worcester, Massachusetts, to the effect that masturbation was "third in point of power to deprive its victim of reason." Beginning with Gove appear admissions by various authors of the universality of the practice; at the same time attempts were not made to explain why the dire consequences which they ascribed to masturbation did not manifest themselves in every case. Gove unconsciously hinted at the naturalness of masturbation in the statement that the greater part of those who communicated with her on the subject had not been taught to masturbate and did not know that anyone else did. At another point she unwittingly intimated that worry was responsible for the symptoms supposedly caused by masturbation itself.

In 1840 an anonymous writer took issue with previous authorities, contending that the disorders attributed to masturbation were not caused directly by it. He declared that they had *no proof* that they were so caused. Here was the first demand for a scientific approach to the whole subject. In the next sentence the writer slipped back into the old groove and described what he considered the one and only disorder due to masturbation, namely dementia praecox or schizophrenia.

Dr. E. T. Brady in 1891 was one of the first to question the part that masturbation was supposed to play in the causation of insanity. While he seemed to have no doubt about the perniciousness of the practice, he did state, "But it is very probable that its importance as an influence has been greatly exaggerated, particularly in connection with the causation of insanity." Modern marriage counselors are still having to deal with the heritage of belief and a carry-over of the old taboos.

In a paper published in 1888 in *Medical News,* Lawson Tait, one of the leading gynecologists of his time, adopted a rather wholesome attitude toward masturbation and sex education. He said, "It is a sad misfortune that all sexual questions are so completely hidden from children at puberty." Apparently he had no doubt that there were evil effects from masturbation, but he raised a serious question as to what those evil effects might be. He was among the first to try to divorce religious morality from a condition that he considered merely physical. He seemed to feel there might be some harm in masturbation so far as the male was concerned, although he said, "The evil effects of masturbation have been greatly overrated." In women he questioned whether or not it was carried on to such an extent as to do any harm. He admitted that there were few boys who failed to masturbate at some time, but he felt the practice was comparatively rare among girls. In this he reflected the attitude of that period, when many considered that females were lacking in passion since they felt they had no need for it. This concept of female sexuality was not exploded until investigators gathered convincing statistics to the contrary at a relatively recent date.

In 1907 Dr. Frederick Sturgis attempted to make a study of the frequency of masturbation without any consideration of its supposed evils or disabling sequelae. His admittedly conservative estimate was that 60 per cent of both sexes masturbate at some time in their lives, but he held that were the whole truth known the figure would be nearer 90 per cent.

The writings of three men have probably had more direct influence upon the thinking and behavior in this country in the last half century than have those of any other writers, largely because their books when published bore the stamp of authority and were generally approved by religious leaders, educators, and social workers. The books of G. Stanley Hall, Winfield Scott Hall, and Sylvanus Stall have probably, in the past, been on the bookshelves in more homes and schools and public libraries than is presently true of modern treatises on the subject. The influence of this last writer has been particularly bad because of the absence of any scientific approach to the subject and the wholly emotional manner in which it was handled. Stall said: "No boy can toy with the exposed portions of his reproductive system without finally suffering very serious consequences." He favored sex education, but in this matter it was with the thought of saving boys from these terrible consequences. He said: "Nothing so much favors the continuance and spread of this awful vice as ignorance, and only by being early and purely taught on this important subject can the coming boys and men be saved from the awful consequences which are ruining morally, mentally, and physically thousands of boys every year." After lecturing on the moral aspects of the subject he tells us that the next to suffer is the nervous system. "In the act of masturbation the nerves are wrought upon in such a manner as to produce most serious results." Then in addition to the mental and moral changes which are supposed to have taken place he details the dreadful physical results.

Stall's chapter on "Self-Abuse" has been quoted because he does not produce one iota of scientific evidence to substantiate any of his statements, yet his influence and that of others like him is still affecting the emotional lives of thousands of people at the present time.

The influence of Freud, the whole psychoanalytic school, and Havelock Ellis more than anyone else have made sexology a godchild of medicine. More specifically for contributions on this subject credit is given to Bernard, Bigelow, Davis, Hamilton, Kinsey, Kirkpatrick, Popenoe, and others.

Two trends are manifest in the literature on masturbation. The first trend is a tendency to consider masturbation in any form, under any circumstances, and with any frequency completely harmless. The writers holding this view knew that the sequelae attributed to it by preceding generations were groundless. Their newly acquired objectivity taught them to view the matter in a different light, to observe that much of animal life masturbates when deprived of any other outlet for its sexual drive. Hence they assumed it to be completely harmless.

The second trend has developed from students interested in psychiatry and psychoanalysis. They began to see new dangers in the practice, such as fixations, repressions, psychoneuroses, maladjustment to the sexual phase of marriage, and other mental effects. Many of these dangers have since been proved false; many are in the process of being so proved. Many of our present writings are still being influenced by the thought that we must not go too far in releasing restrictions lest we encourage complete abandonment, which may lead to possible if not definable untoward results. However, there is a growing accumulation of modern literature which frankly reveals the truth.

What of the prevalence of masturbation? Tissot stated one reason for writing his book was that the practice was so general. Almost without exception, particularly so far as boys were concerned, authors of treatises on this subject have expressed the belief that if it was not universal it was a habit indulged in by the majority of males. (The study of masturbation in females did not come until much later.) Sylvanus Stall said: "I wish I might say to you that but very few have ever known of this vice, but I do not believe that such an assertion would be true." In other words, he, too, accepted that it was pretty generally practiced. It is the one thing about which these early authors were right as proved by studies by W. L. Hughes, Peck and Wells, W. S. Taylor, Kinsey, Exner, Lilburn Merrill, and Dickinson and Beam.

As to the prevalence of masturbation, all of the studies that have been carried on by competent investigators under well-credentialed auspices indicate that well over 90 per cent of all males have had a history of masturbation. While these studies vary somewhat in exactness, running anywhere from 90 per cent to 98 per cent, a study by Kinsey sets the figure at 94+ per cent. There will be little disagreement with this figure on the part of modern students of the subject. In 1929 Dr. Katharine Davis published her study of college women wherein she reported admitted masturbation by 65 per cent of them. Since for most of them to admit masturbation was a matter of confession, 10 per cent might easily be added as a factor of error, as other studies, notably Hamilton's and the present writer's, indicate that the figure among females runs somewhere between 75 per cent and 80 per cent for single women who have reached the age of twenty-five, while Kinsey reports "about 62 per cent of all the females in the sample have masturbated sometime or other during the course of their lives." In both sexes the frequency of the experience varies greatly, but the average single woman will report masturbation from two to three times a month, particularly just before or after her menstrual period, whereas the average single male reports two or three times a week. The Hamilton report shows 49 per cent reported masturbation three or more times a week, and the Kinsey study shows 46 per cent of males who report a frequency of from one to six times weekly or more.

If the histories of men and women who had reached the age of twenty-five were taken from all the studies to date, they would show (1) that masturbation has played a part in the lives of more than 90 per cent of all males and about 70 per cent of all females, with the frequency running from once or twice a month up to several times a week, and (2) that no evidence exists to prove that the greater frequency was any more productive of harm than the lesser.

Since all of this is generally accepted by professional students of the sex life it is a dereliction of responsibility not to bring these facts to the attention of millions of people who could profit by the knowledge. Today two worlds exist—one in which the normality of occasional masturbation for release of tension and for the physical and emotional satisfactions involved is accepted, and the other, a larger world (though admittedly it is growing smaller), in which there is a persistence of the old ideas based on the dogma of the past. That the past still influences present-day thinking on this subject is borne out by a statement made by Dr. Maurice Levine, who says that one misconception is that masturbation causes psychoses.

This is a misconception which has been exceedingly harmful and one which is extraordinarily persistent. In spite of the mental-hygiene teaching of the past fifteen or twenty years, many parents and doctors still believe such incorrect ideas, and still punish and threaten children who masturbate. One child-guidance clinic found recently that about 75 per cent of the parents of its child-patients remembered having threatened the children with the dangers of masturbation. It is important that physicians know that this is a mistake; many still do not.

In overcoming this problem in the larger sense the truth must be told in expressions that do not indicate the bias and prejudice begotten of early training. It is of little avail to try to release a person's fears by admitting the normality of the practice and denying that it has any unhealthy consequences, while at the same time showing a distaste by using such words as, "It isn't nice," "Well-adjusted young people find better things to do," "You should give your attention to more constructive things," and similar condemnations. All such statements are vague, without meaning, and just as productive of emotional conflict as were the consequences attributed to masturbation in the past.

In many instances the feeling of improperness concerning the practice has an untoward effect on personality adjustment which, if not as drastic as were the fears of the past, was definitely unwholesome in its result. Every marriage counselor has met innumerable instances in which the conflict over masturbation and its possible consequences has had a profound result in the lack of sex adjustment in marriage. In personal guidance, counselors run across many cases in which worry over masturbation has been a major factor in maladjustment because of feelings of inadequacy and attitudes of self-condemnation. Whenever a person has not been particularly concerned about physical or mental consequences the very thought that the practice indicated a lack of character development still led to self-castigation and to unwholesome sex attitudes.

MASTURBATION IN INFANCY

Curiosity is a wholesome attribute in the infant. It is natural for the baby to become acquainted with his own body before attempting an extensive exploration of the outside world. In the infant's first half year he will discover his genitals in much the same way that he becomes aware of the existence of fingers and toes. The parent does not need to worry about this practice becoming a habit, for as the baby's awareness grows, he will examine with the same healthy curiosity his widening environment.

The baby may be distracted with a toy if the parent wishes, but this diversion is not necessary. The parent does not want to give the infant the idea that he is naughty or that his genitals are bad. It is important for the growing child to retain a wholesome and natural feeling about his entire body. If extensive attention is drawn to any part of the child's body, he may become preoccupied with it with undesirable effects later on. Any attempt at preventing this natural exploration may result in the child's determining to explore secretly and furtively.

MASTURBATION IN CHILDHOOD

During the ages from three to six there is an early stirring of sexual feeling. Children are physically affectionate and are sociable with people of all ages. They exhibit interest in each other's bodies and occasionally wish to touch or to see them. All this is an important part of normal development.

If the parent discovers the child engaged in sex play by himself or with others, he must check the impulse to show anger or disapproval. Often the child will turn of his own accord to another activity if he is discovered in self or group examination. The parent can suggest some other form of activity in a cheerful tone if his appearance has not checked the child's exploration. During periods of interest in sex a parent may plan activities so that the child and his friends will have plenty of outside occupations. While it is a good idea during this time to have some knowledge of the child's whereabouts and activities (aside from normal parental anxiety), the child should not be made to feel that he is doing anything unusual. Some children will be upset about things their companions do and say. This feeling will be heightened by the presence of older children with misleading information or unhealthy attitudes. The parent should counteract any false facts that the child might learn.

In the event that the child does seem to be preoccupied with his genitals in more than the normal, healthy fashion, the parents should make an attempt to discover the underlying cause of this masturbation. Excessive interest in masturbation may be caused by a physical condition such as adherent tissue or some other irritation that draws the child's attention to his genitals. In that case the physician will correct the condition. If, however, the physician finds that all is normal, the parents should seek to find the underlying psychological cause. Any attempt to correct the symptom without discovering the cause will undoubtedly result in greater tension and make matters worse. In a case of this sort, the parents would be wise to consult a child specialist.

MASTURBATION IN ADOLESCENCE

Masturbation is common as an adolescent practice in both sexes, with all evidence pointing to the fact that there is a higher percentage among males than among females. There is every indication, however, that at the age of fifteen at least 50 per cent of the girls have masturbated and that the percentage increases as the group gets older; there are many more girls masturbating at the age of nineteen or twenty than were doing so in their middle teens. All that can be said about the harmlessness of masturbation in the earlier period can be repeated here. It is true, however, that masturbation itself is likely to take on a somewhat different meaning to the adolescent, as each experience becomes an episode in itself, leading to orgasm, unless this climax is definitely suppressed or inhibited. It is also a psychological as well as a physiological act, as fantasy is a component part of the experience. It is desirable for fantasy construction to be a part of the act; this may make a more complete autoerotic experience, encouraging easier and more successful transition to heterosexual relations than the masturbation which is purely sensory and without imagery.

There is great variety in the reported content of fantasies. Whatever it is, it consists of use of the imagination concerning sexual experience, intensifying the erotism to the point of orgasm. This can be a satisfying experience; it can help to relieve emotional tensions, and it effectively concentrates the sexual sensations in the genital area where they should be located, this being an effect especially to be desired in the female. If fear has not been engendered in the young person's mind he will quickly pass from such an episode to other life activities without particular concern, making the experience helpful and relatively unimportant. Unfortunately, because of the teachings of the past, thousands of young people still find themselves unable to pass from such an experience without deep feelings of anxiety. Consciousness of guilt, feelings of sin, and fear of consequences are the crippling sequelae of those who live in this second world. Thus the feelings of inferiority and self-condemnation, plus the anticipation of eventual harmful consequences, carry over into adult life and often adversely affect the chance for good sex adjustment. Happily, however, the type of sexual incompatibility in marriage which springs from this cause can be eliminated by proper education; this would also be true where it has been a factor in personality maladjustment.

Much credit for the successful application of modern psychology to the problem of masturbation should go to Dr. Walter F. Robie of Baldwinsville, Massachusetts, whose books, *Rational Sex Ethics, The Art of Love,* and *Sex and Life,* first emphasized the modern point of view in this field.

METHODS AND CONSEQUENCES

The physical structure of the male does not admit of a great deal of variety in masturbatory practice, and it is usually accomplished manually. However, some variations are reported, such as making coital movements against the bedclothes, or using a pillow for the purpose, or pressing against objects.

In the girl, however, because her construction permits it, there is considerable variation. While it appears that the use of the finger on the clitoris is the most usual form, running a close second is what has been referred to as thigh-rubbing, in which the girl presses her thighs together or crosses her legs and squeezes the inner muscles of her thighs, thus bringing pressure on the labia and incidentally on the clitoris. At this she may become quite skillful and can prolong the experience or bring herself to orgasm at will. Many girls who use this method, however, report that they stop short of. orgasm. This may be due to the fact that thigh-rubbing is often used as a substitute after admonition by the parent who has observed some digital exploration. A frequent statement of older girls and women is that they remember having been told, "Don't you ever let me catch you touching yourself again." A household term for masturbation is "playing with oneself"; this often develops a concept in the mind of the child that the harm lies in hand contact. The girl, therefore, can indulge in thigh-rubbing with less consciousness of guilt because she is not "playing with herself."

Other methods are also reported, such as pulling panties, nightgown, pajamas, the bed sheet, or other materials tightly between the thighs, then making motions that excite the clitoris. Instrumental masturbation, that of putting something in the vagina, is not as often reported as some of these other methods.

Some forms of masturbation may act as a drawback to marriage adjustment, not because of any harm in the behavior itself, but because the transition from a particular form of masturbation to acquiring satisfactions in intercourse may later become difficult. Girls have reported that they pass from clitoral stimulation to manipulation of the whole vulva, with emphasis upon stimulation of the vaginal orifice, and very quickly make an adjustment to coitus; they often reported that they have orgasm at the first experience or shortly thereafter. Those who for a number of years have used only the clitoris find it more difficult to make such a transition, but where they have been relieved of guilt feelings and have a co-operative and skillful husband such an adjustment will likely be made sometime within the first six months. Those girls who have denied themselves the direct form of masturbation and have used substitutive measures, such as various forms of pressure, or breast rubbing, often force themselves to stop just prior to orgasm because they have developed a fear of the orgasm, having conceived the idea that the wrong or harm lies in the release itself. In such cases, or in any case where orgasm has been suppressed, they may have developed a habit of nonresponse and carry this over into their marital relations, later to report that they have little or no satisfaction in coitus and an inability to come to a climax. In discouraging a form of direct masturbation in children one may be unwittingly encouraging a substitutive form which acts as a deterrent to achieving orgasm in intercourse. Also, the guilt feeling that caused a girl to withdraw from direct fondling of her own organs is likely also to cause her to resist manual stimulation on the part of the husband in his attempts at precoital excitation.

The male who has masturbated with a sense of guilt which has driven him to get it over with as soon as possible and to suppress any accompanying fantasy is likely in consequence to find himself bothered in early marriage by premature ejaculation. The one who has engaged in masturbation reservatus, delaying the orgasm at will, has thus prepared himself to be a more adequate partner by having developed a technique that makes it possible for him to stay with his wife as long as it is necessary for her satisfaction.

SUMMARY

Every sex-education program should include information concerning the normality of masturbation; this should be given to adults as well as to youth because it is through misinformed adults that the old superstitions are perpetuated. The kind of statement to make and stand by should be something as follows: "Masturbation, according to the best medical authorities, causes no harm physically or mentally. Any harm resulting from masturbation is caused entirely by worry or by a sense of guilt due to misinformation."

Topics for further thought:

1. Masturbation appears to be usual among young children, yet our societal values disapprove of attaining sexual pleasure in this way—even for the young. Comment upon this.

2. Masturbation continued on into adulthood is believed to affect the adjustment an individual makes. Discuss this.

Selected reading references

Hohman, Leslie B., and Schaffner, Bertram, "The Sex Lives of Unmarried Men," *American Journal of Sociology*, May, 1947, pp. 501-7. Report of a study of 4600 army draftees from the New York and Baltimore areas. Includes masturbation and other types of sexual activity.

Hunnicutt, C. W., *Answering Children's Questions*, New York, Bureau of Publications, Teachers College, Columbia University, 1949. An inexpensive booklet for parents and teachers that fosters a sound philosophy of sex education.

Kinsey, Alfred C., Pomeroy, Wardell B., and Martin, Clyde, *Sexual Behavior in the Human Male,* Philadelphia, W. B. Saunders Company, 1948.

See Chapter 14, pp. 497-516, for data on patterns of masturbation. For further annotation of this volume see References at end of Chapter 11.

Kinsey, Alfred C., Pomeroy, Wardell B., Martin, Clyde, and Gebhard, Paul H., *Sexual Behavior in the Human Female,* Philadelphia, W. B. Saunders Company, 1953.

See Chapter 5, pp. 132-90, for data on masturbation among women. For further annotation of this volume, see References at end of Chapter 11.

Kirkendall, Lester, "Sound Attitudes toward Sex," *Journal of Social Hygiene,* pp. 241-51.

Stresses the importance of using the new freedom to discuss sex matters to develop positive attitudes.

36 PREPARATION FOR MARRIAGE IN ADOLESCENCE

Katharine Whiteside Taylor

Puberty and adolescence are of unique importance in laying groundwork for really satisfying marital adjustments. There was real wisdom in the ceremonies among primitive peoples that emphasized the great significance of puberty as the dramatic period during which the individual changes from child to young adult. Although the process continues until the child is twenty or thereabouts, puberty as the entry into this important period should really be welcomed rather than ignored or even hidden, as is still too often the case.

THE ROLE OF THE PARENT

Parents often bemoan the fact that young adulthood is approaching, saying, "Isn't it too bad! We are losing our little girl. If only we could keep her sweet and innocent," or "We are keeping our son so busy he won't have time to think about girls. We don't want him to grow up too fast." It is hard for parents to give up the satisfactions of having little children to love and be dependent upon them. But if parents want to help them to the joys of genuine maturity they should look forward to the deeper satisfactions of companionship with mature sons and daughters. They should be able to say with honest enthusiasm, "Isn't it wonderful to have a young woman (or man) in the house! It is so much nicer than when she (or he) was a child. We are proud she (or he) is growing up."

The importance of this cannot be overemphasized. During pubescence and the beginning of adolescence, often continuing for several years, the young person is in the throes of a real conflict within himself about whether it is really better to go on to the greater freedom and joy but greater demands of adulthood or sink back into the easier requirements and safer, well-tried ways of childhood. This struggle may in times of stress be severe. The joys of childhood were very real and what was required of one so much less. Yet in wholesome youngsters the urge toward maturity is strong and will win out if not impeded by undue desires in parents to prolong the joys of having a child look to them alone for guidance and for love.

Even the most understanding and freedom-giving parents may be temporarily rejected during this period of struggle for autonomy and self-direction. Just being near parents during these conflicts is likely to make the young person feel *little,* like a child again, since for many fulfilling years he or she has been their little child. If the parents still derive major satisfactions from keeping their adolescents dependent and in the little-child role psychologically, the young person's revolt must be stronger to save his emerging maturity from destruction or impairment. The wise role for parents then is to accept signs of temporary rejection by adolescents as a normal, even wholesome sign of maturation and give all the leeway to independence consistent with the young person's safety and that of others. With reasonably reliable youngsters this leeway is apt to be wider than most parents tend to realize, and the only way a person's judgment can grow is through independent exercise.

Further, parents must be ready to allow their young adults to do more and more as well as to decide more and more on their own. Teen-agers should also be encouraged to contribute to the home in ways appropriate to their new status. For instance, instead of *helping* get dinner, a teen-ager should be permitted to get it entirely on her own. If a mother is sufficiently mature not to see this as competition for prestige through good cooking, she will welcome such a contribution. So will a father who is really secure in himself welcome his son's wish to take over the full responsibility of caring for the family car instead of just washing it on Saturday afternoon. And such opportunities for accepting more and more responsibility are highly valuable for the young adult, not only for developing his independent abilities, but also in promoting growth toward the true adulthood essential for sustaining marriage.

The opportunity and capacity to contribute in thought and effort in ways recognized as valuable by important persons, including parents, are basic in the young person's establishing the feelings of autonomy and self-worth which underlie healthy growth of personality. While the seeds of these attributes must be sown from earliest childhood on, the onset of puberty brings these growing capacities a new chance to flower.

Until physiological maturity has been reached, the child must be chiefly on the receiving side. The growing body needs to absorb large amounts of food just for building tissue. When maturity has been reached much energy is released for constructive work and creative activity. In like manner, the growing personality must receive an abundance of love, appreciation, and response to grow into even the beginnings of maturity. If growth has progressed wholesomely, puberty marks the point when real love and interest in others outside the family can begin. If parents are to be ready to welcome puberty and help their boys and girls welcome it as a happy step in progress toward maturity and capacity for marriage, they must understand the signs that indicate the process has begun.

RECOGNITION OF MATURATION IN ADOLESCENCE

Since girls reach puberty on an average between eleven and thirteen and boys between twelve and fourteen, some of the internal and external changes may be starting as early as nine in some girls and ten in some boys. The onset of the cycle, however, may start as much as three or four years later for either sex and still be within the normal range.

At the beginning of the cycle there is usually a slowing down of growth, followed by a rapid spurt just before puberty, followed again by a slowing down until physical growth becomes complete. But growth does not proceed evenly in all parts of the body. For example, bones grow more rapidly than muscle tissue, producing the typically awkward length of arms and legs of early adolescence, causing the individual to look ungainly, knock things over, and perhaps even stumble about just when he or she is beginning to be really interested in making a good impression. Differentials in rate of growth also make for temporary disharmony in features. A typical adolescent worry is over a nose that grows out of all proportion to the rest of the face. Added to this, the reorganization of the glandular system often causes pimples, blackheads, and scraggly hair, adding extra complications to the problems of pleasing appearance. Then when the boy's voice starts squeaking unexpectedly and doing other strange things, he is apt to feel he has all the trials there are. Parents who understand what is going on and who welcome the fact their son or daughter is maturing can help the youngster also to an acceptance of, possibly even a cheery attitude toward, the discomforts that mean he or she is becoming a young adult. One boy, for instance, was encouraged to keep tabs with a friend across the street on how many times their voices cracked in an hour. They then laughingly compared notes.

The reorganization of the glandular system often makes for swings in mood and energy level which the whole family needs to understand. Bursts of energy and enthusiasm may be offset by periods of slowing down to the point of being what is called lazy. These sloweddown spells need to be respected, as they are Nature's way of protecting the growing organism from overfatigue. There may be extra strain also because of the fact that all the organs do not grow at the same rate. Indeed, at certain periods heart and lungs may not yet be large enough to carry with ease the new size and length of the body. There may be frequent swings in mood and erratic behavior which are often more difficult to accept than the fluctuations in energy. The young adult may find it decidedly difficult to live with himself. Part of him is eager to grow up, to accept adult responsibility and the normal satisfactions of adult life, including marriage and all it means. Yet the part that is still a child may be frightened at the demands of adulthood and particularly frightened at the thought of sex. The fact that his or her own body is no longer that of a child, but capable of full sex response, may be frightening if the surrounding atmosphere either at home or in the neighborhood has held attitudes that sex is wicked and shameful.

Particularly important for future marital happiness is understanding and acceptance by these young persons of the development of their own sex organs, the appearance of secondary sex characteristics, and the evidence that their capacity to become parents has begun. Serious emotional problems often include shock at the first nocturnal emission or menstruation. One girl who had not been prepared and whose grandmother was dying of cancer, seeing blood on her own underclothing, lay for hours sick with fear that she also was dying of cancer, while all the adults in the family were too busy with the grandmother's needs to notice hers.

Education on reproduction should be given in answer to questions, from the earliest years of childhood on, and if no questions are asked parents should make opportunity to explain, using some of the books now available for parents and also for children.

Girls should be aware of the fact that while menstruation typically occurs monthly there is individual variation even at maturity, and usually considerable irregularity during the first few years, until the function is thoroughly established; also, that the capacity to reproduce is usually not present until several years after the first menstruation. Moreover, girls today should not be burdened with the idea that one is unwell at that time, or that menstruation is a curse which makes one miserable. Indeed, girls and women who have happy, accepting attitudes toward their role as women may actually feel a heightening of energy and well-being during the menstrual period.

Boys should understand that girls may have to refrain from swimming and violent exercise at that time and may need a little extra consideration.

Boys need particularly to understand why they have nocturnal emissions. They may be told that they carry the sperm cells which must be carried over into the mother's body to join with the ovum in hers to form a baby. These are carried in a fluid called semen. But this is not needed until they are ready to become fathers; therefore, from time to time it passes out of the body, not regularly as with girls, but whenever there is a sufficient accumulation.

The young adult should feel he can talk freely to his parents about these problems. The emotions and attitudes parents bring to such discussions are really more important than the words they say. Many parents have hang-overs of unwholesome attitudes from their childhood. They should consciously weed out such attitudes and supplant them with the realization of the deep beauty and sacredness of love between a man and a woman, the creative power which brings new life into the world. One of the best ways to do this, perhaps, is to read aloud together some materials on the subject and, if possible, to attend good lectures in order to be ready to talk it over casually as occasion makes possible in an atmosphere of naturalness and relaxation.

In spite of the fact that relationships change, the relationship between parents and adolescents is fundamental to successful living and in laying the groundwork for happy marriage. In the penetrating study, *Predicting Success or Failure in Marriage,* by Burgess and Cottrell, there were two factors in the histories of happily married people twice as important as any other: a warm sustaining relationship of children with their own parents and of the parents with each other.

CHANGES IN RELATIONSHIP BETWEEN PARENT AND ADOLESCENT

If parents are to be of genuine help, they must understand the normal changes in their own relationship to their adolescent son or daughter, and of the young person's relationships to groups and persons outside the home. In spite of the young person's growing need for independence and his or her tendency to reject both parents for a time, soon after puberty the young adult normally draws close to the parent of the opposite sex, sensing new meaning in the relationship. For a short time, indeed, some of the closeness of infancy may be reactivated. Parents whose own needs are not adequately met may tend to seize on this response and cling to it. This would tend to impede the young adult's maturation.

The Daughter. The daughter becomes increasingly aware of her father and sensitive to his smile and warmth or to his aloofness and disapproval. It is particularly important for a father to understand and accept his daughter's increasing femininity appreciatively. By so doing he builds up her sense of security and feeling of worth. Girls who are secure in their fathers' love and appreciation, yet feel free to develop friendships outside the home, seldom get into sex difficulties. Indeed, serious sex misdemeanors in girls are often found to be a result of insecurity, especially in their relationships with their fathers. As she draws toward her father, the girl is likely for a time to draw away from her mother, resent her suggestions, and even see her as a rival for the attentions of the father. And if the mother is not quite secure as a woman she may resent this new contestant for feminine supremacy in the home.

The daughter is likely to seek feminine ideals in teachers and others outside the home. As she becomes more mature, however, she will turn back to her mother in a new relationship based on real equality which may be deeply satisfying to them both. This happens best where the mother is secure and happy in her own life so that she does not feel rejected and can give her daughter the freedom she needs. A mother who is truly fulfilled as a woman, both in her home and in her community contacts, is most helpful in providing her daughter with a picture of adulthood worth striving for.

The Son. In early adolescence the son tends to draw toward his mother and feels devoted to her in a new way. To a certain extent he relives some of the closeness he felt during infancy. At this time it is particularly necessary for mothers to lead truly fulfilling lives lest they prolong this precious period unduly. It is particularly difficult for unhappy mothers wholeheartedly to approve of their sons' becoming interested in other feminine persons, as they must do if they are to become real men.

At this time also the boy is likely to develop strong antagonism toward his father and to seek masculine patterns outside the home, which is the counterpart of the girl's behavior. And fathers who are not quite secure in their capacity for evoking love may also resent this potent rival for masculine supremacy in the family. A new and deeper understanding and real friendship may be established, however, when the young man has gained full emotional independence.

The boy in one way has an even bigger job of emancipation than the girl, since it is he who must make the living for his future family. The girl in most instances will not need to attain economic independence before she is considered marriageable. It is equally essential, however, for both sexes to become completely freed from childlike dependence upon parents, not only in capabilities and independent judgment, but also from the need to lean upon them emotionally. This emotional emancipation must go two ways to be complete. Parents must be ready to give up dependence upon children for their major satisfactions. Having real fulfillment in marriage and as persons with going lives of their own is the best insurance that the new freedom can be a two-way street.

THE CHILD'S INTEREST IN HIS OWN SEX

As the young adult passes through the stage of attachment to the parent of the opposite sex his main focus shifts for a time to primary interest in his own sex. The first phase is typically a strong sense of group belonging. Out of this group attachment there usually emerges a deep friendship with a member of the same sex. This is sometimes called a crush among girls. It should, however, be accepted by parents and all who deal with young adults as a normal and essential part of their growth toward maturity. It is typically far deeper than the easy friendships of childhood and is usually the young adult's first experience of really loving someone outside his own family. It is, therefore, the first chance to sense deeply the feelings and longings of another and is important in deepening the capacity for emotional response. It may or may not include some degree of physical interest in each other. Its value lies in the depth of real feeling involved and the part that it serves simply as one phase of development.

Appreciation of one's own sex has the additional value of helping establish the young adult's sense of identity also essential to the development of a wholesome personality. The feeling that it is fine to be a member of one's own sex, that one can be as valid and important as a person of the opposite sex, is as necessary for self-acceptance as to accept one's race, creed, and family background as worthy and good.

It is a real tragedy for either a boy or a girl to become fixated at what may be termed this homosexual level, however, even though it is a normal phase to pass through. People are said to be fixated at this level, even if they have never had any interest in physical intimacies, if they still find their greatest satisfaction in being with members of their own sex. Unfortunately this is true of some people who have been married for years and may have had several children. But they may have never established a really mature relationship on a give-and-take basis with their marriage partner. There is in such cases a tragic loss of genuine fulfillment in their lives and lack of genuine security for their children.

RECOGNITION OF NORMAL SEX DEVELOPMENT

Two things are necessary if parents are to make sure that their own young adults pass safely through the homosexual phase into a normal focus upon the opposite sex as the chief center of interest. The first is an abundant exposure to attractive members of the opposite sex. The second is a wholesome education not only about the reproductive process, as mentioned earlier, but in attitudes toward the whole of the relationship of the sexes to each other. One very important phase of this is the attitudes expressed by parents toward their own youngsters' first signs of interest in the opposite sex.

One particularly happily married young man related that when he was about sixteen his father said to him, "Well, Henry! I notice you are beginning to slick down your hair and are asking your mother to press your trousers every few days. And I know what that means. You are getting interested in some of those nice girls you meet at school. And I'm glad you are! There is nothing nicer than having a fine time with really lovely girls, and I want you to have your share of it."

Crude manifestations of interest such as risqué pin-up girls and dirty stories may be a good deal harder for parents to take. But they, too, are quite normal manifestations and are a part of the youngster's self-education in getting used to the contours of the opposite sex. If there is excessive interest in dirty stories, however, it usually means that the youngster has not had enough of the right kind of education, or possibly that he is insecure and tries to build himself up by showing off his sophistication.

The first approach to interest in the opposite sex may be distant and tentative, such as groaning at love scenes at movies, writing for pictures of favorite movie stars, and possibly writing letters to members of the opposite sex at long range whom one has not met. One boy, for instance pinned love notes onto the backs of girls' dresses without their knowing who did it.

Just as with members of the same sex, the first major contacts between members of the opposite sex are typically those in groups. Kissing games are a tentative tryout at intimacy, with the whole group there for protection. There is likely to follow, as the youngsters grow up a bit, considerable experimental hand holding, necking, and kissing. It is a normal manifestation, and usually if parents discuss standards of decency with their youngsters there is little danger that they will go too far. Particularly if they feel secure in their parents' love they will tend to accept their standards. Parents who are not prudish or overly severe will keep the channels open for discussion of such matters, which in itself is a good safeguard. As one wise father said when his son started off on a date, "You are lucky to have such a nice girl to take out. Do everything you can to give her a wonderful time. And it doesn't hurt if you neck just a little. Of course you know where to stop, and I can trust you to do it. The wonderful experience of complete intimacy can be had in the right way only in marriage."

As couples begin to pair off, going-steady relationships start. There is a tendency for these to begin too early in many high schools just because it is the vogue. Such relationships should not be established before they can have the meaning of two people really wanting to know and share each other's lives. Also, they tend to limit contacts and development of personality through varied companionship.

When boys and girls are old enough to enter into such relationships seriously (and that is a matter of maturity rather than chronological age) they may grow thereby in their capacity for mature relatedness on a give-and-take basis. Better than frowning upon such relationships, parents would do well to emphasize emotional sincerity, mutual responsibility and growth together as the sound basis for maintaining them.

That warm interest and love between the sexes be accepted and appreciated as valid and good by every adolescent's parents is an important aid and support in his developing capacity for real intimacy, also now recognized as essential for healthy personal growth. It lies at the very heart of a capacity for real friendship, true marriage, and even for the most fructifying parenthood. Yet it is too often damaged by the projection of parental anxiety regarding the dangers of sex onto children at this very point of the young adult's first awakening to the beauty and power of sex love.

The great moment that parents should be ready to understand and accept is when their children really fall in love. When a boy or girl comes in all aglow, saying, "I have met a person I would just die for!" parents should not derisively say, "Oh! That's just puppy love." Even though the object of such affection may not be worthy of it, the important thing is the feeling inside the heart of the boy or girl. It is a tremendous thing to feel one would be willing to give one's life for another person. It is not an emotion of childhood but an initiation into one of the deepest feelings of adulthood. Even though these first loves usually do not last, they are typically very important steps in growth toward real maturity.

One of the times when understanding parents can be of the greatest help is when the young adult is suffering from what is called a broken heart at the cessation of one of these love affairs. Whether it is because the boy or girl has been turned down or has become disillusioned about the quality of his or her love object, the suffering can be some of the most severe in human experience. Particularly if one has been rejected, parents and other wise counselors can help the young person understand the traits in himself and his partner which caused the break, and re-establish his own sense of worth. Such crises, lived through with understanding, can be factors making for the growth of a person of any age toward greater depth, sensitivity, and appreciation of the utter preciousness of love when it is deep and mutual.

When young adults become seriously interested in marriage, parents should make sure that they have access to books on preparation for marriage. The other chapters in the present volume will be of great value to parents wanting to guide their young folk into lasting marital happiness.

Earnest talks between young adults and their parents can add much in clarifying and underlining what is read. It is a great help, for instance, if parents emphasize and exemplify that marriage is a process that continues over the years and grows deeper and more meaningful as understanding and mutual helpfulness increase; that it is not merely a 50-50 proposition but rather a 100-100 enterprise, with each giving everything he has to making it go; that it is even more important to ask, "What am I giving?" than to wonder, "What am I getting?" It may help to bring out further that there is no discipline like the discipline of love for making us grow toward greater maturity. Life offers no greater motivation for the effort involved than the longing to understand and provide for the comfort and joy of the loved person and to deepen the love that is flowing between.

SUMMARY

Nothing is more important from the point of view of successful marriage than growing up emotionally. This means that a person has learned to carry his full share of responsibility in any situation except when ill, to make decisions upon the basis of his own scheme of values and the reality factors in any situation, and to work out a life pattern that carries sufficient fulfillment so that he does not need to exploit others to gain satisfaction. Further, it means that he has a rich and full capaciy for giving sympathy, tenderness, and love to others, at the same time maintaining his integrity. Therefore, the grownup does not need to be always on the receiving end of a relationship, as is a small child, but is equally ready to give. It means further, however, that a person does not need to be always on the giving side to show his superiority, as in the case with some immature folk, but that he can enter into a reciprocal, interdependent relationship where he both gives and receives when that is desirable. Everyone has times when he is tired or ill, when things have gone wrong, when he does not feel very mature. Each one must realize that all people derive joy from helping. One of the best things about real marriage is that each can find real satisfaction both in giving help and love and in receiving them from the loved person.

Genuine maturity means further that a person does not stop at his own front door, but that his love flows out in ever-widening circles to neighbors, community, and world. In the final analysis everyone pours out effort in work, help, and love not primarily for the prestige, recognition, and response that he gets out of it, but for the real joy of giving what he has to give. Obviously, with this definition of maturity, few attain perfection, nor does it come about quickly. It is rather a process of growth through gaining satisfactions in the use of one's powers, building a satisfying scheme of values, and perhaps most of all through finding satisfying experiences in relationships through giving as well as receiving love.

Topics for further thought:

1. Our society has established certain fundamental rules—some of which are "laws"—regarding marriage. Discuss these rules, showing their importance to society.

2. It is believed that successful families are established by young people who are emotionally and psychologically ready for marriage and are well-matched. Relate this "marital readiness" to adolescent life as it is lived in our society.

Selected reading references

Baruch, Dorothy W., *How to Live with Your Teen-Ager,* New York, Mc-Graw-Hill Book Company, 1953.
Emphasizes understanding between parent and teenager and gives an organized discussion of sex education, outlining the information the parent should impart.

Crawford, John E., and Woodward, Luther E., *Better Ways of Growing Up,* Philadelphia, The Muhlenberg Press, 1948.
Unusually helpful, insightful discussion of the problems besetting teenagers in developing healthy attitudes and sound insights.

Duvall, Evelyn M., *Facts of Life and Love for Teenagers,* New York, Association Press, 1956.
A practical guide for adolescents to problems of dating, courtship, engagement, and marriage.

Duvall, Evelyn M., and Hill, Reuben, *When You Marry,* Boston, D. C. Heath and Company, 1953.

A very readable book on preparation for marriage. Suitable for advanced high-school students and young adults. Gives some re-inforcement to traditional societal values.

Frank, Lawrence K., and Frank, Mary, *Your Adolescent, at Home and in School,* New York, The Viking Press, 1956.
The great value of this book is its illumination of the strengths that are latent in parent-adolescent interactions and the ways they may be released for happy living and sound continuing personal growth in parents as well as in teenagers.

Landis, Judson T., and Landis, Mary G., *Personal Adjustment, Marriage and Family Living,* New York, Prentice-Hall, 1950.
Written for teenagers and designed as a textbook for use in high school. Emphasizes adjustment in the present and wise planning for the future.

Landis, Paul H., *Your Dating Days,* New York, McGraw-Hill Book Company, 1954.
Discusses questions about dating, love, and preparation for marriage of serious concern to young moderns.

37 THE FAMILY COUNCIL

James H. S. Bossard

Tнε problems of parent-child relationships are perennial, but certain recent changes in family situations tend to focus increased attention not only on these problems but also on the social techniques that may be utilized to deal effectively with them. One such device is the family council.

MEANING AND NATURE OF THE FAMILY COUNCIL

The family council, as a more or less formalized meeting of members of a family group, is as old as the primitive family. It changes in form and functions as the family and society in which it operates change.

In Primitive Society. In primitive society the family council is composed of selected representatives of the kinship group, usually the males of adult status. Women sometimes are admitted, but children usually are excluded. In the deliberations of the council, the elders have precedence in decision over the younger. Its ideology is communal, not individualistic, with the survival and welfare of the group as its basic purpose. Customarily there is a definite time, place, personnel, and procedure for its meeting; the range of its deliberations is all-inclusive, from domestic relations to war and crime; the power of its decisions is absolute and complete where the group is isolated from external law, and where not, it acts as an intermediary between the group and the law.

The description which L. Schapera gives of its operation among the Bantu-speaking tribes of South Africa may be cited as an illustration of the family council in primitive society:

Nearly all cases affecting family relations, such as disputes between husband and wife, or the non-fulfillment of kinship obligations, are first discussed by a family council, embracing all the near male relatives of the parties concerned. It is convened and presided over by the senior man of the kinship group. Where women are directly involved the mothers and wives will be included in the council. The matter is, if possible, settled here, and if it is one involving the payment of damages the council will suggest that the usual amount be paid. But it cannot enforce such payment, nor can it inflict any penalty on the offender without his consent. Where the parties cannot come to an agreement, or the offender refuses to accept the decision, the case will be referred to the local court.

In Civil Society. As civil society comes into being, the power of the state and the rights of the individual begin to emerge. The law takes away from the family council its power of decision on matters such as property interest, personal liberty, and criminal behavior. The process of using the council as an intermediary and advisory body, however, standing between the state and the family, survives and seems to do so with greatest vitality in those societies where there is least centralization of government, less concentration of population in large cities, and where the kinship or extended type of the family remains strong and stable. Under the civil code, it was relatively strong in central, southern, and western Europe and in Japan. In these areas it retained many elements of the older pattern, such as selected representatives from the family group, precedence in decisions to elders, and definite arrangements for meeting and procedure. Modifications that came to be accepted were the inclusion of a representative of the law, the selection of a non-family member as president of the council, and the relegation of the family members to a consulting and deliberating role.

Among Immigrant Groups. With the coming of large immigrant groups from these countries, the idea of the family council was brought to the United States. This was most conspicuously true of the French who came to Louisiana. Under the name of the Family Meeting, it was given a legal status in the Civil Code of the state, which it retained, aided by strong popular support, until 1934. Quotations from this code indicate some of its formal features.

Family meetings, in all cases in which they are required by law, for the interest of minors or of other persons, must be composed of at least five relations, or in default of relations, friends of him on whose interests they are called upon to deliberate. . . These relations or friends must be selected from among those domiciled in the parish in which the meeting is held. . . The relations shall be selected according to their proximity, beginning with the nearest. . . The appointment of the members of the family meeting shall be made by the judge. . . The family meeting shall be held before the recorder of the parish, a justice of the peace, or notary public appointed by the judge for the purpose.

The purposes for which the family meeting was held concerned such crises situations as the separation, death, or imprisonment of the parents; the remarriage of a mother; or matters of property in which the child had a stake. Its functions were consultative and deliberative. It had no power of decision.

A less formal type of family council was brought to the New World by other immigrant groups. As ordinarily developed, it took the form of a conclave of several generations and of several degrees of kinship and involved chiefly the right of kinsfolk to have a say about problems of primary family interest, such as business, religion, education, occupations, marriage of the children, control over the children's money, family feuds, and the like. It is seen in its closest likeness to the European model in areas of first settlement, but it keeps its form with difficulty, and for a number of reasons. First, many immigrant families did not migrate as units. If the entire family did come, it often did so piecemeal; in other instances, the complete family unit never was established here. Second, residential mobility in the United States often broke up families, particularly the larger kinship groups. Third, the state and other social agencies make more encroachments upon family rights or take over former family functions. Fourth, immigrant parents are less equipped to cope effectively and intelligently with family problems in the United States and tend to hesitate in the application of older methods.

The Contemporary Form. The contemporary form of family council is a more simplified and informal type than has prevailed in the past. It tends to be a family gathering in which all members participate on a relatively equal footing, at least so far as discussion is concerned, in which differing points of view are aired, with expression of the conflicting claims of individual interest, all against the broader background of family solidarity.

In terms of formalized definition, then, the modern family council may be regarded as a gathering of the family personnel to discuss, advise, deliberate, and, if possible, to agree on matters of common family interest. Its basic implications are that the family is a unified group of interacting personalities, in which each member has his rights, roles, and responsibilities. Applied specifically to the children, it means a rejection of the traditional point of view that they are silent members whose prime duty is that of obedience, and the acceptance of the idea that they are to be regarded as co-operating members in a democratically operating household. True, there still are families where recourse to the council is utilized by an older member to dominate rather than to lead, but these are increasingly out of focus with the mental atmosphere of the times.

Occasionally one hears of modern family councils which are organized in more pretentious manner, with a definite time, place, procedure, rules, and regulations. Father may be the presiding officer; there is a secretary to keep a record of the proceedings; decisions are made formally by majority vote. More and more, however, the contemporary family council dispenses with formalities of this kind and becomes an informal get-together of the family group for joint discussion of its common problems.

CHANGES IN FAMILY SITUATIONS

The preponderant portion of American families are small in size. This affects family counseling in several ways. It permits greater ease, with less formality, in family conferences. Just as small classes permit more effective teaching, so do small families make possible a more satisfactory family council. It encourages the full inclusion of its children, with sufficient opportunity even for the very young ones to participate. Furthermore, the small family emphasizes the personal relations of all its members with each other and the need of adjustment of these relations.

In large families the family council is important in the promotion of family happiness and harmony. In those large families where the father or mother or older brother is a good organizer, leading the family as a project in group living, the children living in these families invariably rate them as happy and satisfactory.

The decline of the patriarchal authority and dominance of the father or oldest male has been a feature of the changing American family, closely associated with changes in the bases and purposes of family living. The authoritarian male family head was a product historically of the time when the family had to be a closely knit and integrated group for purposes of economic production and physical safety. Contemporary economic conditions and prevailing forms of social organization and responsibility no longer require this, and the way is paved for more democratic forms of family life, one of which obviously is the family council.

Contemporary family life tends to be characterized by a diversification in occupations and interests of its members. Father may be a lawyer, Mother is a teacher, Mary is at college, John is in high school, and Jane is attending a specialized private school. This makes, on the one hand, for a richness and variety of backgrounds of the family personnel. Each is a distinct person, and each has his own contribution to make to the family life and its planning. On the other hand, each member of the family, under these conditions, has his own problems, and these may conflict with those of other members or with the interests of the family as a whole. Still another problem is the difficulty of getting all of its members, with their divergent interests, together sufficiently so that the home becomes at least a satisfactory base of operations. The role of the family council, in utilizing effectively this diversified background, its possibility of adjusting conflicting demands and interests, and its potential value as a counterattraction, should be evident.

Another change of the most fundamental importance is the increasing democratization of family life. In part this is the inevitable product of recent changes within the family; in large measure it is but a taking over into the family of concepts that are increasingly emphasized in all segments of American life. To talk constantly about democracy in political life, in industry, in international relations, and then to omit its incorporation into family life is both incongruous and indefensible, if not impossible. Children particularly are alive and susceptible to these "voices in the air." Moreover, they are being given increasingly a training in democratic procedures, in the symbols of expression, and in habits of conferring. Democracy within the family, which is the essence of the family council, comes easily and naturally in keeping with its application in other areas of life.

Contemporary parent-child relationships must be considered against a background of mobile populations and rapid cultural change. The former involves change, often repeated change, from one culture to another, so that members of the family at different age levels come to be conditioned by differing cultural influences and pressures; the latter, by its very nature, increases the cultural differences between successive generations. When these two factors are combined, as has been the case in immigrant families and, to a lesser extent, in country-to-city migrations, the effects upon parent-child conflicts are doubly marked. In such situations of culture differentials between generations, attempts at parental domination tend to defeat themselves. Obviously, co-operative counseling is a far better way out.

All these changes must be considered in relation to the changing functions of the family. Much of the lament over the decline of the family results from a failure to recognize that while older functions of the family are passing newer ones are emerging. These newer functions tend more and more to be of an advising, counseling, administrative nature, through which the family aids the child in the wise selection and effective utilization of the various specialized services that are available. This change is of revolutionary importance in parent-child relationships because it means that leadership in the modern family now calls for the tactful direction of its members to the diverse opportunities and specialized services now open to them. This calls for qualities not of physical dominance but of keen judgment; instead of authoritarian control there must be wise counsel; instead of regulation the demand is for instruction and self-discipline.

ASPECTS OF MODERN FAMILY COUNSELING

Aspects of family life important for the development of family unity include the family meal, family guests, family projects, family ritual.

The Family Meal. The generic importance of the family meal has long been recognized. Christianity has immortalized it in the ceremonial of the Last Supper and renews this recognition endlessly in the communion rite. Dramatists stage it with frequent effectiveness. To the novelist, it is a constant device for character delineation or plot facilitation. The essayist Oliver Wendell Holmes delivered his sage observations around the framework of the breakfast table. Obviously it is important, too, for the student of family life, and particularly of the family council, and for several reasons.

First, the family meal is a distinct aspect of the family's life. In lower-class families especially, the dining room rather than the living room is apt to be the social center of the household. Second, it holds the members of the family together over an extended period of time. The length of time and the details of the occasion naturally vary from one family to another, but in general a family meal is an extended session of the family personnel, with a relatively high rate of attendance. Today, under stress of the differing interests of family members, it may be the only time that its members come together. Third, it is at dinner that the family members are likely to be at their greatest ease, both physically and psychologically. The times that the family is at its best are perhaps most often on the occasions of its more leisured dining, just as the family entertaining at the dining table is the family on exhibition. This more felicitous generalization does not overlook the fact that the family meal also represents at times the family in haste, operating with direct bluntness, or the family at war, disturbing the emotions of its members and upsetting the gastric processes. Fourth, one must recall the continuing repetition of the family meal. Some families meet around the table three times a day; most families do so at least once a day. Over a period of years the simple arithmetic of this is enough to emphasize its quantitative effectiveness. Fifth, the family meal is likely to represent the family in its most democratic mood. Now, more than at other times, the younger members have their opportunity to blossom verbally. Well-fed elders accept with impunity remarks from juveniles which might otherwise not be tolerated, just as Mother has long recognized that Father is most susceptible and generous after a satisfactory dinner. This democratic mood is particularly important in the present connection.

Many features of family life which develop in connection with the family meal are germane to the development of family counseling. Six are summarized briefly.

1. The individual's role in the family group comes to be clearly defined around the family table. Since the entire family is together, relationships between individual members are brought out into the open. Feuding members are seated at opposite sides of the table, for example. Covenants secretly arrived at become manifest. Group choices are made—in seating arrangements, in the serving of food, in the assignment of leftovers, in priorities in conversation.

2. This table audience, both in responses which it gives to and which it withholds from its individual members, carries the greatest weight in the molding of personal traits. Its intimate nature and repetitive force make it often the family's best corrective disciplinarian. Children especially are frank, often quite brutally so, in their reactions to one another, and perhaps nowhere are they so with as much self-assurance as under the protective custody of the family meal.

3. The family meal is a kind of personality clinic, with both students and clients in attendance. Particularly is this true if the family is of

any considerable size. Each member comes to be analyzed, dissected, catalogued, and processed by the other members. This procedure is all the more devastating because it goes on before the entire group. Undesirable traits and personal weakness may be particularly identified and castigated.

4. The family meal, particularly the dinner one, is the clearing-house for most of the family's information, news, and experiences. Jack tells about the substitute teacher; Jane about the neighboring girl's new coat; Dad refers to the fact that Mr. Davis is complaining about the number of government questionnaires and threatens to go out of business; Mother thinks that Bill is coming down with a cold. The family dining table is like a crossroads through which flows the news of the world as the respective members of the family see it and experience it. Much of this traffic of information and ideas flows swiftly and unobtrusively past, noticed more in its absence than in its presence, but it is there for all to see, hear, and assimilate.

5. The family meal is constantly serving as a forum for the discussion of matters of interest and concern to the family members. Questions are asked, answered, or evaded in turn. The range of topics covered may be wide and varied, or monotonous in the recurrence of a few items of interest. Significant for all are the topics meticulously avoided as well as those assiduously discussed. The selection of topics for the family forum is in itself a cultural choice.

6. The family meal serves constantly as an evaluating conference, especially on the experiences, needs, and interests of the family members. There is group discussion. Individual views are expressed, modified, and reconciled often as a family judgment, choice, decision, or attitude emerges. Arrived at experimentally in democratic conference, or imposed by an autocratic parent, these evaluations are absorbed on the basis of their emotional relations to the family, so that the line between the two may often be quite indistinct.

The Family Guest. A second aspect of family life important in this connection grows out of the presence of guests. The role of the guest has long been neglected in the study of the family. A research project completed by the William T. Carter Foundation for Child Development and based on four hundred case documents indicates that this is a serious omission. The outstanding impression from the project as a whole focuses upon the importance of family experience with the guest as source material in the learning (and counseling) process that goes on within the family, with particular reference to its child members. Guests come into the home, generally with some, and often with relatively complete, acceptance by the parents. They are outsiders, but less so than other persons. They constitute a sort of intermediate stage between the child's confined family contacts and the more formal contacts with persons from the world outside. Furthermore, they come to the child's attention on a distinctive plane. They come with the attractiveness of novelty and often with an interpretive coloring by the adults in the family group. Particularly would this be true of the approved guest in upper-class homes, where family entertainment has a relatively selective character. That is to say, guests are invited into the home because the family wants them.

From this it follows that guests often are the agents through which is brought into the home, and to the child's vivid attention, a consciousness of the variety of life, of different people, diverse ideas, contrasting mannerisms and interests. An analysis of 117 autobiographies, in which the authors comment on the role of guests in their families, made as a part of the above-mentioned research project, shows a very general emphasis upon the importance of guests in extending the horizon of beliefs and customs of family members, the introduction of public issues as well as problems of etiquette and other forms of personal behavior, and a knowledge of conflict situations hitherto unknown. At the same time there are frequent references to the fact that guests in the home facilitated comparisons which gave family members a conception of their own family status. Often elders in the family consciously manipulate this use of the guest.

After the guests have left the home, post-mortems may follow. There are analyses, comments, and evaluations concerning many things relating to the guests: their behavior, their occupations, their planes of living, their patterns of expenditures, the attitudes they expressed. Sometimes the family appraisal of these may be made in front of the children and with their participation. Such situations offer an excellent opportunity for the family council to function.

Family Projects. Modern life is rich with opportunities for family projects, which afford an excellent opportunity for the development of family councils. It may be the erection and furnishing of a summer shack, the building of an outdoor grill, the cultivation of a vacant lot or flower bed, the development of a family hobby, or the acquisition of a domestic animal. Many families, for example, have found the training and breeding of a dog a family project exceedingly useful in the training of younger family members in toilet habits, and the education of all in the differences and processes of sex. Or the projects may be more ambitious—a lengthy program for the education of the children, the purchase of a piano, plans for a summer vacation for the family, or the establishment of a business. Concrete projects of the kind indicated above can be made to serve as excellent frameworks for effective family councils.

Family Rituals. Many families develop family rituals. These are certain prescribed patterns of family procedure which come to be accepted by the family members and, in course of time, come to have the support of family tradition. The following brief excerpts from a large collection of family rituals in the book *Ritual in Family Living* illustrate their nature as well as their possibilities for family council.

Every night, when it is possible, I will go into my parents' room prior to retiring and review the day's events. They criticize and give opinions on subjects which to me are problems. I ask questions and also venture ideas. We discuss family affairs, each of us giving a bit to the conversation. This to me is the dearest of all our rituals because it brings me closer to my parents than at any other time, and gives me invaluable aid.

Every Saturday night they would have what they called a "lamb slaughter," which really meant they had a few arguments about anything (all participating), and those who couldn't give much contribution to the discussion they called the slaughter lambs. The children mostly opened the argument asking their father's or mother's opinions about religion, education, love, or anything, but they would wind up arguing with each other. In summer these arguments took place on the porch. When the arguments would become too heated one of the boys would say, "Let's have some music."

The Clark family consisted of father, mother, and two children. The children were of high-school age and were employed each Saturday during the school year. The father's and the children's employment extended into the late hours of Saturday evening. The custom developed early for the family to come together in the kitchen between eleven and twelve o'clock on Saturday evening. Invariably the mother would provide a midnight supper. Earnings of the week were totaled, expenditures were planned, experiences at work were exchanged. Usually these sessions lasted until 2 A.M. on Sunday mornings. After a time they became a family event which each member looked forward to, and made a definite part of the weekly schedule. This ritual continued for a number of years, and now, although the children are married, they still come "home" for the Saturday-night family supper.

The over-all conclusion that emerges from the study of family rituals is their relation to family integration. An integrated family is a well-knit family, one that functions smoothly as a unit. Rituals contribute to this end by accustoming members of a family to do things together. Families are held together best by doing things together.

VALUES OF THE FAMILY COUNCIL

The extent to which the family council obtains as a form of internal family organization in the United States is not known, but a study by W. G. Mather is suggestive in this connection. Analyzing the family histories written by two hundred college students, he identified four types of family control in the following proportions: (1) father dominance, 37.8 per cent; (2) mother dominance, 20.2 per cent; (3) joint dominance by father and mother, 28.4 per cent; (4) family-council control, 13.6 per cent. Whatever the proportion in the population as a whole, its utilization has been extensive enough to justify some tentative conclusion of its possible values. These are stated here in summary form.

1. The family council may serve as an educational device in acquainting all of the members of the group with the family needs and problems. Personal problems are merged into a group problem, and each may see his or her problem and needs in relation to those both of each other member and of the group as a whole.

2. A family group consciousness may be built up through the family council. What is good for the family as a group? How can the family name be upheld? How can the family put its best foot forward? These are considerations that may be involved in the purchase of common possessions, necessitating in turn the curtailment of some individual expenditures. Family achievements that result from co-operative family effort make for family pride. Persons familiar with college and university students will have no difficulty in recalling instances of family planning over a period of years to accomplish the college education of successive members of the family group. Mather's study revealed that family affection, social life, loyalty, solidarity, co-operation, joint use of family property, and celebration of family birthdays and holidays were found in greatest number where the family council prevailed.

3. Increased wisdom of family decisions is possible under the family council. This is so because such decisions are likely to be based on more adequate and complete information. Where each can express

his needs and points of view, the ultimate decision is more likely to recognize the interests of all.

4. Group decisions tend to be supported by group authority. It is not just the authoritarian father but the entire family that expects one to accept its decision. Here is but another illustration of the sociological principle that the group is the best disciplinarian of its individual members.

5. The family council facilitates specialization of role and responsibility within the family. Group organization focuses attention upon individual aptitudes, interests, and knowledge. This in turn often leads to the assignment of responsibilities in such a way as the group considers most advantageous to itself. This again has the added value of establishing duties on the basis of group approval rather than parental domination. Such group specialization is highly meaningful, as students of gang life so clearly reveal. Perhaps the most significant aspect of this is the subtly effective transfer of responsibility for specific functions from older to younger members of the family.

6. Perhaps as significant as any value inherent in the family council is the sense of security it may give to the individual family member. Here is not just a family into which he happened to be born and in which he is made to do things by order of an authoritarian head. This is his family, in which he has his say, in which he co-operates in doing his part. It is a family that does things as a family, and (albeit this may operate below the level of conscious reflection) just as it does things for all, so it may be depended upon to do things for him. The family council satisfies the sense of being wanted, the longing to belong.

Topics for further thought:

1. Our society expects the family to discharge certain basic responsibilities. Mention the most important of these and show how they may be shared—to varying degrees—by both parents and children.

2. Socialization of the child, as well as further development of the personalities of parents, reveals the pattern of interaction within a family. This pattern, in turn, reflects societal standards and values. Analyze this intricate relationship, pointing out ways in which this may be strengthened by the family as well as by society.

Selected reading references

Beasley, Christine, *Democracy in the Home,* New York, Association Press, 1954.

As indicated in the title, this book applies the principles of democracy to virtually all aspects of family living.

Bossard, James H. W., *Parent and Child,* Philadelphia, University of Pennsylvania Press, 1953.

The effects of varying family situations and circumstances upon relationships between parents and children. Derived from analysis of case study materials and interviews.

Bossard, James H. S., and Boll, Eleanor S., *Ritual in Family Living,* Philadelphia, University of Pennsylvania Press, 1950.

The first systematic attempt to analyze family rituals, habits, and customs as they contribute to happiness and family solidarity. Supplements material presented in the present chapter.

Nimkoff, Meyer, *Marriage and the Family,* Cambridge, Houghton Mifflin Company, 1947.

See especially Chapter 20, "The Happy Family," for a broad perspective on the establishment and maintenance of good relations within the family.

Sussman, Marvin B., "The Help Pattern in the Middle Class Family," *American Sociological Review,* February, 1953, pp. 22-8.

Analyzes the relationships between parents and their married children, indicating a high rate of exchange of goods and services between them.

INDEX

Abnormal characteristics, psychology of: American Indians, 88; Bantu customs, 94; berdache, 88; cultural influences on sex norms, 87-9; deviation from heterosexual mores, 95-6; exhibitionism, 94; in Germany, 91; in Greece, 91; homoeroticism, 92; homosexuality, 91, 197, 503-4; incest, 90; in Japan, 91; Keraki Indians, 91; Marquesan culture, 90; masochism, 93; masturbation, 87; men and animals, 93; Mohave Indians, 88; narcissism, 134, 228; norms of social sex-role behavior, 88-9; norms in various cultures, 87-91; "peeping Toms," 94; penal institutions, 91-2; Plains Indians, 88; psychoneurosis, 94; psychosexuality, 93; in New Guinea, 91; rare cases of, 93; reversal of masculine and feminine roles, 88-9; sadism, 93; sex-act perversion, 93-4; sex-object perversion, 90-93; sex reversal, 88; sexual deviation in Western culture, 88-9; voyeurism, 94

Abortion, 401-12; abortifacients, 412; Bourne abortion trial, famous English test case, 409; care and treatment of, 406-8; caused by abnormal reproductive organs, 405; death rate in Russia, 411; in United States, 410; English Abortion Act of 1860, 408; illegal abortion, 410-12; normal, 404; self-induced, 412; spontaneous, 402-6; statistics, 402; superstitions about, 405-6; syphilis not a cause of, 405; therapeutic, 408-10; vitamin E used in treatment of, 407

Abortion Act of 1860, in England, 408

Achondroplasia, mutation rate of, 350

Achondroplastic dwarfism, hereditary cause of, 345; mutation rate of, 350

Activities, see Recreation

Adaptability, see Adjustments

Addams, Jane, 270

Adjustments: childhood and family influence on, 238-9; during engagement, 128-9; factors in maladjustment in marriage, 248-61; importance of background, 238-9; marriage, 128-9, 232-45; personality and temperament, factors for happiness, 236-8, 243-4; sex-adjustment aptitude, 234-5; sexual adjustments in marriage, 215-30; test for marital happiness, 232-5; wedding and honeymoon, 177-86; women's adjustments to marriage, 129, 262-73

Adolescence: age period in physical growth, 421; attachment to one's own sex, 503-4; conflict in respect to status, 44-5; courtship, 144-51, 159; crises in some families, 45; dating, 120-21, 145-9, 161-3; engagement, 128-30, 151-5; going steady, 121, 149-51, 505; in love, 506-7; masturbation, 197, 492-3; maturation and learning, 428-9; medical examination of adolescent girls advised, 170; menstruation, 501; normal sex development, 499-500; parent attachment, 134, 138, 249-53; parents' influence, 134, 117-18, 122, 217-21, 239; petting, 153, 159-61, 163; popularity, desire for, 145-6, 159-60; preparation for marriage, 497-508; problems of, 44; psychology of, 437-40; "puppy love," 142, 461, 506; sex edu-

G